Food

From My

Heart

Food From My Heart

Cuisines of Mexico Remembered and Reimagined

Zarela Martínez

Foreword by Budd Schulberg

MACMILLAN · USA

MACMILLAN
A Simon & Schuster Macmillan Company
15 Columbus Circle
New York, NY 10023

MACMILLAN is a registered trademark of Macmillan, Inc.

Library of Congress Cataloging-in-Publication Data

Martínez, Zarela.
    Food from my heart : cuisines of Mexico remembered and reimagined
    / Zarela Martínez.
        p.   cm.
    Includes bibliographical references and index.
    ISBN 0-02-860361-3 (pbk)
    1. Cookery, Mexican.   2. Mexico—Social life and customs.
I. Title.
TX716.M4M376   1992   92-25392   CIP
641.5972—dc20

Manufactured in the United States of America

10 9 8 7 6 5 4 3 2 1

To my father, who gave me my soul

my mother, who gave me my spirit

and my children, who let me be.

My thanks to Anne Mendelson

for her guidance, knowledge, and wit

in helping this book come together.

Contents

Acknowledgments

To all the people who helped me get to this point in my life (more or less in order of their appearance):

To my mother, Aída Gabilondo; the memory of my father, José Martínez Solano; the memory of my grandparents; my sisters, Aída, Marina, and Clarissa; Loretto Academy and Dominican Convent; Lupe and Nayo Chávez; Caly Álvarez; Malú Fernández; Elisa Southern and Mayo Singh—for helping me grow.

To Lillian Haines, Paul Prudhomme, and Craig Claiborne—for guiding me on my first culinary steps.

To Warner LeRoy; Harley Baldwin; Lew, Beth, and Billy Rudin; Donald Karas; Eddie Schoenfeld; and David Keh—for taking a chance on me.

To the members of the press who have made my food known and understood.

To my aunt and uncle, Panchita and Ernesto Ellis—for making my dream a reality.

To Gary Jacobson, Ed Bonuso, Claude Pastou, Vera Rudzwick, Marissa Sánchez, and all my staff at Zarela—for holding the fort while I worked on this book.

To my customers—for appreciating my food and for their support throughout the years.

To my sons, Rodrigo and Aarón, and my stepchildren Marissa and Spanky—for their understanding and support.

To Max Clemente and Pedro Luis de Aguinaga—for their friendship and for introducing me to a different Mexico.

To Carole Lalli—for first encouraging me to write.

To Jim Dickson—for helping me to conquer my fear of writing and computers and getting me through the difficult early stages of this book.

To Suzanne Hamlin and Paula Wolfert—for bringing Anne Mendelson to me.

To Julie Bloom—for carefully testing my recipes and contributing suggestions.

To all the people who read the manuscript and offered valuable suggestions: Budd Schulberg, Richard Stein, Diana Lissauer, Ned Hamlin, Laurel Gonsalves, Doris Tobias, and Patricia Soliman.

To Richard Fabricant—for running interference for me.

To Pam Hoenig and Bill Rosen—for having faith in an unorthodox book.

Foreword

I n this age of hype, you hear a lot about "Buy one, get one free." But in Zarela Martínez's unique book, *Food From My Heart,* she outdoes the hypesters with the real thing. Buy this book as a collection of recipes of exquisite Mexican cuisine and you get—not surprising to anyone with the good fortune to know her—the colorful personal history of Zarela Martínez. Raised on a great ranch in Chihuahua, a world unto itself that she describes in loving detail, she brings to life a family you won't forget, and a cast of characters that will hold their own against the magic realism of Latin novelists like Gabriel García Márquez and Carlos Fuentes.

This, I realize, is extravagant praise, for García Márquez and Fuentes are two of my favorite contemporary authors. But Zarela happens to be a natural writer, and her prose, like her recipes, reflects high spirit, ingenuity, originality, and a sensual appetite for life.

You will meet and remember her grandparents, and her father, a singular *ranchero* who loves words and reads Joyce's *Finnegans Wake,* a painter and musician who can be by turns a magical charmer and a tormented recluse. Her mother seems to have been the ideal counterpart, strong-minded and independent, who encouraged self-expression on the part of Zarela and her sisters, including a tolerance of and encouragement of their idiosyncracies. There's a rich supporting cast, like the blacksmith Gabriel, who radiates pride, virility, skill, and a love of animals so reciprocated that the ranch dogs, both work-dogs and pets, would follow him everywhere like canine children to the Pied Piper.

In addition to Zarela's lively, in fact impassioned description of her roots, you will find yourself learning through this unique juxtaposition about the Mexican culture and the synergy of pre-Columbian Indian and Spanish cultures that have created the very special and multi-layered world of Mexico. Foods the Spanish had never seen or tasted before, such basic standbys as chiles, corn tortillas, tomatoes, chocolate, and a mouth-watering list of tropical fruits, would now be married to Spanish ingredients unknown to the Aztecs and other conquered empires: pork, olive oil, pomegranate seeds, wheat, rice, peas. The interaction of Spanish and Indian ingredients combined to create a new culture of food.

Zarela's journey from her ranch in Northern Mexico to social worker in El Paso to a master restaurateur in midtown Manhattan is a success story flavored with the *salsas rancheras* of life. To learn how to prepare *Crepas de Chicharrón* (Crêpes Filled with Pork Cracklings) or *Pollo Borracho* (Drunken Chicken) or *Tamales de Mi Ana Linda* (My Grandmother's Chicken Tamales) or hundreds of other mouth-waterers is a treat. But sprinkled through this *Maestra's* collection of seductive recipes are those picaresque personal stories of the origin of these exotic ingredients, a spicy mix that Zarela has put into her own special blender. In warning of the amount of fat in *chorizo,* for instance, you will learn from Zarela that ". . . in defense of the ranch diet, I must say that my great-grandfather, who ate pork and beef practically every day of his life, drank to excess on occasion, smoked cigars, and rarely exercised, lived to be eighty-seven years old."

The ten-page chapter on chiles alone is worth the price of admission to this book! For chef/anthropologist, memoirist Zarela Martínez is telling us: Food is culture is history is pre-history; food is art, food is people, and food is also love—which may go a long way toward explaining the storybook success of Zarela's restaurant reflected in this delicious book so aptly titled *Food From My Heart.*

Budd Schulberg

Introduction

Everyone who has read this book at all its stages has known that it is extremely unconventional. Believe me, I realize that it would have been safer to write a more traditional cookbook, but the things I wanted to say couldn't be pigeonholed. The book took on a life of its own. Finally I threw convention to the winds and wrote what people tell me is several books at once. It is a memoir, a guide to Mexican culinary basics, and a personal recipe collection, all interspersed with glimpse-by-glimpse evocations of Mexican life and culture.

Perhaps the task would have been easier if I had not felt that my own life represents something about Mexico that has not often been portrayed in writing. Everyone who tries to describe us ends up talking about *mestizaje,* literally "intermarriage" or the melding of different heritages since the Spanish invasion in the sixteenth century. The milieu in which I was raised, the spacious northern cattle and wheat country, also "intermarried" with influences from the United States but remains very much a world to itself. It was all I knew until I was eighteen. This is a part of Mexico not known to many in other countries. I hope that I have been able to show how a ranching family from these vast, arid, but beautiful lands lives, worships, celebrates, mourns, and entertains—and how these early experiences melded with other impressions as I learned how much more there is to Mexico.

But I have also tried to arrange things so that you can go first to what interests you. For those who want to learn the whys and wherefores of Mexican cooking, I start off with a detailed introduction to ingredients and a section of master recipes—basic preparations that demonstrate techniques and flavor principles, the steppingstones of my food. You will find yourself referring to this section over and over as you cook with me. Or you may want to skip around, reading about how food is connected with the identity of the Mexican people, from the ancient beliefs about corn and chiles to all kinds of present-day life rituals. If you would rather start with my own story, it begins on page 59 with the chapter "My Roots," and follows the path that took me from my home in Chihuahua and Sonora to Guadalajara, El Paso, explorations of regional Mexico, and at last my restaurant, Zarela, in New York City. This is a memoir of food as well as life experiences, for the recipes that conclude each chapter mirror my development as a chef as I incorporated my growing knowledge of Mexico's many culinary traditions.

Come with me on my voyage of discovery!

What You Must Know To Cook With Us:
Ingredients and Techniques

To understand Mexican culture you must see at first hand how the Catholic faith melded with a system of pagan beliefs to make a uniquely, truly Mexican religion. The same melding holds true for our distinctive cuisine. It is *mestizo*—"hybridized," "of mixed blood," a concept central to our identity—and it took time to develop.

Picture for yourself a moment just before the tragic subjugation of Mexico by Spain began in earnest with the conquest of Tenochtitlán, modern Mexico City, in 1519–20. Before the outbreak of overt war, while the Spanish were in Tenochtitlán supposedly to conduct peaceful negotiations, they beheld the emperor at table. Cortez and his followers were astonished, as they were no doubt meant to be. What they saw was immortalized in Bernal Díaz del Castillo's *True History of the Conquest of New Spain*.

Moctezuma sits enthroned amid servants passing more than three hundred different platters, trays, and dishes of food. There is boar, deer, pheasant, quail, and ocean fish fresh from the coast, brought by a system of relay runners. The emperor chooses what he fancies, the merest fraction of the delicacies. (After all, he went through this two or three times every day.) What he does not eat is passed out to his courtiers. What they do not eat goes to the guards and lower priests. What they do not eat goes to the slaves. The foreigners, accustomed as they are to conquistador rations of cassava bread and salt pork brought from Cuba, try to take notes on foods "so numerous," says Díaz del Castillo, "that I cannot finish naming them in a hurry."

One of the few aspects of the emperor's world that survives to this day in a form Moctezuma would recognize is the food—at least some of it. Many ingredients and dishes have been passed down exactly as they were before the Conquest. Others have come to us through an evolution that is remarkably well documented. The Spanish who first made their way to Moctezuma's table would have noted the lack of pork, olives, olive oil, and distilled liquor. From other accounts we know when these foods and others were introduced. Sometimes we can pin down an actual who-where-and-when for the creation of complex dishes containing Aztec and Spanish foodstuffs. (We know the convent in Puebla where the nuns are said to have invented *mole poblano*, with its mixture of native and European ingredients, to honor the arrival of a sixteenth-century viceroy, and we know the moment in 1821 when *chiles en nogada* first emblazoned the red-white-and-green of the Mexican flag while uniting Spanish pomegranate seeds and walnuts with green poblano chiles.) More often the complex process of *mestizaje* (hybridization) can only be traced in overall outlines.

It was some time before cooks were brought over from Spain, and in the meanwhile the conquerors had to hire or commandeer native cooks to prepare their meals. We know that on their arrival they were immediately introduced to a variety of prepared dishes with corn tortillas. Soon they were tasting chiles, corn in different forms, New World beans, peanuts, tomatoes, chocolate, squash, vanilla, jícama, chayote, mamey, cherimoya, papaya, and white sapote. Three of these were overwhelmingly popular on first taste: vanilla, chocolate, and chiles. Beans, corn, tomatoes, squash, and the Central American fruits were adopted in short order.

As the Spaniards became familiar with the native ingredients, they set about preparing them in European ways—for example, sautéing or frying them, techniques that apparently were not practiced before the introduction of such cooking fats as olive oil, lard, and butter. The first professional European cooks arrived as part of the religious orders sent out from Spain for the purpose of converting the heathen. The holy mission of certain select brothers and sisters was to cook for the viceroys, colonial governors, and princes of the Church. These monks and nuns arrived in Mexico with the seeds or slips of Old World plants such as wheat, rice, carrots, globe onions, peas, almonds, sesame, coriander, citrus fruits, and quinces. (They in turn sent seeds and slips of New World products to their convents around the world.) Those that thrived were soon combined with native ingredients to create new or old-new dishes. After all, Spanish cuisine was itself something of a *mestizo* product. The English novelist Sybille Bedford, who wrote of Mexico in a sometimes acerbic memoir entitled *The Sudden View,* did comment appreciatively on the food.

> The cooking of Mexico belongs loosely to the European Mediterranean. The link was obviously made by the Navigators and Spain; perhaps it was strengthened by some shared oriental affinities. The new food was a graft that took well. It suited the climate and the land, and joined quite naturally with the indigenous roots, just as that Mediterranean tradition itself was a happy hybrid of Greece and Carthage, Gaul and Moor, native corn [wheat] and Persian fruit.

Europeans learned to cook Mexican ingredients their way, while the Indian peoples started cooking European ingredients (including previously unknown meats and poultry brought by the conquerors) their way. As the gilding of Spanish civilization spread over all the former Aztec and Mayan lands, some of the older culinary lore was sadly lost forever. But at the same time something unprecedented was happening for the Spaniards: An element of deliberate "creation" or choice was introduced into the cooking they had taken for granted on their own soil. A new cuisine was now self-consciously being developed at a time when the printed word made it possible to hold up a mirror to change.

This process of synthesis, *mestizaje,* has never stopped since, keeping pace with later historical events. For example, the French occupied Mexico at one point in the nineteenth century and set up the Austrian-born Maximilian as emperor. This is memorialized in our food by our famous breads and pastries, as well as the wide use of crêpes. In Mexico City especially, the breads and wonderful crusty rolls *(bolillos)* have been favorably compared to those of Paris, and we have a roster of Viennese-derived pastries. New ethnic groups arrived in different parts of Mexico, and the local food has also absorbed their contributions. The Germans brought the art of brewing, and today Mexican beers are among the most famous in the world. Lebanese and other immigrants from Muslim lands around the Mediterranean added a note or two in parts of Jalisco and other states. (I know a flaky pastry dish, given to me in Guadalajara, that is uncannily close to the Moroccan *bisteeya* and is known as *turco*.) The Chinese have left subtle culinary traces in the cooking of Acapulco, and sweet-and-sour dishes in different parts of Mexico suggest some Oriental influence. The German-speaking Mennonites who settled in Chihuahua and began making cheese almost disappeared behind the success of their product, which became simply known as *queso de Chihuahua*.

Mexicans have also emigrated to the United States for whatever political, economic, or personal reasons. Here they have adopted certain foodstuffs or dishes, adapted others, chosen and recombined what they found to make new foods. Within Mexico itself, people have come to be interested in different regional traditions, which everybody borrows from and changes at a faster pace than was possible before the speed-of-light communications of the twentieth century. And today there are commercial products from the United States specifically made for the Mexican market, such as Quaker Oats *masa harina*.

All these things are part of the same *mestizo* process begun with the Conquest. My cooking at Zarela in New York is a current example of precisely this process. So is this book.

INGREDIENTS: INDIGENOUS FOODS

All the foods in this by no means exhaustive list were being grown or used on Mexican soil when the Spanish arrived. They are important either to the cooking of the Americas generally or to particular regions of Mexico.

Achiote (annatto seeds). I have a funny association with this ingredient. When people ask me to describe the flavor of achiote, I always say it tastes like dirt—the baked adobe blocks that one of the workmen on our ranch would make every summer with dark pebble-filled mud from the arroyo mixed with straw, golden sticks in the black mud. I have always loved that earth flavor! As a child I would break pieces of adobe from the walls of the cowboys' houses and contentedly suck on them. Something in the earthy, distinctive flavor of achiote brings back that memory, though I hasten to reassure you that it definitely does not taste like mud!

Achiote is really the small, dark red seeds of the annatto tree *(Bixa orellana),* used as a yellow-orange coloring and flavoring agent. You've probably eaten it if you've eaten yellow cheddar cheese. In Mexican cooking it is usually encountered only in certain mixtures of seasonings and spices, either the *recados* discussed on pages 27–28 or the commercial achiote paste *(adobo de achiote)* sold in 4-ounce boxes at Mexican markets. The basic ingredients of achiote paste are usually annatto seeds, garlic, cumin and sometimes other spices, Mexican oregano, and (often) some kind of citrus juice.

Avocado (aguacate) is the fruit of *Persea americana,* a member of the laurel family. It has the Aztec name *ahuacatl,* which means "testicle," and is known in Mexico as the "butter of the poor." Its best-known use is in guacamole. Avocados are generally available in all parts of the United States (especially since the Mexican food craze hit a few years back). I recommend Hass, a small, dark variety. El Fuerte is another flavorful avocado. They have a buttery flavor, less unpleasant fiber, and firmer flesh than the big, green, smooth-skinned varieties preferred by Cubans and other people from the Caribbean. Avocados are full of vitamins C and A. Buy them slightly hard and let them ripen at room temperature for about three days. Never refrigerate an unripe avocado or the flesh will turn black. You should refrigerate a ripe one if you have to hold it for couple of days, but it is, of course, preferable to eat them at their peak. The anise-flavored avocado leaves are also a favorite culinary herb in Mexico.

Beans of the New World or haricot kind *(Phaseolus vulgaris)* were one of the chief sources of protein for the Indian peoples and were swiftly brought by the Spanish and Portuguese to Europe, Africa, and Asia. I can't stress too highly how important beans are to Mexicans, rich and poor. On the ranch where I grew up each of the children had the task of cleaning a big *bandeja* (basin) of beans every day. We would sit outside under the weeping willow and do it after lunch. Even for a Mexican child I must have been unusually bean-minded. On one special occasion when I was two, Mr. Bronson, a good family friend and "angel," took me to the celebrated El Paso del Norte hotel and treated me to my first fancy lunch. I asked for *un plato grande de frijoles*—a big plate of beans. When I was old enough to outgrow an imaginary companion of my very young years, I told everyone that he had drowned in a pot of beans! And for a long time after I had come to New York I hardly felt that a meal was a meal without beans.

Dozens of varieties are popular in Mexico, named often for their color (red, white, black, pinto) or for the supposed place of origin (*e.g., serrano,* from the mountains). All these small beans, when eaten dried, are collectively called *frijoles.* (*Habas* applies to larger beans like limas or European fava beans; the *Phaseolus* beans when eaten as young, immature string beans are called *ejotes.*) Pinto beans are the preferred variety of northern Mexico, black beans in most other parts of the country. They are delicious simmered by themselves (see *Frijoles Charros,* page 93, and *Frijoles de la Olla,* page 43), used in soups or salads, or refried (mashed and recooked in hot lard). Epazote (page 8) is a nice complement to the hearty flavor. In cooking beans, salt is never added until they are somewhat tender, otherwise they will not soften.

Chile. See pages 217–228.

Chocolate. Can you imagine *any* European cuisine without chocolate? It's hard to remember that, like tobacco and turkeys, *Theobroma cacao* was an unknown quantity anywhere east of Mesoamerica until the conquering army sent some back to Spain. Not until the nineteenth century was chocolate industrially processed for use in cake-baking and candy-making. Before then it was generally known in Europe and England as a hot, frothy sweetened beverage made from a hardened paste of roasted ground cacao beans, nuts, and spices. A version in late eighteenth-century editions of Hannah Glasse's *The Art of Cookery* has anise, cinnamon, the black pepper cousin called "long pepper," almonds, pistachios, musk, ambergris, nutmeg, rosewater or orange-flower water, loaf sugar, and "as much achiote as will make it the color of brick." In some ways this was still close to Aztec usage.

The Aztecs, too, knew chocolate as a beverage, though they apparently drank it cold and only sometimes sweetened (with one of the native honeys). To make different versions they pounded the beans with an array of spices and seasonings, from chile to vanilla, and sometimes thickened the mixture with ground corn. Things haven't completely changed. Today Mexicans do prepare some confections and desserts with chocolate, but rich U.S.-style chocoholic cakes and candies (a sort of reverse *mestizo* experience) never became our passion. The most important use of chocolate in modern Mexico is still as a beverage. The chocolate usually sold for this purpose is in grainy, spicy tablets of ground almonds, cacao, sugar, and cinnamon that I think hark back to the early European versions. We drink our chocolate hot now, but we still like to thicken it with ground corn to make the drink called *champurrado.* Another important use of chocolate, also based on pre-Columbian roots, is in some of the more elaborate *moles,* of which *mole poblano* is the most famous.

Mexican sweet chocolate is sold in many Latin American stores; Ibarra is a widely available brand. I urge you to try it for hot chocolate and experiment with other uses. It opens up altogether different chocolate possibilities.

Coconuts (*Cocos nucifera*) probably reached Central and South America centuries ago from the Pacific. They are used in the hot southern areas of Mexico such as Chiapas and Yucatán, and in central states like Veracruz, much as they are in Caribbean cooking. Coconut milk is prepared by steeping grated coconut meat in hot water and squeezing the liquid from the pulp. To grate it yourself, bake a coconut 15 minutes in a 400°F oven and whack it with a hammer to loosen the tough outer covering; peel off the brown covering and grate one medium-sized chunk at a time in a blender, food processor, or on a hand grater. Frozen grated coconut, sold in many Latin American and Filipino markets, is a great convenience; be sure it is unsweetened. Coconut milk can also be made by steeping flaked dried coconut (sold in supermarkets; use the unsweetened variety) in hot water. Canned coconut cream will do in a pinch, though it tends to be full of gloppy additives. Look for brands without propylene glycol, etc.

Corn. See page 191.

Corn husks. One of the important elements in Mexican cuisine is the great range of leaves and husks used as wrappers to cook foods. It is our equivalent of cooking *en papillote,* except that the wrappers lend a distinctive flavor as the contents cook in the wrapping. Corn husks, fresh or dried, are the best-known type of wrapper. They are usually used to make *masa*-filled tamales, but can be used to wrap different vegetables and fish (for example, *Morralitos de Calabacitas,* page 311, or *Tamal de Pescado,* page 183).

They are great for grilling or roasting, as well as baking and simmering. Dried husks, the most widely used, are available in craft stores (make sure they are untreated), and in Latin American groceries and some supermarkets. They are sold in 4-ounce, 8-ounce, and sometimes 1-pound packages. The green husks from fresh ears of corn are also used in different kinds of tamales—for example, to steam a filling of young corn kernels, ground and combined with butter and cheese (*tamal de elote*). Fresh corn leaves, *hojas de milpa,* are another important *tamal* wrapping, particularly in the triangular *corundas* of Michoacán. To prepare dried corn husks for use, soak them in hot or warm water until softened, at least 30 minutes to an hour. I always place *masa* or other fillings on the rough, ridged side of the husk because I like the way it cooks as it sticks to the ridges. However, it is easier to fold them and remove the *tamal* when spread on the smooth side.

Epazote (*Chenopodium ambrosioides*) is an aromatic perennial herb with an assertive, somewhat bitter taste. It grows wild in many parts of the United States—even Central Park in New York City—and has various English names, of which my favorite is "stink-weed." I think epazote is perhaps *the* characteristic Mexican herb. It is especially used in cooking *huitlacoche* (see page 9), squash blossoms, beans, and various stews and soups. It can be bought in specialty food markets, sometimes at farmers' markets in big cities with Hispanic populations, and by mail-order (see page 331).

Hoja santa ("holy leaf," *Piper auritum* or *P. sanctum*), an anise-flavored herb, is another of the characteristic wrappers. It is also known as *hierba santa* or *acuyo* and is used mainly in the south-eastern states and the Mexico City area. The large, dark green leaves, which grow on bushes, are used to wrap food in, *tamal*-style, and to flavor stews and sauces. You may be able to find it in the southwestern United States, or try one of the sources on page 331. It is worth trying to find because it is both delicious and truly important in the pantheon of Mexican seasonings.

Why is it called *hoja santa*? I asked that question of an Indian woman selling herbs in the market at Tuxtla Gutiérrez and she explained that God named it. When the Virgin had the Baby Jesus she was very poor and couldn't afford many diapers. But she had a beautiful big bush in her back yard with large, dark green leaves. She would dry the diapers on this bush, and spread out over the wide leaves they would dry quickly. God blessed the bush and to thank it for helping the Virgin Mary in her time of need, named it *hoja santa*. The same herb-seller told me in a conspiratorial whisper, covering her mouth, that if a woman with female problems steeps a few *hoja santa* leaves in her bath water and soaks herself for half an hour, she will be cured.

Huitlacoche* or *cuitlacoche (*Ustilago maydis*) is corn smut, a type of fungus that invades the growing ears of corn, causing the kernels to swell into gray or blue-black masses. Farmers take vigilant measures against it in the United States, and home gardeners throw away "smutty" ears in disgust. In Mexico we consider it our truffle!

Until now fresh *huitlacoche* has rarely been sold in the United States, though it can be bought in the American Southwest and at some Mexican supermarkets and I hear that it will soon be more widely marketed. When found growing on corn in most parts of this country, it is completely different from the Mexican product. The kernels of American sweet corn yield a milder-flavored *huitlacoche* than Mexican varieties. I hope that fresh *huitlacoche* will one day be widely available throughout the United States, as are such products as the kiwi fruit and jícama. Meanwhile, you have to hunt for it. The demand for it is high in Mexico and the supply is both seasonal and iffy, fluctuating with the amount of rainfall. During high season (July through October), the Herdez canning factory buys what it can and processes it into a wonderful product, sold in 8-ounce cans, which I use thankfully. However, even the canned variety is expensive and not plentiful, particularly in early summer when the previous year's supply is exhausted. My mother has to search constantly for it in supermarkets all over Mexico to keep me supplied in New York City.

Jícama is the tuber of a plant indigenous to Mexico and Central America. The botanical name, *Pachyrhizus erosus,* is derived from the Greek *pachys*—thick and coarse, as in "pachyderm"! It has a crisp texture, somewhere between that of an apple and a raw potato, and a mild, nutty flavor. Low in calories, it is always eaten uncooked or barely cooked. Jerusalem artichokes would be a good substitute if you can't get jícama, but it is becoming more readily available, particularly in the Southwest and diet-crazed California as well as New York (where some people substitute it for water chestnuts in Chinese recipes). Look for firm, clean-looking tubers, heavy for their size and free of mold.

Maguey, inaccurately called "cactus" by some U.S. writers, is actually a general term used for various large succulents of the *Agave* genus with long, thick, tapering leaves *(pencas)* that grow in a rosette pattern around a central "heart." Maguey species grow in many different parts of Mexico from north to south.

Maguey has had many uses since pre-Columbian times, not only in cooking. It is still one of the central plants in Mexican culture. However, the magueys are best known internationally as the source of pulque, mezcal, and tequila (see page 114). One of the most prized natural wrappings used in Mexican cuisine is *mixiote,* obtained by stripping the thin, transparent outer layer from maguey leaves. *Mixiote* is virtually unobtainable in the United States, unless you can get a friend to bring you some from Mexico. Parchment paper would be the closest equivalent. But in any case there are now legal restrictions on the use of *mixiote* because stripping it off the *pencas* kills the whole plant.

The pulque-producing magueys *(Agave salmiana* and *A. mapis-aga)* are also the host plants for another hard-to-obtain ingredient, a kind of burrowing insect larva called *gusano de maguey* (the maguey worm, *Aegiale hesperiaris).* It is considered a great delicacy in Mexico, particularly in the central and southeastern states. (Here I should note that insects were an important part of the pre-Hispanic Mexican diet and that in many regions different kinds of larvae as well as the adults of some ants and cicadalike insects are still a "consuming passion." I have eaten the addictive *chapulines* in Oaxaca—see page 238—and I assure you they are wonderful.) In her *Presencia de la Comida Prehispánica,* Teresa Castelló Yturbide describes how the *gusanos* are harvested by examining the lower leaves of the plant to locate their burrowing tunnels, then carefully cutting off the leaves with a machete so as not to squash the worms. They are removed with a thin implement cut from the edge of the maguey leaf and stored in little bundles of *mixiote* before being roasted on hot coals or toasted on a *comal* (griddle). Maguey worms are considered to be an aphrodisiac and are sold by herb dealers at markets. Despite the difficulty in obtaining them, I have given a favorite recipe of mine, *Salsa de Gusanitos* (page 249), which uses maguey worms that I get from Oaxaca. They have a "smoked" flavor, distinctive and haunting.

Masa. See pages 49–56.

Nopal is a general name for several kinds of cactus with edible paddles and fruit. Various species of the *Opuntia* genus grow wild in different regions, especially central Mexico. There are also cultivated *nopales*. The mild-flavored cactus paddles or *pencas* (the youngest, tenderest, fleshy "leaves") are commonly used as a vegetable. They are covered with thorns, sometimes hard to see, which must be cut out with a knife (gloves must be worn when handling them). Before cooking they are usually cut into strips and simmered briefly in water with a small amount of baking soda or *tequesquite* (see page 13) to reduce their mucilaginous—well, frankly, slimy—quality. If you don't like okra, which has a very similar quality, you may not like *nopales* much. Once cooked, they should be rinsed, first in hot and then in cold water, to remove any still-oozing juice. Cooks in Mexico strain them through a heavy straw basket to drain off the juice; here you can rinse them in a colander. They can then be used as a salad, in a stew, with scrambled eggs (substituting them for the string beans in *Ejotes con Huevo,* page 91), or with a sauce like *Salsa de Chile Colorado* (page 31). The whole *pencas* (unblanched) can also be grilled on a griddle, though be forewarned that they can be slimy. Sliced *nopales,* dethorned and cooked, are sold in cans in Latin American markets, but I don't like them much.

The small, pear-shaped fruits *(tunas),* which grow straight out of the end of the paddles, are known as "cactus pears" or "prickly pears" in English. They may be bright red, pink, magenta, yellow, or greenish. Several species bear sweet fruits that can be eaten in different forms (simply peeled, sliced, and eaten seeds and all, in salads, or in cold fruit drinks). They are also fermented to make a beverage called *colonche,* boiled down into a dense fruit butter called *queso de tuna* ("prickly pear cheese"), and cooked to make a taffylike candy called *melcocha.* A sour variety, *xoconostle,* is used to lend tartness in some stewed dishes. The *tunas* are as treacherously thorned as the cactus paddles. The usual technique for removing the thorns is to cut off both ends and make a shallow lengthwise cut along the fruit so that you can peel off the entire skin, working from the exposed area. They are available in U.S. grocery stores.

"Oregano." From some cookbooks you would gather that Mexicans use oregano as liberally as Greeks and Italians. But the different herbs that go by that name in Mexico are quite unrelated to the *Origanum* species used around the Mediterranean and in the United States. The taste is similar enough to make the confusion understandable, but not wholly interchangeable with European oregano. I don't know whether anyone has sorted out all the confusion, but some years ago the cookbook author Diana Kennedy obtained from the National University of Mexico Botanical Garden a list of at least thirteen species called *orégano*. I have no idea where the varieties I cook with fit into the puzzle. I use two especially. One is simply called Mexican oregano in the United States. It is more full-flavored than European oregano. In the North it grows wild in cattle pastures, so the beef has a wonderful herbed flavor. Mexican oregano can sometimes be found here in herb and spice stores, and is distributed nationally to many supermarkets by McCormick. I also use an herb I've always known as Oaxacan oregano, which is lemony in flavor and tastes totally unlike the other variety. I have not found it for sale in this country, but you may be able to ask a friend to bring back a dried bunch for you from Oaxaca. Otherwise, substitute Greek oregano. Dried whole sprigs keep the flavor longer than broken-leaf oregano, but are unfortunately harder to find. To bring out the flavor, crumble the oregano between your fingers when adding it to any recipe.

Pine nuts (*piñones*). These are actually a bicontinental idea: At the time of the Conquest both the Spanish and Indians had been eating the seeds of their native pine species for centuries. Pine nuts are used like pumpkin seeds and other nuts in sauces, and either ground or whole in sweetmeats and desserts. The most prized variety in Mexico has a salmon-pink color; these are sometimes available in the American Southwest. The flavor is somehow more "piney" than the variety usually sold in this country, which comes from a European species of pine.

Pumpkin seeds (*pepitas, semillas de calabaza*) are one of the favorite snacks of the Mexican people. Vendors sell them hot or cold on almost every street corner, either shelled, fried until puffed up, and salted or simply toasted in the shells, plain or salted. They have become a well-known U.S. nibble as well, particularly among the health-conscious. Pumpkin seeds are a key ingredient in many Mexican dishes, especially toasted or fried and finely ground for certain sauces, where they help to thicken the texture and add flavor. My recipe for *Papadzules* (page 276) is a good example. The Spanish found the Aztecs making sauces with pumpkin seeds that are remarkably close to the modern versions of *pepián* or *pipián* (see page 33). In various *moles* and sauces they are combined with European ingredients like almonds, cloves, and Ceylon cinnamon (for example, *Alcaparrado,* page 257) in the true tradition of the *mestizo* kitchen. In the same vein, the conquerors brought sugar to the New World, and eventually the native pumpkin seeds were combined with this in a kind of nut brittle still popular today, *pepitorias.*

Squash, along with beans, corn, and chiles, was one of the basic elements in the pre-Hispanic diet. In Mexico many kinds of squashes are grown, some never seen in the United States. Most belong to the species *Cucurbita pepo.* Some are eaten when tender and young, like zucchini and yellow summer squash *(calabacitas),* others when fully mature, like pumpkins *(calabazas).* We also preserve squash by peeling it into long ribbons and drying it to make chewy strips called *bichicoris.* Squash blossoms *(flores de calabaza)* are one of the delicacies of Mexican cuisine. Some of their most frequent uses are in *caldo de flor de calabaza* (squash blossom soup), as a filling for stuffed corn tortilla specialties like *quesadillas,* or as cheese-stuffed blossom fritters, coated with egg batter and fried to be served in a good tomato sauce such as *Caldillo de Tomate* (page 36). Though squash blossoms can be purchased in season in some large metropolitan areas, their price is prohibitive. People with vegetable gardens or gardener friends can add the blossoms to soups or cook them as they would *Calabacitas con Queso* (page 90).

Tequesquite or tequizquite is an ancient ingredient that is important to this day in Mexico, though it is not quite reproducible here. It is a mixture of alkaline salts that is collected from lake beds during the dry season. Dissolved in water, it makes *agua de tequesquite.* The indigenous Mexicans used it as an equivalent of regular salt, and for other culinary purposes that still persevere in parts of Mexico. It serves as a leavener in place of commercial baking soda or baking powder. In some areas it is considered essential for giving corn *masa* and other doughs a light, fluffy texture. It is also used in vegetable cookery, as some U.S. cooks would use a pinch of baking soda—for example, to soften dried beans, and to retain the natural color of *nopales* and other vegetables.

Tomatillo (*Physalis ixocarpa*) is known in Mexico as *tomate verde* (green tomato), *tomate de cáscara* (husk tomato), and *miltomate,* though it is not a tomato at all. In actuality it is related to the Cape gooseberry and American ground cherry. In all three of these the fruit (a small to medium-size berry) is encased in a thin, translucent paperlike outer skin that must be removed before cooking. According to Teresa Castelló Yturbide in *Presencia de la Comida Prehispánica,* tomatillo husks furnish a leavening agent when boiled in *agua de tequesquite* (see page 13). The fruit is bright green, yellow-green, or sometimes purple, and can vary in size from a marble to a Ping-Pong ball.

Fresh tomatillos are widely available in specialty groceries and some large supermarkets in the United States. They are also sold in cans, dehusked. (I may be a minority, but I detest canned tomatillos.) The flavor of tomatillos is tart and refreshing and, I find, universally liked. They can be made into much the same kind of relishes, pickles, and raw or cooked sauces as tomatoes, except that their water content is less and the result will be thicker. Cooked tomatillo sauces jell to a curiously solid consistency when cooled, hence the old-fashioned name "jamberry" for the very similar ground cherry.

Tomato or *jitomate* (*Lycopersicon esculentum*) needs no introduction, except to say that the quality of Mexican tomatoes is very good and some of what you find in U.S. markets won't do. Unless truly ripe, flavorful fresh tomatoes are available, you may be better off using a good brand of canned Italian tomatoes for cooked sauces.

My recipes often specify "roasted tomatoes." To roast a tomato, so as to deepen the flavor before adding it to a dish, place it on a heated griddle or cast-iron skillet over high heat and turn so the skin blisters and blackens all over. Or blacken them under a broiler, turning as necessary. Peel off the blackened skin before using. This should be done over a bowl to catch the juice—and don't be religious about removing all the blackened bits. I love the slight smokiness they contribute.

Vanilla (*vainilla*) is one of Mexico's greatest contributions to the world. The "vanilla bean" is actually the fruit of a Central American orchid (*Vanilla planifolia*), which is harvested unripe and subjected to a long fermenting and drying process that brings out its delicious fragrance. Today it is grown as far from its home as Madagascar, Réunion, Tahiti, and Sri Lanka. But as Elizabeth David says in *Spices, Salt and Aromatics in the English Kitchen,* "The best beans still come from Mexico." Vanilla beans are harvested principally in Papantla, Veracruz. Unfortunately, very little Mexican vanilla bean is exported to the United States.

Never use synthetic vanilla extract, which is a crude chemical approximation of the real thing.

INGREDIENTS: OLD WORLD IMPORTS

These did not originate in the Americas, but in one way or another they have become characteristic elements of Mexican cuisine.

Anise (*anís*) is the seed of *Pimpinella anisum,* an herb of the carrot family, and is used very much in the making of Mexican breads, pastries, syrups, sweets, and liqueurs. It also goes into sauces, particularly *moles* like *mole poblano.* The anise used in Mexico is much smaller than that generally available in the United States, with a stronger flavor.

Banana leaves. The Spanish and Portuguese explorers brought different kinds of bananas and plantains (trees of the *Musa* genus) from the Old World tropics to the tropical Americas. Here the huge leaves joined the repertory of native American leaf wrappings for foods. They are used in the most traditional of Yucatecan dishes, *cochinita pibil,* in which a whole suckling pig is marinated in a version of *adobo yucateco* (see page 278), wrapped in banana leaves, and cooked in a *pib,* a hole in the ground. The same method is used for whole fish and chickens. The banana leaves impart a particular flavor and aroma. In the central and southern parts of Mexico they are the most commonly used wrapping for tamales. Packaged banana leaves are sold both fresh and frozen in Caribbean, Filipino, Southeast Asian, and Latin American markets. Look them over carefully and wipe off any powdery white film with a clean damp cloth.

***Canela* (true cinnamon, Ceylon cinnamon).** Here is a major problem of both terminology and taste. I can't stress enough that the product sold as "cinnamon" in U.S. markets is not right for

Mexican food. It actually comes from the cassia tree *(Cinnamomum cassia)* and other strong-flavored members of the cinnamon genus that are disdained in Mexico and many European countries as inferior substitutes for real cinnamon. I refuse to cook with this so-called cinnamon except in certain dishes where its sharpness is acceptable. Mexican cooks insist on a spice known as "true cinnamon" or "Ceylon cinnamon," *Cinnamomum zeylanicum,* which we call *canela*. I had always assumed that it came from Mexico, since I had only seen it there. But it turns out that it is grown in Sri Lanka (formerly Ceylon) and brought into the United States almost exclusively for re-export to Mexico at a hefty markup! Cooks here are literally unaware of its existence.

Wherever one of my recipes specifies *canela,* true cinnamon, I seriously beg you to use it. It differs from U.S. "cinnamon" in both texture and flavor. The bark is softer and thinner, with concentric layers that splinter easily when you break off a piece. The color is medium tan, not reddish brown. The pungent afternotes that U.S. cooks associate with the name "cinnamon" do not belong to our *canela*. It blends subtly with different seasonings and will not drown out other spices like the harsher cassia.

True cinnamon is available (in both powdered and stick form) from a few specialty spice and herb dealers (see page 331). To be sure of what you are getting, specify "Ceylon cinnamon" or "soft stick cinnamon." The ground spice is easier to mistake unless you can smell and taste it—don't buy it unless you are very sure of the sellers and have made them swear up and down that this is Ceylon cinnamon. It is somewhat lighter-colored than the ground cassia. Do *not* buy the sticks or powdered spice sold as *canela* in Cuban and Caribbean stores. It is cassia or another of the substitutes.

If you are obliged to cook with U.S. "cinnamon," you could try to compensate by using one-third to half the amount suggested for the powdered form or by removing the stick from the dish after half the suggested cooking time. I can't say that either of these expedients is very good. There is still a wrong note. Also, please be aware that when one of my recipes calls for putting true cinnamon stick in a blender with other ingredients, using cassia stick is courting disaster because it is too hard and tough. If you don't have the real thing, substitute a little ground U.S. "cinnamon."

Canned milks (evaporated milk, condensed milk). Purists may be surprised at the mention of these ingredients. Of course, all dairy products in Mexico are of European origin, beginning with the first cattle and goats brought by the conquerors. Milk has been drunk in Mexico since the sixteenth century, but not until canning technology was developed in the nineteenth century could milk be safely held for any period of time in the tropics, or easily brought to people in remote areas. Canned milk products quickly became important parts of our cooking in their own right. For most everyday uses, people enjoy not only the convenience but the taste of evaporated milk. Most cafés serve *leche de lata* (canned milk) instead of half-and-half or fresh milk, and use it to make cappuccino. Mother added it to *Calabacitas con Queso* (page 90) and *chile con queso*. Condensed milk, with its flavor of caramelized sugar and milk sugar, is the only thing some cooks will accept when they want the effect of sweetened milk boiled down to a fare-thee-well that is important in many Mexican puddings and custards. My sister Marina's recipe for *Flan—Queso de Nápoles* (page 188) with both evaporated and condensed milk is not some weird aberration!

Cheese, naturally, arrived in Mexico only with dairy animals. We now have cheeses of cow's, goat's, and ewe's milk made in various styles, partly reflecting later ethnic immigrations. There are too many Mexican cheeses to describe here, and unfortunately none is widely available in the United States in versions I can honestly recommend. However, I have had good results with some U.S. substitutions. These are the cheeses I think most important:

Queso añejo means simply "aged cheese," referring usually to something dry enough to be finely grated. The best substitute for the types most often used in Mexico is Parmesan.

Queso fresco ("fresh cheese") is a moist, cream-colored young cheese with a mild flavor (lightly acid, lightly salty) and a crumbly texture that makes it perfect for sprinkling on food. Some brands are found in this country, or you can substitute ricotta salata (sold in Italian markets and cheese stores—not to be confused with the supermarket cartons of fresh ricotta). Be sure not to buy the aged ricotta salata, which is quite different.

Queso Chihuahua or *queso menonita* is a longer-aged cheese probably related to types like Muenster and Tilsiter, introduced by the German Mennonites who came to the state of Chihuahua. For this I generally substitute a white cheddar. (The cheddars labeled "aged" or "sharp" are much more aggressive and will add a different note. Medium-sharp is my preference unless a recipe states otherwise, but use an extra-sharp cheddar if you really love it.)

Queso de bola or *quesillo de Oaxaca* is made from cooked curd pulled into long strings while still hot and rolled into a ball. The closest equivalent, though much saltier, would be a Lebanese or Syrian braided "rope cheese" or "string cheese," if you can find a plain one made without the black nigella seeds.

Asadero ("roasting" or "broiling" cheese), another mild pulled-curd cheese, is, as the name indicates, meant to have its best effect when melted under direct heat. Low-moisture mozzarella is a good substitute.

Requesón is a dry, compact cheese made with part skim milk and part whey. We used to make it on the ranch from the whey left over from making other cheeses. I find that the "hoop cheese" sold in some specialty markets and stores that have low-calorie products for dieters is an almost exact substitute.

Cilantro (*Coriandrum sativum*) must have been an important culinary herb for the Spanish who brought it to Mexico. But oddly enough, since then Spanish cooks have lost all interest in cilantro, while we remain extremely fond of it. It blends well with chiles, tomatoes, and many of our favorite seasonings. You will find it in some groceries and even supermarkets as "Chinese parsley" or "fresh coriander." In Cuban and other Latin American markets it may be called *culantro, culantrillo,* or *cilantrillo.*

Use only the leaves, not the stems, for a more subtle flavor. In most of my recipes, you should measure the cilantro after it has been washed and thoroughly dried.

Dried coriander seed is also used in Mexican cooking. It is part of some ground spice mixtures and is used to flavor some breads and pastries. It is also eaten in the form of *colaciones,* whole coriander seeds coated in sugar and dyed in bright colors that are traditional for the Christmas *posadas* (see page 209). These are exactly like the Elizabethan "comfits"—an example of how our cooking preserves very old elements of European cuisines.

Cloves (*Eugenia caryophylla*). Another of the "sweet" spices brought from Asia via Spain that quickly became one of the standard elements in complex seasoning mixtures like *moles* and *pepianes* and all kinds of braised and simmered meat or poultry dishes. In Spanish they are *clavos de especia* or *clavos de olor* (spice or aromatic "nails," so called from the shape of the dried flower bud).

Cumin. You will probably recognize these tiny dark brown seeds as one of the pervasive (and perhaps overused) flavor notes in Tex-Mex everything. It can be bought powdered, but a small amount of whole cumin seed will contribute more flavor if you first toast it in a small, heavy dry skillet and then grind it yourself (or crush in a mortar). Toasting also brings out the flavor in recipes where the seed is used whole. The plant, *Cuminum cyminum,* was brought from the Mediterranean.

Lard. Since the conquerors introduced Spanish livestock, this has been the favorite Mexican cooking fat. It's the only thing that is right for frying most of the spice mixtures like *moles* and *pepianes,* flavoring refried beans, and making tamales. Until recently, vegetable oils and olive oil were preferred only for a few uses. Now they are becoming more available. For me the smell of good lard recalls the excitement of butchering followed by marathon cooking sessions on our ranch when I was a child (see page 106). You can, of course, substitute any other oil or shortening when lard is called for, but switching cooking fats is like changing the lighting for a photograph and expecting it to look the same. Each kind of fat holds and melds all other flavors in its own way. When I do not sauté in lard, corn oil is my own preference.

For the health-minded, I would like to point out that lard is actually one of the less saturated animal fats. It has a lot of oleic acid, the most important monounsaturated fatty acid.

Olives (*aceitunas*). Some olives and olive oil are produced in Mexico. There might have been more if the colonizing Spaniards had not first started planting olives, then had greedy second thoughts and uprooted the groves in order to make olive oil a Spanish monopoly. Today olive oil enjoys only limited popularity as a cooking fat; people tend to sauté in lard and use blander vegetable oils for salads and frying. (Few Mexican cooks would go out of their way to use extra virgin olive oil; I have sometimes specified extra virgin where it's my personal preference, but in most recipes the grade is unimportant.) But olives are a favorite ingredient in dishes like *Picadillo Dulce* (page 47) or the sauce for Veracruz red snapper, where a sharp, slightly sour accent is desired (see page 37). Only brine-cured green olives, similar to some popular U.S. versions, are used.

Piloncillo. The sugar cane planted by the Spanish in the New World gave rise to several distinctive foods found in Mexico. One of these is our more flavorful equivalent of American brown sugar—the hard cones of unrefined sugar sold as *piloncillo* or *panela*. You can sometimes find these in Latin American markets in large flat cakes or small cones. To use, grate the hard sugar on the fine side of the grater, pulverize it in a food processor, or soften a small amount at a time in water. Dark brown sugar is the closest U.S. substitute.

Plantains. These less-sweet cousins of our familiar yellow bananas reached the New World by the same path. They are a favorite starchy vegetable in all tropical regions and can be found in Latin American or Filipino markets. Mexicans use several kinds; the one I cook with is a large variety that is green when semiripe and later becomes nearly black all over and yielding to the touch. This is the stage when you should buy it—or if you can find only green ones, let them ripen to blackness over a few days.

Plantains, unlike bananas, take a little work to peel. The simplest thing is to cut off the ends with a sharp knife, then make a lengthwise cut through the skin from end to end. Work the skin free using your fingers and the knife tip; cut away any clinging tough fibers.

Rice. Mexican cooking generally uses long-grain rice similar to favorite U.S. brands like Carolina and Uncle Ben's. In my recipes, regular long-grain rice is usually specified when a dish is to be cooked for a fairly short period of time. Where rice undergoes longer cooking, or two separate processes such as being briefly simmered and then cooked in a stuffing or dish, I prefer to use converted rice, which does not split or disintegrate as readily. It is seldom used in Mexico.

In dishes where rice is sautéed before simmering, Mexicans are fanatical about rinsing and rerinsing it until the water runs clear. This is important in the recipe for *Arroz a la Mexicana* (page 94).

Sour cream. Nobody has been able to reduce fresh cultured dairy products to scientific uniformity from one part of the world to another! Our *crema fresca* doesn't taste or feel quite the same as U.S. sour cream, probably because our milk is handled and processed differently and does not support quite the same mix of acid-producing live cultures. It is a little closer to the U.S. brands of crème fraîche, though our version is yellower. Commercial sour cream is used in Tex-Mex and other U.S. versions of Mexican food as a substitute for *crema fresca,* and I use it too, though I would prefer to use the real thing! The recent immigration from Mexico, Guatemala, and El Salvador has led to a better substitute, a type of bottled sour cream manufactured in the United States and sold in Central American groceries under different names such as *crema criolla* or just *crema.* I have had good results with these products. For a flavorful multipurpose sour cream sauce, see page 42.

BASIC PREPARATIONS

Years ago when I first started to cook professionally, my late friend Rosa Green gave me a book called *The Flavor Principle Cookbook,* by Elisabeth Rozin. The book's premise is that in every cuisine there are a few characteristic combinations of flavors—for example, soy sauce, ginger, and rice wine or sherry in Chinese cooking, and tomatoes, olive oil, and cinnamon in Greek cooking. This made me realize that Mexican food, too, rests on a few defining flavors that keep appearing in different ways, whether you are combining a chopped tomato with a couple of seasonings or making a lengthy presentation like *mole negro oaxaqueño.*

For U. S. cooks it can be intimidating to turn to a Mexican recipe and see two dozen ingredients and three pages of steps staring you in the face. The purpose of this section is to show that even complicated-looking recipes are not all that mysterious. They usually turn out to rest on straightforward building blocks, marriages of flavors that we use as the foundation for everything else. It is true that Mexican cooking today—like the food of India, medieval Europe, and the former Aztec empire—has an especially large repertory of rich, many-dimensional flavor combinations

A Note on Salt

When I cook for myself and friends I do what many cooks always do —just add salt without measuring until it tastes right. I am also reluctant to write recipes with hard and fast salt measurements that may be inappropriate for people trying to restrict their intake of sodium. But in many of these basic preparations and some recipes, salt really serves as a spice in a balanced seasoning blend. Without it, other flavors will not come together in the same way. Where I feel salt plays a crucial role, I have given a suggested measurement, usually on the conservative side. You can always start with a smaller amount and increase it (or not) to your own taste.

that take some assembling. But when you become familiar with some basic effects, you will recognize a handful of manageable themes appearing again and again in different variations. The recipes given here will reappear in other dishes in the book, and you will also find that you can apply these approaches creatively to fit different menu plans—so that a sauce you loved with chicken can also be paired with enchiladas, shrimp, or pasta.

In this section, I also indicate some of my own special approaches and try to explain how they relate to traditional Mexican originals. My cooking has evolved over the years in a way strongly rooted in the food of my childhood and in other aspects of Mexican cuisine I later came to know, but with a lot of individual differences. I have developed my own preferred ways of using Mexican cooking techniques to enrich flavors. "Layering" is the word I use to describe what we do at Zarela—not just literally putting a blob of this on top of that in a dish, but presenting different textures and flavors to make them offset and deepen each other.

Seasoning Pastes, Marinades, and Sauces

In most Mexican towns there are market stalls that sell only different kinds of spice mixtures—red, green, yellow, brown, and black mounds heaped up like something on an artist's palette. All will go into different richly sauced dishes reflecting the post-Conquest heritage of mixed Spanish and Mexican approaches.

The main categories of these preparations are *moles, pepianes, adobos,* and *recados*. Don't expect to learn precise definitions of each—they tend to shade into each other, and terms like *recado de adobo* don't help matters. But roughly speaking, *recados* are ground herb-and-spice mixtures ranging from the incredibly simple (at the ranch we used a mixture of garlic and oregano to rub on meat) to rather elaborate combinations of seasonings much like the garam masalas of India. They are especially important in the cooking of Yucatán. *Adobos* generally have dried chiles and (sometimes) vinegar in the seasoning mix and are used to marinate meat, fish, or poultry before roasting or grilling. *Pepianes* and *moles* are names for certain rich, multiflavored sauces usually thickened with ground seeds or nuts. *Pepián,* or *pipián,* is the direct descendant of dishes that the conquerors found Aztec cooks making with pumpkin seeds (nowadays sometimes also with sesame seeds or other nuts; the name is from *pepitas,* which refers to different kinds of seeds). *Moles* are of many types. Some lack the usual nuts or seeds, but some kind of ground chile is usually added for flavor and thickening. They are especially but not exclusively associated with the state of Oaxaca, "the land of the seven *moles.*"

Salsas are yet another complication in the picture. Usually but not invariably, a salsa is added to the food after it is cooked or partly cooked, or served with a dish at the table as a condiment or topping, instead of being intrinsically part of the flavor from the beginning, as is the case with the others.

The ingredients for all kinds of *adobos, recados,* and sauces used to be ground by hand in a mortar (*molcajete*—from the same Aztec root as *mole*). Today the task is accomplished, in all homes with electricity, in a blender. But people still make the sauces by hand when they want to show special honor to a guest. The food processor is satisfactory for some but not all of these mixtures—I confess that I dislike the food processor, and you won't find me recommending it every time a recipe calls for pureeing. It works best for *recados.* The blender is the only thing I recommend for *moles, pepianes,* and salsas.

Mexican Meals and Between Meals

The Mexican meal pattern, in fact the whole structure of the day, reflects the demands of a hot climate and a mostly agrarian lifestyle. There are two major meals, breakfast or brunch and the lengthy mid-afternoon *comida.* (Interestingly, some accounts also report that the Aztecs had two main meals; I've wondered whether the present arrangement may not be a very ancient survival.) Customs are changing a bit as some cities become more nine-to-five oriented and diet-conscious, but our ingrained life rhythms will not vanish any time soon.

Breakfast is typically a big meal. Laborers used to rise early and have a bite to eat (*desayuno*) before going to the fields, then eat a longer second breakfast (*almuerzo*) after a few hours' work. Today in Mexico there is not a rigid distinction between *desayuno* and *almuerzo,* but early morning coffee followed by a late, stick-to-the-ribs breakfast is still the custom. A typical breakfast could include fruit juice, eggs, beans, meat of some sort (for example, chorizo or a small steak), sweet bread or rolls, and coffee or chocolate. Sometimes there is a tortilla dish like *Chilaquiles* (page 312). *Atole,* a sweetened gruel of corn, and *champurrado,* the chocolate version, are great favorites.

The heart of the day is the leisurely *comida* (literally, "meal"), for which businesses obligingly close between two and five in most places to allow the people to go home during the hottest part of the day and eat and relax, or join friends in restaurants. Afternoon closing is less universal in the northern states, but even there the *comida* is commonly taken at home, without an eye or even half an eye on the clock. There is an invariable order of courses: a *sopa aguada* ("liquid" soup, any soup of pourable consistency), a *sopa seca* ("dry soup," meaning rice, pasta, or other starchy foods that cook by absorbing liquid), a *plato fuerte* (main dish of meat, fish, or poultry with some vegetable side dishes), a bean course, and a dessert. Salad is becoming more common now than it was in my late teen years in Guadalajara. Alcoholic beverages rarely accompany the *comida,* except for beer.

The whole idea of this succession of dishes is that the family and friends linger over a series of shared pleasures, savoring the hours around the table together. Maybe old-fashioned Sunday dinners were like this in the United States.

The best part of the tradition is the *sobremesa,* the time after the meal, when you prolong the occasion with stories, jokes, and gossip. When the *sobremesa* leads straight into the evening, it turns into a *parranda,* a drinking party. Some of my fondest memories are of family *parrandas.* We would laugh and tell jokes and my mother would play the piano while we all sang, everyone fighting over whose song would be next. The *parranda* is not really like any drinking party in this country. The idea is not to get smashed, but again, to prolong the party and the fun. There is a saying that the *parranda* has four stages: a toast to friendship, rehashing of grievances, complaints against the powers that be, and, to end the evening, dance and song. A *parranda* is really for drinking (slowly), not for eating. When my mother got impatient or bored with the party and started bringing out something to eat, my grandmother would say, "Aída, don't bring out the food, it will ruin the *parranda.*"

But this is not an everyday sequel to lunch. On ordinary days people eventually go about their business after the *comida* and do not have another real meal. The rest of the day's food usually falls into the snack category, which is a rich one in Mexico and often—not always—supplied outside the home. In most bars it is traditional to have *la hora de la botana* (snack time) in later afternoon. The *botanas* fill the same role as the special little dishes in Spanish *tapas* bars. (There are also family parties at home, *botaneadas,* which feature the same sort of dishes and are a favorite way to entertain on Sunday evenings. During my school years, when we were living in El Paso, Texas, and Agua Prieta, Sonora, Mother would have *botaneadas* on Sundays when my dad's friends would come to watch the football or baseball games on television, and some of his pals from Los Churumbeles de España, a fabulous group of musicians from Spain, would come to play for us.)

Another category of snacks is *antojitos,* literally "little cravings" or "whims," for example, *tortas* (sandwiches), or *masa* preparations like enchiladas, *sopes* (small shallow, round *masa* shells with a filling), or *chalupas* (same idea, but boat-shaped). *Antojitos* usually serve as our quick bite of supper—the quick bite of lunch has not made much headway in Mexico! They are often eaten at street stands or *puestos,* also known as *agachados* or "hunched-over ones." There is no seating, so the customers eat standing up in the street, hunched over the counter. Street food, by the way, is a major part of Mexican life. In any marketplace or town square you can find vendors selling anything, from the wonderful Mexican fresh fruits and fruit drinks to special regional tamales, sweets, or delicious roasted ears of corn with chile and lime juice. The large range of spur-of-the-moment options lends flexibility to the daily routine.

PASTA DE ACHIOTE

Achiote Paste

The most commonly known Yucatecan *recado* is a paste based on ground achiote seeds and other flavorings, bought premixed in market stalls or commercially packaged in bars. It lends flavor and a wonderful orange-red color to many sauces. Here is a home-made version that shows a crucial technique of Mexican cooking—briefly toasting or searing aromatic ingredients to bring out their flavor and fragrance before adding them to a mixture. In Mexico this would be done over a flame, on a small flat griddle called a *comal*. It is a frequent and important step in handling spices, garlic, dried or fresh chiles, and tomatoes.

2 tablespoons lard (see page 19) or vegetable oil

1 cup (about 6 ounces) achiote (see page 4)

3 cups fresh orange juice, heated, or boiling water

1 tablespoon cumin seeds

1 teaspoon black peppercorns

1 tablespoon dried Mexican oregano (see page 11)

4 large garlic cloves, unpeeled

1 teaspoon salt, or to taste

Heat the lard or oil in a small or medium-size skillet over medium-high heat until almost smoking. Add the achiote and sauté, shaking the pan constantly, for 5 minutes. Place the achiote in a heatproof bowl and cover with the orange juice. Let soak overnight in the refrigerator or at least 3 to 4 hours at room temperature. All the liquid should be absorbed and the seeds should be somewhat softened.

Heat a small, heavy skillet or griddle over high heat until a drop of water sizzles on contact. Add the cumin seeds and toast, shaking the pan frequently, until fragrant. Set the toasted seeds aside. Toast the peppercorns in the same manner and set aside. Toast the oregano and set aside. Work carefully while toasting the spices so that they do not scorch; remove them from the pan as soon as their fragrance is released, 1 to 2 minutes. In the same skillet, roast the garlic cloves over high heat, turning several times, until dark on all sides and somewhat softened, 5 to 10 minutes. Peel the garlic and set aside with the spices.

Place the soaked achiote, salt, and spices in a blender or food processor fitted with the steel blade. Grind thoroughly with a pulse motion, adding more water or orange juice, if necessary.

Work in batches, if necessary. The mixture should be a smooth paste. Refrigerate until ready to use.

Can be stored, tightly covered, in the refrigerator several weeks, or indefinitely in small containers in the freezer.

YIELD: ABOUT 3 CUPS

RECADO DE ADOBO BLANCO

White *Recado de Adobo*

The saffron in this recipe represents a U.S. adaptation that I eventually became very fond of. Mexican "saffron" is really safflower, which gives more or less the same color but does not have the subtle flavor and wonderful fragrance of true saffron. It is, however, quite inexpensive and can be used in generous quantities. I have gotten used to using saffron in this country the way we would use "Mexican saffron," probably more lavishly than everyone will care to. For my own purposes, I would probably make this *recado* with 1 teaspoon of saffron. *Recados* like this and the following *Recado de Adobo Colorado* can also be prepared using a mortar and pestle; follow the directions below but pound the spices in a mortar with the roasted and peeled garlic.

This mixture can be used to marinate chicken or fish, spread on heavier meats to be barbecued or roasted, or used to flavor stews.

3 tablespoons black peppercorns	1 teaspoon cumin seeds
1 teaspoon dried Mexican oregano (see page 11)	1 teaspoon coriander seeds
	¼ to ½ teaspoon saffron threads
8 cloves	6 garlic cloves, unpeeled

Heat a small, heavy skillet or griddle over medium-high heat until a drop of water sizzles on contact. Add the peppercorns and toast, shaking the pan often, until the aroma is released, 1 to 2 minutes. Set aside. Toast the oregano, cloves, cumin seeds, and coriander seeds in the same way, working with one spice at a time and setting it aside with the pepper as soon as it turns fragrant. Be careful not to scorch the spices; shake the pan often as you work.

Crumble the saffron between your fingers and add it to the toasted seasonings. Grind the mixture to a fine powder in a spice grinder or electric coffee grinder, working in batches if necessary.

In the same skillet over high heat, roast the garlic cloves, turning several times, until dark on all sides and somewhat softened, 5 to 10 minutes. Peel and finely chop the roasted garlic, then combine with the ground spices.

Can be stored, tightly covered, in the refrigerator up to 2 weeks, or indefinitely in the freezer.

YIELD: ⅓ TO ½ CUP

RECADO DE ADOBO COLORADO

Red Recado de Adobo

Use this the same way as *Recado de Adobo Blanco* (page 27), except that it is a little more suited to light foods such as chicken, pork, and fish.

1 tablespoon black peppercorns
1 teaspoon dried Mexican oregano (see page 11)
1 teaspoon cumin seeds
8 cloves

1 piece (2 inches) true (Ceylon) cinnamon (see page 15) or 1 piece (1 inch) U.S. "cinnamon"
3 garlic cloves, unpeeled
1 teaspoon Pasta de Achiote (see page 26)

Heat a small, heavy skillet or griddle over medium-high heat until a drop of water sizzles on contact. Add the peppercorns and toast, shaking the pan often, until their aroma is released, 1 to 2 minutes. Set aside. Toast the oregano, cumin seeds, cloves, and cinnamon in the same way, working with one spice at a time and setting it aside with the pepper as soon as it turns fragrant. Be careful not to scorch the spices; shake the pan often as you work. Grind the toasted spices to a fine powder in a spice grinder or electric coffee mill.

In the same skillet over medium-high heat, roast the garlic cloves, turning several times, until blackened in spots on all sides and somewhat softened, 10 to 15 minutes. Peel and finely chop the roasted garlic. Combine with the achiote paste and ground spices.

Can be stored, tightly covered, for up to 2 weeks in the refrigerator, or indefinitely in the freezer.

YIELD: ¼ TO ⅓ CUP

RECAUDO

This concept is not the same thing as *recado* (although that and its Caribbean counterpart *recaito* must go back to the same root). It is probably related to the lengthier Spanish *sofrito,* which involves onions and garlic slowly cooked in olive oil and then simmered with tomatoes. Variations are found all around the Mediterannean. The *recaudo* is the same general idea except that the usual Mexican cooking fat would be lard or a bland vegetable oil. It is the beginning of innumerable dishes and is also a wonderful multipurpose enrichment added to sauces and soups at a later stage; I rely very strongly on this enriching technique in my own cooking. You will frequently find a quick *recaudo* used (whether by name or not) in the recipes in this book. I recommend it for partly offsetting the failings of canned chicken stock. When used as an enrichment, the *recaudo* should be simmered at least 5 or 10 minutes in the sauce or soup to communicate its flavor (strain it out if you need a clear broth or smooth texture, puree in the blender if you want the *recaudo* to lend a little body).

The basic formula for a *recaudo* is as follows: Heat 2 tablespoons lard (see page 19) or vegetable oil in a medium-size heavy skillet over medium-high heat until hot but not smoking. Add 1 medium-size onion, thinly sliced or chopped (about 1 cup chopped onion) and 1 to 2 minced garlic cloves. Cook, stirring, until the onion is golden, 2 to 3 minutes. Add 1 chopped large, ripe red tomato. (The tomato can be roasted first for extra flavor, or used as is. See page 14 for instructions.) Continue to cook, stirring, until the liquid is mostly evaporated and the mixture begins to have a somewhat saucelike consistency, about 4 to 5 minutes. Use at once. This makes about 1½ cups. For about ¾ cup, use 1 tablespoon lard or oil, 1 small onion, 1 garlic clove, and 1 medium-size tomato.

ADOBO DE CHILE COLORADO

Red Chile
Adobo

The flavor of this typical marinade/coating will depend on the hotness and the variety of the chiles used. The recipe illustrates one technique of preparing dried chiles so as to soften them and enrich the flavor, by first frying them in hot fat (being careful *never* to scorch—the dish will have a horrible bitter taste) and then soaking them in hot water. In only a few recipes are dried chiles just put in the dish as is. Usually they are roasted on a griddle, fried, or softened in hot water, or some combination of these steps.

This *adobo* is good brushed on pork, grilled chicken, and *Pescado Estilo Playa* (page 135) or other fish. It also lends some real interest to Tex-Mex chili con carne. I use it as the spicy part of the complex fruit sauce in *Manchamanteles de Pollo* (page 95).

2 tablespoons lard (see page 19) or vegetable oil
4 medium-hot whole dried red chiles, either ancho, guajillo, or dried Anaheim (see pages 223–225), stems intact

1½ cups boiling water
1 large garlic clove, peeled and finely minced
1 teaspoon dried Mexican oregano (see page 11)
1 cup water

Heat the lard or oil in a small or medium-size heavy skillet over medium heat until rippling. Fry the whole chiles, one at a time, turning several times with tongs, until puffed and red or slightly orange in color, 30 to 60 seconds. *Be careful not to let them burn!*

As the chiles are done, add them to the boiling water in a bowl. Let soak until softened, about 10 minutes. Push them down if they float. Drain.

Pull or cut off the chile tops and scrape out the seeds. Discard the tops and seeds. Place the soaked chile pods in a blender with the garlic, oregano, and 1 cup water. Process to a smooth puree. Add a little more water if desired to facilitate blending, but the sauce should be thick.

Place a medium-mesh sieve over a bowl. Pour the paste into the sieve and force it through with a wooden spoon, scraping and rubbing to push through as much of the solids as possible. Discard any bits that won't go through.

Can be stored, tightly covered, in the refrigerator up to a month, or indefinitely in the freezer.

YIELD: ¾ TO 1 CUP (DEPENDING ON THE AMOUNT LOST IN SIEVING)

SALSA DE CHILE COLORADO

Red Chile Sauce

This is probably the most versatile of the red chile sauces. It also shows two important techniques. To develop the flavor of the dried chiles while softening them and taking away any bitterness, they are washed, quickly heated on a griddle to dry and briefly toast them, and soaked in hot water. Learn to recognize the moment when they are fragrant but not scorched—this is something you'll be encountering in many dishes. Scorched chiles will turn the entire dish bitter and unusable. The other technique to note is one that I have made an even more special point of in my own cooking: After the sauce has been pureed, it is finished by being cooked in a small amount of hot fat. This kind of final sautéing is an important addition to flavor in dozens of dishes we serve at Zarela. It both deepens and melds the effects of separate ingredients. This particular chile sauce is also bound with a roux, which is not true of all.

This sauce can be used to make red enchiladas, *enchiladas rojas,* with any preferred filling. It is used with cooked pork to make *Carne con Chile Colorado* (page 105) and to season *pozole* (hominy soup with pork and chicken), *menudo* (tripe soup), and northern-style tamales. We also used it with string beans or potatoes to make simple Lenten dishes (see page 106). In that case the sauce is cooked with vegetable oil and water instead of lard and chicken stock.

6 ounces large, medium-hot whole dried red chiles, either ancho, guajillo, or Anaheim (see page 223–225)
Boiling water to cover
2 teaspoons dried Mexican oregano (see page 11)
3 garlic cloves, peeled

2 cups water, Caldo de Pollo (see page 44), or pork stock (page 46), or as needed
2 tablespoons lard (see page 19) or vegetable oil
1½ tablespoons flour
1 teaspoon salt, or to taste

Heat a griddle or heavy skillet over medium-high heat, until a drop of water sizzles on contact. Meanwhile, remove the stems and seeds from the chiles while rinsing them under cold running water. Place them in the griddle and toast, three or four at a time, just until the aroma is released, 30 to 60 seconds. Be careful not to burn them. Place the chiles in a bowl and cover with the boiling water. Let soak until softened, about 10 minutes. Drain the chiles and discard the liquid.

Place the chiles, oregano, 2 of the garlic cloves, and the water in a blender and process to a smooth puree. Add more water or stock if it is too thick for the blender. With a wooden spoon or pusher, work the puree through a medium-mesh sieve into a bowl, pushing and scraping to get all you can. Discard any solids that will not go through. You may want to pour in a little more liquid to help rinse the sauce through the sieve.

In a heavy, medium-size saucepan, heat the lard or oil over medium-high heat until rippling. Add the remaining garlic and brown in the hot fat, pressing down with the back of a cooking spoon to release the flavor. Remove and discard the garlic. Add the flour to the hot fat and cook, stirring constantly, until golden. Add the strained chile puree and salt to the pan and reduce the heat to low. It will splatter as you pour it in—be careful. Cook over low heat, stirring often, until the raw taste is gone and the flavor of the chiles has mellowed, about 10 minutes.

Can be stored, tightly covered, in the refrigerator up to a week, or indefinitely in the freezer.

YIELD: ABOUT 2 CUPS

Variation:

My mother has a shortcut version of *salsa de chile colorado* that I sometimes use, replacing the whole dried chiles with powdered red chile. Not, I beg you, U.S. cayenne pepper or "chili powder"! Be sure to get pure powdered red chile, available at spice and gourmet stores (see page 226). Because it is sometimes a little harsh-flavored, she adds vinegar and sugar, which can be omitted or varied to taste. Pour about 1 cup boiling water over ½ cup powdered chile; stir in 2 to 3 tablespoons cider vinegar if desired, 1 teaspoon dried Mexican oregano, salt to taste, 1 teaspoon sugar if desired, and 2 to 3 crushed garlic cloves. In a heavy, medium-size saucepan, heat 2 tablespoons lard or vegetable oil and brown 1 garlic clove as described above. Remove and discard garlic. Add the powdered chile mixture to the pan, thin with water or broth to desired consistency, reduce the heat to low, and cook, stirring often, until the harshness of the chile is slightly mellowed, 5 to 10 minutes. Taste for seasoning and add a little more vinegar and sugar if desired. Let sit a few minutes to blend the flavors. My mother sprinkles 1 tablespoon of chile seeds on top, which picks up the flavor; use the loose seeds that always fall out of packaged dried red chiles.

You can also vary *salsa de chile colorado* by adding 3 or 4 large roasted ripe tomatoes (see page 14 for roasting technique) pureed with the dried chiles and garlic, as is done at Restaurant La Hacienda in El Paso, Texas.

PEPIÁN

Pumpkin-Seed Sauce

I have been eating this version of *pepián* (also spelled *pipián*) ever since I can remember. My mother used to serve it with green beans, *nopalitos* (cactus paddles, page 11), or cooked veal tongue. It's also good with *Pollo Guisado* (page 45), but in this case the chicken should be a little chunky, not finely shredded. We often serve it at Zarela as a very subtle accompaniment to grilled duck breast, but it is also wonderful with rack of lamb.

Fresh, good tomatoes are imperative in this sauce. Don't expect it to be fiery; you can spike it with more red chile sauce or *adobo*, but the mixture should be subtle. Serve the completed dish with a piquant table sauce like *Pico de Gallo Norteño* (page 40) on the side.

3 to 4 tablespoons lard (see page 19) or vegetable oil, or as needed

1 cup shelled raw pumpkin seeds (about 4 ounces)

4 large ripe, red tomatoes (2½ to 3 pounds), roasted (see page 14)

2 garlic cloves, peeled

3 cups Caldo de Pollo Casero (see page 45)

3 tablespoons Adobo de Chile Colorado (see page 29) or Salsa de Chile Colorado (page 31)

Salt to taste

Heat 2 tablespoons of the lard or oil in a heavy medium-size skillet over high heat until hot but not smoking. Add the pumpkin seeds, lower the heat to medium, and cook, shaking the pan and stirring constantly, until the seeds start to pop and take on a nutty fragrance, 1 to 2 minutes. Do not let them darken, or they will make the sauce bitter (discard any that browned too fast). Set the seeds aside. If any of the oil remains unabsorbed, reserve that separately.

Puree the roasted tomatoes in a blender with 1 clove of the garlic.

Transfer to a bowl large enough to hold all the ingredients. Combine the pumpkin seeds, the remaining garlic, and the chicken stock in the blender. Process to a smooth puree, working in batches if necessary. Add to the tomato mixture and stir to combine.

In a heavy medium-size saucepan, heat another 2 tablespoons lard or oil (using any remaining from the frying of the pumpkin seeds) until hot but not quite smoking. Add the puree and *adobo*. Stir to combine and bring to a boil, stirring occasionally. It will now be fairly thin, like medium cream. Season with salt. Reduce the heat to low and simmer, uncovered, stirring occasionally, until the mixture thickens, about 10 minutes. Don't let it scorch; it will thicken from the bottom.

Can be kept, tightly covered, in the refrigerator up to a week, or indefinitely in the freezer. I find that the flavor is, if anything, better after a day or two.

YIELD: ABOUT 4 CUPS

MOLE DE ALMENDRAS

Almond *Mole*

To many U.S. cooks *mole* means *mole poblano,* the sumptuous chocolate-enriched turkey or chicken fricassee that was popularized here a few decades ago by teachers like the late Michael Field. But there are many kinds of *moles,* all descended from the *mollis* that were well established when the conquerors arrived. This is a simple example of the *mole* concept, which does well as a sauce for many meats, from turkey or roast veal to lamb. It is also delicious with enchiladas. This same *mole* takes on an even richer flavor in braised dishes when it is used to deglaze the pan drippings from browning meat or poultry, which is then added to the *mole* to finish cooking.

1 cup whole unblanched almonds (5 ounces)
4 medium-hot whole dried red chiles, either ancho, guajillo, or Anaheim (see pages 223–225), stems intact
Boiling water to cover

2 hard-boiled large egg yolks
1 teaspoon aniseed
1 teaspoon ground true (Ceylon) cinnamon (see page 15), preferably freshly ground in a spice grinder, or ½ teaspoon U.S. "cinnamon"

1 teaspoon salt, or to taste
A generous grinding of black
   pepper
1 tablespoon sugar
2 to 3 cups Caldo de Pollo (page
   44) or Caldo de Pollo Casero
   (page 45)

¼ cup lard (see page 19) or
   vegetable oil
2 tablespoons cider vinegar

Toast the almonds in a shallow baking pan in a preheated 350°F oven until they have a rich, roasted fragrance, about 15 minutes. Check that they do not burn.

Wash the dried chiles under cold running water. Remove the tops, seeds, and veins. Heat a griddle or heavy medium-size skillet over high heat until a drop of water sizzles on contact. Place the chiles on the griddle and let them dry about 30 seconds; turn and let the other side dry 20 to 30 seconds. Be careful not to scorch. Remove the chiles to a small bowl, cover with boiling water, and let soak until softened, about 10 minutes. Drain.

Place the chiles in a blender with the toasted almonds, egg yolks, aniseed, cinnamon, salt, pepper, sugar, and 2 cups of the chicken stock. Process until thoroughly pureed, adding up to 1 cup additional chicken stock if needed to facilitate blending. The mixture should be somewhat thicker than cream. Work in batches if necessary.

Heat the lard or oil in a heavy, medium-size sauté pan or saucepan. Add the *mole* mixture and vinegar. Bring to a simmer and cook over low heat about 15 minutes, stirring often and watching that the mixture doesn't burn. Note that the mixture will thicken somewhat on cooking; add a little stock or water if desired to thin it to the original consistency when reheating.

Can be stored, tightly covered, up to 2 weeks in the refrigerator, or indefinitely in the freezer.

YIELD: ABOUT 2½ CUPS

PASTA DE CHIPOTLE

Chipotle Paste   This is not a traditional sauce but an improvisation I've happily been using for a number of years. I include it here because canned chipotle chiles are an easy introduction to two delicious flavors that will enlarge your understanding of Mexican food: smoked dried chile peppers and the version of *adobo* in which they are canned. When the two are blended to a paste, they are a nearly effortless example of a versatile spicy *adobo*.

There are few recipes that I use as much as this. I rub chipotle paste on fish or chicken for grilling (see *Salmón Ahumado al Chipotle,* page 326); use it if desired in place of *adobo de chile colorado* in *Pescado Estilo Playa,* page 135. I combine it with sour cream or mayonnaise to make cold sauces. And I haven't begun to explore all the possibilities. You are sure to find more as you experiment.

1 can (8 ounces) chiles chipotles en adobo (see page 224)	**1 tablespoon dried Mexican oregano (see page 11)**
4 to 5 garlic cloves, minced (about 2 tablespoons)	**2 tablespoons vegetable oil or olive oil**

Place the chipotle chiles and their sauce in a blender or food processor fitted with the steel blade. Process until pureed, about 1 minute. Add the garlic, oregano, and oil and process on pulse until combined but still slightly chunky.

Can be stored, tightly covered, in the refrigerator up to 3 weeks. I do not recommend freezing.

YIELD: ABOUT 1 CUP

CALDILLO DE TOMATE

Light Tomato

Sauce

This is a good sauce in its own right, but it is also one of those basic formulas that can be transformed in the handling. A good *caldillo de tomate* is the basis of many a Mexican sauce and provides the flavor basis for countless soups and other dishes. It is a traditional sauce for *chiles rellenos* (for example, the vegetarian version on page 251). I like to use the enriching technique of sautéing the mixture in one or two tablespoons of lard or butter if it is going to go into a dish as a flavoring agent. The simple addition of chiles, herbs, and spices (for example, cumin, cloves, or Mexican oregano) also puts a new spin on it. But in any case, the flavor of the tomatoes should always stand out, which is why it is crucial that they be at their peak of ripeness and that they be roasted before cooking in the sauce.

¼ cup lard (see page 19) or vegetable oil

1⅓ cups diced onion (1 medium to medium-large onion)

4 garlic cloves, peeled and minced (about 2 tablespoons)

3 pounds ripe, red tomatoes (4 to 5 large or about 8 medium)

Salt and sugar to taste

Roast the tomatoes by blackening them on all sides in a heavy skillet or in a griddle over high heat, or blacken under a broiler, turning several times. They should be well blistered. Remove the blackened skins, working over a bowl to catch any juice. Break the tomatoes into large pieces with your hands; do not seed.

Heat the lard in a medium-large saucepan over high heat until very hot but not smoking. Add the onion and garlic and cook 1 minute, stirring. Reduce the heat to medium and cook, stirring occasionally, until the onion is translucent and a little softened, about 5 minutes. Add the tomatoes and simmer another 5 minutes. Season with salt; if the sauce is too acid for your taste, offset it with a little sugar. Let the mixture cool.

Place the cooled tomato mixture in a blender, in batches if necessary. Blend until smoothly pureed, about 1 minute. With a wooden spoon or pusher, work the puree through a medium-mesh sieve into a bowl. Discard any solids that won't go through. Alternatively, puree in a food mill.

Can be stored, tightly covered, in the refrigerator up to 3 days, or indefinitely in the freezer.

YIELD: ABOUT 2 CUPS

SALSA VERACRUZANA

Veracruz-Style Sauce

This is one of the culinary basics of Mexican cooking that preserves the Spanish heritage in a nearly pure form, as shown by the olive oil, olives, and bay leaves. Originally from the coastal state of Veracruz where the Spaniards first landed, it has become a classic sauce throughout Mexico, especially with red snapper (*huachinango*) or other fish. It can also be used with braised tongue, fried calamari (we do this at Zarela), pork chops, and chicken. It makes a delicious sauce for pasta, too. Some cooks add sliced cooked potatoes and/or capers; I use pickled jalapeños.

½ cup extra virgin olive oil	½ cup pimiento-stuffed green
3 bay leaves	olives, sliced
4 to 5 garlic cloves, minced	½ cup mild pickled jalapeño
(about 2 tablespoons)	chiles (see page 225), sliced
1 medium-size onion, thinly	Freshly ground black pepper to
sliced (about 1 cup)	taste
1 can (28 ounces) whole Italian	Pinch of sugar (optional)
tomatoes with their juice	

Heat the oil in a heavy, medium-size Dutch oven or saucepan over medium-high heat until very hot but not quite smoking. Add 1 of the bay leaves and heat several minutes to perfume the oil; remove and discard the bay leaf. Add the garlic and onion and cook, stirring occasionally, until the onion is translucent, about 3 minutes. Add the tomatoes, breaking them up with your hands. Add the olives, jalapeños, and the remaining bay leaves. Stir well to combine. Bring to a boil, reduce the heat to medium, and cook for 5 minutes, stirring occasionally. Taste for seasoning. Add the black pepper and sugar. (Salt probably will not be necessary since the olives already have a lot.) Simmer another 2 minutes to mingle the flavors.

Can be stored, tightly covered, in the refrigerator 1 week, or in the freezer up to 1 month.

YIELD: ABOUT 5 CUPS

SALSA DE TOMATILLO/SALSA VERDE

Tomatillo

Sauce

This simple sauce, which is obviously a near relative of the raw tomatillo sauce (see page 41) and the *Pico de Gallo Norteño* (page 40), is another example of the extra dimension added by quickly sautéing an aromatic mixture in a small amount of hot fat. (In this case I prefer butter or corn oil. I think lard overpowers the delicacy of the tomatillos.) Notice also how the tomatillos will thicken and jell when pureed and cooked, one reason for their popularity in sauces.

The uses of this sauce are infinite. It is not only an excellent table sauce, but wonderful in *Chilaquiles* (page 312) and *enchiladas verdes*. My mother uses it in a delicious layered crêpe dish.

I don't care much for canned tomatillos, but they are better than nothing. Omit the simmering step and add drained canned tomatillos directly to the blender. They need no additional liquid.

1½ pounds fresh tomatillos (see page 14), husks removed (about 16 to 20 large tomatillos) or 2 cans (15-ounces each), drained

2 small onions, chopped (about ¾ cup)

2 garlic cloves, peeled

2 to 3 fresh or canned jalapeños, tops removed but not seeded

1 cup loosely packed fresh cilantro leaves (1 large bunch cilantro, leaves stripped)

1 teaspoon sugar

Salt to taste

2 tablespoons unsalted butter or vegetable oil

Place the fresh tomatillos in a medium-size saucepan and add water to cover. Bring to a boil and cook, uncovered, over high heat until the tomatillos change color, about 5 minutes. Stir them occasionally to be sure all cook evenly. Drain, reserving 1 cup of the cooking liquid. You can proceed with the sauce right away or let the tomatillos cool if it suits your schedule better.

Place the tomatillos in a blender with the reserved liquid. Add the chopped onion, garlic, jalapeños, cilantro, sugar, and salt and process until thoroughly pureed, about 1 minute. The sauce can be served at once as a condiment, or kept up to 1 day, tightly covered, in the refrigerator. But for the richer and longer-keeping version I prefer, heat the butter or oil over high heat in a medium-size saucepan. When the butter is hot and bubbling or the oil ripples, add the tomatillo mixture, reduce the heat to medium, and cook, stirring occasionally, until slightly thickened, 5 to 8 minutes. Serve hot or at room temperature.

The sautéed version can be kept, tightly covered, 2 to 3 days in the refrigerator, though it will lose something in flavor. This sauce does not freeze well.

YIELD: ABOUT 4 CUPS

Salsa De Tomatillo Con Tortilla
Tomatillo Sauce with Corn Tortilla

In sauces to be served hot, corn tortillas are often used as a thickener. The flavor combines nicely with the tomatillos and cilantro. Proceed as for *Salsa de Tomatillo,* but after cooking and draining the tomatillos, heat ¼ cup vegetable oil in a small, heavy skillet over high heat until hot but not quite smoking and fry 1 packaged corn tortilla just until it colors lightly, about 1 minute. (Do not let it brown or it will be bitter.) Remove the tortilla, drain on paper towels, and when cool enough to handle, break into pieces. Add the broken pieces to the blender and puree along with the other ingredients; proceed with the rest of the recipe.

PICO DE GALLO NORTEÑO

Uncooked

Tomato Salsa

This is an example of a *salsa fresca* or *salsa cruda*—"fresh" or "raw" sauce, meaning an uncooked sauce to be used as a condiment at table or street stall. There are many variations on *salsa cruda,* but this simple version is known everywhere. *Pico de gallo* (rooster's beak) is what we call it in northern Mexico—but don't confuse it with the salad eaten under that name in Guadalajara and Mexico City (see page 128). It can be served with almost any kind of dish—beans, eggs, tortillas, and various *antojitos* (snacks), or meat, fish, or poultry. The two imperatives are that the tomatoes must be truly ripe and sweet and that the sauce should be eaten at once. If you must, you can hold it for up to 2 hours refrigerated and tightly covered, but it loses its magic fast. But all is not lost if some is left over; it can be quickly sautéed in a little lard, butter, or vegetable oil to be served in a more durable reincarnation. In fact, it's probably the sauce I use most in this manner.

For the right slightly coarse texture, the ingredients should be chopped separately by hand. The only thing I sometimes do by food processor is the chiles. Try to find fresh ones, by the way; canned jalapeños will work but aren't ideal in a sauce supposed to be sparkling fresh. In a pinch, I have used the chiles from Asian markets or the ones called *ají* in South American markets. All of these vary in hotness and must be added to taste.

**2 to 4 fresh chiles, either jala-
peño or serrano (see pages
225 and 226) or to taste, tops
removed but not seeded
1 garlic clove, peeled
4 large ripe, red tomatoes,
peeled but not seeded (about
2½ pounds)**

**6 to 8 scallions with part of
green tops
¼ cup (loosely packed) fresh
cilantro leaves
1 teaspoon dried Mexican oregano (see page 11), or to taste,
crumbled
Juice of 1 large lime
Salt to taste**

With a large sharp knife, chop the chiles very fine. Mince the
garlic. Coarsely chop the tomatoes. Finely chop the scallions and
cilantro. Place the garlic, tomatoes, scallions, and cilantro in a
large bowl. If the tomatoes are very dry and juiceless, gradually
add up to ½ cup cold water to achieve a light salsa consistency.
Stir to mix the ingredients. Add the chiles a little at a time, tasting,
until it is as hot as you like. Add the oregano, then squeeze the
lime juice into the salsa; gradually add salt to taste. Use at once.
YIELD: ABOUT 4 CUPS

SALSA CRUDA DE TOMATILLO

Uncooked

Tomatillo

Sauce

Most restaurants and street stands have a red sauce (*Pico de Gallo
Norteño,* page 40, or another tomato sauce) and a green sauce on
the table to be added to taste. Green sauce, *salsa verde,* is most often
made with tomatillos, cilantro, and hot chiles. There are different
variations, cooked and uncooked. This version is very close to the
Northern *pico de gallo,* but with the pleasantly tart edge of tomatillo.

**1 pound fresh tomatillos (see
page 14), husks removed
(about 12 large tomatillos)
1 small onion, chopped (about
½ cup)
1 garlic clove, minced**

**1 to 2 fresh chiles, either jala-
peño or serrano (see pages
225 and 226), tops removed
but unseeded
½ cup loosely packed fresh
cilantro leaves
⅓ to ½ cup water, as needed
Pinch of sugar
Salt to taste**

Place the tomatillos in a blender with the onion, garlic, chiles, cilantro, and ⅓ cup water. Blend with a pulse motion until not quite smoothly pureed (a slightly chunkiness is one of its charms). Add more water if necessary to produce a light salsa texture. Add the sugar and season with salt. Serve at once.

YIELD: 2½ TO 3 CUPS

CREMA AGRIA PREPARADA

Aromatic Sour
Cream Mixture

This is an endlessly adaptable formula for which American sour cream, though unlike the cream of my childhood, works well. I use it to make *Chilaquiles* (page 312), crab enchiladas (*Enchiladas de Cangrejo,* page 181), my famous rice casserole, *Arroz con Crema y Poblanos* (page 172), and as a dip or sauce for fried oysters, fish, shrimp, or crudités.

Preparada is a hard word to translate. It usually indicates that an ingredient has been "elaborated," or converted into something a little different in the handling. The very flavorful Mexican cream is generally used plain; in my own cooking I have developed this nontraditional "prepared" version based on a sour-cream mixture used by one of my early teachers, Lillian Haines.

2 cups cultured sour cream
1 small onion, finely chopped
   (about ½ cup)
1 small garlic clove, minced

2 tablespoons finely chopped
   fresh cilantro leaves
Salt to taste

Combine all the ingredients and let rest 5 minutes to blend the flavors. This loses its freshness quickly but can be held, tightly covered, a couple of days in the refrigerator.

YIELD: SLIGHTLY MORE THAN 2 CUPS

FRIJOLES DE LA OLLA

Pot-cooked Beans

Every Mexican home has a special glazed pottery *olla* (pot) for the basic cooked beans—*frijoles de la olla*. It's as simple a dish as you could find, but there are some rules. It is important not to add salt until the beans are partway done, otherwise they will not be tender. If you need to add more water during the cooking, make sure it is boiling hot, otherwise the beans will be dark and unappealing.

Many people add a sprig of epazote to the cooking water for beans—there's a theory that it reduces their gassy properties, and in any case the flavor complements the earthy quality of the beans. In the north of Mexico *frijoles de la olla* are customarily served with a splash of vinegar and oil, a little crumbled Mexican oregano, and some *Pico de Gallo Norteño* (page 40) or chopped onion.

I always make *frijoles de la olla* with pinto beans, but you can use any preferred kind. In my experience pinto beans cook a lot faster than the also popular black beans, though any batch may be different. You can use the same method to cook a well-loved Old World import, chick peas. But note that they will take longer to cook and even when they are done the skins are so tough that Mexicans often rub off the skin before using cooked chick peas in a recipe.

1 pound pinto or other dried beans

1 large sprig epazote (see page 8), optional

2 teaspoons to 1 tablespoon salt, or to taste

Carefully pick over the beans to remove any foreign particles. Place them in a colander and rinse under cold water. Place the beans in a large, deep saucepan or Dutch oven and add enough cold water to cover by at least 1 inch, about 8 cups. Add the epazote and bring to a boil over high heat; reduce the heat to medium-low, partly cover the pot, and cook 20 to 25 minutes, until about half done (they will be somewhat chalky and dense inside). Add salt and check the water level, adding more hot water if the beans seem to be getting dry; there should always be at least ½ inch of water covering the beans.

Continue to cook until the beans are tender, occasionally checking the water level and adding a little more hot water if necessary. Time will vary greatly depending on the age and condition of the beans—as little as 45 minutes if they are fairly fresh, or more than 1½ hours for old, dried-out beans. The liquid should never be completely absorbed; when the beans are cooked they should be a little soupy. Do not drain unless beans are to be used in another recipe; *frijoles de la olla* are always served with a little of the cooking liquid.

YIELD: ABOUT 7 TO 8 CUPS

CALDO DE POLLO

Chicken Stock

Homemade stock is an important part of our cuisine, but it is not like the rich stocks of the classical French and Italian kitchens. Real Mexican cooking uses a light chicken stock meant to subtly enhance rather than overpower dishes in which it is used. We also often use the stock from boiled pork. Beef and veal stock are less frequent and more likely to be used for European-style sauces and soups. I have tailored this simple recipe for *caldo de pollo* to produce a bonus: the cooked chicken meat that is one of the most versatile ingredients in my kitchen. Luckily, the 3- to 4-pound chickens sold in every U.S. supermarket cook so quickly that they do very well for this double-barreled effort. You can, of course, make the stock from chicken wings and backs if a whole chicken doesn't fit your plans.

To deepen the flavor of *caldo de pollo* (but without turning it into something more like the European stocks), I like to use still another variant of my favorite enriching technique (see below, *Caldo de Pollo Casero*). In recipes calling simply for "chicken stock" you can use any good chicken stock or broth that you have on hand. When *Caldo de Pollo* and *Caldo de Pollo Casero* are called for, please use these particular stocks.

1 chicken (3½ pounds) or 3 pounds chicken wings and backs
1 medium-size onion, unpeeled
3 garlic cloves, unpeeled
1 carrot, scrubbed but unpeeled

1 celery stalk or leafy tops of 3 celery stalks
2 bay leaves
1 teaspoon black peppercorns
Salt to taste
10 cups water

The chicken can be left whole or cut up into 6 to 8 pieces. Combine all the ingredients in a medium-large pot or Dutch oven. Bring to a boil over high heat. Reduce the heat at once to low. Simmer, partly covered, until the meat is barely tender, about 30 minutes. Remove the chicken from the stock. Strain through a fine sieve and skim the fat, discarding the solids in the sieve.

Can be stored, tightly covered, 4 to 5 days in the refrigerator, or indefinitely in the freezer.

YIELD: 8 TO 9 CUPS (MORE OR LESS, DEPENDING ON WIDTH OF YOUR POT)

Caldo de Pollo Casero
Homestyle Chicken Stock

In medium-size sauté pan or skillet, heat 2 tablespoons lard or vegetable oil over medium-high heat until not quite smoking. Add 1 cup coarsely chopped onion (1 medium-size onion) and 1 minced medium-size garlic clove. Cook, stirring, until the onion begins to color, about 2 minutes. Add 1 chopped medium-size ripe, red tomato, and cook 3 minutes. Have 8 cups *Caldo de Pollo* (recipe above) just at the boiling point in a deep pan. Add the onion mixture to the boiling stock, turn the heat to low, and simmer, uncovered, 10 minutes. Strain through a sieve and discard the solids.

YIELD: 8 TO 9 CUPS

POLLO GUISADO

Poached and
Sautéed
Chicken

This is one of my real standbys, the basis of many dishes at Zarela. As the chicken emerges from the stockpot it is plain poached chicken, ready to be pulled into shreds and used as is. You can do this if you want—but I always take it one step further for the extra depth and dimension of flavor that is so important to my food. I sauté the shredded chicken with onion and garlic to bring out a richer dimension. If for some reason I'm on a diet and use the plain poached chicken, I use lots of herbs and spices when I add it to a recipe!

Pollo guisado is an incredibly useful ingredient. You can use it to make tamales, *flautas,* and many kinds of enchiladas. I love it in *Chilaquiles* (page 312). You can also prepare it with the same olive-raisin combination described in the variation for *Picadillo Dulce* (see *Picadillo de Pollo*, page 48).

2 tablespoons lard (see page 19) or vegetable oil	**Chicken from Caldo de Pollo (see page 44), meat pulled from bones and shredded**
1 small onion, finely chopped (about ½ cup)	**Salt and freshly ground black pepper to taste**
1 small garlic clove, finely minced	

Heat the lard or oil in a large saucepan or wide sauté pan over medium heat until hot but not smoking. Add the onion and garlic and cook, stirring, until translucent. Add the shredded chicken, stirring well to distribute the ingredients. Season with salt and pepper and let cook 5 minutes, stirring occasionally, to blend the flavors.
YIELD: ABOUT 3 CUPS

CARNE DE PUERCO COCIDA

Cooked Pork

Butt

This is a basic way to cook pork butt to produce both the cooked meat and stock for recipes such as *Tamales con Chile Colorado* (page 216) and *Pastel Sole de Vega* (page 255). The cooled stock will be used to moisten and flavor the *masa*. You can also sauté the shredded meat with a *recaudo* (see page 29) and use to fill *Gorditas* (page 161) or *Sopes* (page 124), or use in place of the chicken in *Flautas* (page 174).

To store the shredded meat, pour just enough of the cooled, strained pork stock into the storage container to cover it. This helps keep it from drying out.

2½ pounds boneless pork butt in one piece, trimmed of all but a thin layer of fat	**1 teaspoon black peppercorns**
	4 large bay leaves
1 whole head of garlic, unpeeled, cut crosswise in half	**1 teaspoon salt, or to taste**

Place the pork butt in a large Dutch oven or medium-size stockpot. Add the garlic, peppercorns, bay leaves, and salt. Add enough cold water to cover by at least 3 inches. Bring just to a boil on high heat, quickly reduce the heat to medium-low, and let simmer, partly covered, skimming any froth from the top during the first 15 to 20 minutes of cooking. A piece this size should be well cooked but not dried out in 1½ to 2 hours. Remove from the stock and let cool to room temperature. When cool, pull the meat into fine shreds.

Strain and degrease the stock (it will be easier to remove fat when thoroughly chilled).

Can be kept, tightly covered, 2 days in the refrigerator if degreased at once, up to 1 week if you leave the top layer of fat on it until ready to use. The stock also freezes well.

YIELD: ABOUT 3 CUPS OF SHREDDED MEAT AND 3 CUPS OF STOCK

PICADILLO DULCE

"Sweet"
Spiced
Ground Meat

This is one of the recipes you meet everywhere in Mexican cooking (often with the meat hand-shredded instead of ground). There is nothing New World about the ingredients unless you count the optional potato. But *picadillo dulce* features two of the most characteristic Mexican flavor combinations: true cinnamon, clove, and cumin; and raisins, green olives, and, in many versions, almonds. Perhaps this is one of the Mexican survivals of medieval Spanish cuisine, also shown, I believe, in the integral importance of sweetness as an element in much of our savory cooking. In any case, it is wonderfully versatile. *Picadillo dulce* is a favorite filling for tacos and burritos. I use it to stuff Christmas turkey, marinated ancho chiles (see page 224), and the fabulous hollowed-out Edam cheese of Yucatán. I have also tasted it in the sugar-coated pastries of Chihuahua, *empanadas de Santa Rita*.

For this recipe (and, you will notice, many others) I prefer to grind the Ceylon cinnamon fresh in a spice or coffee grinder instead of using it preground. The difference is really startling. And because I dislike the smell of grease rendering too fast out of meat, I start off the ground beef or pork with a cup of water, which evaporates in the cooking.

½ cup golden raisins

½ cup dry sherry, heated

1½ pounds very lean ground beef, pork, or any combination of the two

1 cup water

2 large garlic cloves, minced

1 medium-large onion, finely chopped (about 1½ cups)

1 jar (6 ounces) sliced pimiento-stuffed green olives, drained and sliced (about 1 cup)

2 teaspoons ground cumin

1½ teaspoons ground true (Ceylon) cinnamon (see page 15) or ½ teaspoon U.S. "cinnamon"

1 teaspoon freshly ground black pepper

½ teaspoon ground cloves

Salt to taste

OPTIONAL

1 medium-sized boiling potato (Red Bliss or other thin-skinned variety), peeled, finely diced, simmered in boiling water until not quite tender (about 5 minutes), and drained

1 cup toasted (see page 35) slivered blanched almonds

Combine the raisins and hot sherry in a small bowl and let soften at least 20 minutes. Meanwhile, heat a large skillet over high heat. Add the ground meat and water, bring to a brisk simmer, and cook, uncovered, stirring occasionally, until the grease begins to render, about 2 minutes, breaking up the meat with a fork or cooking spoon. Continue to cook on high heat until the water is evaporated, then add the garlic and onion and let simmer another 2 minutes. Add the plumped raisins and sherry together with the remaining ingredients, except the almonds. Reduce heat to low and simmer, uncovered, until the flavors are well melded, about 5 more minutes. The meat must not be overcooked. Garnish with the almonds before serving.

Can be kept, tightly covered, in the refrigerator up to 3 days. Can be frozen up to a month, but omit the almonds until serving time.

YIELD: 4 MAIN-COURSE SERVINGS

Picadillo de Pollo

To make this versatile alternative to beef or pork *picadillo,* soak the raisins in the hot sherry as described above. Prepare *Pollo Guisado* (page 45), instead of the ground pork or beef; stir in the raisins and sherry, olives, spices, and salt (no potato). Cook 5 minutes, stirring frequently, until the flavors are well melded. Garnish if desired with the toasted sliced almonds before serving.

Masa and *Masa* Preparations

The staff of life for most Mexicans is still just what it was before Cortez's army ate their first tortillas in 1519: a preparation of dried corn kernels soaked in an alkaline solution of slaked lime until they swell and undergo a crucial chemical change that vastly enhances their food value. (For more on the history of corn, see pages 191–199.) When not used whole for dishes like *pozole,* the softened and cooked kernels are ground up to produce a moist mixture that Mexicans call simply *masa,* or dough, the basis of all corn tortillas and most tamales.

It is possible to make your own *masa* from scratch using dried corn, quicklime or slaked lime, and a special mill, but I don't think the effort is worthwhile when most large U.S. cities are within reach of at least one large tortilla factory selling its own fresh-ground *masa* by the pound. There are probably hundreds of them in this country; for a short list of suppliers see Mail-Order Sources, page 335. Fresh *masa* sours very quickly and cannot be kept more than a couple of days in the refrigerator. However, it freezes well. Store tightly wrapped in the freezer for up to a month. I generally double-wrap it, first in a layer of plastic wrap and then in aluminum foil.

You can usually buy *masa* ground to different levels of fineness. I recommend finely ground for tortillas, coarsely ground for *tamales*.

If you cannot find a source in your area, an equivalent of fresh *masa* that is fairly good for most purposes and excellent for some can be prepared from *masa harina,* literally "flour for *masa.*" This is made from fresh *masa* that has been allowed to dry and ground to a coarse flour. It is manufactured in this country and distributed nationwide in 5-pound packages by the Quaker Oats Company (see page 332 for the address). To substitute *masa harina* for fresh *masa,* reconstitute it with water or stock as indicated below under Basic *Tamal* Dough and *Tortillas de Maíz,* or follow special directions in individual recipes.

Please note that *masa harina* is NOT the same thing as U.S. cornmeal, which never has received the all-important alkali treatment.

BASIC TAMAL DOUGH

As I explain elsewhere, there are dozens of dishes called tamales with nothing in common except that they are folded before being cooked in a wrapping, usually corn husks or banana leaves (see Tamales, page 228). This particular formula, in which *masa* is beaten very light with lard and chicken (or sometimes pork) stock, makes probably the most versatile *tamal* dough. The important things to bear in mind are that no matter what quantity you make, you will almost always use the same proportion by weight of *masa* to lard—in my recipes, 3 to 1—and that the mixture must be beaten until it is not just light but practically ethereal.

> ### A Note on Weighing
> I am a great believer in kitchen scales. Most U.S. cooks use only cups and spoons to measure ingredients, and I've deferred to this practice. But there are cases where the scale tells you what's important—for example, in making doughs for tamales, where the ratio of fat to be beaten into a prepared *masa* dough is generally 1:3 by weight. For this reason I include weight measurements along with cup measurements in some recipes. In nearly all such cases the weight measurement is really the more precise.

Though the amount of salt may seem excessive, a lot of the salt will be lost when the mixture is steamed inside the *tamal* wrapping. You can reduce the amount somewhat, but remember that the particular flavor of *masa* in tamales is complemented by salt.

3 pounds fresh masa (ask for coarsely ground)
or
4½ cups masa harina and 4 to 5 cups warm Caldo de Pollo (page 44) plus more as needed

1 pound lard (preferably non-hydrogenated and without preservatives)
2½ tablespoons salt

Set fresh *masa* aside, if using. If using *masa harina,* place it in a large bowl and reconstitute by adding 4 cups warm stock. Beat with a wooden spoon or mix with your hands until you have a stiff, smooth dough like a medium-pliable bread dough. Use a little more stock if necessary, but the mixture should not be loose.

Beat the lard in a large bowl with an electric mixer on medium speed until very fluffy and fully aerated, about 3 minutes. It may take longer if your mixer is not powerful (a heavy-duty machine such as a KitchenAid is best). The best alternative to a mixer is not a spoon but your bare hand: whip and beat the lard with a rapid folding motion until you feel it lightening, and continue to whip until it is fluffy and full of air. It should be as light as butter creamed for the lightest butter cake.

Still mixing on medium speed, begin adding the *masa* a handful at a time. Stop to scrape down the sides of the bowl with a rubber spatula as necessary. Alternatively, beat in the *masa* using your bare hand as a whipping and folding tool. If the mixture becomes too stiff to beat, add up to 1 cup tepid chicken or pork stock a little at a time. When all the *masa* has been incorporated, the mixture should be very light and delicate, the texture of buttercream frosting. Beat in the salt.

The mixture is now ready to be spread onto corn husks, banana leaves, or other wrappers and steamed.

FILLING AND STEAMING TAMALES

There are different ways of shaping tamales, but the two methods given here will serve as general guidelines for the most versatile forms of corn-husk and banana-leaf tamales. Follow the quantities given in the individual recipes.

Corn-husk tamales. Place the dried corn husks (see page 7) in a large bowl and cover with boiling water. Let soak 30 minutes or longer. Drain and select as many as you can of the larger pieces, being careful not to open the crinkled leaves of the core that are full of corn silk. Select some of the better-looking middle-sized or narrow pieces, which you will be pasting together as necessary. Pat the husks dry.

Working with a few at a time, fill and fold them as follows. Place a large husk on the counter. With a spatula, spread ¼ to ⅓ cup of *masa* mixture across the lower (wide) end of the husk, covering it from side to side and extending about halfway up toward the narrow tip. If there is a meat, chicken, or other filling, place about 1 heaping tablespoon of filling in the center of the *masa* mixture. Either roll the *tamal* up lengthwise and fold in half, or first fold the right third over to the center and then fold the left side over it (figures 1 and 2), then fold up the narrow end even with the wide end so the *tamal* is folded roughly in half crosswise (figure 3). Smaller husks will take less *masa* mixture and filling. If necessary, use a bit of *masa* to paste together a couple of husks too small to use by themselves. As they are finished, place the tamales on a baking sheet until ready to steam. (They can be refrigerated, covered with plastic wrap, up to a day, or frozen for one month.)

Have a steamer with a basket or steaming insert ready, or improvise your own arrangement. A cake rack propped on top of sawed-off tin cans in a large stockpot or Dutch oven with a tight-fitting lid is one possibility. My own preferred stratagem is to place the tamales directly on the bottom of a large Dutch oven, leaning teepee-style against a central prop like a large ball of wadded-up aluminum foil. In any case, arrange the tamales with their open ends facing upward. Place some of the unused corn husks (and/or a wrung-out wet tea towel) over the tamales to help absorb steam. Pour boiling water into the bottom of the steamer to a depth of at least 1 inch; if using my teepee arrangement,

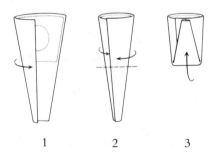

1   2   3

carefully pour about 1 inch of boiling water into the bottom of the pot. (Don't worry—if the tamales have been tightly wrapped they will not leak.) Cover tightly and bring quickly to a full boil over high heat. Reduce the heat to medium-low to maintain a gentle bubbling. Cook for about 1 hour, replenishing with boiling water as necessary (remember that water will evaporate faster in a wider pot). Remove the steamer basket (or uncover the Dutch oven) and let the tamales stand 10 minutes before serving.

Banana-leaf tamales. I am very fond of the fragrant quality imparted by banana leaves, and suggest that you sometimes experiment by substituting them for corn husks in *tamal* recipes.

Banana leaves are generally sold in packets, in enormous squares that should be trimmed to the desired size with kitchen scissors (thaw the leaves first if frozen, and wipe off any powdery residue). A good size for most purposes is a rectangle about 14 x 11 inches. Place about ¾ cup of prepared *masa* mixture in the center of the leaf; spread it out into an oval or rectangle about 4 x 3 inches and about ½ inch thick. If using a meat or other filling, place 1 to 3 tablespoons in the center of the *masa* oval. Fold over the right and left edges of the banana leaf so that they meet in the center, overlapping slightly. Fold the top and bottom edges in the same way. You should have a neat flat package about 4 x 5 inches. Fasten by tying with a thin strip torn off another banana leaf.

In this case you want the tamales to lie flat on the steaming rack, well above the boiling water. Stack them in layers as necessary, seam side up. Place some extra banana leaves on top to help absorb steam. Pour boiling water into the bottom of the steamer to a depth of at least 1 inch; cover tightly. Bring quickly to a full boil over high heat, then reduce the heat to medium-low to maintain a gentle bubbling. Cook for about 1 hour, replenishing with boiling water as necessary (remember that water will evaporate faster in a wider pot). Remove the steaming rack or insert and let the tamales stand 10 minutes before serving.

TORTILLAS DE MAÍZ

Corn Tortillas

Unlike *tamal,* which was the Spaniards' attempt to pronounce the Aztec word *tamalli, tortilla* is a Spanish word—though one that often leads American tourists into trouble in Spain, where it refers only to omelets! The original meaning was a little round, flat cake, and in Mexico the word eventually came to refer primarily to thin cakes of prepared *masa* baked on a griddle or a softer equivalent made with wheat flour.

One legacy of the Mexican food craze in the United States is that you can now buy packaged corn and flour tortillas at many or most supermarkets. They are a mixed blessing. Usually commercial corn tortillas are much thinner and drier than homemade versions. I use them (only brands made with 100 percent corn) for some purposes, like tostadas, *flautas,* and taco shells—anything where they are going to be fried. (Because they are thinner, they don't absorb as much grease.) Where they are to be used as an accompaniment to the meal the way you would use bread, it is imperative to use homemade tortillas—the commercial ones curl up and dry out in no time flat, and will never have the fine flavor or ability to soak up other flavors that you want.

This is a basic recipe for corn tortillas shaped with a tortilla press (available in Latin American and some specialty gourmet stores). Yes, it is possible to shape tortillas by hand, as women in Mexico have done for centuries, but the press is inexpensive and will greatly hasten the tortilla-making careers of some who would otherwise struggle vainly for the knack. If you have no press, you can resort to the trick described below.

2 cups masa harina	*or*
1 cup plus 2 to 4 tablespoons warm water, or as needed	**1 pound fresh masa (ask for finely ground)**

Before you begin, prepare an anti-stick liner for the tortilla press by cutting open two sides of a medium-size (about 6 inches square) heavy-duty plastic bag, such as a zip-closing freezer storage bag, to make a rectangle at least 12 x 6 inches.

In a medium-size bowl, combine the *masa harina* and 1 cup of the warm water. Using a wooden spoon or your bare hands, mix to form a smooth dough with a consistency like a somewhat stiff bread dough. Add a little more water if necessary. If using fresh *masa*, place it in a bowl and work it with wet hands to check the consistency. If it is crumbly, work in water, a tablespoon at a time, with your hands, until it holds together.

Dampen your hands as necessary with cool water, shaking off the excess. Shape the dough into 10 to 12 Ping-Pong–size balls. Keep them covered with a damp tea towel while you work, to prevent them from drying out.

Heat a griddle or cast-iron skillet over high heat until a drop of water sizzles on contact. Quickly grease the griddle by pouring a little vegetable oil on a paper towel and rubbing it over the surface. Adjust the heat as necessary to remain constant while you work.

Open the tortilla press and place your plastic liner in it with the creased edge next to the hinge. Place a ball of dough in the center of the press between the two flaps of plastic. Lower the top of the press and press down on the handle to make a tortilla between 5 and 6 inches in diameter and about 1/16 inch thick. Open the press. Peel off the top flap of plastic, lift out the tortilla, and peel away the bottom flap, dampening your hands again if necessary.

My one suggestion for shaping tortillas without a press works only if you have a small, round heavy object with a perfectly flat bottom like a very small cast-iron skillet. Place the plastic liner directly on the counter. Place a ball of dough between the two flaps. Being super-careful not to tilt the weight unevenly, press straight down with the bottom of the skillet to form a flat 5- to 6-inch tortilla. Carefully peel off the top flap of plastic, then peel away the tortilla from the bottom flap.

Place the tortilla on the hot griddle and cook until lightly flecked with brown on the underside, about 1½ minutes. Turn with a spatula (I use my fingers) and cook 1 to 1½ minutes on the other side. Now encourage it to puff up slightly (if it hasn't puffed by itself) by quickly pressing down on the top with a bunched-up tea towel or a weight such as a heavy can. Flip it over and quickly press the other side. (If using a cast-iron skillet, be *very* careful not to brush against the hot sides as you do this!) Remove the tortilla with a spatula to a plate, wrapping snugly in a napkin or tea towel. Repeat with the remaining balls of dough, stacking and covering the tortillas as they are done.

Fresh corn tortillas are best used at once. I don't recommend freezing them—it can be done but they will never be the same.
YIELD: 10 TO 12 SMALL (5- TO 6-INCH) TORTILLAS

NOTE: Leftover tortillas are as important in Mexican homes as leftover bread is in the homes of thrifty European cooks. You could practically write a book on the subject. They are pulverized to make a thickening for sauces. Cut into strips or triangles, air-dried, and fried in hot lard or oil to crisp them, they go into dishes like *Chilaquiles* (page 312). Or they are eaten in their own right with a salsa as tostadas. For some of these uses my recipes usually suggest commercial tortillas, on the assumption that not many U.S. cooks will ordinarily have leftover homemade tortillas on hand.

TORTILLAS DE HARINA

Flour Tortillas

This Europeanized (but now totally Mexican) takeoff on the pre-Columbian tortilla idea was made possible by the Spanish introduction of pigs (for lard) and wheat, which grew beautifully in parts of the north-central regions. In my childhood in the North we had corn tortillas every day for lunch, but at night my mother usually served flour tortillas. By then solid vegetable shortenings, such as Crisco, had overtaken lard in popularity because of the nice supple consistency they lend to the dough.

I wish I could get flour here as good as that grown and milled in Mexico. It just seems to have more flavor and character. Even the color is warmer, not so pallid. You may want to experiment with flours from smaller mills in this country that supply amateur bread bakers. For tortillas, however, you want an all-purpose flour rather than the hard-wheat flours usually sold for bread-making. I get good results with Hecker's or Pillsbury all-purpose unbleached flour.

6 cups unbleached all-purpose flour
1½ teaspoons salt
1 teaspoon baking powder

1 cup solid vegetable shortening
1½ to 2 cups water warmed to 115°F (warmer than lukewarm, but not hot)

Combine the flour, salt, and baking powder in a large mixing bowl. With two knives or your fingers, cut or rub the shortening into the flour until the mixture resembles coarse crumbs. Slowly pour 1½ cups of the warm water into the mixture, at the same time working the ingredients together with your fingers. When all the water has been added, continue to work the mixture with both hands until it gathers together in a ball. The object is a somewhat soft but not sticky dough. Add a little more water if necessary, but the dough is not terribly "forgiving" of adjustments. Turn the dough onto a lightly floured surface and knead gently until smooth and silky, about 5 minutes.

Divide the dough into 4 equal pieces and make 12 equal-sized balls from each piece. (For larger—6-inch—tortillas divide each quarter of the dough into 6 rather than 12 pieces.) Work with one piece at a time, keeping the others covered with a tea towel to prevent them from drying out. Shape each ball of dough in your fingers as follows—the process is easier to carry out than to describe. Flatten the ball slightly and hold it in your two hands with your thumbs on the top side and other fingers underneath. Lightly pull the dough out from the center on all sides, not stretching it much, but pulling it enough so that you can tuck down the edges between your thumbs and first two fingers to produce a somewhat rounded shape. (It's as if a flattish mushroom cap had fat edges you could tuck down, pulling and pushing to round the shape.) Cover the shaped piece of dough with a damp towel. Continue until you have shaped every ball of dough, keeping the completed ones covered. Let rest 20 minutes, covered.

On a lightly floured surface using a small, lightly floured rolling pin, roll out a ball of dough to a circle about ¹⁄₁₆ inch thick and 4 inches in diameter. Repeat with 3 more balls of dough, covering them with a towel as you are done. Be ready to cook them quickly.

Heat an ungreased griddle or cast-iron skillet over medium-high heat until a drop of water sizzles on contact. Place a tortilla on the griddle and cook until the underside is speckled with brown spots and small bubbles appear on the top, about 30 seconds. Turn the tortilla with a spatula and cook the other side until it is also speckled, about 30 seconds more. Now encourage it to puff slightly by quickly pressing it first on one side and then the other with a bunched-up tea towel or a weight such as a heavy can. (If using a cast-iron skillet, be *very* careful to avoid brushing the hot sides with your hand!) Remove to a plate, let cool slightly, and wrap snugly in a napkin or tea towel. Repeat with the remaining balls of dough, rolling, cooking, stacking, and covering them as they are done.

YIELD: 48 SMALL (4-INCH) OR 24 LARGE (6-INCH) TORTILLAS

NOTE: Tortillas should be used quickly, but can be reheated very successfully. Wrap in aluminum foil and place on a baking sheet in a preheated 300°F oven until heated through, about 5 minutes. A second method is to reheat them one at a time on a hot griddle. Or heat them (stacked, not individually) in a microwave oven 30 to 40 seconds. Flour tortillas freeze beautifully.

My Roots: El Rancho (The Ranch)

I have not loved anything as much or with such passion as the ranch. It is an integral part of my being, and I would not be as I am without having lived there those marvelous years of my childhood.

It was 1931 when the land came into the hands of my mother's family, one of the ranching families of northern Mexico that have had close ties (and often property) on both sides of the border for generations. Ranchers of varied national backgrounds mingle on close terms in Sonora, Chihuahua, Arizona, New Mexico, and Texas, and some of our dearest friends were descended from a wave of British fortune-seekers who came to the north of Mexico in the nineteenth century.

One of these immigrants, a certain Lord Delaval James Beresford, founded our ranch after leaving Ireland, where we gather he was some sort of black sheep and had the misfortune of not being the first-born. He came to the New World, but at some point en route he was supposed to have fallen ill with malaria and been nursed back to health by a mulatto woman named Florida—"Lady Flora," in our family version of the story. They made their way to the El Paso area and set up house, something just not done by mixed-race couples at that time (around 1880). The scandal drove them to Chihuahua, where many English and Scots had settled. Here they acquired large properties, one of which was San Pedro de Ojitos, Saint Peter of the Springs, where they raised Percheron horses to be sent back to Scotland. The horses were branded with the double triangle which my mother was later to inherit.

San Pedro sits at the very start of the Sierra Madre, in Geronimo territory, in a valley surrounded by majestic mountains with evergreens, cactus, mountain lions, and bears, the perfect location for the fort it was originally meant to be. Apache attacks were still common when Lord Beresford arrived. The square structure of the house, with its two turrets, is English. The walls are three feet thick and impenetrable. The slanted tin roof is a later addition—my grandfather loved to hear rain pounding on tin roofs and installed them on all his houses. On windy nights the towering elm trees would sweep against the tin roof at San Pedro with a sound like long skirts swooshing.

When Lord Beresford died, Florida returned to El Paso and lived there until her death, but it was a mistake. She died longing to go back to the ranch. She is buried in Concordia Cemetery in the center of El Paso, but her spirit haunts San Pedro. When we were children, our nanny, Doña Sabina, a tall, skinny Apache woman very much like the "old maid" of the card game, with a figure exactly like Olive Oyl's, would frighten us with stories of how "Lady Flora" (we never called her anything else) still visited the house. We would lie in the dark hearing the ghost of Lady Flora pace the roof, her skirts rubbing against it. She would never rest in peace.

After Lady Flora's death, San Pedro was sold to another British aristocrat, Lord Urmston, before coming into the possession of my grandfather, Hilario Gabilondo, "Papá Lalito." The Gabilondos have been in Mexico since about 1840. In that year my great-great grandfather, also named Hilario Gabilondo, arrived to visit his brother, Bernardo, who had settled in Caborca, Sonora. Hilario stayed there for a time but soon moved to Mexico City, where he enlisted in the National Guard. He returned to live in Caborca years later, by now with the rank of major. At the battle of Caborca in 1857 he was to hold back the American troops known in Mexico as *filibusteros* and prevent them from taking possession of the state. He is known in Mexican history books as *"el héroe de Caborca."*

His son Rafael, my great-grandfather, served as an adviser on livestock during the presidency of his good friend and compadre, Álvaro Obregón (1920–24) and that of Plutarco Elías Calles (1924–27). Papá Rafael was a diamond-in-the-rough type, variously a bootlegger, cattle rancher, kingmaker, and patron of the arts. He was short in height, a dandy with a lusty spirit. He was prone to drink too much on occasion and would then forget to button the fly of his well-tailored suit. One day he showed up at the Palacio Municipal in Mexico City to visit his friend the President and asked his secretary if he could see *el mocho* (a slang word used to describe someone who has lost a leg or, like President Obregón, an arm). The flustered secretary rushed into the President's office and nervously announced that there was a visitor who wanted to see *el manco*.

President Obregón asked, "Has he been drinking?"

"Yes."

"Does he have a *barriga* [a big stomach]?"

"Yes."

"Is his fly open?"

"Yes."

"Send him in, he's my compadre!"

Papá Rafael had extensive land holdings in the northern states. His son, Hilario, acquired more property in a large swath of Sonora. San Pedro, which the two of them bought in 1931, was one of his easternmost holdings, across the border of Sonora-Chihuahua.

He married a distant cousin, the beautiful Ana Acuña Corella. The Corella women were known for their beauty and spirit—and also for their many boyfriends, a reputation that Grandfather's maiden sisters were in no danger of sharing. Except for the gorgeous red-haired Tía Janda (Alexandra), who was the inspiration for one of Mexico's famous waltzes, the Alejandra, the Gabilondo sisters were not awfully good-looking. Ana did not mind belaboring the point on occasion. My grandfather was once extolling the virtue of his sisters while criticizing one of the Corella women who had just dumped a man. My grandmother fired back a reply to the effect of "Do you know why your sisters are so virtuous? Because they are too ugly to have anyone covet them!"

She was in no danger of such a fate, being admired by all. My grandfather was absolutely devoted to her. They had first started courting around 1915, in the aftermath of the Mexican revolution. Many Mexican families, including the entire Gabilondo clan, moved to the United States to avoid the troubles. Grandfather asked for Ana's hand in marriage so that she and her mother could join the clan in California until things calmed down, and it was in

California that they were married, at a church in Santa Monica. (Years later they went looking for the spot and couldn't find it. Papá Lalito told Ana not to worry, he would build her her own chapel in honor of her patron saint, St. Anne, the grandmother of Jesus, on their ranch of Santa Anita. But he was adamant that he didn't want to see any statue of an ugly, old St. Anne—*"La quiero con tu cara bonita,"* "I want her with your beautiful face.")

After they were married my great-grandmother came to live with them, and Grandmother continued to be waited on hand and foot by both her mother and her husband. When they first came back from California and were living in the Sonora mountains on their first ranch, "Oaxaca" (no relation to Oaxaca state), with their first child, she used to love to bathe in the river. My grandfather would carry the baby to her to nurse right there in the middle of the river. Their romance never lost its first glow. When he died, she told me that they had always slept like *cucharitas*—little spoons.

"Ana Linda" (Beautiful Ana, as she was always called) and Papá Lalito had four children. My uncle and godfather, Hilario, "Nino Lalito," was the youngest, preceded by my Tía Letizia, Tía Panchita, and my mother, Aída, who married José Martínez Solano in 1945.

We don't know as much about the Martínez family as about the Gabilondos, maybe because more of the family history was lost during the upheavals of the Revolution when *porfiristas* (members of the government of the ousted Porfirio Díaz) were fleeing to the safety of Texas, California, and Arizona. Also, the Martínez clan tended to be more reticent about themselves than my mother's family.

My parents settled for a time in Columbus, New Mexico. Their oldest son, my brother Antero, died shortly after birth, a casualty of the medical shortages during the world war, and Mother was inconsolable. It was my grandfather who knew the only thing that would assuage her grief. She had been the oldest child herself, and he had raised her as if she were a son. She had spent many hours with him on his ranches learning to handle horses and cattle. She had driven his tractor and his two-ton truck, and she loved the land. (Papá Lalito often said that he would rather have a daughter who was a whore than one who was lazy.) My grandfather gave her his prize property, San Pedro de Ojitos.

My parents had returned to Mexico and were living in Agua

Prieta, Sonora, when I, the next child, was born. (It was imperative that I be born in Mexico so the property could be put in my name.) We moved to the ranch when I was still a baby, and I lived there year round until the age of eight, when I was packed off to boarding school in El Paso. My earliest memories of it are isolated fragments. A baby coyote I had as a pet. The outhouse and gas lamps with their smell of petroleum. The large tin tubs set in front of the roaring fire for my bath. The vastness of the property and the elm trees all around the house. The large rock formation at the top of the highest mountain, which I promptly named El Trono del Rey (The King's Throne). My dream to ride there became an obsession. My mother tells me I talked about nothing else for a long time.

I loved San Pedro more than anything or anyone. My joy in it was total. It was a working ranch with a big staff of cowboys and household help, all of whom made much of me when I was small. Mother says that I did not speak a word until I was two, but then in complete sentences. There simply was no need for me to talk because everyone would jump when I pointed at something. As a baby I went from arm to arm, from cowboy to nanny, Mother and Father. I would sit with the cowboys, in someone's arms, while they had dinner. They would give me coffee from their big enamel spoons and I would slurp it down. Mother just gave up on sanitizing anything for me.

The cowboys or their kids would take me for long rides on their horses. I rode on horseback myself, on a tiny handmade saddle, before I could walk. The horseback rhythm became a part of me. When I was maybe two or three my father gave me a horse that I named Ramitos (Little Twigs). He was gentle and sweet, his face white and his body a shiny tan. How I loved him! Often in the early days, before I was sent away to school, I would ride with Father around the ranch and into the mountains, checking the barbed-wire fences and making sure there were no *cercos caídos* (fallen fences). Papa told me stories about the Apaches, and I was thrilled when I found an entire rock wall with Indian paintings on the side of the arroyo we called "El Apache." We would dig *montezumas* (a local name for molehills or mounds) where entire families were buried with their worldly possessions. There was beautiful pottery, mostly off-white with red-and-black designs, huge *molcajetes* and *manos* (mortars and pestles), *metates* (square stones for grinding corn), and arrowheads.

Sometimes we rode in silence, lost in thought. My heart would fill and almost burst with the beauty. My father carried a rifle (I, too, when I was a little older) in case our thoughts were disturbed by a coyote attacking a calf, or an attack by a rabid bear or wild boar.

My parents gave all of us—I was followed by Aída, Marina, and Clarissa—different things. My father, I know now, was beset with a losing inner struggle. But his wit and originality will always be among the happiest memories of my life. He was a man who took joy in all civilized pleasures and expected the finest as if it was the most natural thing in the world. It was characteristic of Father and his love of quality that he would eat only from china and with cloth napkins. Once at the dinner table Father's sister and her husband, Tía Mela and Tío Pepe Janeiro, were marveling (in English) over my mother's cooking. "Aída, you could cook for a king," gushed Tía Mela.

"She does," Father replied.

Father was clever in both English and Spanish. He read a lot in both languages and excelled at puns and word games in either tongue. (I recall another dinner with our parents' dear friends, Tío Mike and Tía Súqui Padilla—they were *tíos de cariño,* or uncle and aunt by affection—where Mother had prepared one of our favorite meals, leg of lamb with a curry sauce of her own invention, served with white rice and homemade chutney. My Tía Súqui, a lovely, very dramatic woman whose gestures and voice at all times were high theater, outdid herself in constantly telling Mother how absolutely delicious every bite was. Father finally looked up and said "Súqui, don't get curried away!") He did English triple acrostics in pen. He spoke with a thick accent, but his English vocabulary was perfect and he loved words. He spent hours poring over his dictionary, learning meanings and roots for pure enjoyment. He also had a fund of words and phrases in Arabic and Italian, mostly not so nice, which we children thought were hilarious.

My sister Aída and I used to revel in his sometimes stabbing irony, most often at poor Mother's expense. She would ignore us and simply raise an eyebrow in disgust. But all of us felt the sting of his wit from time to time. He used to take Aída and me, along with any guests—there was always a gang of kids on hand—out to shoot prairie dogs and hares. (It was good for the ranch, necessary conservation, since the large colonies in the flatlands beneath the rolling hills and mountains wrecked the land by eating the grass, roots and all. Cows and horses would get their legs caught and broken in the entrances to their warrens and would have to be sacrificed.) One time he took five of us in the back of the pickup truck to shoot prairie dogs and gave each of us four shots. We each took our turn, and in twenty shots not one of us killed a single dog. Father turned to us in disgust and said, "The San Pedro Dogs twenty, The Idiots nothing!"

In anything he enjoyed, Father was a connoisseur. His tastes in reading ran among other things to Ian Fleming, P. G. Wodehouse, and Rex Stout (on whom he got me hooked; one summer I read twenty-four Nero Wolfe mysteries, intrigued by this heavyset gourmand who raised orchids). He loved *Ivanhoe, Anthony Adverse*—and, inveterate punster that he was, James Joyce. He often called people "Zósimo" or "Zósima," after a name that had caught his fancy in *Finnegans Wake*. He read poetry out loud to us, and translations of Japanese haiku. He loved Spanish poetry as well. His favorite character in literature was El Cid, Don Rodrigo Díaz de Vivar. (One of my sons is named Rodrigo in his honor.) He loved philosophy and taught us to think and reason by posing questions and possibilities.

Father was a lover of opera (especially when Enrico Caruso was the tenor) and Spanish zarzuelas (especially when they were sung by the very young Alfredo Kraus). The Gabilondo family had always been music-lovers also, and music was responsible for two of my sisters' names: Marina, named for a zarzuela, and Aída, named like my mother before her for the opera. ("Zarela" was Mother's tribute to her very good friend from Ensenada, Zarela Migrand, who worked with her as a translator for American military intelligence during World War II. Clarissa is a Corella family name.) Father played the organ and Mother plays the piano. They used to perform duets, mostly after dinner, and this usually ended with all of us singing around the piano.

Father was a painter, too. His den was a haven, his studio. His rule was that we were never to go in there uninvited. (The other ironclad rule was that we were never to slam any door for two hours after lunch while he took his nap.) There he painted pictures, mostly portraits and still lifes, in great detail. In my New York living room today hangs one of Father's landscapes of the ranch. He was blind in his left eye and painted very close to the canvas, using a very thin brush. He had the Martínez family shakes and tremors, so he would steady his hand by resting it on a billiard cue that was just the right height. When he wasn't painting with his cue he played bumper pool with it, and he taught us the game when we were very young. We would put chalk on the cue so as not to scratch the felt and rub resin on our hands so the cue would not slip.

Everything I remember about Father absolutely speaks of a *bohemio,* as people who explored a lot of artistic and other interests were called in my younger years. There were many such people among our family friends in northern Mexico in those days. He built a woodworking shop, and he himself made a lot of our furniture. He got a metal detector to search the property (in vain) for buried treasure. He raised plants, even orchids, in our *invernadero* (hothouse), which separated his den from ours. Here he also built a ceiling-high cage for parrots and exotic birds like toucans that he raised. He also raised miniature Philippine roosters and hens, and rabbits for cooking.

He was a fanatic for building stone barbecue ovens for all sorts of specialized uses, some to smoke meats, others for specific types of grilling, even one that was a rock-lined hole in the ground with a metal cover, a sort of modern version of one of the oldest methods of cooking. I think one of his inspirations was the special ovens in which the Chinese roast pork. (There was a restaurant we always went to in Mexicali where this was a specialty.) He would experiment with different ingredients to lend flavor to his barbecues. He tried household preserving methods—making corned beef and head cheese from scratch, that sort of thing. He made wine with raisins and I don't remember what else. His early mornings were spent in the vegetable garden, where he grew asparagus and wild strawberries, Syrian cucumbers (the long, thin variety with ridged, tough skin), and all kinds of squash.

Father loved the ranch. It permitted him to live the life he wanted, not so much work as exuberant self-expression. It was San Pedro's solitude that permitted this. Freedom is, of course, only one side of solitude; the other is loneliness. My father drank too much and was often surly and ill-tempered. He would retreat when angry and would not tell anyone why. It was very hard on all of us. I never knew whether I pleased him or not. Sometimes he would reprimand me by saying, *"¡Cómo eres tontita!"* ("My, what a little fool you are!"). It hurt worse than a spanking.

My father was a man of great charm and engaging personality—people would just fall under his magic. But he was also a tormented, complicated man. Suffering from cancer, he withdrew into a deeper isolation and let the disease kill him by inches, more or less untreated. I can only say that he left me a tremendous legacy.

Mother gave me a different legacy—a sense of self. She celebrated our individuality and fostered it. She did not spoil us at all—in fact she was quite hard on us. But she always told Father that a woman's life could be very hard and that she wanted her daughters at least to have a happy childhood. On that she spared no expense. If we were depressed, she thought nothing of driving us nine hours to the beach in La Jolla, California (where Ana Linda had a home), to sit on the boulders and listen to the breakers to soothe our troubled thoughts. She told Father we were going to Tucson for the weekend, and flew us to Washington to see the cherry trees in bloom. She planned a trip to Utah so we could snowmobile. She brought us to New York to have breakfast in bed at the Plaza. It was not that Mother believed in casually indulging expensive whims. It was that she thought nothing was more important for children than building an album of unforgettable experiences.

She always made us feel beautiful. She let us dress any way we wanted and wear any makeup we chose. For a time Marina decided to wear an Indian headband and eyeglass rims with no glass in them. (This was before it became fashionable in the hippie era.) That was fine. Aída used to wear peacock-blue eyeliner an eighth of an inch wide and that was fine, too. We were all allowed to perform uninterrupted. We loved to sing and dance. Aída was not very accomplished in these areas, and Father would say, *"No cantes, mijita"* ("Don't sing, darling!"). However, she was given fencing lessons so she could also perform. Mother and Father encouraged us to tell stories and jokes, and everyone got equal time. (When we wanted to say something and someone was talking, we would raise our hand and say, *"Pido la palabra"*—"May I say a word?") The greatest lesson those ranch years gave us is a respect and love for the art of conversation.

Mother insisted that we be very independent. When I was eight years old, she left me at the immigration office at the Arizona border to get my own crossing card (required for Mexican citizens). She blithely told me that she was going to the hairdresser and would pick me up in about four hours! I got the card. Later she would send my sisters off by themselves to Tucson to do shopping. When I was fourteen she sent me to La Jolla to drive my grandmother back to the ranch (I had learned to drive when I was twelve). Grandmother's dog and her cook, Ramón, were the only other passengers. I needed a pillow to see traffic and reach the pedals in her big Cadillac.

Mother expected us to be very strong and would not allow weaknesses. If we fell off the horse we were made to get back up immediately. We were expected always to conquer our fears and face them head on. Sometimes she would demonstrate with an act how foolish it was to be afraid. On our frequent trips over the dirt roads, grasshoppers would jump into our Willys International and we would scream in fright. Mother once got a huge one in her hand and pretended to saddle it with a miniature saddle, bridle, and reins. Our fear dissipated in delight.

We were tended as small children by a series of nannies. As a baby I was the charge of "Nana" Lencha, who was very young and radiantly beautiful. She looked like Grace Kelly—golden blond hair and green eyes. If we were ever in the city, people would stop us to look at the disparate pair. I lost her because of her looks. When she was just fifteen a dashing cowboy named Bachi came along and swept her off her feet and onto his horse and *se la robó*—which is what we say when a man elopes with his bride.

After Aída's birth we were cared for by the Olive Oylish Doña Sabina. She was already old when she came to us. You could hear her muscles creak when she walked. She suffered from miserable varicose veins, and wore lisle stockings knotted at the knee, her swollen feet pushed into tennis shoes. Doña Sabina loved to frighten us—in jest, making us roar with laughter. I have a mental picture of how she would turn her baggy eyelids inside out to reveal the red veins, brandish her pair of sewing scissors, lie on the cot with her lanky legs kicking in the air. Aída would refuse to eat her morning egg unless Doña Sabina performed an egg-laying ritual. She would cackle and make a commotion like a broody-hen at the moment of triumph and miraculously produce the egg!

Our first schooling was at home. Mother taught us to read and write English with the Calvert School system. This program was very popular with missionaries and was used by all the ranchers to prepare their children for eventual boarding school. All of us were to receive some schooling, as Mother had, in El Paso.

I was sent there at the age of eight, to Jesus and Mary Academy. I did not go gently. The confined world of rote lessons, schedules, penances, and conformity just killed me. I brooded and cried constantly. I would scream to the nuns that I wished I was a horse so I could run free. I finally semi-accepted my fate when I made a friend in Sister Luz del Carmelo, who loved me and tried very hard to tame this wild ranch-raised spirit. Sister Luz del Carmelo was the granddaughter of General Porfirio Díaz, for many years president (or rather dictator) of Mexico. Her stories about growing up took me far from San Pedro, to the Palacio de Chapultepec during the long second term of Don Porfirio.

After three years at Jesus and Mary I was ready for my mother's old school, Loretto Academy. By the time I was in my teens we were all in Loretto, and my parents—who had been living the year around at the ranch since I was tiny—bought a house in El Paso to be closer to us during the winters. Several years later they moved back to Sonora, to Agua Prieta, the city of my birth. By now Father was living at the ranch much of the time by himself.

The ranch was still my spiritual home, too. Throughout our school years we would go back there for all school vacations and the entire summer. That time is precious in memory partly because the work itself, the ranch life, got into my blood like the rhythm of the horse. The other part I treasure is the aura of celebration and friendship that filled our summers. My parents loved to have guests. Every summer at least three or four grown-up couples and ten children stayed with us—that is, the parents just paid long visits, while the children usually stayed the whole summer.

Since growing up I have come to realize that the essence of Mexican hospitality is to socialize with an epic-scale family of relatives and friends. It is true not just of the wealthy families, but from one end to the other of the social scale. But while other people usually get together once a week, usually on Sunday, when the entire family gathers together for lunch, we had guests the entire summer. And we children learned a lot from our part in the summer's hospitality—to play, listen, share, respect, consider, and be gracious and fair. We learned the male-female roles when we played *comiditas,* literally "little meals," in the playhouse Father had built for us out of the same stone as the house, with a miniature wood-burning stove and an exact baby replica of our kitchen table. The boys would chop wood and bring it in and the girls would cook. Fighting was strictly forbidden, as was tattling (*chirimolear*). We were expected to work out our differences without parental interference. It was a school of life.

The adults would have cocktail afternoons, listening to opera, telling stories and jokes, seated in lawn chairs around the *rueda,* a raised circular flower bed my father had built to grow exotic flowers and wild strawberries. Sometimes they let the children sit with them. My parents' friends always had a lot to talk about. We loved the grownup jokes—there's a crazy quality in Mexican humor that is completely lost when you try to explain it. Some kind of surreal imagination must be built into us.

Later everyone would congregate to watch the CBS evening news in Papá's den. Our one television set got only the one channel and the reception was extremely poor—so bad that we had to divine what was happening! When my grandmother saw all of us laughing hysterically at comedy programs that mostly consisted of "snow" populated with fuzzy figures she looked as if she was watching a roomful of lunatics. The adults played canasta, gin rummy, or bumper pool. Mother cooked elaborate meals. (Whenever she cooked, all the girls, and some of the boys, clustered around, notebook in hand, to learn her recipes. I just found a journal from the summer I was fourteen with recipes for chop suey, Chinese almond chicken, paella, lasagne, spaghetti, curry, chicken Provençal, and many Mexican dishes.) If there weren't too many people, we sat at the dining room table, set with Royal Delft china, beautiful silverware, and always cloth napkins. Father was uncompromising on the subject of plastic plates and paper napkins. On every cupboard Mother had glued pictures of perfect table settings so the housekeepers would know how to set a formal table for every conceivable kind of meal. All this on a ranch a hundred miles from civilization, with absolutely no shops around!

After the meal everyone either went back outside to talk more, play the guitar, and sing, or migrated to the living room, where Mother and Father played duets on piano and organ while we sang along.

My parents were serene in the face of occupying armies of children, but sometimes needed a breather. Then they would put all or some of the children on horses and send us off to visit either an aunt or grandmother on a nearby ranch. We would pack our clothes in duffel bags, tie them to the backs of our saddles, and stay two or three days. Tía Letizia was stricter than my parents and we were all petrified of her, but her son Manuel and his friends were careless, crazy, and fun. We played hide-and-seek on horses, riding bareback, very dangerous. We had another death-defying game, too. The house was located on flatland—*el llano*—cut across by arroyos that were six to twelve feet deep. Two riders raced bareback, at full speed, down the arroyo bed. The other team was waiting atop the arroyo bank. As you raced by, they would jump onto each horse and try to wrestle the other off. That is, if they happened to land right, they would try to wrestle you off! It's a miracle we weren't all killed.

Often we would be sent off to visit my oldest friends, Carmela and Bilo Wallace, at their ancient hacienda of Corralitos near Casas Grandes, Chihuahua. This was a longer journey, at least three or four hours by jeep or pickup truck. Corralitos is as historic as San Pedro, or more. It was built two hundred years ago by a Spanish family, the Lujáns, and eventually came into the possession of my godfather, "Nino Bill" Wallace, whose family had also arrived with the early English and Scots migration into the region. We spent many happy times at Corralitos. Every year there would be a big bash on July 4, with friends coming from all over for prayers and mass, dances and meals, to celebrate the feast day of Our Lady of Refuge, Nuestra Señora del Refugio, the patron saint of the ranch. The hacienda of Corralitos was much larger than San Pedro, big enough to be considered a small town, and at one time even had its own mint and a big staff of mostly Chinese employees (there were also many Chinese settlers in the nineteenth century, originally brought by the railroads). When we were young we used to roam the property to look for old coins and bullets, remnants of the many fights with the Indians. We often found arrowheads and pottery, which we hid from our families. (In Mexico everything that is under the ground belongs to the government, and helping yourself to it is forbidden.)

July 26 was always another celebration, my grandmother's feast day. In Mexico the feast day honoring the saint for whom you are named is more important than your own birthday. My grandmother was Ana, and at the feast of St. Anne friends and relatives, distant or not, descended from everywhere on my grandmother's ranch of Santa Anita, a short ride from San Pedro. That annual party lasted at least three days. There were sixteen bedrooms, and the kids would sleep in huge dormitories. Grandfather, Papá Lalito, would bring in two groups of musicians, one for the cowboys

and workers with their families and one for the Gabilondo and Corella guests. A Piper Comanche airplane flew in the priest from Casas Grandes or sometimes Janos for confessions, baptisms, marriages, and a beautiful Mass. It might be the only time all year a priest went to those remote parts, and he did a good business. Grandmother would try to get all the cowboys who had *arrejuntado* (sort of settled down with women during the year) to get married by the Church.

On the eve of her feast day the cowboys would get together and serenade her. Her grandchildren gave her another *serenata* that same night, with everyone either playing an instrument or singing. (I don't know how good we were, but Grandmother was always touched deeply.) Two steers and a hog would be slaughtered. There was fabulous food: tamales, chorizo, *carne adobada* (pork marinated in a red *adobo* mixture), and *revolcado,* a pork and red chile stew garnished with the seeds from the chiles. Three meals a day for all those people—an incredible amount of work! But my grandmother's wonderful cook, Ramón, who worshipped her, never complained. He was pleased to be able to give joy. When Ana Linda died, Ramón died soon afterward.

The lessons I absorbed through play and celebration are one part of what the ranch life meant to me as a child, but what I really enjoyed was the actual work of the ranch—the horse- and cattle-centered routine that I was part of from the time I could ride. Most often, my guests would not want to go out with the cowboys to work, preferring to play. They did not share that feeling of literally, physically belonging to a place and landscape that you can experience but never describe to one who has not known it.

Just as my mother was raised to be a hands-on rancher, I grew up learning the work like a boy. Every year when I came back from school the cowboys would present me with a brand-new saddle blanket made from the wool of our sheep. Every year they would make me a *riata* (lariat), woven thinly so that it would not hurt my hands, and a small leather whip. (I learned to kill rattlesnakes with the twelve-inch whip, and when we went out on horses with guests I knew that my father was praying for an opportunity to show off my skill.) By the time I was fourteen I was busting broncos. It was a thrill to work with a horse in a corral, one on one. The first step was to lasso the horse and hold the rope closely, patting and talking soothingly to him. It would take a number of days for the horse to familiarize himself with my voice and not get startled when I touched him. Then I would go on to teach him how to respond to the tugging of the rope and learn to follow me. After that came putting on first gunny sacks and later saddle blankets until he learned not to throw them off.

Before I could progress to the saddle, I had to break him in to having a tight cinch around his middle, and that is a difficult step. Depending on the animal, it could take a month of regular handling for the horse to be ready for the saddle. Once he was used to the weight of the saddle, he had to learn to have a bridle in his mouth and recognize the commands of the reins. Finally he was ready for riding. The first time a horse feels the weight of the body, he bucks, and you have to be ready so as to not fall. You can hold on by the saddle horn, but it is better to use the muscles of the inner legs. Once that is mastered, you can go on to teaching the gaits.

It took me a while to find the horse that would be truly mine. The second horse I was given after I outgrew the gentle Ramitos was a dapple-gray quarter horse. Friendly and only mildly challenging, he certainly did not live up to his name, Capricho (caprice—I was always fond of lyrical names!). He was the perfect interim horse for the period when I was starting to ride long hours with the cowboys, but I soon grew restless.

Who should come to my aid and give me my greatest gift but Bachi, the cowboy who long ago had robbed me of my Nana Lencha! Bachi had come to work for us and the whole family was living on the ranch. One summer when I returned from school, Bachi gave me a horse whom I named El Travieso (The Naughty One) and who unfortunately lived up to the name. He was not particularly attractive or good, having the annoying habit of constantly shaking and bobbing his head back and forth. This was very tiring, and I grew to resent him. But one morning we took a ride on the hills near Bachi and Lencha's house, at La Agua Zarca, one of the outposts on our property, and I saw another horse and fell in love. He too was Bachi's—a glorious creature, bucking and galloping, with a flowing black mane and a dark, shiny brown coat. I just had to have him. Bachi warned me that this horse was untamable and that he had thrown off every cowboy who tried to ride him. He had been christened Desprecio—something that nobody wanted—and for good reason. I insisted, and we took him home. The entire household came out to watch me try to mount him. Fortunately Desprecio took an immediate liking to me and from then on would allow only me to ride him. I have loved few people as much as I loved that horse.

Desprecio turned out to be an excellent work horse, and we always took part in the cattle roundups. These were held in October and May to brand the calves, neuter them, dehorn them, and cut their ears. Every rancher has his own brand (my parents' brand was a double triangle, my grandfather's a diamond with an H in it, and mine 7+—for the sake of memory I have named my two corporations Seven Plus and Diamond H) and must notch the ears in a certain way for easy identification. If the calf was male and was to be sold to a dealer to be fattened for beef, he was neutered and his horns would be removed. When I was very young, this was still done by using a horrible contraption to cut them off at the roots. Thankfully, later this was achieved by the simple application of an acid. After dehorning came *el desahije* (separation)—the bittersweet time when we had to take the calves from their mothers. If you didn't, the calf would continue to suck at the teat, the cow would have trouble getting pregnant, and the calf would take a long time to learn to eat grass and would not grow to a good weight. Desprecio was great at maneuvering the calves away—he was a good *cortador* or "cutter," jumping expertly from one side of the calf to the other to effect the separation. We kept the cows in the corral the night of the *desahije,* to be taken to a distant pasture the following morning. The night would be filled with the desperate cries of the mothers, aching from their unmilked teats and the anguish of losing their young.

The roundups were thrilling. The smells and sounds of hundreds of cows, the songs and yells of the herd-leading cowboy (usually *el caporal,* the head cowboy), that were so important to setting the right pace and avoiding a stampede. Extra cowboys would be brought in to help, and a ranch cook was hired for the occasion. This had to be done way in advance to guarantee the best one—it was a competitive business! The wood wagon was transformed into a chuckwagon, which would be set up near the corral. The food was traditional chuckwagon fare, mostly spicy beef or pork stews, beans, and biscuits made in heavy cast-iron Dutch ovens suspended on a bar over the coals on different levels to get just the right amount of heat. The cowboys would hunker down and eat their food in that position, their chaps dragging on the dirt. I loved all of it.

When we weren't busy, Desprecio and I spent a lot of time by ourselves. I would get up at dawn and sit on the wooden fence in front of the house until the *remuda,* the relay of work horses, would be brought down from the hills to the corral to be saddled. The name *remuda* ("switch" or "replacement") derives from the fact that the horses were alternated to rest between heavy work days.

The dairy cows would already be at the gates, desperate to be milked. One of the cowboys' wives would bring a hot enamel pot of coffee and a batch of big cups, and we would add the milk directly from the cows' teats. It would foam up like cappuccino. Then I would approach Desprecio and talk to him in a soothing voice until he separated himself from the other horses. I'd grab his mane, jump on him bareback and without a bridle, and hurry to the house to saddle him and make our getaway for the day or morning. I loved to ride alone, singing, brooding, reciting poetry, talking to Desprecio. I used to wonder what would happen if he answered me back. It sounds strange, but I think Desprecio took the place of my imaginary companion Alicio, whom I spent much time talking to when I was smaller. We explored the entire ranch this way. We would visit the cowboys' *estancias* (outposts). If we came to a dammed-up place in the mountain arroyos, I would jump in, clothes and all, and swim, almost sinking from the weight of my jeans. If the arroyos were full, as they often were, Desprecio would swim across. Together we fulfilled my dream of visiting El Trono del Rey, the rock formation I had christened. It was a wonderful time in my life, probably the best I have known.

The years we lived on the ranch are so deeply fixed in my memory and emotions that sometimes it seems San Pedro is still ours, but it is not. After my midteens my father began to spend long periods of time there alone in increasing seclusion. The last years of his life were unhappy ones for all of us—particularly Mother, who had come to live there as a solace for her first great loss. In the end she came to hate the ranch, associating it only with sorrow. Shortly after Father died, she sold it to Aída's now ex-husband, and it has changed hands twice since.

It was my first great heartbreak. I still am not over it. I know now how it was that Lady Flora left San Pedro in body but not in spirit.

Rain

For the rancher, rain means a good year. More basically, it can mean survival. We pray for, sing to, and rejoice in rain.

Dry spells come in cycles, usually every fifteen years. They are terrible for ranchers, because cattle are ordinarily range-fed, and the government allows each rancher to have only the number of cattle the land can support by calculating different factors, including average yearly rainfall. Any lesser amount is potential disaster.

On our ranch, San Pedro de Ojitos, the ratio was ten hectares (about twenty-five acres) of land per head of cattle, very good for the generally arid North. We had an unusually good natural water supply because of the *ojitos* (springs) all over our land. But in bad years we would still have to buy feed and rent *pipas* (water trucks) and gather the cattle to feed them and give them their water in troughs. All of this is very melancholy, because you know if it keeps up you are going to lose many in spite of your efforts.

The crucial time is late June, around the time of the fiesta of San Juan (St. John). In winter the cattle are not in as much danger. They go into the lee of the mountains, where they are sheltered from the extreme cold and the winds, and where there is always plenty to eat. When warm weather comes, the flies and mosquitoes drive them out to graze on the open *llanos* (flatlands). The mesquite is blooming then, and that is what they can feed on until the rain brings new grass.

A hill overlooked our house, at the top of which stood a cross. Every year in June when we started worrying about the rains, my mother would send my sisters and me, along with any visiting cousins and friends and the cowboys' children, up there in late afternoon to pray for rain. (This also got rid of us for a while!) Or she would make us kneel down after supper and pray a novena or rosary. For some reason or other, this often sent us into fits of hysterical laughter.

When we would go out to ride, we would tie heavy rain ponchos to our saddles in the hope that the rain would catch us. What a sight we must have been as we returned in the rain—a troop of ten to fifteen children galloping on horseback, our hats tied firmly under our chins, all in bright yellow rubberized capes flapping in the wind and rain.

Each day at a set time we reported our rainfall, or lack of it, to a central office in Ciudad Juárez by short-wave radio. The rest of the six to eight minutes allotted to us we used to swap reports with other ranches about rain. All the ranchers know the short-wave schedule; family, friends, and neighbors tune in regularly to talk rain.

When the rains came, each of us had a special way of celebrating. After the first heavy rainfall Grandfather, Papá Lalito, would come out in his shorts in the middle of the night and yell exuberantly while shooting his gun in the air. He was the one who put tin roofs on all the ranch buildings on his properties so he could really hear the rain thunder down.

After the first rain my father, more reserved, would take my mother breakfast in bed.

I would lie in bed, under the covers, the window open and the curtain blowing, watching the thunder and lightning in the distance. And oh, that smell! After the rain, the arroyo flowed outside my window, roaring and laughing, the toads singing and the cows celebrating, bucking and mooing. What joy!

After it rained we would go *en famille* in the jeep to see which dams were filling up as the water rushed down from the mountains. The dams are part of the rancher's thinking ahead to keep the land in equilibrium. The land, including the spots where the cattle gather because of dammed-up water, must be rotated at intervals to let grass grow and to offer protection to the cattle. We kept building dams in likely spots all over the property because you must have a good supply of water everywhere. During the dry season, my father scouted the land for new places where water was likely to accumulate. You don't expect all of them to last forever in our climate and landscape. If one of them was in danger of breaking, which happens regularly in lands with heavy erosion, the cowboys would fortify them with rocks. If one of the John Deere tractors was nearby, they used it. Otherwise they tied lassos around the rocks and hauled them with horses. Sometimes there was nothing that could be done, and the force of the water broke the retaining wall. If this could not be repaired before the next rain you had to let it go for the season, and with it sometimes went the surrounding pasture.

One summer, while we were celebrating my grandmother's feast date in late July, it rained so tremendously that my grandfather insisted on going out with my father to check on the dams. Santa Anita, their ranch, is mostly located on *los llanos* (the flatlands). They are significantly more arid than the mountains, so when it rains the dirt roads become impassable with the mud. They had gone out expecting to make just a short cruise, and got

stuck in the mud. They wasted a lot of gasoline and soon found themselves with an empty tank. My father volunteered to walk back to the ranch house, but my grandfather insisted on doing so and left my father to wait. By now night had fallen. The silence was total.

All of a sudden he saw distant headlights coming in his direction and breathed a sigh of relief. As the two perfectly spaced lights got nearer, my father realized that there was no sound of a motor. The hairs stood up on his arms from sheer fright. The lights came up to him and passed him on either side and went silently on into the darkness. My father had been visited by the famous *luces llaneras,* eerie and fascinating, which I suppose must be like an *ignis fatuus,* or will o' the wisp. My mother tells me they are a kind of phosphorescence from dissolving minerals in the skeletons of dead animals. Since then I have seen them myself, a fluorescent-looking radiance that can either be spread over an entire field or focused to look as sharp as a spotlight. The only disturbing thing about the rainy season!

Maestro Gabriel

This is my small homage to Maestro Gabriel, my link with the history of the land I grew up on. We lost him only a few years ago. As best we could tell, he was about a hundred ten years old. He claimed to remember Cochise and Geronimo.

My family ranched for many years on land where the Apache and other Indians had wintered in the old times, before Spanish and British ranchers moved into northern Mexico. My great-grandfather, Rafael Gabilondo, took in a seven-year-old Yaqui Indian orphan to work on his ranch of "Oaxaca" in Sonora state.

When Rafael died, Gabriel went to work with my grandfather, Papá Lalito, who had several ranches in Chihuahua and Sonora. In the late 1940s my mother, who had known Gabriel from the time she was born, brought him to our ranch of San Pedro de Ojitos as a *maestro herrero*—master blacksmith—when she and my father moved there with me, then a new baby. Like all artisans in Mexico he was invariably called Maestro.

Maestro Gabriel made all the horseshoes for the ranch. He fixed the axles for the *carros de mulas* (mule wagons) that transported firewood between different parts of the ranch. He would make hinges for the gates and doors. The ranch smithy, his domain, was

Mañana Syndrome

Once there was an American who owned a cattle ranch in the northern state of Sinaloa. He invited a friend from the United States to visit and see the property. Riding around the ranch, they came on a construction job in progress—and progress and progress and progress. The owner explained that work on the project had been going on for two years and no end was in sight yet.

The friend was not slow to moralize about Mexican inefficiency: "Everything is *mañana* here. That's why things don't get done." One of the workers was listening and spoke up: "Do you know what's wrong with you gringos? You think *mañana* means tomorrow. It only means *not now!*"

I could not put it better. Do things get done in Mexico? Yes, they do. Do they get done "on time?" Seldom.

Most people from the United States are totally exasperated by the chronic lateness of Mexicans. But this is not due to laziness or inefficiency, just a different philosophy of time. In Mexico no one gets too upset about anybody being tardy. You might make an appointment with the plumber or carpenter but you don't really expect them to show up that day, much less on time, just some time. "On time"—it's an arrogant, possessive concept if you stop to think about it! In Mexico it is actually very rude to be "on time." When I first lived in New York I used to get furious when everyone showed up on time for my parties, and those who did usually ended up having to mop the bathroom.

For Mexicans, it is unimportant to be punctual because there is no reason to interrupt one thing you're doing, especially if it is important or fun, just to meet an appointment to do something else. This attitude is also rooted in our fatalism. For us, most events are predetermined, and there is no point in a scheduled routine or discipline. The past is gone, the present we can play with, and the future will come in its own time.

We're not much impressed by arguments meant to show that we would live in more prosperous efficiency if only we rushed to a mentality of the stopwatch. My great-grandfather, Papá Rafael, was a sturdy, hard-drinking individualist and sometime politician who lived his own life at his own pace. One day a younger fellow rancher and neighbor, Bill Wallace (who also happened to be one of my godfathers), took a U.S. cattle-buyer to see some of Papá Rafael's stock. The prospective buyer was lanky, bowlegged, and ruddy, an archetypal redneck cowboy. For some reason my great-grandfather instinctively and immediately disliked him and told Nino Bill that he did not speak English that day. Poor Nino Bill had to translate the entire conversation.

"This gentleman wants to see your cattle, Don Rafael," said Bill.

Rafael replied in Spanish, "Tell him to come back tomorrow," and peacefully dragged on his cigar.

The prospective buyer said in English, "Look at him! Drinking and dragging on his cigar. This man owns this land? Everything is *mañana* here, that's why they never get ahead."

Papá Rafael had had enough. He spat out, in perfect English, "Listen, you long-legged SOB! You see that cow going by? Well, one of them can keep me in liquor for one whole year and I've got thousands of them!"

Now, that's what I call a healthy sense of proportion. My great-grandfather knew a lot more about life than the stopwatch contingent!

at the back of the house. Over the embers hung a barbecuelike contraption with a bellows on one side that looked like a food mill. When the fire went down, he would turn the handle of the bellows and the embers would glow again. He also used to make the charcoal for the ranch in his shop, using the scrub oak that grew all over.

I only knew him old, yet he radiated virility. From a very young age I was fascinated to watch him pound the glowing pieces of hot iron, bending them to his will. I loved his smell of wood and dogs and hot metal. He had the most beautiful face, dark and weathered, with a narrow angular jaw, square-cut cheekbones, straight hair, a long mustache, and a broad, flat nose. I spent hours watching him. I did not understand at the time that Maestro, for some reason, loved my attention beyond anybody's, that he considered my presence as much of an honor as I considered his.

The ranch had wood-burning stoves and a fireplace in every room. When there was no blacksmithing to do, Maestro was the woodchopper. I took to keeping him company, riding out in his wagon, searching out already fallen trees while Maestro felled the standing ones. After bringing the trees back in the wagon, he would chop the wood into different-sized pieces for the stoves and fireplaces, stacking some in the kitchen and some on the *zaguán* (porch), where my sisters and cousins would take what they needed for their rooms. But not me! The Maestro himself would bring firewood into my room. He insisted on doing it every time, whether I needed it or not. My room perpetually had ceiling-high stacks of logs. He himself would lay the roaring fire so my room would be nice and warm. I was very young, but I knew that Maestro was unique and that our friendship was different from his relationship with others. He must then have been eighty or more.

Animals loved the old blacksmith. How he would talk to the mules! They would cock an ear and bray in greeting when he got close. On the ranch, all the dogs would immediately and irrevocably attach themselves to Maestro. We were a family of dog lovers, and my father was always getting special breeds—hunting dogs for some specific kind of game, work dogs for particular ranch chores, or pets for us children. But no dog ever paid the slightest attention to my poor father, while Maestro walked everywhere on his great bowed legs followed by a pack of assorted dogs, including maybe a few Weimaraners and a collie and a basset hound.

One day when he was alone making a horseshoe, Maestro Gabriel caught a metal splinter in his eye. He never cried out, never said a word. It was two days before we found out and rushed him for medical attention to a nearby town. The doctor said that the eye was lost but there was no infection. Maestro Gabriel said he knew that. And I thought, this is how a man is supposed to be.

We took to sharing a special treat. Every afternoon he came to the *casa grande,* the ranch house, to eat the afternoon snack (*merienda*) with me. (He was the only worker on the ranch thus invited.) Socorro, the housekeeper, could sometimes be persuaded to make her delicious sweet yeast rolls, or Lupita, the cook, would make tortillas, or sometimes my mother made *Semitas* (page 109), a sconelike bread. We spread them with fresh-churned butter and lots of homemade peach jam. Maestro liked his steaming enamelware cup of coffee sweetened with lots of sugar, and he liked to slurp it down while keeping the spoon in the big cup pinned down by his thumb. I imitated him. Looking back, I realize it must have made my mother shudder, but she never said a word.

Through him I had my first role of importance, whether I understood it or not. My relationship with Maestro Gabriel stood for the respect that his character and his lifetime of service had earned from the whole family, living and dead. It is a hard thing to explain in the United States, where "service" implies anything but mutual respect.

When I came home from school vacations I would immediately rush to say hello to Maestro, and he would tell me, *"Mira, ¡qué bonita vienes—gorda, gorda!"* ("Look how pretty you've come back, plump, plump!" Ranch people equate plump with pretty.) From then on Gabriel promoted me. He was very old by this time. He now called me La Patroncita (The Little Boss). There came a time when no one else could give him an order unless it came through me. I remember my father, quite amused, telling me to please ask Maestro to make some charcoal for our evening barbecue or we weren't going to have dinner.

Many years later, when I was first married and living in El Paso, I went on a weight-loss campaign and came back to visit the ranch with my husband, feeling very svelte and glamorous. I rushed to Maestro expecting delighted compliments. He looked me over with his good eye, frowned, and wanted to know why I was so thin and sickly. I told him I was stylish, not sickly! I further informed him that I worked hard and wanted to be slender like this. It made him furious.

"Aren't you married?" he demanded. "What good is the man if he can't keep you plump and pretty?"

He refused to talk to my husband for the entire visit.

I knew that it would not be long before I lost him when I found him using two axes for canes. His death was my last goodbye to a part of my childhood, but not to my memory of having been given an honor and importance beyond my years.

HORCHATA DE ARROZ

Cold Rice
Drink

If you travel to Mexico, you will see many street stands selling only fresh cold beverages (see *Aguas Frescas y Preparados,* page 141). Most are made from fresh fruit. This, which like the French *orgeat* must go back to some medieval Mediterranean original, is the mysterious white one that you will see in the glass jugs. It's one of my favorite flavors. My son Rodrigo always begs me to make this refreshing drink, which is still a favorite remedy for children with digestive upsets.

1 cup rice
1 piece (2 inches) true (Ceylon) cinnamon stick (see page 15) or 1 piece (1 inch) U.S. "cinnamon"
2 cups boiling water
5 to 6 cups cold water
Juice of ½ lime

1 teaspoon ground true (Ceylon) cinnamon, preferably freshly ground in a spice grinder, or ½ teaspoon ground U.S. "cinnamon"
3 to 4 tablespoons sugar, or to taste

Place the rice and cinnamon stick in a small saucepan. Add the boiling water and let soak until the water is white and milky. Bring to a boil over medium-high heat. Reduce the heat to low and simmer, uncovered, until partly softened but not fluffed up, about 15 minutes. Discard the cinnamon stick and let the rice cool, covered. Working in several batches, puree the rice mixture in a blender or food mill. The mixture may be sticky and hard to work with; use the cold water a little at a time if necessary to thin. With a wooden spoon or pusher, force the mixture through a medium-mesh sieve (you can use more of the cold water to help rinse it through). Combine the strained pureed rice with the lime juice, ground cinnamon, and sugar to taste. Add the remaining cold water gradually until the *horchata* is the consistency of a not-too-heavy cream soup (use a little more if desired). Taste and add more sugar, lime juice, or cinnamon if desired, but the flavor should be delicate and slightly bland. Chill thoroughly or serve with ice.

YIELD: ABOUT 1½ QUARTS

SOPA CALDOSA DE FIDEOS

Pilaf-Style
Noodle Soup

I do not know why, but in Mexico pasta is generally browned in hot oil or butter before the liquid is added—the same technique as for the French *pilaf de nouilles*—whether the dish is to be eaten pilaf-style or as a soup. In this soup (which I must have eaten a thousand times while I was growing up and love as much now as I did then), the pasta that is used is a kind of thin noodle sold in little nests under the name of fideos. If you cannot find them in Latin American stores, look for Italian fidelini, which are the same thing. In a pinch, substitute thin vermicelli. Cooking times may vary quite a bit for different brands.

¼ cup vegetable oil
½ pound fideos (nested thin egg noodles), fidelini, or vermicelli
1 small onion, finely chopped (about ½ cup)
1 medium-size ripe, red tomato, roasted (see page 14), peeled, and chopped (if ripe tomatoes aren't available, use ½ cup canned tomato puree)

2 garlic cloves, minced
10 cups Caldo de Pollo (see page 44)
Salt and freshly ground black pepper to taste
5 large sprigs fresh cilantro leaves, chopped
¼ cup finely diced white cheddar cheese

Heat the oil in a large Dutch oven over medium heat until hot but not quite smoking. Add the fideos and brown on first one, then other side. (If using vermicelli, stir-fry to brown quickly on all sides.) Lift the noodles from the oil and drain on paper towels.

Discard the oil in the pan, leaving only a light film. Add the onion, tomato, and garlic and cook, stirring, 2 to 3 minutes over medium-high heat. Add the chicken stock and bring to a boil. Season with salt and pepper, reduce the heat to low, and simmer 5 minutes. Add the noodles and cilantro and simmer until the noodles are just done, 3 to 6 minutes (slightly longer for vermicelli). Serve at once with a few cubes of cheese sprinkled over each bowl.

YIELD: 6 TO 8 SERVINGS

SOPA DE CREPAS

Layered Crêpe Dish

This is an example of a *sopa seca,* or "dry soup," a category that will be less baffling if you follow the Mexican reasoning that starchy ingredients like rice, pasta, or crêpes turn into a "soup" when they absorb liquid in cooking. My mother perfected a version of this dish—a takeoff on more traditional filled crêpe dishes—and always served it for parties. It has a lot of the "layering" of flavors that I love and have adopted in my own cooking. My contribution was to make a layered casserole instead of rolled crêpes and to experiment with part *masa harina* or cornmeal in the crêpe batter. Another departure is that my mother's version used canned deviled ham, which many people don't care for (though I think it's delicious).

24 Crepas de Maíz (recipe follows)
1 package (10 ounces) frozen chopped spinach or 1 pound fresh spinach, thoroughly rinsed and trimmed of woody stems
⅓ cup vegetable oil
2 garlic cloves, minced

1 medium-small onion, finely chopped (about ¾ cup)
1 pound boiled ham, ground
3 or more (to taste) pickled jalapeño chiles (see page 225) from 8-ounce can, finely chopped, plus juice from can (about ⅓ cup)
2 cups sour cream

⅓ cup chopped fresh cilantro
leaves
Salt to taste, optional
1 to 2 tablespoons milk, optional

**1 pound sharp white cheddar
cheese, shredded (about 4
cups)**

Make the crêpes, stacking as they are done; reserve, covered with a clean cloth.

Cook the spinach according to package directions and drain thoroughly. (If using fresh spinach, cook over high heat in a tight-lidded pot, using only the water that clings to the washed leaves, just until wilted, 3 to 5 minutes; drain thoroughly and chop roughly with a heavy knife.) Squeeze the spinach between your hands to remove as much moisture as possible.

Heat the oil in a medium-size skillet over medium-high heat. Add the garlic and most of the chopped onion (reserve about ¼ cup to use later). Cook 2 to 3 minutes, stirring often. Add the spinach, toss to combine well, and cook 5 minutes, stirring occasionally. Set aside.

Combine the ground ham, chopped jalapeños, and the juice from the jalapeños in a medium-size bowl. Set aside.

Combine the sour cream, cilantro, and remaining chopped onion in a small bowl. If desired, add a little salt (but not if the ham is strongly salty). If the sour cream is very thick, thin the mixture with 1 to 2 tablespoons milk. Set aside.

Preheat the oven to 325°F. To assemble the casserole, butter a 13 x 9-inch Pyrex baking dish (or other baking dish with sides about 2 inches high). Line the bottom with 8 crêpes. Spread with one third of the sour cream mixture. Cover this with half of the ham mixture. Sprinkle the ham with half of the spinach. Cover the spinach with one third of the shredded cheese. Cover the cheese with 8 more crêpes and repeat the layering: half the remaining sour cream mixture, all the remaining ham and spinach mixtures, and half the remaining shredded cheese. For the final layer, add the remaining 8 crêpes and top with the remaining sour cream and cheese.

Bake until heated through (insert a knife in the center to check), about 30 minues. Let stand about 10 minutes.

Can be made ahead (up through assembling the casserole) and refrigerated, tightly covered, several hours or overnight, or made ahead and stored in the freezer up to 2 weeks. (Do not thaw before cooking; add 10 to 15 minutes to the baking time.)

YIELDS: 8 OR MORE SERVINGS

CREPAS DE MAÍZ

Corn Crêpes

When I started experimenting with different versions of crêpe recipes, I tried various proportions of cornmeal or *masa harina* to flour. This version was developed by Ed Bonuso, pastry chef at Zarela.

1 cup sifted unbleached all-purpose flour
¾ cup finely ground yellow cornmeal
Pinch of salt
4 large eggs

2 cups half-and-half
1 cup milk
⅔ cup (about 10 tablespoons) unsalted butter, melted, or as needed

Combine the flour and cornmeal in a large bowl. Add the salt, then stir in the eggs.

Combine the half-and-half with the milk. With a whisk or portable electric hand mixer on low speed, begin adding the liquid to the batter. The consistency should be that of heavy cream; add as much liquid as you need to in order to achieve this. Whisk in ¼ cup of the melted butter. Let rest for 30 minutes, then strain the batter through a fine sieve to remove any lumps.

Heat a 6-inch crêpe pan or small skillet over medium-high heat. Brush with a small amount of the remaining melted butter. Pour in just enough of the batter to coat the hot pan evenly (1 to 1½ tablespoons) and cook over medium-high heat just until set enough to flip easily. Cook the other side until barely browned, a few seconds more. Remove to a platter and cover with a clean cloth. Repeat, brushing pan each time with melted butter, until all the batter is used (you may need a little more melted butter for the last few crêpes). Stack and cover the crêpes as they are done, either by letting them cool slightly before stacking or placing sheets of waxed paper between them.

YIELD: 2½ TO 3 DOZEN 6-INCH CRÊPES

PAPAS CON CHILE VERDE

Potatoes with

Green Chile

This brings back many memories of good friends—Lupe and Nayo Chávez, who lived about a city block away from our house on the ranch and have known me forever, since I was a small child and Nayo was working for my grandfather. Nayo says he first met me in the corral when I was two, and my first words to him were *"Cójeme el mayate"* ("catch that bug for me!") (It was one of the beautiful iridescent green bugs that like to hide in cow patties. We loved to tie a thread under their wings, twirl them around, and let them try to fly. Not a very humane amusement, but we were not so enlightened then!)

When I was growing up, we practically lived at their house. We would go over there after lunch and Lupe "la de Nayo" (in Mexico, we often refer to a married woman by calling her "la de" so-and-so), would tell us the story of their courtship and elopement. We insisted on hearing it at least once a week. At Lupe's I would do all the things they couldn't get me to do at home when I was a child. We used to do embroidery together, all sorts of things in bright Mexican colors. She also taught me to iron using heavy cast-iron irons. Or in late afternoons during the summer we would walk around the rolling hills looking for *pitayas* (the fruit of a ground-hugging thorny cactus) or *manzanitas* (a berry that grows on shrubs and is mostly pit, but oh, so delicious). When the *capulines* (a sort of wild cherry) ripened we would ride out on horses and pick them. We kids used to eat so many we really got sick. Acorns were another favorite—we enjoyed eating even the worms, which you feel squeeching when you bite into them!

Anyhow, I probably never had better friends. Lupe and Nayo were my rock of Gibraltar when I was going through the obligatory 1960s' adolescence. By then they were living on an *ejido*—a type of government-allotted parcel of land that is a loaded political subject in modern Mexico; they were meant as a land-reform measure. The government expropriates plots of land from large landowners and turns them over to rural families to farm as they wish. It was always a sore point with my family and every other rancher who had had land taken for *ejidos*. So my parents were less than thrilled when during one stormy patch I went to live with Lupe and Nayo on the *ejido* that used to be family land.

Lupe and Nayo listened to me moan, groan, and be miserable,

but they never complained. They pulled me through my depression and I can never thank them enough.

Lupe is also a great ranch cook, and I learned her recipes. She was giving me instructions once on how dark to toast the flour for a roux we were making and she said, *"Hasta que esté del color de una cucaracha"* ("Until it is the color of a cockroach!") I think about it every time I toast flour and always strive to get that particular color.

Lupe used to make this simple but irresistible dish with potatoes and fresh green chiles. It's a good filling for burritos with freshly made flour tortillas—a form in which I met it years later when I was working as a social worker in El Paso. Every morning a woman would come to our offices at morning break time, bringing a batch of burritos with eggs and chorizo and another batch filled with these potatoes. This version makes a great portable lunch.

2 pounds boiling potatoes (Red Bliss or other thin-skinned variety; about 5 to 6 large potatoes), peeled and cut into ½-inch cubes

¼ cup lard (see page 19) or vegetable oil

1 small onion, sliced or chopped (about ½ cup chopped)

2 garlic cloves, minced

2 fresh jalapeño chiles (see page 225), or to taste, tops removed but not seeded, finely chopped

½ cup shredded white cheddar cheese, optional

Salt and freshly ground black pepper to taste

In a large saucepan, bring to a boil enough salted water to cover the potatoes. Drop in the potatoes and cook until almost done but still a little crunchy, about 5 minutes. Drain and reserve.

Heat the lard or oil in a large skillet over high heat until hot but not quite smoking. Reduce the heat slightly and add the onion, garlic, and jalapeños. Cook, stirring, until the onion is golden, 2 to 3 minutes. Add the drained potatoes and reduce the heat to medium. Cook, tossing occasionally, until the potatoes are golden, about 5 minutes. They should be just tender, not mushy. Add the cheese, stir thoroughly to combine, and cook just until the cheese melts. Season with salt and pepper and serve immediately as a vegetable or filling for burritos.

YIELD: 4 SERVINGS AS A SIDE DISH; TO FILL ABOUT 6 TORTILLAS (DEPENDING ON THEIR SIZE)

PAPAS CON CHORIZO

Potatoes with

Homemade

Sausage

This is a terrific breakfast or brunch dish. Potatoes go wonderfully with the flavors of chorizo.

3 medium-size boiling potatoes (Red Bliss or other thin-skinned variety; about 1 pound total), peeled and cut into ¼-inch dice

3 tablespoons vegetable oil

1 small onion, finely chopped (about ½ cup)

2 garlic cloves, finely minced

1 cup (about 4 ounces) home-made chorizo mixture (see page 106)

In a medium-size saucepan, bring enough salted water to cover the potatoes to a boil. Drop in the potatoes and cook until almost done but still slightly crunchy, about 5 minutes. Drain and reserve.

Heat the oil in a medium-size sauté pan or skillet over medium-high heat until very hot but not quite smoking. Reduce the heat slightly and add the onion and garlic. Cook, stirring often, until the onion is golden, 2 to 3 minutes. Add the drained potatoes and reduce the heat to medium. Cook, stirring occasionally, another 3 to 5 minutes.

Add the chorizo, stirring to break it up and distribute it. Cook, stirring, another 5 minutes. Serve at once.

YIELD: 4 SERVINGS AS A SIDE DISH OR 2 AS A BREAKFAST MAIN DISH

CALABACITAS CON QUESO

Zucchini with

Cheese

When we were growing up we ate this dish at least once a week and sometimes more when it was harvest time. We would groan every time we saw it. Now, though, I love it, and not only because it reminds me of home.

1½ pounds zucchini (5 to 6 young, tender zucchini), scrubbed but not peeled, cut into ¼-inch dice
1 cup water
Salt and freshly ground black pepper to taste
2 tablespoons vegetable oil
1 large garlic clove, minced
1 medium-size onion, finely chopped (about 1 cup)
1 large ripe, red tomato or 2 small ones (about ¾ pound), chopped

2 cups fresh corn kernels cut from the cob, or 1 package (10 ounces) frozen corn, or 1 can (16 ounces) plain corn kernels, drained
2 poblano chiles (see page 226), roasted (page 227), peeled, and finely chopped
1 can (5 ounces) evaporated milk or ⅓ cup heavy cream
½ pound white cheddar cheese, finely diced (about 2 cups)

Place the diced zucchini in a medium-size saucepan with the water; season lightly with salt and pepper. Bring to a boil and simmer, covered, over medium heat until slightly tender but still crunchy, about 2 minutes. Set aside without draining.

Heat the oil in a large skillet over high heat until hot but not quite smoking. Reduce the heat slightly; add the garlic and onion and cook, stirring, until the onion is translucent, about 2 minutes. Stir in the tomato and cook until its liquid is partly evaporated, about 5 minutes. Stir in the corn and poblanos and simmer 5 minutes more.

Add the undrained zucchini and evaporated milk to the corn-chile mixture and bring to a boil. Reduce the heat to low, stir in the diced cheese, and cook just until the cheese melts. Serve immediately.

YIELD: 4 TO 6 SERVINGS

EJOTES CON HUEVO

String Beans with Egg

This is another dish well remembered from childhood—we ate a lot of good vegetable dishes at the ranch! The beans must be tossed very quickly with the sauce and egg, almost as if you were stir-frying. It's a good way of using leftover *pico de gallo norteño* and works well with other blanched vegetables.

I like to strain the egg before adding it to the beans, because I detest the taste of soft egg white bits. Most people will probably find this unnecessary.

1 pound fresh string beans, trimmed, strings removed if necessary, and cut into 1-inch pieces
2 tablespoons butter or vegetable oil

1 cup Pico de Gallo Norteño (see page 40)
1 large egg
Salt and freshly ground black pepper to taste

In a large pot of rapidly boiling water, blanch the beans until slightly tender but still crunchy, about 2 minutes. Drain thoroughly.

Heat the butter in a large skillet over high heat until hot and bubbling, or the oil until rippling. Add the *pico de gallo* and cook, stirring, until the liquid is nearly evaporated, about 2 minutes. Add the drained beans and cook, tossing rapidly, 1½ to 2 minutes. Meanwhile, beat the egg in a small bowl. Add to the mixture in the skillet and cook, tossing and stirring, just until the egg is set, a minute or less. Season with salt and pepper and serve immediately.

YIELD: 4 SERVINGS AS A SIDE DISH

ESPINACAS

Wilted Spinach

This dish always brings back memories of the wild greens that we gathered to cook on the ranch. We called them *quelites,* a name applied in Mexico to various sorts of leafy green plants. Our *quelites* always grew around water holes and were a little like young dandelion greens, a little like kale, but not really like either. This was one of our favorite ways of preparing them. Nowadays I often use oil for the sautéing, but on the ranch we always used bacon grease.

Mother used to make *quelites* with cooked beans, and that was delicious too. If you want to try spinach in this way, add 1 cup cooked dried beans to the hot fat along with the tomato, scallions, garlic, and jalapeño. Cook to heat through over medium-high heat, then add the spinach and cook, stirring constantly, just until wilted.

2 to 3 tablespoons bacon grease or vegetable oil
1 medium-size ripe, red tomato, chopped
3 scallions, white and some of green part, finely chopped
1 garlic clove, minced
1 fresh jalapeño chile (see page 225), or to taste, top removed, seeded if desired, and finely chopped

2 tablespoons chopped fresh cilantro leaves (1 to 2 large sprigs)
1 package (10 ounces) fresh spinach or same amount loose, well rinsed and woody stems trimmed
Salt to taste

Heat the bacon grease or oil in a large, wide skillet over high heat until a drop of water sizzles on contact. Add the tomato, scallions, garlic, jalapeño, and cilantro and cook, stirring rapidly, for about 30 seconds. Add the spinach in large handfuls, stirring to distribute. Cook the spinach, uncovered, just until wilted; season with salt and serve at once.

YIELD: 4 SERVINGS

FRIJOLES CHARROS

Beans
Cowboy Style

A favorite Sunday afternoon activity in Ciudad Juárez, across the border from El Paso, is to go out to the outskirts of the city and eat *tacos al carbón*. They are sold in small but very clean stands. The atmosphere is festive and totally Mexican, with whole families sitting around long oilcloth-covered tables and strolling bands of musicians, usually mariachis or trios. The meat (beef or pork) is charcoal-broiled, cut with lightning speed into tiny squares, placed in a soft, freshly made corn tortilla with sprigs of cilantro, and usually downed with a cold bottle of beer or bottled soft drinks. The accompaniments are roasted scallions and these *frijoles charros*—heaven! You can serve these beans with any grilled or barbecued beef. *Charros* means "cowboy-style," except that *charros* are not exactly cowboys but members of exclusive clubs or societies that colorfully enact rodeo feats in elaborate costumes.

Canned beans are acceptable in a few of my bean dishes, but definitely not here!

1 pound cooked (but still firm) pinto beans (see page 43)
1 bottle (12 ounces) dark Mexican beer or other dark beer
4 pickled jalapeño chiles (see page 225), or to taste, finely chopped
3 tablespoons lard (see page 19) or bacon drippings

1 medium-small onion, finely chopped (about ⅔ cup)
2 small garlic cloves, minced
2 medium-large ripe, red tomatoes, coarsely chopped (about 2 cups)
Salt and freshly ground black pepper to taste

For this recipe the pinto beans should be slightly undercooked (be sure to use plenty of liquid in cooking). Drain them and place in a large bean pot or Dutch oven with the beer and chopped jalapeños. Bring to a boil.

While the beans are heating, heat the lard or drippings in a medium-size saucepan or sauté pan over high heat until fragrant. Add the onion and garlic and cook, stirring, until the onion is translucent, 2 to 3 minutes. Add the tomato and cook 5 minutes more, stirring occasionally. Add the mixture to the beans, bring to a boil, and reduce the heat to low. Simmer, partly covered, until the flavors are melded, about 10 minutes.

YIELD: 6 OR MORE SERVINGS AS A SIDE DISH

ARROZ A LA MEXICANA

Rice

Mexican Style

On the ranch we always called this *sopa de arroz,* but more people will have met it under *arroz a la mexicana.*

Mexicans are fanatical about soaking and rinsing rice before cooking. Some of the time I go along with the no-rinse, vitamin-conscious approach in the United States, but not for this dish. I have tried and the rice just doesn't come out the same—the grains don't have that clean, separated effect. Chinese people say the same thing.

If you include peas, don't use tiny new peas. They will be fatally overcooked.

2 cups long-grain rice
½ cup vegetable oil
1 medium-size onion, finely chopped (about 1 cup)
2 large ripe, red tomatoes, roasted (see page 14) and peeled

2 large garlic cloves, coarsely chopped
2 sprigs fresh cilantro leaves
1 to 1½ cups shelled fresh peas, optional
3 cups hot Caldo de Pollo (see page 44) or water
Salt to taste

Place the rice in a bowl or saucepan, cover with very hot tap water (130°F or hotter), and let soak for 15 minutes. Pour into a colander and rinse with cold running water until the water runs clear. Drain thoroughly.

In a heavy medium-size saucepan or Dutch oven with a tight-fitting lid, heat the oil over medium heat until rippling. Add the rice. Reduce the heat slightly and cook, stirring and tossing the rice constantly, for 10 to 12 minutes. At first it will tend to stick; later it will turn translucent and sound like sand. When ready, the rice will be golden. Drain off as much excess oil as possible.

Puree the onion, tomatoes, garlic, and cilantro together in a

blender or food processor and add to the rice mixture. Season with salt and cook, uncovered, for 2 to 3 minutes. Add the peas, then stir in the hot chicken stock. Cover tightly and reduce the heat to low. Cook for 15 minutes, remove from the heat, and let sit in a warm place, tightly covered, for 8 to 10 minutes before serving.
YIELD: 6 TO 8 SERVINGS

MANCHAMANTELES DE POLLO

Braised Chicken in Spicy Fruit Sauce

This was one of the first dishes I tasted that piqued my curiosity about food from other parts of Mexico. I was introduced to it in my high school years, when we were living in Agua Prieta and I would come home on weekends. Often we would have Sunday meals with my parents' dear friends the Orozcos, who came from the distant and mysterious state of Chiapas. Through them I became partly acquainted with what was to me an exotic cuisine. The Orozcos fed us *manchamanteles,* which means "tablecloth-stainer"—the tablecloth really did get stained when we ate it! It was wonderful, rich and complicated, with a thick, succulent texture and different notes of sweet-tart fruit, fragrant spices, and chile. We would dip the chicken pieces in more of the sauce and suck blissfully. It has been one of my favorites ever since.

One bite and you will understand how I knew this was a different world from the northern Mexican foods I had grown up with. Later I would become familiar with many of the rich, compelling flavors of central and southern Mexico, but this still recalls to me the early sense of novelty.

There are many versions of *manchamanteles* in Mexico, using different kinds of fruit and different sweet/hot proportions. Some are thickened with ground nuts. The usual meats are chicken, pork, or a combination of both, and it is traditional to cook the meat (first browned or not) and sauce together from the beginning. But I often like to make the sauce by itself and serve it with separately cooked meats—for example, roast duck, as we do at Zarela. This recipe is an in-between version. The fruit sauce is cooked first and the chicken browned separately before it finishes cooking in the sauce.

⅔ to ¾ cup vegetable oil

1 medium-size onion, sliced into thin half-moons (about 1 cup)

2 large garlic cloves, minced

1 can (28 ounces) whole tomatoes, with juice

2 bay leaves

½ to 1 teaspoon freshly ground black pepper or to taste, plus a little more for seasoning chicken

1 to 2 teaspoons salt, or to taste

¼ to ⅓ teaspoon ground cloves

1½ teaspoons ground true (Ceylon) cinnamon (see page 15), preferably freshly ground in a spice grinder, or ½ teaspoon ground U.S. "cinnamon"

1 teaspoon ground cumin

1 teaspoon dried Mexican oregano (see page 11), crumbled

½ cup dried apricots, sliced

¾ cup pitted dried prunes, whole or sliced

½ cup golden raisins

1 can (20 ounces) unsweetened pineapple chunks, with juice

½ cup dry sherry or red wine

1 tablespoon cider vinegar

1 cup Adobo de Chile Colorado (see page 29)

2 chickens (about 3½ pounds each), each cut into 6 to 8 pieces

1 to 2 medium-size tart apples, such as Granny Smith, cored and cut into eighths

1 to 2 tablespoons butter, optional

1 large ripe plantain (see page 20), peeled and sliced, optional

Cinnamon sugar, made with 1 tablespoon sugar to 1 teaspoon (or to taste) ground cinnamon, optional

Heat 2 tablespoons of the oil in a heavy, medium-size saucepan over medium-high heat until hot but not quite smoking. Add the onion and garlic and cook, stirring, until golden and translucent, 3 to 4 minutes. Add the tomatoes, breaking them up with your hand. Add the bay leaves, ½ teaspoon of the black pepper,

1 teaspoon of the salt, the cloves, cinnamon, cumin, and oregano. Bring to a boil, then reduce the heat to low and simmer, uncovered, 10 to 12 minutes. Working in batches if necessary, puree the mixture in a blender and transfer to a large Dutch oven.

Bring the pureed sauce to a boil over high heat, adding the dried fruits, pineapple with its juices, sherry or red wine, and vinegar while it heats. Let simmer a minute, then add the *adobo*. Taste for seasoning and add more salt if desired. (I like to use quite a bit, to balance the sweet-sour effect of the fruit.) Reduce the heat to medium-low and simmer the sauce, uncovered, about 10 minutes (see note). While it cooks, heat about ½ cup oil in a large heavy skillet over high heat until almost smoking. Sprinkle the chicken pieces on all sides with salt and pepper. Working with 3 to 4 pieces at a time, brown the chicken on both sides (add a little more oil to the skillet if necessary). As they are browned, add them to the simmering sauce (see note). Add the apple pieces to the sauce and chicken. Let the sauce return to a boil and simmer, covered, until the chicken is cooked through, 25 to 30 minutes. Serve with corn tortillas.

If you wish to garnish, melt the butter in a medium-size saucepan over medium heat. When the butter begins to bubble, add the plantain slices and cook, stirring, until golden on both sides. Sprinkle with the cinnamon sugar and arrange over the *manchamanteles*.

NOTE: If preparing the sauce to be used with separately cooked meat, simmer, uncovered, 15 minutes or longer instead of 10, first adding the apple pieces; the longer simmering will remove the raw taste of the chiles.

Manchamanteles can also be finished in a preheated 350°F oven after the meat is browned and added to the sauce. Bake 35 to 40 minutes.

Manchamanteles de Cerdo
Pork *Manchamanteles*

Prepare the sauce as instructed above, but substitute 3 pounds country-style pork ribs for the chicken, browning them well and adding them to the sauce with the apples as described above. Simmer, covered, over medium heat until the meat is tender, about 30 minutes.

YIELD: 6 TO 8 SERVINGS

POLLO BORRACHO

"Drunken"
Chicken

This is another recipe from our neighbors, the Chávez family. They owned a still (La Vinata) that made *sotol,* the northern version of mezcal (see page 115). In fact, the only access to the still was through our ranch. When I was going through my time of troubles, Lupe would reply to my despair by making fresh orange juice and serving it to me with a large dose of *sotol.* (I also vividly remember how once, when I must have been about fifteen, she put some dried corn kernels in a wet gunny sack and let them sprout. She then proceeded to ferment it somehow and made the most wonderful corn liquor. It was mild and sweet at first, but it got stronger by the day and we got sillier.)

Amelia Chávez, Nayo's sister, devised this recipe using their *sotol.* But since it is completely unobtainable from anywhere but private stills like theirs, I substitute tequila. (Of course the alcohol boils off in cooking, leaving only the flavor.) The level of vinegar in this sweet-and-sour dish would not be considered excessive by many Mexicans, but it may be a bit much for some people here. Begin with a small amount and add more to taste. Amelia's version also contained pickled whole serrano chiles, which produced a very *picante* dish.

½ cup golden raisins
½ cup dry sherry, heated
½ cup flour
¼ teaspoon salt, or to taste
¼ teaspoon freshly ground white pepper, or to taste
1 small chicken (about 3½ pounds), cut into 6 to 8 pieces
½ cup corn oil or other vegetable oil
1 medium-size onion, thinly sliced (about 1 cup)

3 large garlic cloves, minced
½ cup blanched whole almonds
½ cup whole pimiento-stuffed green olives
1 tablespoon cornstarch
1½ cups Caldo de Pollo (see page 44)
1 cup tequila (preferably Sauza or Herradura)
⅓ to 1 cup distilled white vinegar
1 tablespoon sugar

Place the raisins in a small bowl and pour the hot sherry over them. Let sit at least 20 minutes to soften the raisins. Meanwhile, combine the flour, salt, and pepper on a flat plate or dish. Roll the chicken pieces in the flour to coat evenly. Heat the oil in a large skillet over medium-high heat until not quite smoking. Fry the chicken pieces until well browned on the outside but not cooked within, about 10 minutes. (Work with two skillets if you don't have one big enough to hold all the pieces comfortably.) Place the browned chicken in a baking dish or Dutch oven with a tight-fitting lid. Set aside while you make the sauce.

Discard all but about 2 tablespoons of fat from the skillet. Add the onion and garlic and cook over medium heat, scraping the pan to dislodge any browned bits of chicken, until the onion is golden and translucent, 3 to 4 minutes. Add the almonds and cook, stirring occasionally, for another 2 minutes. Add the olives and plumped raisins with any unabsorbed sherry; cook, stirring occasionally, another 2 minutes.

Preheat the oven to 350°F.

In a small bowl, dissolve the cornstarch in about ¼ cup of the chicken stock. Add the rest of the stock to the skillet along with the tequila and bring to a simmer over medium heat, stirring and scraping. Add ⅓ cup of the vinegar to the mixture along with the sugar; stir to combine and taste to judge the effect. Continue to add vinegar (up to 1 cup in all) until the desired tartness is achieved.

Stir in the cornstarch mixture. Let it boil, then reduce the heat to low and simmer until the sauce thickens and the flavors meld, about 10 minutes.

Pour the sauce over the chicken. Cover the baking dish and bake until the chicken is tender but not overcooked, about 20 minutes.

YIELD: 4 SERVINGS

TAMALES DE MI ANA LINDA

My Grandmother's Chicken Tamales

My mother's mother, Ana Acuña Corella, was a beauty of legendary charm, tall and curvaceous, with regal carriage, auburn hair, and green eyes. She had a waltz composed in her honor, and there were beautiful stories about her romance with my grandfather. Everyone called her Ana Linda (Beautiful Ana).

My grandmother had an earthy sense of humor. She always said that she loved *gentes con pasado* (people with a past). When she found me sitting splayed like a man with one leg over the arm of a chair—after all, I was wearing jeans—she would say, *"Mijita, ¡imagínate cómo te verías sí estuviéras desnuda!"* ("My daughter, imagine how you would look if you were nude!")

When my sisters and I were children, we loved to hear her tell the joke about the grandmother who is taking care of her grandchildren. They beg for a bedtime story. She begins, "There was once a beautiful girl named Cinderella."

"Not that one!" say her grandchildren.

So she starts another: "Once upon a time, there was a beautiful girl and her name was Snow White."

"Grandmother, not that one!"

"All right," she says. "There was a lovely girl named Sleeping Beauty."

"Oh, Grandma, not again!"

"So tell me what story you children want to hear."

"Please tell us about the time you were a whore in Chicago!"

In my last memory of Ana Linda, two days before she died, she is lying on her bed wearing blue silk pajamas. She has one leg raised, pointing up, and is rubbing it. She turns to me and says, "When I get well, we are going to Sea World to see the dolphins."

This is a recipe that she taught my mother and that has always been a favorite in our family. Tamales are not as difficult to prepare as they may first seem, and these are exceptionally delicious. The chicken filling, as you can see, is closely related to the basic *Picadillo de Pollo* on page 48, which can be used instead for a milder, less piquant filling.

Before you begin to cook, make sure you have a workable steamer arrangement and be prepared to follow the general directions for wrapping and steaming tamales on page 51.

1 pound dried corn husks (see page 7)

FOR THE FILLING
½ cup golden raisins
½ cup dry sherry, heated
3 tablespoons lard (see page 19) or vegetable oil
1 medium-size onion, finely chopped (about 1 cup)
2 large garlic cloves, minced

3 medium-size or 2 fairly large ripe, red tomatoes, roasted (see page 14), peeled, and seeded (1½ cups tomato pulp)
3 fresh chiles, either Anaheim or poblano (see pages 223 and 226), roasted (page 227), peeled, and finely chopped, or 2 cans (4 ounces each) chopped green chiles, drained and finely chopped

3 cups shredded cooked chicken (from one 3½-pound chicken—see page 44)

½ cup halved pimiento-stuffed green olives

2 teaspoons dried Mexican oregano (see page 11), crumbled

Salt and freshly ground black pepper to taste

⅓ cup chicken stock, or as needed

Basic Tamal Dough (page 50)

Place the corn husks in a large bowl, cover with boiling water, and let soak at least 1 hour.

In a small bowl, soak the raisins in the hot sherry until fully plumped, at least 20 minutes.

Heat the lard or oil in a large saucepan or sauté pan over high heat until very hot but not quite smoking. Add the onion and garlic; reduce the heat to medium and cook, stirring to prevent scorching, 2 to 3 minutes. Add the tomatoes and chiles and cook another 2 minutes, stirring occasionally. Add the shredded chicken; toss to mix with the other ingredients and cook 5 minutes, stirring often to distribute evenly. Add the plumped raisins and the olives. Stir in the oregano; season with salt and pepper. If the filling is too dry, moisten with a little chicken stock. Cook a few more minutes over low heat, stirring often, to meld the flavors. Remove from the heat and let cool.

Drain the corn husks and select 50 to 60 of the better-looking pieces. Fill, wrap, and steam the tamales as explained on pages 51–53.

YIELD: 45 TO 50 TAMALES

LENGUA EN FIAMBRE

Cold Tongue Platter

This is another old friend. My mother often prepared tongue *en fiambre*—cold, with an assortment of vegetables and a vinaigrette. (Probably the olive oil suggests a Spanish origin.) The same presentation is used to make beef, pork, or chicken *en fiambre*. We usually had tongue unless there was some leftover roast beef. Experiment with any preferred cold cooked meat, but do not chill—it should be served at room temperature.

The only bothersome part of this dish is cooking the vegetables. Each must be separately added to boiling salted water and just lightly cooked, then drained and quickly cooled. Have all the vegetables ready before you start the final preparation.

2 veal tongues (about 1 pound each)
2 quarts water
6 bay leaves
1 tablespoon black peppercorns
Salt to taste

FOR THE VINAIGRETTE
2 garlic cloves, peeled
1 teaspoon salt, or to taste
Freshly ground black pepper to taste
½ cup white wine vinegar
1½ cups olive oil

FOR THE VEGETABLES
2 large boiling potatoes (Red Bliss or other thin-skinned variety)
2 medium-large zucchini, thinly sliced
1 package (10 ounces) frozen string beans (or use fresh)
1 package (10 ounces) frozen peas and carrots (or use fresh)

Place the veal tongues in a large saucepan with the water, bay leaves, peppercorns, and salt. Bring to a boil, reduce the heat to low, and simmer, partly covered, until tender, about 1 hour. Drain and let cool.

While the tongue cooks, make the vinaigrette. Crush the garlic to a paste in a small bowl with the salt. Whisk in the pepper, vinegar, and olive oil. Set aside.

When the tongue is completely cool, skin it and cut into thin slices. In a shallow bowl, toss the tongue slices in the vinaigrette and let marinate for 30 minutes. Drain the slices, reserving the vinaigrette.

Meanwhile, prepare the vegetables. Place the potatoes in boiling salted water to cover and cook until barely tender, about 20 minutes. Peel while hot and cut into thin slices. Cook the sliced zucchini in boiling salted water until barely tender, just a few minutes. Plunge into ice water to stop the cooking and drain. Cook the string beans in boiling salted water until still slightly crisp. Plunge into ice water to stop the cooking and drain. Do the same with the peas and carrots. Toss the cooked potatoes in the reserved vinaigrette till coated, then drain—reserving the vinaigrette—and set aside. Do the same with string beans, zucchini, and peas and carrots, draining each vegetable and reserving separately.

Place the tongue slices in overlapping circles at the center of a serving platter, arranging them compactly enough so that everything else can be arranged in concentric circles around them. Place a ring of sliced potatoes, slightly overlapping, around the tongue. Arrange the string beans around the potatoes. Place a ring of zucchini slices, slightly overlapping, around the string beans. Finish with a ring of carrots and peas.

YIELD: 6 SERVINGS AS A MAIN DISH

ALBÓNDIGAS DE MI MAMA

Meatballs Like Mama Makes

This recipe calls to mind the *llaves* (outdoor water faucets) on the ranch, which were always surrounded with patches of *yerba buena*—"good herb," or mint. Whenever my mother made *albóndigas* I would be sent out to pick some fresh for the soup. She always served it with freshly made corn tortillas, *salsa casera* (homestyle sauce), and refried beans with *asadero* ("roasting" cheese; the nearest thing here would be mozzarella).

Whenever my mother comes to visit, I always ask her to make me these *albóndigas*. I have tried to serve them at the restaurant, but people can't seem to get excited about meatball soup. Too bad—it's a fabulous soup. The meatballs freeze well, by the way, and reheat wonderfully.

¼ cup masa harina (see page 49)
¼ cup warm water
1 pound lean ground beef or ½ pound each lean ground pork and beef
¾ teaspoon salt, or to taste
Freshly ground black pepper to taste
4 garlic cloves, 3 minced and 1 left whole
¼ cup lard (see page 19) or vegetable oil
1 tablespoon flour
8 cups Caldo de Pollo Casero (see page 45)

4 medium-size scallions, white and some of green part, chopped
1 large ripe, red tomato, roasted (see page 14), peeled, and chopped (or ¼ cup canned tomato puree if good tomatoes are not available)
2 fresh chiles, Anaheim (see page 223) or (for hotter flavor) jalapeño (page 225), roasted (page 227), peeled, and finely chopped
3 tablespoons finely chopped fresh cilantro leaves
3 tablespoons finely chopped fresh mint leaves

In a large bowl, combine the *masa harina* with the warm water. Add the ground meat, ½ teaspoon of the salt (optional), a generous grinding of black pepper, and one minced garlic clove. Mix these ingredients with your hands and shape into tiny balls, between the size of a large marble and a small walnut. (The mixture makes 40 to 45 small meatballs.) Set aside.

Heat 2 tablespoons of the lard or oil in a small skillet over medium-high heat. Add the whole garlic clove and let cook 20 to 30 seconds to flavor the fat, pressing down on it with the back of a cooking spoon. Remove and discard the garlic. Turn off the heat, add the flour to the hot fat, and quickly stir to combine with a wooden spoon or whisk. Turn the heat to medium and cook, stirring constantly to smooth out lumps, until the mixture is golden, about 1 minute.

Meanwhile, have the stock heating in a large (at least 6-quart), deep saucepan or Dutch oven. Just before it boils, add a little hot stock to the browned flour mixture and whisk or stir to eliminate lumps. Pour the mixture into the hot stock and bring to a boil, whisking or stirring with a wooden spoon to keep it from lumping. Reduce the heat to medium-low and simmer the stock, uncovered, 5 minutes. It will thicken just slightly. Season with a little salt and pepper, being careful not to overseason (the meatballs will add more salt).

Make a *recaudo:* Heat the remaining lard or oil in a large skillet over medium-high heat until very hot but not quite smoking. Add the chopped scallion, roasted tomato, roasted chiles, and remaining minced garlic. Reduce the heat a little and cook, stirring frequently, for 2 minutes. Add the sautéed mixture to the stock, then add the cilantro and mint. Reduce the heat to low and simmer, uncovered, another 5 minutes. Add the meatballs, let the stock return to a boil, and simmer, uncovered, for 15 minutes. Correct the seasonings and serve.

YIELD: AT LEAST 6 TO 8 SERVINGS AS A MAIN-DISH SOUP, MORE AS A FIRST COURSE

CARNE CON CHILE COLORADO

Pork with Red

Chile Sauce

This is one of the best uses of the ever-useful *Salsa de Chile Colorado* (page 31). I hope it gives you further inspirations. The basic idea will always be the same: Brown or partly cook a meat or vegetable, then finish cooking it in the chile sauce.

This recipe also makes a good filling for burritos or tacos. In that case, cut the meat and potato (if you want it) into smaller cubes.

2 tablespoons lard (see page 19) or vegetable oil

1½ pounds lean boneless pork butt or leg, cut into 1-inch cubes

1 large garlic clove, minced

2 cups Salsa de Chile Colorado (see page 31)

1 large potato, peeled, cut into ½-inch cubes, and cooked in boiling salted water until still somewhat crunchy, about 5 minutes, optional

Heat the lard or oil in a large sauté pan or saucepan over high heat until very hot but not quite smoking. Cook the pork, stirring, until golden on all sides, regulating the heat so as not to burn it. Add the garlic when the meat is just partly browned (it burns easily if added earlier). Add the chile sauce and potato, bring to a boil, reduce the heat to medium; simmer, covered, over medium heat until the meat is tender but not overcooked, about 25 minutes.

YIELD: 4 SERVINGS

NOTE: My mother made any number of dishes *con chile colorado,* especially meatless dishes for Lent. Two of our favorites were blanched *nopales* (see page 11) rinsed and cut into strips, then briefly simmered in the sauce, and blanched string beans given the same treatment to produce *ejotes con chile colorado.* We also loved *papas con chile colorado,* lightly blanched cubed potatoes fried in lard, salted and peppered, and simmered in the sauce. When my parents first got the ranch, they had no money, and my mother would often make a meal out of these potatoes, frying up the peelings in the same way to give to the cowboys. Between you and me, the latter were better!

CHORIZO

Some of my earliest ranch memories are of the butchering/cooking sessions that followed every time we slaughtered a hog. This was always cause for celebration because all the women of the ranch congregated in our kitchen to help, laugh, and gossip, and everyone got something to take home afterward. Everything—I mean *everything*—was used and converted into some delicacy. There would be big tubs sitting over a barbecue pit to render the fat. This produced scrumptious *chicharrones* (cracklings) with crunchy bits of meat sticking to the crispy fat. I would eat all the meat and throw away the fat; my sister Aída would eat the fat and throw away the meat! The blood, heart, and liver would go to make *morcilla* (blood sausage). I never developed a taste for it, but everybody else loved it. The feet were pickled. We made delicious tamales with the cooked meat from the head and butt. The loin

was saved to be roasted or barbecued for company. As for the legs, my mother would slice one leg into thin steaks for *carne adobada* (made with a version of *salsa de chile colorado* brushed on the meat to marinate before cooking—still one of my favorites). My dad would take another to make a ham. A third went to the cowboys for a great chile con carne. The fourth leg was dedicated to this chorizo.

Today I duplicate some of our ranch recipes using U.S. pork, but the quality is very different. The pork here is so lean and so bland that you have to treat it almost like veal. The only cut that really works when you need a lot of flavor and texture is pork butt. The truth is that the pork we raised had a lot more fat, which is the vehicle of meat flavor. If you must avoid it, chorizo is not for you. But in defense of the ranch diet, I must say that my great-grandfather, who ate pork and beef practically every day of his life, drank to excess on occasion, smoked cigars, and rarely exercised, lived to be eighty-seven years old.

I don't recommend trying to reduce the proportion of fat in the chorizo mixture. Ask the butcher to give you 3 parts lean meat (preferably butt) to 1 part fat. This recipe is for a large amount, which is meant to be lightly cooked as soon as the mixture has rested overnight, then frozen in convenient-sized batches for later use. It has dozens of uses. Chorizo mixture is cooked with potatoes (see *Papas con Chorizo,* page 89), scrambled eggs, or cheese. In Mexico it is also stuffed into casings and aged to make wonderful air-dried sausages. I think the fresh sausage mixture is a more practical option for most U.S. cooks. The recipe can easily be halved.

5 pounds ground pork (3:1 ratio of lean to fat)

4 ounces pure powdered red chile (see page 226), stirred to a paste with ½ to ¾ cup boiling water

¼ cup cider vinegar

¼ cup dry sherry or red wine

4 to 5 large garlic cloves, minced (about 2 tablespoons)

1 tablespoon salt, or to taste

2 tablespoons dried Mexican oregano (see page 11), crumbled

2 teaspoons ground true (Ceylon) cinnamon (see page 15), preferably freshly ground in a spice grinder, or ½ to ¾ teaspoon ground U.S. "cinnamon"

1 teaspoon freshly ground black pepper (coarse grind)

1 teaspoon ground cloves

1 teaspoon sugar

2 to 3 tablespoons lard (see page 19)

In large bowl, combine all the ingredients except the lard. Mix with your hands to distribute the seasonings evenly. Let rest, covered, overnight in the refrigerator.

The next day, prepare to cook the mixture. Melt the lard in a large skillet over medium heat. (This is to get the cooking started; the meat will provide its own cooking fat as you proceed.) Working in batches and being careful not to crowd the skillet, cook the chorizo mixture about 5 minutes, stirring often to cook evenly. Remove each batch to a bowl as it is done. When all the mixture has been sautéed, drain as much fat as you can from the cooked meat. Let cool to room temperature.

Pack the cooled mixture into heavy-duty plastic bags (it's probably smart to use several different sizes, depending on how much you will be using at one time). Unless planning to use within a day or two, freeze at once; it can be stored up to 2 months in the freezer.

YIELD: ABOUT 5½ POUNDS

SEMITAS

Little Biscuits

On the ranch we never had bread as such. We were far from any bakery, and the sweet rolls sometimes baked by my mother or the housekeeper and cook, Socorro and Lupita, did not take the place of plain bread. Our daily bread was corn or flour tortillas. But we were also fond of these little *semitas,* which are made with a dough very like that for tortillas, except that the liquid is milk and there is a larger amount of baking powder.

3 cups unbleached all-purpose flour	**¾ to 1 cup milk warmed to 115°F (warmer than lukewarm, but not hot)**
1 teaspoon salt	
1½ teaspoons baking powder	**Vegetable oil as needed**
½ cup solid vegetable shortening	

Combine the flour, salt, and baking powder in a medium-size bowl. With your fingers or two knives, rub or cut in the shortening until the mixture resembles coarse crumbs. Slowly pour in about ¾ cup of the warmed milk, at the same time working the ingredients together with your fingers. Add more milk if necessary to make the mixture gather together into a pliable but not sticky dough. Knead on a lightly floured counter until the dough is smooth and silky, about 5 minutes. Let it rest, covered with a damp cloth, for 15 minutes. Preheat the oven to 400°F.

Shape the dough into 12 equal-sized balls about 1½ inches across. (While you work, keep the dough and completed balls covered, to prevent them from drying out.) Shape each ball of dough as follows: Hold a ball in both hands, thumbs on top and fingers underneath. With your fingers, lightly pull and push the dough out from the center to make a slightly flattened shape like a big mushroom cap, slightly more than 3 inches across.

Lightly grease a baking sheet with oil. Flatten each ball of dough on the baking sheet to make a circle about 4 inches across. Lightly oil your fingers and rub a little oil over the tops of the *semitas.* (At the ranch we used bacon grease—delicious!) Prick them all over with a fork. Bake until golden, 12 to 15 minutes. Serve at once with butter or fruit preserves.
YIELD: 12 SEMITAS

HUEVOS A LA MEXICANA

Scrambled Eggs with Salsa

I have never cared much for eggs, and when I was a child this was the only form in which my mother could get me to swallow them. Here the salsa is made fresh for the dish, but you can also use any leftover salsa.

1½ to 2 cups vegetable oil for frying, or as needed, plus 3 tablespoons for cooking the salsa and eggs
3 commercial corn tortillas, cut into ½-inch strips (about 2 cups)
1 large garlic clove, minced
3 large scallions, white and some of green part, finely chopped

1 large ripe, red tomato, finely chopped
2 to 3 fresh jalapeño chiles (see page 225), or to taste, tops removed but not seeded and finely chopped
3 tablespoons finely chopped fresh cilantro leaves
8 large eggs, thoroughly beaten
Salt and freshly ground black pepper to taste

Pour the oil into a large skillet to a depth of about 1 inch. Heat over high heat until very hot but not quite smoking (a tortilla strip dropped into the oil should sizzle). Fry the tortilla strips about 30 seconds, working in batches if necessary so the oil temperature doesn't drop. Lift from the pan and drain on paper towels.

In another large skillet, heat the 3 tablespoons oil over high heat until not quite smoking. Add the garlic and scallions and cook 1 minute, stirring. Add the tomato, jalapeños, and cilantro, reduce heat to medium, and cook 5 minutes, stirring occasionally.

Add the eggs and cook another 2 minutes, stirring to scramble. Add the tortilla strips, stir to combine, and season with salt and pepper. Cook, stirring, until the eggs are done to your taste, another couple of minutes or longer. (I confess I can't stand "creamy" scrambled eggs!)

YIELD: 4 TO 6 SERVINGS

Guadalajara Learning Opportunities

Until I was eighteen, my culinary and other horizons were closely centered on northern Mexico and the southwestern United States. Perhaps I would never have set out to explore the food of regions beyond my own if it had not been for parental veto of my original plans. When I graduated from my mother's old school, Loretto Academy, in El Paso, I announced that I wanted to go to college in the United States—Stanford University and Webster College in Missouri were my first choices. My parents refused, saying that they wanted me to go to a Mexican school so as not to lose touch with my roots. The real reason, I am sure, is that it was the 1960s and they were afraid I would turn into a hippie. So I found myself, like many daughters of "good" Mexican families, at a sort of finishing school whose mission was to prepare me to be the perfect housewife—the Instituto Familiar y Social in Guadalajara, the capital of Jalisco state. It was the first time I had lived away from home in Mexico. Part of the reason for selecting a school in Guadalajara was that we had good family friends there—the Aragóns, who had lived in Agua Prieta while I was in high school—who my parents knew would keep an eye on me.

I disdained the Instituto at the time, and lasted there only a year. The curriculum consisted of things like shadow embroidery, papier-mâché, crocheting, sewing (including making your own patterns), ways of cleaning and removing stains, etiquette, conversational arts—and cooking! The thinking was not that we would actually be doing any sort of housework ourselves, but that we needed to know how to do it so that we could supervise and instruct our servants. I thought much of this was superficial, unimportant, silly, and profoundly unintellectual. After a year I persuaded my parents that I needed something more stimulating, and Father transferred me to another school in Guadalajara, the Instituto Tecnológico y de Estudios Superiores de Occidente—Mexicans love long titles—where I studied mass communications. In all I spent five years in Guadalajara.

Life is funny—the skills I learned while looking down my nose at the Instituto Familiar y Social have stuck with me. I wish I had the time for embroidering. Ditto making tiny flowers with *migajón de pan,* a pliable dough made by mixing glue and bread crumbs, or oil-painting waxed flowers. Working with my hands is relaxing. My twin sons frequently give me occasion to revive those handy stain-removal skills. My housekeepers stay with me for years, too, and that may be a tribute to what I was taught about unobtrusive guidance. I never became the perfect housewife, however!

My exposure to Jaliscan (and other) food was even more of an influence. It would shock the Instituto Familiar y Social to know that it turned out to be a vocational school for me, something no one could have foreseen. But it was there that I first learned to cook food totally different from what I was used to at home—surprising and delicious. I learned recipes from the most basic to the most unusual: quick cakes and candies, wonderful combinations of fruits and meats, pork in every guise, delicate ice creams. I didn't fully realize it at the time, but the Instituto and its conscientious faculty of maiden ladies excited my curiosity about food and started my quest for new and better recipes. It helped that at the same time I was encountering some of these new dishes at friends' homes.

During this time I lived mostly in a series of boardinghouses. Only briefly did I live in an apartment of my own, which was considered terribly daring for a young lady. I was very aware of the rigid social atmosphere of the *provincias,* the provinces away from Mexico City and the more Americanized north. In my teens in Juárez, El Paso, and Agua Prieta there certainly were limits to what I was allowed to do, but I had a lively social life and danced and partied (at supervised dances and outings within our circle of friends) to my heart's content. Here (though for the first time I socialized with people from many parts of Mexico) the boardinghouse atmosphere hung heavy, and I saw boys only with a chaperone or in the confines of a group. I found the meal pattern of central Mexico unfamiliar, too. In the North we are somewhat closer to U.S. lifestyles, especially in regard to eating hours. I didn't like the long wait from breakfast (heartier than I wanted to face) to the mid- or late afternoon *comida* (main meal), and in some places the boardinghouse fare was monotonous. But in others it was great. I still have fond memories of a rice dish with green poblano chiles and a spicy, probably very thrifty, black bean soup that I first ate at the boardinghouse tables.

Something that used to enliven our existence were the different kinds of whistles that announced the arrival of this or that service. One whistle meant the postman had come, another the knife grinder, and so on. Two of the whistles we eagerly listened for were the one that heralded a man selling roasted yams at about six in the afternoon, and another for a vendor with muslin-covered tubs of ears of corn to be eaten with powdered chile and lime juice.

The Aragóns and relatives of our old family friends Tío Mike and Tía Súqui Padilla helped me see more of Guadalajara and its food. It is a beautiful, stately sixteenth-century Spanish city, but with a very violent past. In Jalisco the *conquistadores* met much resistance from the local peoples and exterminated them even more thoroughly than in other parts of Mexico. Intermarriage was forbidden. This is why the food became more Europeanized—not just Spanish, but colored by many layers of immigration—than that of most regions. To me it was and is fascinating. When our family friends took me to some of the Guadalajara restaurants, I realized that one reason the food at places like the celebrated Los Cazadores (The Hunters) seemed strange to me was that the meat was butchered into totally different cuts than it had been on the ranch. We had been used to U.S.-style steaks and roasts, which were not eaten at all in Jalisco. What was popular were things like beef round or pork shoulder cut into *chuletas,* or cutlets. I was also introduced to dishes that are not necessarily Jaliscan but that were new then to me. My skimpy knowledge of fish and shellfish was broadened by the Guadalajara *fondas* (simple eateries) serving only *mariscos* (seafood).

Best of all was the Mercado de San Juan de Dios in Guadalajara, one of the great markets of the world. It is built on several levels—a kaleidoscope of activity and color when you look down from the top floor. For me it was one amazing discovery after another. Piles of vegetables and fruits I'd never seen before, stalls with different kinds of herbs and remedies, flower stalls and candy sellers. I spent a lot of time there because every student at the Instituto Familiar y Social had to buy her own ingredients for cooking classes, as well as things like thread, yard goods, lace, etc., for other classes.

At the Mercado the prepared foods are sold on the second level, dished out of big *cazuelas* (the Mexican pottery casseroles) at colorful tiled islands with their own seating areas. (My mother, when she visited, would always say we should head for the most crowded one with no place to sit.) I remember marveling at the wonderful things Jaliscans did with pork. I loved the local version of *pozole* (hominy stew) made with both chicken and pork. *Tacos de cabeza* (made with the meat from a beef head) was another happy discovery. I still think about the market (now called the Mercado de Libertad), and I try to recapture some of its vivid atmosphere for catered parties in New York, with marketplace banners and cooks working at little stalls in full view.

So there was more compensation than I could have expected for my being sent to Guadalajara instead of Palo Alto or St. Louis. I did not have any idea of cooking on a professional level, but when I returned to the North in my early twenties I had acquired a broader perspective on cooking and a willingness to experiment. And then it was my turn to teach Mother some things!

The recipes in this chapter are ones that have been with me, either in their original form or with later adaptations, since my time in Jalisco.

Tequila and Margaritas

"*¿Cuál es su gracia?*" asked the elderly, mustachioed Indian at the pulque stand in the little town of Ixtapan de la Sal in Mexico state. In my part of the North, *gracia* means talent, in the sense of a gift for your chosen work. Thinking he was asking about my profession, I told him I was a restaurateur.

"No—what is your *name?*"

We can still stymie each other in Mexico with our odd regional usages. Even customs that are spread almost the length and breadth of the country have their local words and ways. The stuff my friend Laurie and I were drinking that rainy morning in the marketplace of the ancient Aztec spa town (known for its baths of mineral-rich mud) was as new to me as to any other tourist—as unfamiliar as the clientele of five Indian men and one woman, all smoking cigarettes rolled in corn husks. Pulque is still as localized as beer might have been in Shakespeare's England. I could probably have found it being made that day on the edge of town, out of almost the same maguey plants I remember from my childhood in the North.

Maguey, or botanically *Agave,* is one of the great Mexican plants, as important in its way as corn and chiles. From ancient times people have built houses and woven cloth out of maguey. They have also used the plant to construct different versions of what *Joy of Cooking* calls The Gulp of Mexico. The simplest, oldest maguey beverage is pulque, which the Aztecs were drinking when Cortez arrived. Unlike chocolate, the thick, milky-looking beverage was drunk by commoners. It was made much as it is today, by fermenting the sweet, clear, colorless liquid that accumulates in the heart of the plant. The long, thick leaves, or *pencas,* as fierce-looking as giant sword blades, grow in a rosette-like formation out of a central reservoir shallowly rooted in the soil. The Aztecs had learned to fool the plant into producing more of the sweet *aguamiel* ("honey water") by cutting the flower stalk just before it blossomed and tapping the heart. In several weeks it would become mildly alcoholic—enough to have created a small subpopulation of pre-Hispanic boozers! The Spanish took to the new drink with interest. It is still the poor man's drink of Mexico. In most areas except the North, pulque shops, or *pulquerías,* are as much of an institution as the neighborhood bar in a working-class U.S. town.

We didn't drink pulque in the North, maybe because the kinds of magueys that grow there yield a different kind of sap. But I have vivid memories of our local maguey beverage. The Spanish, who arrived just as the knowledge of distilling was spreading across Europe, tried this craft on the new product with great success. In most parts of Mexico the liquor distilled from *aguamiel* is known as mezcal. It is produced principally in the state of Oaxaca, where bottled mezcal is often sold with a special piece of local color in the bottle—one of the maguey worms that live in the plant. Our maguey liquor in Chihuahua was called *sotol* and was illegally distilled here and there in the neighborhood. Near our ranch was a still owned by my first serious boyfriend, Caly Álvarez, the nephew of my dear friends Lupe and Nayo Chávez. I loved to visit the still, but I would always have to hound my father for permission. I had no idea making moonshine was illegal—I thought Father was just being whimsical! The liquor was distilled in big copper pots and kettles. It tasted fresh and inoffensive straight out of the pipes. What I really loved was to eat the cooked maguey hearts. I can't describe the flavor. It was like nothing else except the sweet essence of tequila.

The best-known version of agave liquor in the United States is tequila, which I probably would have learned about anyhow but got a head start on because of my friend Judy. Judy Smilgus Sauza was one of my classmates at the Instituto Tecnológico y de Estudios Superiores in Guadalajara. We became friends and she invited me to visit her home. Little did I know that the experience would stand me in good stead in my future career! The Sauza factory in the town of Tequila, Jalisco state, makes what many connoisseurs consider the finest of all tequilas.

Judy's home in Tequila, about an hour's drive away from Guadalajara, was an ancient white hacienda, with arches and a heavy wooden gate concealing the splendor inside. I only vaguely remember the meal and the company, but there are lasting impressions of an endless table with beautiful cotton placemats (handmade by the difficult technique called *deshilado,* where patterns are created by pulling out threads from the tight-woven fabric) and antique Talavera china (service for twenty-four). The patriarch of the family sat at the head of the table and I next to him—probably so he could inspect Judy's new friend. (The family was very strict and Judy, like me, is a free spirit.) Luckily I was a credit to my mother's upbringing! I got him talking about tequila and extracted a promise to take me to the factory. I was fascinated with the process and asked many questions. Now, of course, I know much more.

Real tequila is produced only from a single variety of maguey—*Agave tequilana* 'Weber', blue variety. This plant flourishes in the dry, volcanic soil around the town of Tequila (named for a tribe that lived in the area). As far as the eye can see as you drive through the desertlike countryside around Tequila, the rolling hills are planted in beautiful symmetry with the blue magueys. According to the Mexican government *normas* (legal specifications), agave for tequila must be grown either in Jalisco or any of three other states that have appropriate growing conditions (Michoacán, Nayarit, and Tamaulipas). The product from Jalisco is considered the best. Cane sugar and other sugars may be added to the *aguamiel* to assist fermentation, but only to the amount of 49 percent of the total sugars. At least 51 percent must come from the agave itself. There are only two tequila makers I know of—Herradura and Sauza—who produce some 100 percent agave tequila.

The fermented juice is distilled twice. When tequila comes out of the still it is 150 proof (75 percent alcohol by volume). White tequila, the most popular variety, is bottled at once after having been diluted to 110 proof with distilled water. Some is shipped in large vats to the United States and bottled here, usually cut to 80 proof. There are other categories that undergo further aging. Gold tequila, also called *reposado,* is aged about six months in redwood vats before bottling. *Tequila añejo* (aged tequila), which undergoes still more aging, is mostly consumed in Mexico, where its much stronger flavor is appreciated. Super-premium varieties, like Cuervo 1800 and Sauza 3 Generaciones, are aged in oak whiskey barrels that lend a distinctive flavor. Today the United States is the greatest consumer of tequila, most of it in the popular margarita cocktail. In 1986, 47 million liters were produced in the Jalisco area, and only 15 million were consumed in Mexico. No tequila at all is made outside of Mexico, though I understand the Japanese are processing a synthetic tequila. The Mexican government has fought this under international patent laws because it considers the liquor and its name part of the national patrimony since 1795, when José María Cuervo won an exclusive government patent to produce *vino mezcal de tequila.* Though Cuervo is the oldest existing company and we sell a lot of it at my restaurant, my personal favorite is Herradura.

Every night I hear my bartenders and waiters ask the customers if they would like their margaritas straight up, on the rocks, or frozen. Larry Cano, founder of the popular El Torito restaurant chain, told me that he invented the frozen variety, a sort of adult Slurpee. When I asked him where margaritas originated in the first place, he answered, "In heaven!" I think heaven came up with the idea some time in the late 1940s.

My margarita recipe is the traditional one. The proportions are what matter, and it can be doubled, tripled, or whatever, at will.

1½ parts white tequila   **1 part fresh lime juice**
1 part Cointreau or Triple Sec

Combine all the ingredients and shake in a cocktail shaker.

Courtship and Marriage

People who did not grow up in Mexico would find it hard to understand the attitudes toward young girls that still prevailed in my youth. Of course much has changed in my lifetime, especially with more unmarried girls starting to join the work force, but I would say that even now there is a degree of protectiveness and romantic theater incredibly different from anything in U.S. society.

One did not go out on dates without a chaperone when I was in my teens, and in many families girls are still strictly supervised. In our northern ranching circles with close ties to the United States, women probably had an amount of authority and independence that they would not have had in most of the provinces. (Both my mother and I were brought up to ranch work as if we had been oldest sons.) But we also were expected to meet very proper expectations. There was never any question of girls and boys socializing off somewhere by themselves. We were always supposed to be in groups. Among our friends in the Ciudad Juárez/El Paso area, this meant *tardeadas* (afternoon dance parties, usually on Sundays) at the *casinos* (social clubs). They were supervised by eagle-eyed relatives like my Nino Lalo, who once forcibly took me off the dance floor when I was dancing with a charming rogue we were all crazy about.

My sisters and I had a certain amount of freedom in one respect: We were encouraged to bring friends home, as many and as often as we wanted. My mother would often let us party until morning. It was very innocent partying—we would tell jokes and stories all night until Lupita, the cook, started a breakfast of eggs with chorizo, refried beans, and flour tortillas at six in the morning. My mother rightly believed that it was better to have ten or twelve teenage guests in plain view at home than one teenager out on the town.

Respectable girls got no closer to being out on the town than going to meet their dates at the big party-atmosphere Wednesday and Sunday serenades in the town square of Agua Prieta. Groups of girls would walk around the plaza in one direction, boys in the other, eyeing each other anxiously. When you met up with your date, you detached yourself from your group and would walk around the plaza with him—not holding hands, of course, unless it was really serious! Or we might go to street dances, with the traffic blocked off by cattle trucks (the mayor was always someone's relative and would give us permission to close the street) and music by a hired *grupo norteño* (northern country band).

When I did go on something closer to the U.S. idea of a date, my parents would always insist on sending along one of my friends or—worse yet—sisters. (Aída would make my life miserable by loudly cracking a big wad of gum or chewing pork cracklings; Marina was so pretty and charming that my date would spend the entire time talking to her. And both would tease me afterward about whatever I had said or done.) Even when I was in college in Guadalajara, I never went out with a boy unchaperoned. It would have been disaster for my reputation otherwise. I spent about two years there going with a boy named Ricardo, and a lot of our outings consisted of going to Sunday Mass and then to lunch with his mother. I dreaded those rides, with her sitting in the middle of the car between us.

So there were not many opportunities for private romantic moments in a young lady's life at that time, and girls and boys are still expected to remain in the family household under the watchful eye of their parents until they marry. Public romantic moments are something else. We have many kinds of dramatic, ritual self-expression in Mexico. We are more comfortable with such displays than people in this country. Even now a *serenata* with a group of hired musicians is a favorite way for a young man to make his feelings known to his beloved, and the entire neighborhood, on either a preplanned (for birthdays, anniversaries, or feast days) or an impromptu basis. The spur-of-the-moment serenade is a whole ritual that starts with the man choosing his special friends to accompany him for moral support. They go down to the town square and pick one of the different groups of strolling musicians that are always ready to play. *"¡Vámonos, muchachos!"* they tell the musicians, and all drive to the girl's house to be part of the moment.

There are other occasions for serenades, too—for example, children serenade their mothers or grandmothers on occasions like Mother's Day, birthdays, and saints' days. Husbands mark important days in the same way. But romantic serenades to court a girl are not only the best known, they are a whole language to themselves, expressing different stages of the relationship. There used to be (and in some places still is) a corresponding language of responses by the girl—for example, leaving the curtains of her window open to say that she favored his suit or shut to say that she wasn't interested. It used to be possible to conduct much of a courtship by serenade. There are happy, lyrical ones, eloquent ones of hurt (usually accompanied by too much liquor) if the girl has broken off the relationship, and serenades of tender reconciliation.

My Guadalajara boyfriend, Ricardo, was a great serenader. He fancied his own guitar playing and would often come to my window himself with a couple of musician friends. (Most serenade groups are just a trio.) Sometimes he hired mariachi bands. Being given to grand gestures, he once showed up with a group called La Rondalla Tapatía (The Guadalajara Strolling Musicians), with twenty-seven guitars and twenty-seven wonderful voices, to make up after we had quarreled. But this extravagance couldn't hold a candle to our family story of my great-grandfather, who once sent a band of musicians on a whole day's journey by donkey in order to serenade my great-grandmother with one hundred pesos' worth of his favorite song. My great-great-grandmother, the story goes, saw the weary band arrive at some awful hour and insisted on bringing them into the kitchen for a meal before letting them proceed then and there with *"Le Pido al Cielo"* ("I Implore Heaven").

Because young men and women were so seldom permitted to enjoy quieter forms of romance alone, some parts of the courtship traditionally fell to the parents. My case was different because by the time I married I had achieved more of an independent life than most girls in the regional towns. I had a job and an apartment of my own in El Paso and had come a long distance from the sheltered attitudes of a few years before. But even now the custom remains of having the parents of the groom formally call on the parents of the bride to ask for her hand in marriage. In some regions the *pedimento,* or "asking," takes several visits, with the groom's parents bringing presents like baskets of bread or bottles of liquor and the bride's parents putting up *pro forma* arguments against the match—why would you want such a no-good lazy girl as our daughter anyway? (For a wonderful account of many customs common earlier in the century that have not yet disappeared, see Frances Toor's *A Treasury of Mexican Folkways.*)

After agreement is reached, there are lengthy and complicated preparations, mostly for the church wedding. (In Mexico the religious ceremony is not valid in the eyes of the government, so there must be two separate ceremonies.) Three weeks before the wedding the couple must appear in church to kneel before the priest and solemnly swear that they are free to marry. The girl is expected to be a virgin or to do penance if she is not. By my time premarital instruction on religious and parental responsibilities was also required in our diocese.

In most families the *boda civil* (civil wedding) is a simple affair, though sometimes it can be more elaborate. People pride themselves on getting the highest possible government official to preside at the ceremony, and there is a lengthy series of *brindises* (toasts) afterward, with a beautiful speech by the family orator—in my case, my Tío Mike Padilla, who stutters terribly in everyday life but is magically cured when he gets up on the podium. Many people hold the *boda civil* the night before the *boda religiosa,* using it as a sort of rehearsal for the church ceremony.

The *boda religiosa* is always the main event. As with many Mexican religious observances, people commonly enlist the aid of "godparents"—*padrinos* and *madrinas.* These titles are given both to your two sets of regular godparents (those who stood at your baptism and those who stood at your confirmation) and to the friends who agree to help a family perform any important rite. With poorer people, this may go a long way toward defraying the cost. But it is also considered an honor among people of all social standings to act as "godfather" or "godmother" for the different responsibilities of a wedding. There is a *madrina de ramo,* who either provides or is asked to carry one of the bridal bouquets— yes, bouquets. It is traditional for the bride to carry a bouquet of fresh flowers while the *madrina* carries another of beautiful silk flowers and wax orange blossoms which will be left before the image of the Virgin. The *padrinos de lazo* are in charge of the symbol of "tying the knot"—the *lazo,* which can take the form of a rope of flowers, a rosarylike string of beads, or silken cord, and which is formed into one large loop or two intertwined circles and placed over the shoulders of the couple to signify their union. The *padrinos de arras* are the "godparents" who provide thirteen gold or silver coins. At the altar the groom takes the coins and lets them run through his fingers into his bride's, to tell her that from that moment on he will support her. The money is left at the church to be used for charity or made into a bracelet to be given by the husband to the wife on their first anniversary, as a symbol of sharing.

Perhaps because of the expense of the traditional wedding, in poorer villages the couple often elope. The groom comes with a group of his friends and *se la roba*—he takes her away. The parents get angry or make a show of it (everybody may be halfway in on the act anyway), then accept the marriage and celebrate. But a proper wedding celebration is carried out over at least several days with no expense spared. For a big wedding people start arriving days ahead of time, with parties at different houses all week. There was a huge assemblage of friends and family for my wedding, though my husband and I did not have the most lavish traditional touches. We were married on a February day in a small and poor chapel in a Juárez *asilo* (old-age home) that my family had contributed to and come to love very much—several other weddings of family and friends had been held there, and I had fond associations with it. Instead of a beautiful choir and orchestra performing classics, we chose for music the Mass for mariachis. This nonconformist gesture may have been appropriate in one sense— etymologists think the word *mariachi* is a corruption of the French *mariage,* perhaps from the rage for having mariachi bands play at celebrations like weddings in the court of the Emperor Maximilian—but it was not a hit with the priest. When he came up to the altar, he said under his breath, "You want to get me fired? You know you cannot have a sung Mass during Lent!" I confess that I had known this perfectly well but had wanted to have the mariachis play anyway. But the priest went through the ceremony, and afterwards as is customary my husband led me to the high altar, where the bride traditionally kneels down below the image of the Virgin and prays that she will be fertile, a good wife and mother. (A childhood friend of ours in Agua Prieta who has a beautiful operatic voice knelt before the Virgin at her wedding and, instead of praying, sang the Ave Maria. There was not a dry eye in the house.)

After the bride has prayed, it is time for the main feasting. Usually the groom's parents provide the liquor and sometimes the food, with or without help from the real or extra godparents. The classic meat for weddings was and often still is turkey. In the state of Mexico turkeys used to figure in a part of the festivities called *bailar el guajalote* ("doing the turkey dance"), with some of the participants either carrying a live turkey to the festivities or decking out a cooked one with touches like a cigarette stuck in its beak. In upper-class or more Americanized circles the menu may be dominated by things like cold buffet meats or *volovanes* (little pastry shells filled with creamed foods, like vol-au-vents). But in the villages people still serve festive dishes that have been traditional for centuries. Tamales and *mole,* usually made with chicken or turkey, are the unquestioned favorites. According to the Spanish friar Sahagún who wrote down everything he could find about the Aztecs, the prelude to a wedding was that "They made tamales all night and all day for two or three days, and hardly slept at all." Just so today in the villages, all the women of the family make hundreds of tamales for a wedding. The type of *tamal* may vary from region to region, but wherever the old ways persist, you find people who would not dream of having a wedding without tamales.

CUERNITOS DE MERMELADA

Jam-Filled

Crescents

Many Mexican weddings are accompanied by *fruta de horno,* literally "fruit of the oven"—a cornucopia of small baked sweetmeats and pastries, often ordered from convents that specialize in these delicacies. This is a favorite in Chihuahua.

1½ cups pecan meats
2½ cups unbleached all-purpose flour
½ teaspoon salt
1 cup (2 sticks; ½ pound) unsalted butter, chilled

2 large eggs, separated
4 tablespoons ice water, or as needed
¾ cup pineapple preserves
1 cup confectioners' sugar, sifted

Preheat the oven to 325°F.

Chop the pecans finely with a heavy knife and set aside.

Sift the flour and salt together into a mixing bowl. Cut in the butter with two knives or a pastry blender until the mixture is like coarse, crumbly sand. Add the egg yolks and mix gently with a fork or wooden spoon. Add the ice water a little at a time, working it in just until the mixture comes together in a dough. (Alternatively, cream the well-chilled butter in a food processor fitted with the steel blade. Add the flour and process to the consistency of coarse, crumbly sand. Add the egg yolks and process for a few seconds; trickle in the ice water a little at a time, processing in an on-off motion just until the mixture comes together in a dough.

Do not overprocess or it will become greasy.) Wrap in plastic wrap and refrigerate until thoroughly chilled, about 30 minutes.

Shape the dough into 36 balls about the size of small walnuts. Working with a rolling pin on a very lightly floured surface, roll each ball out into a 2½- to 3-inch circle. Place a dab of jam (slightly more than ½ teaspoon) in the center of each circle. Fold one third of the circle over the center, fold from the other side to enclose the jam, and roll into a cigar shape. Twist the cigar into a crescent, pinching all edges to seal well.

Beat the egg whites until frothy in a small bowl. Dip the crescents into the beaten whites, letting any excess trickle back into the bowl. Lightly roll the coated crescents in the chopped pecans. Place on an ungreased baking sheet and bake until golden, 17 to 20 minutes. Let the cookies cool slightly and roll in confectioners' sugar.

YIELD: 3 DOZEN COOKIES

SOPES

Masa Tartlets

I would not eat *sopes* at all for eighteen years because they brought me back too completely to the boardinghouse where my sister Marina and I lived with thirteen other boarders during my last two college years. One taste of a *sope,* the delicious Mexican snack, and I was right back in Guadalajara, aged about twenty and endlessly reliving the same dismal scenario.

The house is airy, spacious, and comfortable and is run efficiently—but by three unhappy women dressed in mourning, all in black, except for one pair of pink terry-cloth slippers. The owner and proprietress is old, dignified, sour-faced, ill-tempered Doña Mercedes (middle-class but with pretensions of great gentility), who organizes everything by commands accompanied by rapping on the tile floor with her cane. Her only son has died recently in an automobile accident, leaving Doña Mercedes in grief, which she passes on by making life even more miserable for the widow, her daughter-in-law Magda, whom she holds responsible for the death.

Magda is a beautiful, earthy woman with, despite everything, a quick humor and deep laugh. She miraculously has a fabulous figure despite her eight children, ranging in age from twelve years to three months, all of them living in the house, too. She was pregnant with the youngest when her husband died. She had no alternative at all to living with her mother-in-law. The arrangement condemns her to servitude and humiliation. Doña Mercedes endlessly reminds all of us that Magda is low-class and Doña Mercedes had always objected to the marriage. Her son was too good for Magda, so Magda killed him! Perfectly logical.

Despite her humor and beauty, Magda is deeply depressed. She deals with it by working from dawn to dusk, getting her children ready for school, and helping them with their homework when they come home, all this between shopping and cooking the *comida* (afternoon meal) for the house. Her food is delicious. But her mother-in-law never has a good word to say to her or about her.

The third woman is the poor relation, completing this triptych of miserable frustration. Carmelita, distant cousin of Doña Mercedes, shuffles around in the pink terry slippers muttering prayers and lamentations, a dust rag in her hand, ever solicitous of her benefactress and the boarders. She is resident maid, laundress, and morning-and-night cook, and has a silly laugh. She never complains about anything specific, she is only too happy to help. She just steadily bemoans everything under her breath—the cosmos, fate, destiny.

She makes the boarders big, heavy breakfasts that I'm not used to and have trouble getting down. So Carmelita makes me her version of a *ponche,* in this case a hearty blender-drink of raw eggs, milk, vanilla, Ceylon cinnamon, and bananas. She stands over me until I drink it all down.

I don't drink *ponches* any more, for the same reason I stopped eating *sopes.*

Since our Guadalajara college budget didn't allow frequent eating out, we were pretty much condemned to eat all our meals in the boardinghouse. Carmelita was not an original or inventive or even varied cook. We ate *sopes* at least three times a week. Luckily, since I started making them for my frequent dinner parties in Manhattan, *sopes* are acquiring better associations for me. They are delicious, versatile appetizers, always a favorite with my guests.

The basic procedure is easier to do than to describe! Small, thicker-than-usual tortillas are griddle-baked, then quickly formed into the shape of miniature tartlets by crimping up the edges into a slightly raised rim while the dough is still just warm enough to

be malleable. They are then fried and served with any filling of your choice.

Sopes are usually made with a regular tortilla dough of corn *masa.* The flour in this recipe is my own addition. It makes the dough silkier and less likely to become hard and brittle in frying.

2 cups masa harina (see page 49)	**1 teaspoon baking powder**
1 cup unbleached all-purpose flour	**¼ cup lard (see page 19) or vegetable shortening**
1 teaspoon salt	**1½ cups hot water, or as needed**
	Vegetable oil for frying

Combine the *masa harina,* flour, salt, and baking powder in a mixing bowl. Work in the lard with your fingertips or a pastry blender until thoroughly incorporated; the mixture should be like crumbly sand. Add 1 cup of the hot water and stir to mix; gradually add just enough more water to form a soft but not wet dough. You will need more or less water depending on the humidity and the condition of the flour.

Divide the dough into thirds; working with one part at a time and keeping the remaining dough covered with a moist tea towel, divide each third into five pieces and form them into Ping-Pong–sized balls. Flatten each ball with your hand to make a round a little more than 2 inches in diameter and about ⅛ inch thick. Cover with a moist towel as they are made, to keep them from drying out. If not using immediately, be sure to keep well covered.

Heat a large, heavy griddle or cast-iron skillet over medium-high heat and rub with an oil-soaked paper towel. When smoking lightly, place about 4 rounds on the griddle. Adjust the heat as necessary to keep the *sopes* from darkening too fast. Cook for about 30 seconds on one side and turn with a spatula; the cooked side should be golden (no darker). Cook the other side until golden. The *sopes* will puff up slightly from trapped steam. Remove from the griddle.

When each *sope* is just cool enough to handle, crimp up the edge with your fingers to make a raised rim like a shallow tartlet. Cook and shape the remaining *sopes,* working with about 4 at a time.

Heat a medium-size skillet over high heat and pour in vegetable oil to a depth of about ½ inch. When rippling but not smoking, add 3 or 4 *sopes* to the pan and fry until golden but not brittle, about 30 seconds on each side. Adjust the heat as necessary to keep from scorching them. Drain on paper towels as they are done.

While the *sopes* are still hot, fill with any of the following fillings: *Picadillo Dulce* (page 47), *Salpicón de Huachinango* (page 160), *Pollo Guisado* (page 45), or *Papas con Chorizo* (page 89). Also suitable are refried beans, shredded cheese, sautéed chorizo (page 106)—use your imagination. Top with a spoonful of any fresh salsa you like (*Salsa Cruda de Tomatillo,* page 41, is particularly good) and a sprinkling of crumbled ricotta salata (my substitute for *queso fresco*) or other grated aged cheese mixed with chopped scallion tops. Another delicious alternative is to top the filling with a spoonful of *Pepián Verde de Tampico* (page 328) and the crumbled cheese and scallions. Serve at once, hot (you should make just a few at a time, not the whole batch at once).

YIELD: 15 SOPES

NOTE: *Sopes* can be made ahead up to the point of griddle-baking and shaping, and held as long as 3 hours before frying. Immediately after shaping, place them in a bowl or on a baking sheet and cover tightly with aluminum foil or plastic wrap. When ready to serve, proceed with the frying and filling.

A larger version of *sopes,* called *pellizcadas,* native to Puebla state, is made by substituting large corn tortillas (about 5 inches in diameter, made a little on the thick side) for the small ones. Griddle-bake, shape, and fill as described above.

ENSALADA PICO DE GALLO

Cucumber, Jícama, and Fruit Salad

Until I came to Guadalajara, I knew *pico de gallo* as an uncooked table sauce like the one on page 40. However, in the central region of Mexico, *pico de gallo* refers to this salad. It is sold from vendor carts in paper cones, and the fruit, which is always cut in decorative shapes, is changed according to what is in season. The cucumbers are essential, though.

Part of what makes the *pico de gallo* salad exciting is one of the classic Mexican combinations of flavors—fresh-squeezed lime juice and powdered hot red chile. This combination is used a lot in street food, such as roasted ears of corn. (A simple and wonderful idea for party crudités is to dip slices of jícama all over in lime juice and then dip one end in powdered red chile.) Here it also helps marry the different flavors of sweet fruit and bland vegetables. This version of the salad, conceived by my Mexico City friend, the painter Xavier Esqueda, contains an unorthodox note in the onion, garlic, and olive oil, which I think add a nice twist. But don't use extra virgin oil—it will overpower the fruit.

The salad is particularly good when watermelons are at their peak.

1 garlic clove, minced
¼ cup pure or "light" olive oil
¼ cup fresh lime juice
1 small red onion, finely chopped (about ½ cup)
½ teaspoon salt, or to taste
1 pound seedless oranges, mangoes, or crisp tart apples, or 2 pounds watermelon or other melon

1 medium-small jícama (see page 9; about 1 pound), peeled and thinly sliced or finely diced
2 large cucumbers (about 1 pound), thinly sliced into rounds
1 tablespoon minced fresh chile piquín (see page 226) or pure powdered red chile (page 226)

Combine the garlic and olive oil in small bowl; let steep about 15 minutes. Combine the lime juice, onion, and salt in a second small bowl. Let rest 5 minutes while you prepare the fruit.

Peel the oranges, mangoes, or apples. Core or seed as necessary and cut into fine dice, thin slices, or other preferred shapes. If using melon, scoop out the flesh with a melon baller or cut into any desired shapes.

Place the fruit, jícama, and cucumber in a salad bowl and toss with the minced or powdered chile. Add the garlic-oil and onion-lime juice mixtures and toss to combine thoroughly. Serve chilled.
YIELD: 4 TO 6 SERVINGS

CALDO DE FRIJOL NEGRO

Black Bean
Soup

The first boardinghouses I lived in in Guadalajara had some really wonderful food. This soup became a favorite of mine. When made with water and vegetable oil, it's an excellent vegetarian dish.

3 tablespoons lard (see page 19)
   or vegetable oil
2 large garlic cloves, finely
   chopped (about 1 tablespoon)
1 medium-size onion, finely
   chopped (about 1 cup)
3 small carrots, thinly sliced
1 large celery stalk with leafy
   top, chopped
2 fresh chiles, either jalapeño or
   serrano (see pages 225 and
   226), tops removed but not
   seeded, sliced into rings; or
   use canned jalapeños
2 bay leaves

2 tablespoons chopped fresh
   cilantro leaves
1½ teaspoons dried Mexican
   oregano (see page 11),
   crumbled
6 cups water or chicken stock
1 pound dried black beans,
   picked over, soaked overnight
   in water to cover (or according
   to package directions), and
   drained
2 dried or canned chipotle chiles
   (see page 224)
Salt and freshly ground black
   pepper to taste

Heat the lard or oil in a Dutch oven or small soup pot over medium-high heat until hot but not quite smoking. Add the garlic and onion and cook, stirring occasionally, until the onion is golden and translucent, about 3 minutes. Add the carrots, celery, jalapeños, bay leaves, cilantro, and oregano. Reduce the heat to low and cook, uncovered, for 15 minutes, stirring occasionally.

Add the water or stock, drained beans, and chipotle chiles and bring to a boil. Reduce the heat to medium-low and simmer, partly covered, for 45 minutes. Season with salt and pepper; continue to simmer until the beans are tender, another 45 minutes to

1 hour. (Time will vary depending on the age and storage conditions of the beans.) Let cool slightly and remove the bay leaves. Remove the chipotle chiles also if you prefer the soup not too spicy, or leave them in for a little extra kick.

Working in two batches, puree the soup in a blender or food processor. Transfer to a saucepan and bring back to a boil, stirring often. Serve immediately with crisp-fried corn tortilla strips.

YIELD: 4 TO 6 SERVINGS AS A MAIN DISH

CALDO TLALPEÑO

Soup from

Tlalpan

In Guadalajara I encountered not only Jaliscan recipes but dishes from different parts of Mexico. This delicious soup from Tlalpan, a suburb of Mexico City, is one that I remember having with my parents when they came to Guadalajara on a visit during my student years. Little did any of us foresee that the recipe would be my contribution to an affair of state when Queen Elizabeth visited President Reagan in California in 1983!

If using the optional canned chick-peas, drain and rinse under cold water in a colander.

8 cups Caldo de Pollo Casero (see page 45)

2 whole, bone-in chicken breasts (about 1 pound)

2 tablespoons lard (see page 19) or vegetable oil

1 small onion, chopped (about ½ cup)

1 garlic clove, crushed

1 medium-size ripe, red tomato, peeled, seeded, and finely chopped

1 or 2 canned chiles chipotles en adobo (see page 224)

Salt to taste

2 medium-size firm, ripe avocados (preferably the black-skinned Hass variety), peeled, pitted, and cut into thin strips

8 radishes, trimmed and thinly sliced

2 scallions, white and some of green part, thinly sliced

8 ounces Muenster or white cheddar cheese, cut into ¼-inch cubes

1 cup canned or cooked (see page 43) chick peas, skins rubbed off between your fingers, optional

2 limes, cut into wedges

Bring the stock to a boil in a large, heavy saucepan over high heat. Add the chicken breasts and reduce the heat to low. Simmer, uncovered, until the chicken is fork tender, about 20 minutes. Transfer to a plate; when cool enough to handle, remove and discard the skin and bones. Pull the chicken into shreds and reserve, covered. Reserve the stock in the saucepan.

Heat the lard or oil in a small, heavy skillet over medium-high heat until rippling. Add the onion and garlic and cook, stirring, until the onion is translucent, about 4 minutes. Add the chopped tomato and cook, uncovered, stirring frequently, until somewhat concentrated, about 5 minutes.

Puree the chipotle chiles in a blender with ½ cup of the reserved chicken stock. Add the chipotle mixture and tomato mixture to the rest of the stock; simmer, uncovered, over low heat for 15 minutes. Let sit off the heat briefly; strain through a sieve and return to the saucepan. Bring to a boil over medium heat. Taste for seasoning and add salt if desired.

Divide the shredded chicken, avocado strips, radishes, scallions, cheese, and chick peas among 8 warmed soup bowls. Ladle the flavored stock into the bowls and serve immediately with lime wedges on the side.

YIELD: 8 SERVINGS

SOPA JULIANA

Vegetable

Soup

The word *juliana,* in Mexican cooking, refers to dishes that contain mainly combinations of vegetables. It is important to julienne or dice the vegetables uniformly to achieve the proper presentation of this healthful soup. The Worcestershire sauce typifies the frequent use of bottled sauces to season soups and other dishes in Mexican cooking. Adjust the amount as you please, but the flavor belongs there.

I like to top this soup with a dollop of crème fraîche as a substitute for Mexican cream; U.S. sour cream will break up and spoil the appearance of the dish. When we ate it at the boardinghouses where I lived as a student, it was served also with uncooked tomato salsa (like *Pico de Gallo Norteño*, page 40) and freshly made corn tortillas.

3 garlic cloves, peeled

1 medium-size onion, peeled

½ pound carrots, peeled

1 medium-small boiling potato (Red Bliss or other thin-skinned variety), peeled

1 pound zucchini

¼ pound fresh string beans, strings removed if necessary

1 pound fresh spinach, stems removed, well washed, and patted dry

1 large ripe, red tomato, roasted and peeled (see page 14)

3 tablespoons vegetable oil

¼ pound fresh shelled peas

8 cups Caldo de Pollo (see page 44)

2 tablespoons Worcestershire sauce

Salt and freshly ground black pepper to taste

1 lime, sliced

½ cup crème fraîche or Mexican-type sour cream (see page 21), optional

Prepare the vegetables as follows, setting each aside separately. Mince the garlic. Cut the onion, carrots, potato, and zucchini into ¼-inch dice. Cut the string beans into short lengths (preferably ¼ inch, but no longer than 1 inch). Roughly chop the spinach and tomato.

Heat 2 tablespoons of the oil in a soup pot or large Dutch oven over medium-high heat. Cook the onion and garlic for 3 minutes, stirring often. Add the carrots, string beans, peas, and potatoes and cook, stirring, 3 to 5 minutes over medium heat. Add the chicken stock and Worcestershire; season with salt and pepper. Bring to a boil, reduce the heat to medium-low, and simmer until the vegetables are tender, about 15 minutes.

Meanwhile, heat the remaining tablespoon of oil in a skillet over medium-high heat. Add the zucchini, spinach, and tomato and cook 3 minutes, stirring. Five minutes before the other vegetables are done, add the zucchini, spinach, and tomato to the soup. Serve immediately, garnished with the lime slices. Serve with a dab of crème fraîche, if desired.

YIELD: 4 SERVINGS AS A MAIN DISH, 6 AS A SOUP COURSE

NOTE: If using tiny new peas (*petits pois*), sauté them along with the zucchini, spinach, and tomato.

ARROZ VERDE

Green Rice

This was one of the dishes I became familiar with in the board-inghouses where I lived in Guadalajara.

6 fresh chiles, either poblano or
    Anaheim (see pages 226 and
    223), roasted (page 227)
1 medium-size onion, diced
    (about 1 cup)
1 garlic clove, peeled

3½ cups **Caldo de Pollo Casero**
    (see page 45)
¼ cup vegetable oil
1½ cups rice
3 sprigs fresh epazote (see page
    8) or cilantro, chopped
Salt to taste

Place the roasted chiles in a plastic or brown paper bag and let rest 10 minutes. Peel, seed, and chop 5 of the chiles, reserving 1 for garnish.

Place the chopped chiles in a blender or food processor fitted with the steel blade. Puree with the onion, garlic, and ½ cup of the chicken stock. Set aside.

Heat the oil in a medium-size saucepan over medium-high heat until it begins to ripple. Add the rice and cook, stirring often, until golden, about 5 minutes. Pour off the excess oil. Add the pureed chile mixture and bring to a boil. Add the remaining chicken stock, the epazote, and salt and bring to a boil; reduce the heat at once to very low and cover the pan tightly. Cook for 20 minutes. Serve at once, garnished with the remaining chile cut into strips.

YIELD: 4 TO 6 SERVINGS

LANGOSTINOS TÍA CUQUITA

Tía Cuquita's Langoustines

I met Doña Cuquita, an old-fashioned matron with three unmarried daughters, while I was studying in Guadalajara. Doña Cuquita was stern-looking, with hair in a bun and little glasses on the tip of her nose, but this appearance belied a heart of gold. Her oldest daughter, also named Cuquita, took a liking to me and welcomed the opportunity to practice her English. They often invited me to their family *comidas,* and what delicious lunches they were! Doña Cuquita was a fabulous cook, and kind enough always to give me her recipes for the dishes we ate.

These *langostinos* were part of a memorable meal. Unfortunately, it is hard to get fresh *langostinos,* a prized type of small lobsterlike marine shellfish. They are similar to the East Atlantic and Mediterranean langoustines, also called Dublin Bay prawns or Norway lobsters and sometimes sold in specialty fish markets. You might need to substitute either very large shrimps or prawns (like the Asian freshwater prawns widely sold in U.S. fish stores). The flat-leaf Italian parsley is used a lot in Mexican recipes; we call it *perejil.*

2 pounds fresh langoustines, lobsterettes, Asian freshwater prawns, or "colossal" (10 or fewer to a pound) shrimp
Salt and freshly ground white pepper to taste
½ cup fresh lime juice
6 garlic cloves, peeled
¼ cup fresh Italian (flat-leaf) parsley leaves
½ cup dry white wine, or as needed
3 tablespoons butter

Leave the langoustines or giant shrimp in the shell; rinse well under cold running water. With a small sharp knife, slit open the belly enough to hold a small amount of stuffing. Sprinkle the inside of the belly with a little salt and pepper, then with lime juice.

Mince the garlic and parsley together very fine and place in a small bowl. Gradually add just enough white wine to moisten them. Stuff a little of this mixture into the incision in each langoustine.

In a sauté pan or saucepan with a tight-fitting lid and large enough to hold the langoustines comfortably in one layer, heat the

butter over high heat until fragrant and sizzling. Arrange the langoustines in the pan. Cook, covered, adjusting the heat as necessary, just until the langoustines are opaque, 4 to 5 minutes.
YIELD: 4 TO 6 SERVINGS

PESCADO ESTILO PLAYA

Jalisco-Style Fish in Sauce

Years ago, while I was studying in Guadalajara, I experienced for the first time one of the great treats of going to the beach at Puerto Vallarta—eating freshly caught local fish, threaded on sticks and grilled over an open fire on the beach. The fish are quite large and served simply with bottled red chile sauce and lime. The flavor stayed with me and I developed this refreshing, lively sauce—though how much of the present recipe is my own invention and how much I gleaned from now-forgotten cookbooks, I'm not really sure!

FOR THE SAUCE
½ cup fresh lime juice
¼ cup chopped fresh cilantro
2 fresh chiles, either jalapeño or serrano (see page 225 and 226) or more to taste, tops removed but not seeded, finely chopped; or use canned jalapeños
½ small onion, finely chopped (about ⅓ cup)
1 to 1½ cups cold water, or as needed

Salt to taste

FOR THE FISH
4 small red snappers, sea bass, or brook trout (about 1 pound each), cleaned and scaled, heads left on
1 cup Pasta de Chipotle (see page 35) or Adobo de Chile Colorado (page 29)
Salt and freshly ground white pepper to taste

To make the sauce, combine the lime juice, cilantro, chiles, and onion in a small bowl. Gradually stir in enough cold water to achieve the texture of a thin sauce. Season with salt. Refrigerate while you prepare the fish. (The sauce will lose its freshness if held more than a few hours.)

Rinse the fish under cold running water to remove any stray scales or traces of blood. Pat dry. Rub the fish inside and out with the chipotle paste or *adobo,* covering everything except the heads. Sprinkle with salt and pepper. Let rest 1 hour in the refrigerator.

Preheat the grill or broiler. Grill as close as possible to the coals or source of heat (4 to 6 inches away) for 3 to 4 minutes on each side. Serve at once with the lime-cilantro sauce.

YIELD: 4 SERVINGS

NOTE: The fish can also be baked in a preheated 400°F oven for 15 minutes.

CARNITAS

Pork Nuggets

Actually, my first encounter with this famous dish was as a child visiting Tijuana with my uncle Ernie. We ate *carnitas* at a restaurant that was like a thatched hut with open sides. In my college years I found that it is one of the great specialites of Jalisco.

Four pounds of pork may sound like a lot, but it will shrink tremendously as the fat renders out of it in baking. The orange juice is my own addition.

¼ to ⅓ cup lard (see page 19) or
    vegetable oil, or as needed
4 pounds lean boneless pork
    butt or leg, cut into 1½-inch
    cubes

Salt and freshly ground black
    pepper to taste
Zest of 1 or 2 oranges, finely
    chopped or slivered
¾ cup fresh orange juice

In a large, heavy Dutch oven with a tight-fitting lid, heat 3 to 4 tablespoons of the lard or oil over high heat until almost smoking. Add about one third of the pork (just enough to fit in one layer). Season lightly with salt and pepper and scatter one third of the orange zest over it. Reduce the heat to medium-high and cook, uncovered, stirring occasionally and adjusting the heat as necessary, until the pork is browned and crisp on all sides, 15 to 20 minutes. Remove the meat to a large bowl and reserve. Cook the remaining pork in two batches in the same manner, adding another 1 or 2 tablespoons of lard if necessary.

Drain off the excess fat from the Dutch oven; return the browned meat to the pan, add the orange juice, and bring to a boil over high heat, stirring frequently to coat the meat on all sides. Reduce the heat to medium and simmer, uncovered, until the liquid reduces to a syrupy glaze, 10 to 15 minutes. While the orange juice is reducing, preheat the oven to 300°F. Bake, tightly covered, until the meat is very tender but chewy, about 40 minutes.

Drain off the fat that has accumulated and serve the *carnitas* hot, with hot flour or corn tortillas and any kind of salsa.

YIELD: 6 TO 8 SERVINGS

TORTAS AHOGADAS

Jalisco-Style
Hot Roast Pork
Sandwiches

Tortas are not only "cakes" or things in the shape of round cakes, but sandwiches. These wonderful open-faced sandwiches are traditional in Jalisco state. I have not seen them elsewhere. I became addicted to them after I persuaded my parents to transfer me from the perfect-housewife "finishing school" to the Instituto Tecnológico y de Estudios Superiores de Occidente in Guadalajara. The school cafeteria had a great cook who used to make this garlicky, spicy version of *tortas ahogadas*. It was so delicious that the taste haunted me for ten years, until I duplicated it from memory. It is a great winter party dish.

Good French rolls are the closest equivalent of the Mexican *bolillos,* which deserve a book in their own right. Mexican wheat and bread flour are of very high quality. Since the short, doomed reign of the Emperor Maximilian in the 1860s, Mexican bakeries have been producing many types of bread and rolls at least as good as those of Paris or Vienna. (For a fascinating account, see the chapter "La Panadería" in Diana Kennedy's *Recipes from the Regional Cooks of Mexico*). Anyone who visits Mexico without sampling some of the breads is missing one of the national glories. Every state has its own interpretation of *bolillos,* but they are universally wonderful. I have a prejudice in favor of the version in Chihuahua state (where the wheat is especially good), but the Jaliscan rolls are good too.

The word *ahogada* means "drowned," and the sandwiches should literally be swimming in the sauce. Ladle it on generously.

8 garlic cloves, minced
1 tablespoon dried Mexican oregano (see page 11), crumbled
Salt and freshly ground black pepper to taste
1 boneless pork butt (about 4½ pounds)
6 crusty French rolls

3 to 4 cups Salsa de Chipotle (recipe follows)
1 cup Crema Agria Preparada (see page 42)
1 ripe avocado (preferably the black-skinned Hass variety), peeled, pitted, and cut lengthwise into thin slivers

Preheat the oven to 475°F. Combine the garlic, oregano, and a little salt and pepper. With a small sharp knife, make gashes an inch deep all over the roast and fill with the garlic mixture. Rub the outside of the roast with more salt and pepper. Place the meat in a shallow roasting pan and bake at 475°F for 20 minutes, to seal in the juices. Lower the heat to 350°F and continue to bake until tender and thoroughly cooked, about 2 hours and 15 minutes. An instant-reading thermometer inserted into the thickest part should register 170°F. Remove from the oven and let rest 20 minutes. Carve into thin slices.

Warm the rolls briefly in the oven and slice in half lengthwise. Remove some of the inside if desired to make room for the filling. Spoon 2 tablespoons of the *salsa de chipotle* over each roll half. Arrange the pork slices on top. Drench each with about ¼ cup more sauce, then dot with 1 tablespoon of the prepared sour cream. Garnish with avocado slices and serve immediately, allowing two open-faced sandwich halves per serving.

YIELD: 8 TO 10 SERVINGS AS A LUNCHEON DISH—BUT THEY'RE SO GOOD THEY MIGHT NOT GO THAT FAR

SALSA DE CHIPOTLE

Chipotle

Sauce

This is a very versatile sauce. *Tortas Ahogadas* (recipe above) would not be the same without it, but it has many other possible uses. At Restaurant Pardiños in Veracruz and Mexico City it is served with shrimp. My mother makes wonderful meatballs in it. Experiment!

2 tablespoons lard (see page 19) or vegetable oil

2 large garlic cloves, minced

1 medium-size onion, chopped (about 1 cup)

Pan drippings from roast pork for Tortas Ahogadas (see page 137), optional

2½ to 3 pounds very ripe, red tomatoes (5 to 6 large tomatoes) or 1 can (28 ounces) whole tomatoes (plain, without added puree)

2 to 3 canned chiles chipotles en adobo (see page 224) with a little of the sauce that clings to them

1½ teaspoons dried Mexican oregano (see page 11)

Pinch of sugar

½ teaspoon salt, or to taste

Heat the lard or oil in a medium-size saucepan over medium-high heat until almost smoking. Add the onion and garlic and cook, stirring often, until the onion is translucent, 2 to 3 minutes. Add the remaining ingredients. Stir thoroughly to combine and simmer, uncovered, over low heat 10 to 15 minutes, stirring often. Puree the sauce in a blender or food processor. With a wooden spoon or pusher, force it through a sieve, discarding any solids.

If you want a milder sauce, remove all or some of chipotle chiles before pureeing.

Keeps, tightly covered, up to 3 days in the refrigerator or indefinitely in the freezer.

YIELD: 3 TO 4 CUPS

TORTA DE ELOTE

Savory Corn Bread

At the Instituto Familiar y Social, I learned to make a zucchini dish with a consistency something like a moist, cakey bread, called *torta de calabacitas*. Over the years I've found it a good basis for departure like this version made with corn. Because rice flour has no gluten, it will not rise to be as light as if it were made with wheat flour. I sometimes take the batter and use it to fill roasted and peeled whole poblanos, then bake until they puff, and serve as a side dish.

3 cups fresh, frozen (thawed), or drained canned corn kernels	**1 teaspoon salt**
1 cup (2 sticks; ½ pound) un-salted butter or margarine	**½ pound white cheddar cheese, shredded (about 2 cups)**
2 tablespoons sugar	**4 ounces poblano chiles (see page 226), roasted (page 227), tops removed, seeded, and diced (2 or 3 chiles, to make about ½ cup diced)**
3 large eggs	
1½ cups rice flour	
1 tablespoon baking powder	

Working in batches if necessary, grind the corn by pulsing it in a blender until coarsely crushed but not pureed. Set aside.

Preheat the oven to 325°F.

In a large bowl, cream the butter by hand or with an electric mixer at medium speed until light and fluffy. Add the sugar, 1 tablespoon at a time. Add the eggs, one by one, beating after each addition to incorporate thoroughly.

Sift the flour, baking powder, and salt together and add to the creamed mixture in two parts, beating on low speed until each is well incorporated. With a spatula or large spoon, fold the ground corn into the batter. Fold in the shredded cheese and diced poblano chiles.

Butter and lightly dust with cornstarch a 13 x 9-inch Pyrex baking dish. Pour in the mixture and bake until puffed and golden, about 30 minutes. A toothpick inserted in the center should come out clean.

YIELD: 6 TO 8 SERVINGS AS A SIDE DISH

TORTA DE ZANAHORIA
Carrot Casserole

This further experiment with the basic zucchini *torta* from my student years is made just the same as Torta de Elote (recipe above) except for two departures. Instead of the corn, use 1 chayote or mirliton squash (simmered in a small saucepan with salted water to cover for 5 minutes or until slightly tender but still crunchy, then peeled and diced when cool) and 1 pound shredded peeled carrots. Fold in the diced chayote and shredded carrots after the flour and baking powder, and proceed as above. I sometimes make this version in the form of muffins, baked in buttered and cornstarch-dusted muffin tins at 375°F for 15 minutes. It will make 12 muffins.

ROMPOPE

Mexican

Eggnog

Rompope is the super-rich eggnog of Mexico. This recipe, which I first encountered in Guadalajara, is a simple version that can be turned into a dessert topping simply by reducing the amount of fresh milk to obtain the desired consistency.

1 can (14 ounces) condensed milk   **6 large egg yolks**
Same amount of fresh milk; use   **6 ounces dark rum**
   the can to measure

Place the condensed milk, fresh milk, and egg yolks in a blender and process for 30 seconds, or until smoothly mixed. Add the rum and process for 30 more seconds. Chill thoroughly before serving.
YIELD: 6 TO 8 SERVINGS

AGUAS FRESCAS Y PREPARADOS
Mexican Fresh Fruitades and Pureed Fruit Drinks

One of the things that made the biggest impression on me in Jalisco was the incredible wealth of fresh cold beverages sold everywhere at street stalls. They are one of the real treasures of Mexican food. Actually, I had known a few examples from childhood. We used to love the cold sweet rice drink, *Horchata de Arroz* (page 82), and in summer my mother would make us save the seeds of cantaloupes and other melons so she could make another kind of *horchata* with the pureed seeds and a *canela* (Ceylon cinnamon) tea. That is delicious, too.

But as a student in Guadalajara I was amazed to find a huge, exotic range of refreshing cold drinks, mostly made out of fresh fruit, though there is a version from alfalfa! In later travels I came to understand that these *aguas frescas* and *preparados* are part of the landscape all over Mexico. (On my first visit to the southern state of Tabasco I sampled a drink made from the unlikely but delicious combination of the wandering-jew plant with fresh lime juice, water, sugar, and ice—the only thing that can bring relief from Tabasco's oppressive heat.) They were a revelation to me in 1966.

I remember the marketplace stands, and the stalls along the underground crosswalks beneath a plaza in the center of town, each with round glass containers full of perfectly ripe papayas, pineapples, guavas, strawberries, mamey, guanábana, black sapodilla, watermelon, and other seasonal fruit. Freshly cut fruit was set out on the spic-and-span counters. And the aromas! At the boardinghouses where I lived, our meals were served with cold drinks, usually made from Jamaica flower (red hibiscus, a most beautiful color) or different melons or citrus fruits.

The *aguas frescas* resemble limeades or other fruitades, often varied with exotic flavors such as chía (the seed of a plant related to sage) or tamarind, my favorite. (For an elaborate, unusual *agua fresca* associated with the feast of Candlemas, see page 203.) Fruit is also whipped in a blender to produce the pureed *preparados,* which often have milk added so as to resemble fruit-flavored milkshakes or "smoothies." I recommend experimenting with both, using whatever fresh fruit is best in the market and varying the flavor with lime juice and sugar to your taste. You may not be able to duplicate the rainbow of fruit at the Guadalajara stands, but you can certainly invent some healthful and delicious drinks.

PREPARADO DE FRESA O DE PLÁTANO

Strawberry or

Banana

"Smoothie"

At the Instituto Familiar y Social I was taught this basic formula for fruit *preparados.* You can substitute any other fruit you have available; vary the amount of sugar according to how sweet the fruit is. It's so simple that you hardly even need a recipe once you've tried one example; I suggest you explore the frozen tropical fruit pulps in Latin American markets and come up with your own favorite *preparados* or *aguas frescas.*

½ pint fresh strawberries, hulled
and sliced (about 1 cup)
or
1 small, ripe banana, peeled and
sliced

1 cup milk or ice water
4 ice cubes
1 to 2 tablespoons sugar, or to
taste

Combine all the ingredients in a blender and process until smoothly pureed.

YIELD: 1 SERVING

AGUA FRESCA DE TAMARINDO

Cold Tamarind

Drink

I remember the tall tamarind trees that grew around Yelapa, a small fishing village about an hour south of Puerto Vallarta in Jalisco. This is another example of Asian influence—a tropical fruit brought to Latin America from India. The long brown pods contain a sticky, acid pulp that is one of the most wonderful tropical flavors. (You may have tasted it in southern Indian or Thai dishes.) Until recently tamarind was seldom available in the United States except as a leathery dried paste that had to be softened in water and usually strained to eliminate seeds and fibers. Now stores in Central American neighborhoods are starting to carry a product that is simpler to use for *aguas frescas*, the prestrained frozen tamarind pulp called for in this recipe. A 14-ounce package has about 2 cups of pulp. I like it on the tart side; you may prefer more sugar.

1 package (14 ounces) frozen
tamarind pulp, thawed

2 cups water, or as needed
¼ cup sugar, or to taste

In a mixing bowl or pitcher, stir to combine all the ingredients thoroughly. Serve chilled.

YIELD: ABOUT 1 QUART

PASTEL DE NUEZ

Pecan Cake

This is one of the popular Mexican desserts that I learned at the Instituto Familiar y Social in Guadalajara. It is especially beloved in the central region of Mexico. The texture is dense and moist, something like that of a fruitcake, and the cake requires long baking. In Mexico it is usually served with *cajeta,* the rich caramel sauce of sweetened boiled-down milk, generally goat's milk, that is named for the *cajetas* (flat wooden boxes) in which it is sold. In my pantry I always have some Mexican *cajeta,* often the famous variety from Celaya in the state of Guanajuato, or a kind that is *envinada* (enriched with sherry). In many Latin American markets you can buy a similar product under the name of *dulce de leche.* By the way, non-Mexicans may look horrified if you say *cajeta,* which has a terribly lewd connotation in some parts of Latin America! Lacking a source of *cajeta,* frost the cake with raisin icing or a simple sugar glaze.

1½ cups shelled pecan halves (about 6 ounces)	2 large eggs, separated
1¼ cups (2½ sticks; 10 ounces) unsalted butter, at room temperature	2½ cups unbleached all-purpose flour
	1½ teaspoons baking powder
1½ cups sugar	1 teaspoon salt
1 teaspoon pure vanilla extract	1 cup half-and-half

Preheat the oven to 325°F. Butter and flour a 10-inch Bundt pan, shaking off any excess flour.

In a single layer on an ungreased baking sheet, toast the pecans until fragrant, about 15 minutes. Cool to room temperature and grind finely in a nut grinder. Set aside. Adjust the oven heat to 350°F.

In a large mixing bowl, cream the butter and sugar together with an electric mixer until light and fluffy. Add the vanilla and beat another 30 seconds to incorporate. Add the egg yolks, one at a time, beating well after each addition.

Sift the flour, baking powder, and salt into a second bowl.

In another bowl combine the ground pecans and half-and-half, stirring to moisten thoroughly. Add one third of the dry ingredients to the butter mixture and beat to incorporate well, then add one third of the pecan mixture and beat well. Repeat, alternating thirds of the remaining dry ingredients and nut mixture and scraping down the sides of the bowl as necessary, until all has been added.

Whip the egg whites with an electric mixer until stiff peaks form. With a spatula, gently fold about a third of the beaten whites into the batter, then fold in the rest until no streaks are visible.

Pour the batter into the Bundt pan. Bake until a toothpick inserted in the center comes out clean, about 1½ hours. Let cool in the pan 10 to 15 minutes before unmolding. Cool completely on a rack.

YIELD: 1 CAKE; 8 TO 10 SERVINGS

BETÚN DE PASAS

Raisin Icing

Most people will not be able to obtain *cajeta,* but *Pastel de Nuez* (page 144) also goes well with this variant of a seven-minute icing—actually very close to a favorite Maida Heatter recipe—that I learned on the ranch.

½ cup dark raisins	3 tablespoons cold water
½ cup dark rum, heated	1 teaspoon fresh lemon juice
2 large egg whites	Dash of salt
¾ cup sugar	1 teaspoon pure vanilla extract

In a small bowl, cover the raisins with the hot rum and let stand until plumped, about 20 minutes. Drain the raisins of any remaining rum and pour into a food processor fitted with the steel blade and process until finely chopped. Set aside.

Combine the egg whites, sugar, water, lemon juice, and salt in the top of a double boiler over hot water. Set the double boiler over medium heat and beat the mixture with an electric mixer on high speed for 5 minutes. It will become foamy, then glossy and firm enough to stand in peaks when the beaters are lifted. Transfer to a mixing bowl, add the vanilla, and continue to beat on high speed for another 1 to 2 minutes. Add the chopped raisins and fold them in thoroughly. Frost the cake at once.

YIELD: ABOUT 2½ CUPS

PASTEL RÁPIDO

Quick Butter Cake

This is another of the recipes that I learned at the Instituto Familiar y Social—a versatile, simple, delicious cake with a texture a little like that of pound cake. It needs no icing except (if you like) a simple confectioner's sugar glaze.

3 tablespoons dark rum, heated
¼ cup dark raisins
1 cup (2 sticks; ½ pound) un-salted butter, at room temp-erature
¾ cup plus 1 tablespoon sugar

3 large eggs, at room temp-erature
2¼ cups unbleached all-purpose flour
2 teaspoons baking powder
½ teaspoon salt

Pour the hot rum over the raisins in a small bowl and let steep at least 15 minutes.

Meanwhile, preheat the oven to 350°F. Butter and flour a 10-inch Bundt pan, shaking off any excess flour.

Cream the butter by hand or with an electric mixer at medium speed in a large mixing bowl until light and fluffy. Add the sugar, about ⅓ cup at a time, continuing to beat at medium speed. Beat until the mixture is very fluffy, about 4 to 5 minutes. Add the eggs, one at a time, beating well after each addition. Beat the batter about another 3 minutes. Fold in the raisins and rum with a spatula.

Sift the flour, baking powder, and salt together three times. Add to the batter a little at a time, folding gently with a spatula until thoroughly combined.

Pour the batter into the Bundt pan. Bake until a toothpick inserted in the center comes out clean, 30 to 35 minutes. Let cool in the pan about 10 minutes before unmolding. Cool completely on a rack.

YIELD: 1 CAKE; 8 TO 10 SERVINGS

ROLLO DE DÁTIL Y NUEZ

Date-Nut Roll

I hadn't thought about this chewy confection for years until I was working on the Guadalajara recipes for this book and suddenly had a memory of it in an ancient notebook from the Instituto Familiar y Social. Sure enough, there it was, just as I remembered it—dense, very sweet, but a little fruity from the dates.

The original recipe was all in metric weight and volume measurements.

1 cup plus 2 tablespoons sugar
1 cup milk
1 pound pitted dates, coarsely chopped (about 2 cups)

1 pound pecan meats, coarsely broken up (about 4 cups)

Have ready a big dishtowel wrung out in cold water and laid flat.

In a small heavy saucepan, cook the sugar and milk to the soft-ball stage (238°F on a candy thermometer) over medium-high heat. Add the dates and cook 5 minutes, stirring. First the milk will look curdled, then the mixture will become sticky and hard to stir. After exactly 5 minutes, remove from the heat and beat in the pecans.

Scrape out the mixture into the center of the dampened dishtowel and use the towel to roll the hot candy into a long (about 18 inches) cylinder. Place a long piece of heatproof plastic wrap on the counter. Unroll the nut mixture onto this, roll up tightly, and let cool. When completely cool, refrigerate; unwrap and cut into ⅓-inch slices when ready to serve.

Will keep, tightly wrapped, in the refrigerator 1 week.

YIELD: ONE 18-INCH ROLL; ABOUT 50 SLICES

BOLITAS DE CHOCOLATE

Chocolate Balls

This was one of my early acquisitions at the Instituto Familiar y Social. It's a case where Mexican chocolate would not be appropriate—it's too grainy, never having undergone the same pulverizing and emulsifying processes as ordinary commercial chocolate.

4 ounces milk chocolate
1 teaspoon butter
½ cup condensed milk
½ teaspoon ground true (Ceylon) cinnamon (see page 15), or a large pinch of U.S. "cinnamon"

½ teaspoon pure vanilla extract
Crushed pecans, optional

Melt the chocolate in the top of a double boiler over simmering water. Add the butter and whisk in the condensed milk, cinnamon, and vanilla. Stir until thoroughly combined. Refrigerate the mixture until firm enough to shape into small balls (about walnut-size), about 2 hours. Roll in crushed pecans, if desired.

Can be stored, covered with plastic wrap, in the refrigerator 2 to 3 days. Do not double this recipe.

YIELD: ABOUT 20 BALLS

Experiments and Surprises

I left Guadalajara in 1971 with no clear idea of what I wanted to do next. It was one of the floundering, unhappy times a lot of young people went through in those days, during or after college. Up to that time my life had been governed by a strict code of rules and ethics that no longer applied in the whole distressing shift of values that was going on then in the world. I was unable to think of any future plans at all and was just generally unstrung.

Cooking helped me through this bad period. My father and I spent a lot of time alone together, holed up on the ranch. The two of us would go into the kitchen and cook for hours, experimenting with everything under the sun. But mostly not Mexican! My Tía Panchita, my mother's sister, gave us a lot of the Lebanese recipes she had learned when she married my Tío Ernesto Ellis, whose family was Lebanese. (There are a lot of Middle Easterners in Mexico.) We made Arabic bread, pomegranate jelly, baby eggplants stuffed with walnuts, grilled loin of lamb with the lamb tripes wrapped around it.

We also cooked a lot out of *Gourmet* and other magazines. We had the big *Gourmet Cookbook* and would tackle anything we could find. We fooled around with different kinds of roasting and grilling, or corning our own beef with whole heads of roast garlic. We loved big productions. Sometimes we had fights about just how to make the food. I'd be cooking something and my father would start in with "Don't you think it would be a good idea if we added a little such-and-such," and I'd say, "Papá—*out!* You're not making it, I'm making it."

We stayed there about two years, until Father decided that the self-imposed isolation of the ranch was not good for me and made me get out and face the real world in El Paso. He was right—I did pull out of my crisis, though life was not easy and Father himself was very ill. He died of cancer in 1974. Meanwhile, I had got a job first as a secretary and then as a medical social worker for the Texas Department of Human Resources, and then in 1975 I married Adolfo Sánchez, a widower with three young children.

I went on experimenting as Papá and I had together. I served ambitious international gourmet recipes that my housekeeper thought were a pain in the neck. In the end I was not the one to realize that my hobby could become my career. It was my sister Aída who inspired me. She was married then to a very wealthy man in Ciudad Juárez, and they entertained constantly. To help out I began preparing meals for Aída's parties, usually for at least twenty people. I was avidly reading cookbooks and trying dishes from all parts of the world. My husband and I were not at all well off, and when I learned that I was pregnant with twins, we were desperately looking for ideas for extra income. Aída's brainstorm was for me to start cooking and catering for money, on a regular basis.

I couldn't set up as a professional at once, of course, but I did make a start that winter with a lot of Christmas-cookie baking. After my sons Aarón and Rodrigo were born in February 1976, I really threw myself into Aída's suggestion. All my family—most of all, my mother—enthusiastically joined in. It became the career focus I hadn't found before.

I had an incredible amount to learn. My mother offered to pay for real lessons, as much study in as many places as I needed to master the craft. At that point my idea was to build an international gourmet repertoire, and the cooking schools we looked to were in the United States. When the twins were about six months old I found an excellent California teacher/chef, Lillian Haines. With her I learned basic realities, like equipment, cost estimates, portion sizes, purchasing, and dealing with suppliers. I also took her "International Foods" course, with segments on many different cuisines. When we got to Mexican food I was prepared for the worst, because not one restaurant in Beverly Hills served anything

I recognized as Mexican no matter what they called it. Much to my surprise, Lillian's recipes were delicious and true.

I began a small business in El Paso—not easy, as I was also still a full-time social worker with a full caseload. But I persevered. I even started handling some accounts for Pete Singh Produce, a big El Paso distributor, in exchange for some of the fruits and vegetables I needed for my business. My sister Clarissa was my only employee, and she proved to be a great asset. (When once asked what she did for me, she replied, "Everything Zarela hates to do!") Everyone I knew helped in my furious, never-ending search for recipes. Friends gave me books and got their mothers or grandmothers to give me very old recipes that had been in their families for generations. My mother was now remarried and traveling often to Mexico City and central Mexico with my stepfather. Wherever they went she looked for unusual dishes and reported them to me. When I was able to travel myself, I incessantly scouted out recipes from all parts of Mexico.

My sister Marina was a help, too. She had also been in Guadalajara in my last couple of student years. In our boardinghouse was a young man named Joel Díaz de León, from the state of Aguascalientes. Even though Marina was only fourteen, he immediately fell in love with her. Four years later they were married. On our visits to Joel's family in their home town of Calvillo (the Mexican guava capital—you start to smell the guavas about a mile out of the city), we tasted all kinds of dishes new to us. Later, as a newlywed living in San Luís Potosí, Marina refined the art of cooking with little money. She learned her mother-in-law's recipes and sent them on to me when I needed every idea I could get my hands on for the business.

I soon developed a regular clientele, mostly from the El Paso medical community, where I had a lot of contacts from my work. (My mother, no slouch herself in the contacts department, got me one of my first jobs by announcing to a doctor's wife sitting next to her in the beauty parlor that her daughter was a caterer.) I had a great success with a luncheon for the El Paso Medical Society and promptly found myself flooded with requests. Still, it was some years before I was able to quit my social-work job and devote myself full time to catering. What free moments I was able to fit in I spent continuing to take classes around the United States.

Though I knew a lot about Mexican cooking, I still thought of myself as an eclectic gourmet caterer. One of my typical catered parties from those days might have featured a chicken dish from Julie Sahni's *Classic Indian Cooking,* a Chinese vegetable stir-fry, and a great Mexican rice casserole I'd learned, *Arroz con Crema y Poblanos* (page 172). A popular item at bar mitzvahs was elegant little tea sandwiches with a spread of roasted Anaheim chiles cooked down almost to a paste and mixed with a little mayonnaise! I did a lot of layered casseroles that were good for big parties, often adapting rolled crêpe or enchilada recipes to a simpler casserole format. I also started to understand more about the way flavors worked, the way a well-constructed dish can give you a complex of distinct flavor sensations, from creamy to tart to aromatic to hot, in each bite.

I had finally quit my job and gone into the business full-time when my career suddenly took an abrupt Cinderella-Zarela turn. My good angel was Chef Paul Prudhomme of K-Paul's in New Orleans. Late in February 1981, I found myself there because my mother and I had had a couple of planned visits to U.S. cooking schools fall through. We decided to salvage something from the trip by visiting all the restaurants we could, looking for potential additions to my repertoire. (We both have an ability to duplicate most things we have tasted from memory.) We had already eaten four meals on the day we passed K-Paul's, but we went in anyhow and they sat us in front of Paul. We had the most marvelous meal. My mother had the Sticky Chicken and I ate a dish of three small fillets (veal, pork, and beef). I was painfully shy in those days, and when my mother urged me to go up and talk to Paul Prudhomme, I was terrified. But with my mother's coaxing I got up my courage and introduced myself.

Paul was wonderful. He asked me about myself and listened with sympathy when I told him how the restaurant-school I'd started out to visit in New Orleans, hoping to acquire new dishes, had turned out to be a waste of time and money. Before I knew it, he had offered to teach me something about Cajun food from his own vast knowledge. In return he asked me to teach him some Mexican dishes. For the next three days I cooked at K-Paul's. We had a great hit with one of the recipes Lillian Haines had taught me, *Enchiladas de Cangrejo* (page 181). Everything else we tried was well received, too. By the time I went back to El Paso, Paul and I were fast friends.

We chatted a few times by phone to stay in touch, and during one call Paul told me that he had been invited to cook at a dinner for the Maîtres Cuisiniers de France at Tavern on the Green in New York. Mother half-kiddingly suggested that I offer my services as a dishwasher, to get to go along with him. I said, *"Mother!"* and declined the suggestion. But two weeks later I had a phone call that floored me. Paul told me that the party had got so big that he would not be able to do his food as it should be done. So they were changing the concept to a buffet showcasing American regional cooking (one of the first presentations of this kind—the idea would be almost commonplace a few years later). Would I do the Mexican-inspired food?

I was not a confident person at that stage. I told Paul I couldn't possibly do it—I didn't even know how to chop an onion the way chefs do.

"You don't have to," said Paul. "You are the *chef*! You can ask a prep cook to bring you a chopped onion."

So I agreed. I asked that Mother be allowed to accompany me, as I had about one third of her repertoire. On March 21, one month to the day after we had wandered into K-Paul's, we were at work in the kitchen at Tavern on the Green. Neither of us had ever been inside a restaurant kitchen, and there we were, not ten blocks from a fantastic suite that had been rented for us at the Essex House, learning from Pierre Franey how to chop a scallion double-quick. We made Lillian's crab enchiladas again, *salpicón de carne* (a sort of hash of shredded beef), enchiladas with red chile sauce. Every dish was a hit. They were served in an incredibly beautiful buffet presentation, with silver chafing dishes, candles, and flowers galore amid a fairyland of chandeliers, Tiffany glass, and red carpets.

We had never been to such an event, let alone participated in one. I was so inexperienced that when we were called to the Crystal Room after the meal and everyone stood up and clapped amid exploding flashbulbs, I never imagined it was for me. I innocently sat down at a table and Suzanne Hamlin, then food correspondent for the New York *Daily News,* had to tell me to stand up and acknowledge the applause. I burst into tears.

Needless to say, this was a watershed. One month before, I had been a small-time caterer looking for new recipes to serve the El Paso Medical Society. Suddenly I was a star at a national media event, with heady compliments and talk of major-league career opportunities flowing all around me. Paul was my anchor to re-

ality. He took time to talk over the whole experience with me. He helped me learn what to say to the reporters and interviewers. Above all he warned me not to let the moment's triumph go to my head—that this was never-never land and I would have to go back to bridge luncheons and bar mitzvahs in El Paso, paying bills and working hard. Then and at every stage Paul would be there with the advice I needed and the sane, steady perspective I couldn't have provided for myself.

I had been offered a tremendous opportunity, but it was up to me to build on it. Long before, Lillian Haines had told me that the most important asset I could have in my business was an identity—my own approach and convictions, which people would recognize as soon as they walked into one of my parties and ate my food. The more I learned as a young caterer, the more defined my cooking had become. It was my feeling for Mexican food that Paul and others had recognized as unusual and somehow individual. (I don't need to say that my mother's talent and support had also been a huge part of the triumph.) I was able to present a solidly rooted but personal, vivid version of a great cuisine that had received only fifth-rate imitations in most cities of the United States—in those days, especially New York. (A Fodor's guide from around that time commented that the Mexican food available in the United States bore the same uncomfortable resemblance to real Mexican cooking as a howling monkey has to man.) I saw that I had something real to offer.

But I kept my feet on the ground as Paul had advised. I went back to my business in El Paso, turning down some restaurant and other offers that had been made to me in different parts of the country. Nothing really happened. But after about a year I felt I was ready to make something happen. So I called Warner LeRoy, who had been very kind to us at Tavern on the Green, and asked whether he'd like to have a party and let me cook for him. It was a great success and another turning point—because Warner reintroduced me to Craig Claiborne of *The New York Times,* whom I'd barely met at the Maîtres Cuisiniers dinner. Craig, too, was generous and sympathetic from the first. Not only did he ask me to his East Hampton home to prepare a dinner that he wrote up in an article titled "Memorable Dishes from a Mexican Master Chef," but I became one of the lucky chefs from all over the world invited to participate in a grand potluck luncheon celebrating his sixty-second birthday (September 4, 1982) and the publication of his autobiography, *A Feast Made for Laughter*. My contribution to that memorable meal was *Camarones al Ajillo* (page 179), one of the dishes I had so busily gathered when I first decided to start cooking professionally. I met many other food writers who would take an interest in my ideas about Mexican food, and some of whom would become good friends. I began coming often to New York to cook for parties—at my own expense—and to introduce a version of Mexican cuisine that was a revelation to most people. It was an investment of time and money that has repaid me many times over.

Several months after Craig's party came another bombshell invitation—this time from the White House. President Reagan's staff had contacted Craig about the menu for a dinner to honor Queen Elizabeth II at the Reagan ranch in California. They wanted a recipe for a light, fresh Mexican soup. Craig referred them to me in El Paso. I supplied a recipe (and the ingredients) for *Caldo Tlalpeño* (page 130), which I had first encountered during my college days. It brought more publicity—and it brought me an invitation to cook for the international economic summit conference in Williamsburg, Virginia, in May 1983. Craig was serving as special consultant for the occasion, and there was to be a series of menus featuring regional American specialties and the work of people like Paul Prudhomme, Wolfgang Puck, Maida Heatter, and Leo Steiner of the Carnegie Delicatessen in New York. I was asked to prepare the closing luncheon, which was to be served alfresco on the lawn of Basset Hall, the Rockefellers' Williamsburg home. Because of the outdoor presentation and because we had been asked to make only limited use of the kitchen facilities in the historic house, the planners requested that I devise some courses that would be prepared with only a grill. We—once more, I had asked that Mother be allowed to share the experience with me—settled on an eclectic menu including corn bread filled with Texas chili con carne, tamales with pork and red chile sauce, the stuffed beef fillet known as *Tapado Tlaxcala* (page 185), a *tamal* presentation of fish that was invented on the spur of the moment (page 183), and an original vegetarian version of stuffed poblano chiles.

"Unforgettable" hardly conveys the event. To this day I can clearly see the late spring Virginia afternoon, with a light mist creeping over the grass. Secret Service men, security checks, and tasters (no kidding!) were all over. President Reagan, in a brown cowboy dress suit with cowboy boots, took off his jacket, rolled up his shirtsleeves, and led the conversation with a charisma obvious even from across the lawn while the seven heads of state dug in to my food at the round table under a yellow awning. Midway through the proceedings, Prime Minister Trudeau of Canada sent a messenger to congratulate me on the meal. Afterward I stood in a reception line with all the other chefs while the seven heads of state moved past to greet us. Then I sat on the lawn of the beautiful apartment building where we had been staying and stared speechlessly for two hours at the St. James River. My friend Alex Baker, who had accompanied me, broke into my reverie to ask, "What are you going to do *now*, Zarela?"

By now I had come to a now-or-never decision. Craig Claiborne and others had given me great help and encouragement. Privately I knew that I could see my cooking developing, becoming more confident and individual as I worked. Not long after the first White House invitation I had decided I was ready to move on from my business in El Paso, where I had long since been separated from my husband. That spring I took my sons out of school in Texas. With a grand total of $12,000 in hand, I packed up my van and a few possessions and drove to New York and into a $2,000 monthly rent. It was a crazy gamble, but I knew I had to do it.

I was helped by some of the consultants and developers I had met on earlier New York trips, as well as media coverage like an article in *Cuisine* magazine that appeared around this time. I did not have a good idea of what I was going to do next—or, rather, I had too many. For more than a year I pursued several false starts, barely supporting myself and the boys through the catering. What grateful memories I have of my friends Lew, Beth, and Billy Rudin helping me through this period with many commissions and recommendations beyond the call of duty.

But eventually my path led to the best thing I could have gotten—my first real restaurant experience. I was asked to devise the menu and recipes at a new Mexican restaurant being opened by the restaurateur David Keh in mid-Manhattan.

The new venture, Café Marimba, was probably the most beautiful restaurant in New York, an incredible fantasy-setting with dazzling arches, a tiled fountain, and great lighting effects. David and his associate, Eddie Schoenfeld, had hired a lot of high-powered talent, including the restaurant consultant Barbara Kafka.

When Café Marimba opened at the end of 1984 it made quite a splash. It was Mexican food unlike anything to be found in the city. For me Café Marimba turned out to be a way station rather than a destiny—but it was an absolutely invaluable learning experience.

In all the years I had spent as a caterer and guest chef, I had never seen the daily routine of a working restaurant kitchen. I knew nothing. I had no idea how different processes and personnel had to fit into a line, or how to plan quantities. We developed the menu by having me cook my dishes the way I would at home and then having an experienced chef, John Terzac, translate them to restaurant methods and proportions. Eddie Schoenfeld patiently undertook to fill me in on what I didn't know about day-to-day operations, which was everything. From him I learned the innumerable details of seating and "dressing" a room, hiring and training and motivating staff, handling customers at good moments and bad, gauging U.S. menu preferences, and so forth. Not to mention self-control instead of the emotional outbursts I was sometimes prone to.

As for the food, it was another step forward in my development of a flexible but sound culinary style, a way of cooking that would be my own "voice." I was familiar now with New York resources and the tastes of the city dining public—I knew they were eager to encounter something other than enchiladas, tacos, and burritos. I had always had an inherent grasp of the basic Mexican flavor principles that have to be honored for the food to mean anything. But my understanding of how techniques influence flavors had deepened. So I was able to improvise, to remain faithful to the character of a dish when I was obliged to substitute one important ingredient for another. It was now that I began to experiment with a kind of synthesis of Mexican cooking, mixing varied elements when my instinct told me they would complement each other. In my cooking, I was ready to take on the role of an interpreter between different worlds.

The recipes in this chapter derive from some of the exploring and repertoire-building that took place in stages as I came back from college, decided on food as a career, and first tried my wings in New York.

CREPAS DE CHICHARRÓN

Crêpes Filled with Pork Cracklings

I remember eating pork cracklings, *chicharrones,* whenever we butchered at the ranch. They are a beloved snack everywhere in Mexico and are usually eaten with bottled red hot sauce and fresh lime juice. Butcher shops and street stalls sell them fresh and crisp. This recipe is a little eclectic, because the usual way of serving *chicharrón* filling would be in *antojitos* (snacks) like tacos, *Sopes* (page 124), and *Gorditas* (page 161). Use packaged pork rinds, unless you can get good fresh-made cracklings from Latin American butchers.

2 tablespoons corn oil
2 scallions, white and some of green part, finely chopped
2 garlic cloves, minced
1 large ripe, red tomato, chopped
2 fresh chiles, jalapeño or serrano (see pages 225 and 226), tops removed but not seeded, finely chopped

2 tablespoons chopped fresh cilantro leaves
3 cups coarsely crumbled pork cracklings or rinds (about 2 ounces)
Salt, optional
8 Crepas de Maíz (see page 86)

Heat the oil in a medium-size sauté pan or skillet over high heat until hot but not quite smoking. Add the scallions and garlic and cook 2 minutes, stirring. Add the chopped tomato, chiles, and cilantro and stir well to combine. Reduce the heat to medium-low and simmer until the liquid is partly evaporated, about 3 more minutes. Add the pork cracklings and stir to combine. Taste the mixture and add salt if desired. Cook 5 more minutes, stirring occasionally.

Fill the crêpes with the mixture and serve with *Salsa Ranchera* (page 308) or *Caldillo de Tomate* (page 36).

YIELD: 4 SERVINGS AS A FIRST COURSE

ALITAS DE POLLO EN SALSA DE CHIPOTLE

Chicken Wings
with Chipotle
Sauce

One of my two favorite aunts, my Tía Panchita Ellis, taught me to make this sauce long before I thought of cooking professionally. Tía Panchita is slightly eccentric, totally lovable, and a fabulous cook. She entertains a lot and insists on total organization and minimum fuss. I learned a lot from her and used to be fascinated with the Lebanese dishes she would make for my uncle Ernie. The two of them are the "angels" who later made my restaurant Zarela financially possible for me.

This sauce may be prepared one day in advance and can be used in endless combinations. It is wonderful on fresh pasta and with cooked peeled shrimp. I have used it as a dip for crudités, as a sauce for crisp, barely cooked vegetables, and in place of mayonnaise in chicken salad.

2 pounds chicken wings
2 bay leaves
2 garlic cloves, peeled
1 small onion, peeled
6 black peppercorns
Salt to taste

FOR THE SAUCE
1 cup sour cream
1 cup mayonnaise

2 canned chiles chipotles en
adobo (see page 224), or to
taste, pureed in a blender or
food processor
1 garlic clove, finely minced
¼ cup chopped scallion (white
part only) or onion
1 tablespoon chopped fresh
cilantro leaves

With a small sharp knife, cut each chicken wing into 3 joints. Discard the wing tips or save for soup stock. Place the larger wing joints in a deep saucepan or small Dutch oven. Cover with cold water. Add the bay leaves, garlic, onion, peppercorns, and salt. Bring to a boil, reduce the heat to medium-low, and simmer partly covered until cooked through, 15 to 20 minutes. Do not overcook. Allow to cool in the broth. Drain, remove the skin, and pat dry with paper towels. (Reserve the broth for another use.)

Prepare the sauce by combining all the ingredients in a medium-size bowl. Serve the chicken wings warm or cold as a finger-food appetizer, either covered with or accompanied by the chipotle sauce.

YIELD: 8 SERVINGS AS APPETIZER; ABOUT 2 CUPS SAUCE

SALPICÓN DE HUACHINANGO

Red Snapper Hash

This recipe has become my signature dish, but actually I adapted it from one of the dishes my mother found when everyone was passing recipes on to me in El Paso. It was originally done with crab, but here the cost would be prohibitive for what was originally a simple dish from a bar in Tampico, Tamaulipas state.

The story is this: My stepfather and my mother were in Tampico on a business trip. My Tío Chacha is a nosher. (We call him *tío*—uncle—because we have known him since we were children.) He would rather eat snacks than regular meals and always finds the bars that have the best *botanas* (snacks to accompany drinks, like the Spanish *tapas*). In this case he was directed to a place located in front of a cemetery and called El Porvenir (That Which Is to Come). The logo announced, *Se está mejor aquí que en frente*—"you rest better here than across the street"—and another notice advised that neither women nor military personnel were allowed inside. So my stepfather had to go in and buy the *botanas* and beer, and they ate outside, sitting on the back of their pickup truck with a beautiful view of the cemetery.

It makes me cringe to think of U.S. "cinnamon" (actually the harsh-flavored cassia) in this dish, but if you must use it reduce the amount of cinnamon to ½ teaspoon.

½ cup (1 stick; ¼ pound) unsalted butter

6 large garlic cloves, finely
minced

6 to 7 scallions, white and some
of green part, minced (about
1 cup)

3 medium-sized ripe, red tomatoes, chopped (about 2½ cups)

3 fresh chiles, either jalapeño or
serrano (see pages 225 and
226), stems removed but not
seeded, finely chopped

¼ cup chopped fresh cilantro
leaves

1½ teaspoons ground true (Ceylon) cinnamon (page 15), preferably freshly ground in a
spice grinder

½ teaspoon ground cloves

2 teaspoons ground cumin

1 teaspoon salt, or to taste

2½ pounds red snapper fillets,
skinned and small bones removed with tweezers

Choose a heavy skillet (preferably nonstick) that will be large enough to hold the fish in one layer. Melt half the butter over medium heat. When the foam subsides, add half the minced garlic and cook 1 minute, stirring constantly. Add the scallions and cook 1 minute longer, stirring often. Add the tomatoes, chiles, cilantro, spices, and a little salt; stir well to combine. Cook, stirring often, until the sauce is slightly concentrated, about 5 minutes.

Cut the fish fillets into halves or several large pieces, depending on their size. Place them in the pan in one layer. Adjusting the heat to maintain a low simmer, poach the fish, uncovered, just until the flesh begins to turn opaque, 1 minute. Carefully turn the fillets with a spatula and poach on the other side for about 1 minute more; the flesh should still be slightly undercooked. Allow them to cool in the sauce.

When the fish is cool enough to handle, pull the flesh into shreds with your fingers. Carefully remove any bones that may be left. If the sauce looks watery, drain off a little of the juice.

Heat the remaining butter in a second large skillet over medium heat until hot and bubbling. Add the remaining garlic and cook for 1 minute, stirring. Add the shredded fish and sauce; cook just until heated through.

Serve with freshly made corn tortillas or crisp-fried tortilla chips.

YIELD: 6 TO 8 SERVINGS AS A FIRST COURSE, MORE AS A TACO FILLING

GORDITAS

"Little Fat Ones"

Gorditas were a favorite way to entertain in Juárez. My sister Clarissa had friends who would hire a woman to come to their house and make *gorditas* for parties. So I started doing them for my clients, with great success—people love watching a steady stream of fresh hot *gorditas* being produced. They can be served with any preferred filling—I suggest *Picadillo Dulce* (page 47), *Salpicón de Huachinango* (page 160), *Ropa Vieja* (page 175), or *Papas con Chorizo* (page 89).

In Guadalajara we used to see a version of *gorditas,* but very tiny, not a third of the size. They called them *aspirinas*—"aspirins."

2 cups masa harina (page 49)

½ cup unbleached all-purpose flour

1 teaspoon baking powder

1 teaspoon salt, or to taste

1¼ cups warm water, or as needed

½ cup grated aged cheese (queso añejo—see page 17—or Parmesan)

Vegetable oil for deep frying (at least 6 cups)

1½ cups (approximately) preferred filling (see page 161)

FOR GARNISH

1 cup finely shredded cabbage mixed with ¼ cup cider vinegar, seasoned with salt and pepper to taste

½ cup grated aged cheese (queso añejo or Parmesan)

Pico de Gallo Norteño (see page 40)

In a bowl, thoroughly combine the *masa harina,* flour, baking powder, and salt. Stirring with your hand, add the water, a little at a time, using only enough to produce a fairly soft, pliable but not sticky dough. Knead in the grated cheese.

Divide the dough into 24 balls. Keeping the dough covered with a slightly damp cloth before and after shaping, flatten each ball and shape into a round, cookielike pastry about 2½ inches in diameter, with the edges slightly squared. (Wet your hands in a little water to make it easier to handle the dough.)

Heat the oil to 350°F in a deep-fryer or heavy, deep skillet over high heat. Add the *gorditas* in batches of 3 or 4 at a time, watching to be sure that the temperature remains constant. Cook until they are crisp and golden brown (1 to 2 minutes). When done, they will rise to the top and be slightly puffed. Remove and drain on paper towels.

As each batch is done, split the hot *gorditas* partly open. Stuff each with about 1 tablespoon of the chosen filling. Garnish with a small amount of the cabbage, a touch of grated cheese, and a spoonful or so of *pico de gallo.*

YIELD: 24 GORDITAS

JÍCAMA ESCABECHADA

Jícama Relish

Lillian Haines, my teacher in California, had a variation on a traditional Mexican vegetable *escabeche* that became one of my most useful accompaniments. The chipotle and olive oil are her additions. So is cutting the vegetables into fine dice (about ¼ inch) instead of slicing them on the bias.

At the restaurant we serve this with the grill-smoked salmon (page 326).

1 small carrot, peeled and finely diced

1 small zucchini, scrubbed and finely diced

1 medium-size jícama (see page 9—1½ to 2 pounds), peeled and finely diced

1 medium-size onion, finely chopped (about 1 cup)

4 garlic cloves, minced

1 canned chile chipotle en adobo (see page 224), seeded and minced

1 bay leaf

6 black peppercorns

1 teaspoon salt, or to taste

1 teaspoon dried Mexican oregano (see page 11), crumbled

2 tablespoons chopped fresh cilantro leaves

½ cup distilled white vinegar

½ cup water

⅓ cup extra virgin olive oil

Blanch the diced carrot in boiling water for 2 to 3 minutes. Drain thoroughly. Place all the ingredients in an earthenware or glass bowl and toss to combine. Let marinate, refrigerated, at least 4 hours or preferably overnight. Serve at room temperature.

Can be stored, tightly covered, in the refrigerator for up to a week.

YIELD: 4 SERVINGS (ABOUT 6 CUPS)

ENSALADA DE CHICHARRÓN

Pork Crackling Salad

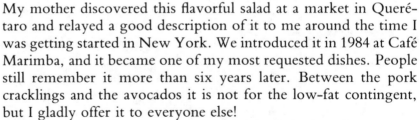

My mother discovered this flavorful salad at a market in Querétaro and relayed a good description of it to me around the time I was getting started in New York. We introduced it in 1984 at Café Marimba, and it became one of my most requested dishes. People still remember it more than six years later. Between the pork cracklings and the avocados it is not for the low-fat contingent, but I gladly offer it to everyone else!

I make the salad with packaged pork rinds, but you can use fresh *chicharrones* bought from a butcher in Latin American neighborhoods.

1 medium-size ripe, red tomato, peeled, seeded, and chopped

3 to 4 scallions, white and some of green part, finely chopped

1 or 2 fresh chiles, either jalapeño or serrano (see pages 225 and 226), tops removed but not seeded, finely chopped

2 tablespoons finely chopped fresh cilantro leaves

½ cup mayonnaise

Salt to taste

2 ripe, firm avocados, preferably the black-skinned Hass variety

3 cups pork cracklings or rinds (about 2 ounces), broken into large (about 1-inch) pieces

In a medium-size bowl, combine chopped tomato, scallions, chiles, and cilantro with the mayonnaise. Taste and add salt if desired. Let rest 15 minutes.

Peel the avocados and cut into ½-inch cubes. Add the avocados and cracklings to the tomato mixture, toss to combine well, and serve immediately.

YIELD: 4 TO 6 SERVINGS

ENSALADA DE JÍCAMA Y BERROS

Jícama-

Watercress

Salad

Salads were not a big thing in Mexican meals during my Guadalajara days. Around the late seventies there seemed to be an upsurge of interest, just when I was starting my catering business in El Paso and looking for ideas. Suddenly people were doing unusual combinations like this exotic and unexpected salad my mother scouted out in Mexico City.

Do not soak the julienned jícama in cold water if you have to hold it for more than a few minutes. Soaking removes its natural sweetness. It will not discolor; just refrigerate in a small bowl covered with a damp cloth.

3 bunches watercress
2 tablespoons salted butter
½ cup pine nuts (see note)

1 small jícama, about ¾ pound
(see page 9 and note)
Vinagreta de Zarela (recipe follows)

Strip off and discard the tough watercress stems. Rinse well and pat dry.

Heat the butter in a small skillet over low heat until fragrant and bubbling. Add the pine nuts and cook just until golden brown, stirring occasionally and watching that they don't burn. Remove from the pan and drain on paper towels.

Peel the tough outer skin from the jícama. Cut into either julienne strips or longer sticks about 3 × ¼ × ¼ inches.

Arrange the watercress on a large platter. Arrange the jícama strips decoratively over the watercress. Pour the dressing over the salad and sprinkle with the toasted pine nuts.

YIELD: 4 TO 6 SERVINGS

NOTE: ½ cup sesame seeds, toasted until just brown in a dry skillet over medium-low heat, can be substituted for the pine nuts. If jícama is unavailable, substitute 8 ounces of raw mushrooms, trimmed, cleaned, and thinly sliced.

VINAGRETA DE ZARELA

Zarela's Vinaigrette

Maggi seasoning is one of the most commonly used condiments in Mexico. Gary Jacobson, the chef at Zarela, says he has seen people putting it on pizza in Mexico City. We even use it to make a drink called *el petrolero*—"the oil man."

When we first opened Café Marimba in 1984, I was working with a "purist" executive chef who refused to use the Maggi seasoning called for in the recipe unless I took full blame or credit (as the case might be) for this awful deed. So we called it "Zarela's vinaigrette."

½ cup distilled white vinegar
2 garlic cloves, crushed
1 tablespoon Maggi seasoning

Freshly ground white pepper to taste
Salt to taste, optional
1 cup vegetable oil

In a small bowl, whisk the vinegar with the garlic, Maggi seasoning, and pepper. Taste for seasoning and add salt if desired (the Maggi seasoning already has a lot). Whisk in the oil, a little at a time, until well combined.

YIELD: ABOUT 1½ CUPS

ENSALADA DE PIÑA Y CHILE MORRÓN

Pineapple-Bell Pepper Salad

Another dish I added to my repertoire around this time was an unusual salad from Taboada, a natural spring and spa near San Miguel de Allende in the central state of Guanajuato. I have retained the splendid combination of pineapple, bell peppers, and a garlicky vinaigrette, but have changed the presentation and added red bell peppers to the green.

1 small to medium-size ripe pineapple (about 4 pounds)
2 medium-size red bell peppers,
cored, seeded, and cut into ½-
inch strips

2 medium-size green bell peppers, cored, seeded, and cut
into ½-inch strips

Cut off the pineapple crown and cut the pineapple lengthwise into quarters. Trim away the core. With a sharp knife, peel each quarter by cutting away the skin from the flesh (but not too close to the rind) in one piece, leaving a narrow "boat" that will serve as a decorative container. Cut the flesh into medium (½-inch) dice or triangular chunks.

In a large bowl, combine the pepper strips and pineapple. Add the dressing and toss to distribute. Let stand at room temperature 15 minutes to blend the flavors.

To serve, place a pineapple "boat" on each salad plate and arrange one quarter of the pineapple mixture in it. Sprinkle with the sesame seeds and serve.

YIELD: 4 SERVINGS

CALDO FRÍO DE AGUACATE MARGARITA

Margarita
Jameson's
Cold Avocado
Soup

This soup was served on a visit to friends of my mother and stepfather. Margarita and Juan Jameson, both of old Mexican *familias de abolengo* (blueblood families), welcomed us in their beautiful apartment in the hills of Mexico City with a marvelous *comida* consisting of cold avocado soup, pan-fried chicken breasts, sweet-and-sour marinated ancho chiles (see *Chiles Anchos Nana Luz,* recipe follows), and olive-size new potatoes in a tomatillo sauce. A simple and refreshing mango pudding completed the meal.

I was overjoyed to discover this easy-to-make soup. I had always tasted avocado soup in super-rich versions with lots of heavy cream. Here the consistency is delicate, not so overpowering. As a bonus, the recipe is versatile. You can easily adapt it by adding poached shrimp and scallops and replacing the chicken stock with fish or shrimp stock. Or convert the dish into a sauce for shrimp or fish or a dip for crudités by adding another avocado and using just enough stock to thin to the desired consistency.

Begin the soup far enough ahead of time to chill and degrease the tomato-flavored broth.

2 tablespoons unsalted butter or vegetable oil
1 small onion, finely chopped (about ½ cup)
2 garlic cloves, minced
1 medium-large ripe, red tomato, peeled, seeded, and chopped (about 1 cup pulp)
4 cups Caldo de Pollo Casero (see page 45)
2 very ripe avocados (preferably the black-skinned Hass variety)
½ cup (loosely packed) fresh cilantro leaves

2 fresh chiles, either jalapeño or serrano (see pages 225 and 226), tops removed, seeded, and roughly chopped; or use canned jalapeños
1 teaspoon salt, or to taste

FOR THE GARNISH (OPTIONAL)
Crema Agria Preparada (see page 42) or plain sour cream
Salmon caviar
Chopped scallion tops
Shoestring tortilla strips, fried crisp in oil or lard (see page 19)

Heat the butter or oil in a medium-size skillet or sauté pan over medium heat until very hot. Add the onion and garlic and cook, stirring, for 2 minutes. Stir in the chopped tomato and cook another 3 minutes.

Combine the chicken stock and tomato mixture in a medium-size saucepan. Bring to a boil, reduce the heat to medium-low, and simmer, uncovered, for about 10 minutes. Let cool to lukewarm, then strain into a bowl through a medium-mesh sieve and refrigerate until well chilled. Remove any fat that has congealed on top.

Peel and seed the avocados. In two batches or as necessary, puree the avocados and chilled tomato broth in a blender or food processor with the cilantro and chiles until smooth. Chill the mixture again if it seems too warm; taste for seasoning and add salt to taste.

Serve in a tureen with the garnishes passed separately in small bowls, or in individual soup plates with a dollop of sour cream (topped, if desired, with a few grains of salmon caviar) in the middle and a sprinkling of scallion greens. (I like to make a thin crescent of scallions on one side.) Tortilla strips should be added individually at the last minute so they will be crisp.

YIELD: 6 TO 8 SERVINGS

CHILES ANCHOS NANA LUZ

Marinated Ancho Chiles a la Luz Barreras

This is another of the wonderful dishes shared by Margarita Jameson. But first let's have a word about *nanas*—especially Nana Luz, Sra. Luz Barreras, who prepared that excellent luncheon!

The word *nana* has a special meaning to us who grew up in Mexico and were lucky enough to have a *nana*. It refers to your nurse, nanny, or caretaker and always brings to my mind the security of childhood and the nurturing I received from my Nana Lencha. Most *nanas* stay with their charges for life—if they marry, their husbands are also taken into the family—and have a special place in the home, a sort of adviser, cheerleader, and confidante. Their influence increases in proportion to the number of years they have been with the family. Nana Luz has taken care of Juan Jameson for forty years and proudly states that she has been with *el joven* (the young man) since he was at home. She washed and cooked for him and, when he married Margarita, went with the young couple to continue caring for him. Today she is at least in her late seventies, an amiable but quietly assertive woman who, though still quite "the servant" as is traditional in Mexican households, is self-assured and proud of her position in the home. I was amused to see how Margarita has learned to get up from the table and go ask Nana to clear the plates or bring another course instead of summoning her by the customary bell—Nana says that only prisoners and animals answer to a bell!

In many ways this typifies the difference between Mexican and U.S. attitudes toward servants. Here there tends to be something uncomfortable in the relationship of employers and "household help"; it doesn't seem right or natural for either side, maybe because of some lingering puritanism. In Mexico there are real bonds of respect and a sense that those who work in a household have their own authority—especially *nanas*! You do not just open your mouth and talk back to them, even when you are grown up. For fifty years Vicki has advised, scolded, directed, and organized the entire family of my Nino Lalo (my mother's only brother and my godfather). She is the senior *nana* of the family. Socorro has been with my sister Clarissa since Clarissa was five years old, and Soco now takes care of my nieces, Nadia and Bea, and rules the whole family with an iron fist. These women, who have been part of a household for several generations, occupy a special position. Nana

Luz, for example, does not cook everyday meals for Juan and Margarita these days. It was a mark of respect for our visit that she prepared a simple but very elegant *comida*.

4 cups water

1½ cups cider vinegar

4 ounces piloncillo (see page 20) or 1 cup firmly packed dark brown sugar

5 cloves

8 allspice berries

8 black peppercorns

8 large garlic cloves, peeled

4 ounces ancho chiles (see page 224; about 8 chiles)

Place all ingredients, except chiles, in a heavy, medium saucepan and bring to a boil over high heat. Reduce the heat to medium and cook, uncovered, for 20 minutes, until somewhat reduced.

While the marinade is reducing, look over the chiles. If they are very brittle, place them in a steamer basket or platform and steam in a tightly covered saucepan over boiling water just long enough to make them slightly flexible. (Alternatively, wet the chiles slightly and place them in a plastic bag; microwave on full power for 30 to 40 seconds.) With a small, sharp knife, make a small (about 1½ inches) lengthwise slit in each chile and carefully remove the seeds and veins, taking care not to split the chile any more. Rinse under cold running water, drain, and add to the boiling marinade. Cook 1 to 3 minutes until the chiles are soft but not falling apart; the exact timing will vary according to the age and condition of the chiles.

Place the chiles and marinade in a nonreactive bowl or container (stainless steel, glass, earthenware) and let stand at room temperature for at least 3 hours or preferably overnight.

Nana Luz simply drained the chiles and served them as they were (no need to remove the spices), as a delicious accompaniment to chicken breasts. They are also good this way with pork. But I often like to stuff them with different fillings—for example, *Picadillo Dulce* (page 47) or shredded cheese mixed with scallions—and use them as a main dish. Once during a late night foray into the refrigerator, I even came up with an international extravaganza featuring these marinated chiles, farmer's cheese, purple onion, and lettuce in pita bread, and I loved it.

Can be stored tightly covered, in the refrigerator up to 2 weeks.

YIELD: 8 SERVINGS AS A SIDE DISH. IF STUFFED WITH A SUBSTANTIAL FILLING, THE SAME AMOUNT WILL SERVE 4 AS A MAIN DISH

MACARRONES CON SALSA POBLANA

Pasta with Poblano Sauce

My sister Marina learned this recipe from her mother-in-law and sent it to me when I first started catering.

1 medium-size onion, unpeeled, roasted until dark on all sides on a griddle over high heat or under a broiler

3 garlic cloves, unpeeled, roasted until dark on all sides on a griddle over high heat or under a broiler

4 poblano chiles (see page 226), roasted (page 227), peeled, and seeded

2 tablespoons finely chopped fresh epazote (see page 8) or cilantro leaves

½ cup heavy cream

½ teaspoon salt, or to taste

1 pound fusilli, rotelle, or other pasta suitably shaped for "catching" sauce

½ cup (1 stick; ¼ pound) unsalted butter, cut into small pieces

½ pound white cheddar cheese, shredded (about 2 cups)

Peel the blackened skin from the onion and garlic. Puree the poblanos, onion, garlic, and epazote in a blender or food processor with the heavy cream; add more cream or a small amount of water if necessary to facilitate blending. Add the salt.

Cook the pasta according to package directions and drain.

Preheat the oven to 350°F (see note). Butter a 1½-quart heatproof dish. Add half the pasta; dot with half the butter, half the sauce, and half the cheese. Repeat with the remaining ingredients. Bake until heated through, about 25 minutes. (Note: If using a Pyrex dish, set the oven at 325°F.)

YIELD: 4 SERVINGS

ARROZ CON CREMA Y POBLANOS

Creamy Rice Casserole with Poblano Chiles

When I came back to the North, it seemed as if every party I went to in Juárez featured this dish. There was a very good reason: It was a specialty of one caterer whom everyone was using! When I became a caterer myself, I rapidly discovered that it is a superior party dish because it is delicious, economical, and holds well so that it can easily be preassembled and reheated just prior to serving. What I immediately liked about it was the "layers" or different dimensions of flavor that were beginning to be important to me: creamy rice, mildly piquant poblanos, crunchy corn kernels, and the refreshing aftertaste of the cilantro in the sour-cream mixture.

4 cups water
1 tablespoon butter
2 teaspoons salt, or to taste
2 cups converted rice
2 tablespoons vegetable oil
1 small onion, chopped (about ½ cup)
1 garlic clove, minced
2 poblano chiles (see page 226), roasted (page 227), peeled, seeded, deveined, and diced

2 cups fresh corn kernels, or 1 package (10 ounces) frozen corn kernels, thawed, or 1 can (16 ounces) corn, drained
1½ cups Crema Agria Preparada (see page 42)
½ pound white cheddar cheese, shredded (about 2 cups)

Bring the water to a boil in a medium-size saucepan over high heat and add the butter and salt. When the butter has melted, add the rice and bring back to a boil. Reduce the heat to very low, cover the saucepan tightly, and cook for 20 minutes. Remove the rice from the pan and spread on a baking sheet to cool, or allow to cool in the pan uncovered.

Meanwhile, preheat the oven to 350°F (see note).

Heat the oil in a heavy skillet over medium-high heat until very hot but not quite smoking. Reduce the heat to medium, add the chopped onion and garlic, and cook, stirring, until wilted, 2 to 3 minutes. Add the poblanos and cook, stirring, for 1 minute. Let cool, then combine with the rice. Mix in the corn, sour cream mixture, and shredded cheese.

Pour the mixture into a heatproof baking dish or casserole and bake until heated through, about 30 minutes. (Note: if using a Pyrex baking dish, set the oven at 325°F.)

YIELD: 6 SERVINGS

CREPAS DE HUITLACOCHE

Layered Crêpe

Dish with

Huitlacoche

I first encountered a version of crêpes with *huitlacoche,* the prized Mexican corn fungus, on a trip to Mexico City while I was living in El Paso. They were traditional rolled crêpes with a sautéed *huitlacoche* filling. The version I evolved is typical of the layered casseroles I experimented with as a young caterer.

My mother was also captivated with the *huitlacoche* mixture. She likes to use it as a filling for *quesadillas,* using only one can of *huitlacoche* and the optional chopped spinach. At the restaurant we serve this good (and much less expensive) version of the mixture, minus the crêpes or *quesadillas,* as a bed for scallops. The buttery flavor of the scallops is delicious with the *huitlacoche.*

3 tablespoons vegetable oil or lard (see page 19)

1 medium-size onion, finely minced (about 1 cup)

2 large cloves garlic, minced (about 1 tablespoon)

3 poblano chiles (see page 226), roasted (page 227), peeled, and seeded, finely chopped

1 package (10 ounces) frozen chopped spinach, thawed and squeezed dry, optional

2 cans (8 ounces each) huitlacoche (see page 9), or 1 pound fresh

2 tablespoons fresh or dried epazote (see page 8) or fresh cilantro leaves, chopped

Salt and freshly ground black pepper to taste

24 Crepas de Maíz (see page 86)

2 cups Crema Agria Preparada (see page 42)

1 pound white cheddar cheese, shredded (about 4 cups)

Heat the vegetable oil or lard in a medium-size skillet over medium-high heat until very hot but not quite smoking. Add the onion and garlic and cook, stirring often, until the onion is translucent, about 3 minutes. Add the chopped poblanos, and stir well to combine. Cook for 2 minutes, stirring occasionally. Add the spinach and *huitlacoche,* and epazote. Stir well to combine, reduce the heat to medium-low, and cook another 5 minutes, stirring often. Season with salt and pepper. Let cool.

To assemble the dish, place a layer of 8 crêpes in a round 10-inch or 13 × 9-inch rectangular baking dish. Spread with a third of the sour cream mixture. Cover with half of the sautéed *huitlacoche* mixture and a third of the shredded cheese. Repeat with 8 more crêpes, half of the remaining sour cream, the remaining huitlacoche mixture, and half of the remaining shredded cheese. Finish with the remaining 8 crêpes, sour cream, and shredded cheese. The dish can be baked at once or held several hours or overnight in the refrigerator, tightly covered.

Preheat the oven to 350°F. Cover the dish tightly with aluminum foil and bake for 20 to 25 minutes. Remove the foil and bake until golden and heated through, another 10 minutes.

YIELD: 6 TO 8 SERVINGS

FLAUTAS

Rolled Chicken Tacos

I think in my childhood we would simply have called these *taquitos.* By the later 1970s tortillas rolled into cylinders around a filling and deep-fried had become very popular with U.S. audiences under the name of *flautas* ("flutes"). I made them a lot in the El Paso business, and they are one of the most popular items at Zarela and in my catering business.

Flautas can be made with shredded beef as well as chicken and can be served with any hot salsa or guacamole. You can make them ahead of time, cover them thoroughly with plastic wrap, and fry at the last moment. It is important that there be plenty of oil and that it be at the right temperature, so that they do not absorb too much.

16 packaged corn tortillas   **Vegetable oil for deep frying**
3 cups Pollo Guisado (page 45)

Soften the tortillas so they can be rolled easily. The best method is to place them in a small plastic bag and microwave on full power for 30 to 40 seconds (depending on the wattage of the oven). It is best to microwave no more than 4 at a time since they will harden again if held too long. Alternatively, place the tortillas in a steamer basket or on an improvised steaming platform and steam, covered, over boiling water until softened. Keep covered after steaming.

Work quickly with the softened tortillas, no more than 4 at a time. Place approximately 2 tablespoons of the shredded chicken mixture in the center of each tortilla and roll into a tight cylinder. Secure with a toothpick. As they are filled and rolled, place them in another plastic bag and reserve until all the *flautas* are rolled and you are ready to fry. (This is to prevent the tortillas from cracking.)

Heat the oil to 350°F in large deep-fryer or heavy saucepan. Fry the *flautas* 2 or 3 at a time until golden, about 5 minutes. Drain on paper towels and serve at once.

YIELD: 16 FLAUTAS

ROPA VIEJA

"Old Clothes"

Ropa vieja is a traditional Spanish dish that has migrated to many Latin American countries including Cuba, Peru, and Mexico. Each country has its own version, with different ingredients and presentations, but all involve some kind of shredded cooked meat—sometimes beef, sometimes pork. This version comes from Kika, my housekeeper in El Paso when I was first married. She had also been the nanny of my stepdaughter, Marissa, who used to follow her around like a shadow. I remember a very tiny Marissa standing next to Kika while she chopped onions in the kitchen and saying, *"Kika, ¿por qué lloro?"* ("Why am I crying?")

Kika was a natural cook. I learned from her, but it was definitely not reciprocal. When I cooked and tried to teach her some recipe, she would say, "Don't teach me how to make that because next you are going to ask me to make it!"

Ropa vieja can be made ahead of time and reheated. It is best served with beans and freshly made flour tortillas. The Maggi seasoning in the recipe, by the way, is something that many Mexican cooks use as a slightly salty accent, a little analogous to soy or Worcestershire sauce.

Some markets with a large Jewish clientele carry a cut of beef known as "deckel," which pulls easily into long shreds when cooked. If you can get it, it is far cheaper than flank steak.

3 pounds flank steak
8 garlic cloves, peeled
6 black peppercorns
Salt to taste
8 Anaheim or 6 poblano chiles (see page 223 or 226), roasted (page 227), peeled, seeded, and thinly sliced
2 fresh chiles, jalapeño or serrano (see pages 225 and 226), roasted (see page 227), peeled, seeded, and thinly sliced, optional

¼ cup vegetable oil
1 large onion, sliced into thin half-moons (about 2 cups)
2 teaspoons ground cumin (or toast whole cumin seed—page 19—and grind in a mortar)
1 teaspoon Maggi seasoning
Tortillas de Harina (see page 56)

Place the flank steak in a large, deep saucepan or Dutch oven with 6 of the garlic cloves and the peppercorns, and season with salt. Add cold water barely to cover and bring to a simmer over low heat. Cook, partly covered, until the meat is tender, about 1½ hours. Remove from the heat and let the meat cool in its own broth. When cool enough to handle, remove the meat from the broth and pull into fine shreds with your fingers or two forks. Strain the broth; return the shredded meat and strained broth to the saucepan.

Heat the vegetable oil in a large, heavy skillet over medium heat until rippling. Crush the remaining garlic cloves with the flat of a knife blade, add to the oil, and cook, stirring, until fragrant, about 1 minute. Add the onion and cook, stirring often, until the onion is translucent and slightly softened, 2 to 3 minutes. Add the chiles and cook, stirring occasionally, another 2 minutes.

Add the chile-onion mixture to the shredded meat. Add the

cumin and Maggi seasoning and bring to a boil. Cook over medium-low heat until the meat is heated through and the flavors are blended. Serve with flour tortillas.

Can be kept, tightly covered, in the refrigerator up to 3 days, or indefinitely in the freezer.

YIELD: 6 TO 8 SERVINGS AS A MAIN DISH

FAJITAS

Grilled Skirt Steak

In the last few years fajitas have become immensely popular throughout the United States thanks to the Mexican, or supposedly Mexican, restaurant chains. The word refers to the formerly very cheap cut of beef just above the tenderloin, often called skirt steak. It resembles a belt, or *fajo*. In northern Mexico the same cut is known as *arrachera*. The U.S. fajita craze has driven up the price of skirt steak and spawned a bunch of dishes marinated and cooked in the same way and fashionably though inappropriately called "shrimp fajitas," "chicken fajitas," etc.

All this fuss amuses me somewhat, because I have my own memories of fajitas suddenly coming on the scene in El Paso around the late 1970s. I was working very hard to make a go of my catering, selling produce in a small way to help support the business. In those days one of the big produce distributors in El Paso used to have regular Saturday afternoon cookouts at his warehouse with his truckers, who were from the area of Nuevo León and Brownsville, Texas. They had rigged up a grill using sawed-up halves of heavy metal barrels, and every Saturday they would make fajitas while everyone asked Mayo Singh, "*Where* did you get this?" Soon every stylish cook from Texas to Maine was "discovering" fajitas!

Most home charcoal broilers do not get hot enough to make fajitas as good as the restaurant versions. If you are good at grilling, though, the results can be delicious. I suggest using mesquite, which gets hotter than most charcoals, and, if your grill does not have a cover, covering the meat during grilling with something like a large baking sheet to help trap the heat. Place the grilling rack in the closest position to the coals. I do not recommend making fajitas in an oven broiler.

2 pounds skirt steak, trimmed of all fat	Freshly ground black pepper to taste
1 cup fresh lime juice (about 6 limes)	Salt to taste

Place the meat in a glass bowl or other nonreactive container. Add the lime juice, season generously with pepper, and marinate, turning the meat occasionally, at room temperature for at least 1 hour (preferably 2 to 3 hours) or refrigerated overnight.

Prepare the grill and heat the charcoal until ashen. Drain the meat well and pat dry. Season with salt on both sides. Grill the meat for about 3 minutes on each side, or until done to your taste. Quickly cut into convenient-sized serving pieces.

Serve with flour tortillas, refried beans, guacamole, and salsa.

YIELD: 4 SERVINGS

RAJAS CON CREMA

Chile Strips in

Creamy

Cheese Sauce

This often accompanies grilled meats. It is also good with either flour or fresh corn tortillas. In Mexico the cheese would be *asadero* or "roasting" cheese, which is of the same general type as mozzarella and makes nice, long strings when it melts.

6 fresh chiles, either poblano or Anaheim (see pages 226 and 223), roasted or fried (page 227), peeled, and seeded; or 2 cans (4 ounces each) whole long green chiles, drained and rinsed with cold water	1 garlic clove
	1 medium-size white onion, sliced into thin half-moons (about 1 cup)
	1 pound low-moisture mozzarella cheese, cut into small dice (about 4 cups)
2 tablespoons lard (see page 19) or vegetable oil	2 cups half-and-half

Cut the chiles lengthwise into strips about ¼ inch wide.

Heat the lard or oil in a large saucepan over high heat until rippling. Add the garlic and cook, stirring, 1 to 2 minutes, pressing the garlic with the back of a spoon to release the flavor. Remove the garlic and discard. Reduce the heat slightly; add the onion and cook for 3 minutes, stirring occasionally. Add the chile strips and cook for 3 minutes, stirring occasionally. Add the diced cheese and reduce the heat to medium-low. Add the half-and-half and continue to cook just until the cream is heated through and the cheese starts to melt.

Can be served at once or held at room temperature several hours and reheated, but the sauce should not reach a boil or it will break up.

YIELD: 6 SERVINGS

CAMARONES AL AJILLO

Shrimp with

Garlic Sauce

This recipe came to me in an amusing manner during my early period of looking for professional inspirations by sampling restaurant dishes. My mother and I went to eat in a wonderful seafood restaurant in Mexico City called Pardiños (an offshoot of Restaurant Pardiños in Boca del Río, Veracruz, which is a definite must for any traveler). I ordered *langostinos al ajillo,* langoustines with garlic sauce, and immediately fell in love with the exciting combination of flavors—garlic, olive oil (much used in Veracruz cooking), both fresh and dried chiles, and something else I couldn't identify. I begged the waiter to ask the chef to give me the secret of the recipe. The chef refused.

But the waiter was sly and eager to please. So he waited and watched while the chef made my second order of the same dish. The waiter came back and confided, "He splashed olive oil into the frying pan and added garlic."

"There's something else in there," I insisted. "I'll come back tomorrow and I'll give you a hundred pesos"—of course this was *before* devaluation!—"if you find out the secret."

Money talks, and the next day I learned the secret was powdered consommé base—much to the horror of my purist friends. (When the magazine *Cuisine* did a feature story on me, they refused to print the recipe with the powdered consommé base and substituted a reduction made by boiling about a tankful of chicken stock down to two tablespoons. The flavor was acceptable, but not the same.)

I happily continue to make the dish with this frowned-upon ingredient, but I vary it by using any kind of shellfish—langoustines, lobster, shrimp, soft-shelled crab, or crab claws (which make a great appetizer). I have also refined the original by steeping the garlic and dried chiles in the olive oil before cooking. There are other recipes for a similar dish called *setas al ajillo* that call for large mushroom caps, like Portobello or shiitake, instead of the shellfish.

4 to 5 large garlic cloves, finely minced (about 2 tablespoons)
1 tablespoon Knorr Swiss or other chicken stock base
1½ cups extra virgin olive oil
6 dried chiles, either guajillo or Anaheim (see pages 225 and 223), about 5 ounces

4 fresh chiles, either Anaheim or poblano (see pages 223 and 226), about 8 ounces
2 pounds large (16-count) shrimp in the shell
Salt to taste
Juice of 1 lime

In a small bowl, combine the garlic and chicken stock base with the oil and let sit, preferably overnight.

Cut off the tops and stems of both the dried and fresh chiles and remove the seeds, being careful not to break the pods apart. Cut the chiles crosswise into ¼-inch rings. Marinate the dried chiles in the oil and garlic mixture for several hours. Set aside the fresh chiles.

Devein the shrimp by slitting through the shells down the center of the backs with a small, sharp knife and removing the dark vein with the knife tip. Leave the shrimp in their shells. Rinse, pat dry with paper towels, and set aside.

Remove half the dried chiles and garlic from the oil mixture with a slotted spoon; reserve. Heat the remaining oil, chiles, and garlic in a deep, heavy skillet over medium-high heat. When the oil is rippling, add half the fresh chiles and half the shrimp. Fry, turning the shrimp once, until they turn pink, 2 to 3 minutes on each side. Remove the shrimp and other solids with a slotted spoon. Repeat with the remaining shrimp, the rest of the fresh chiles, and the reserved garlic and dried chiles. Taste and add salt if needed (some chicken base is already very salty). Sprinkle with lime juice and serve immediately.

In Mexico the shrimp are served in the oil, but with American figure-consciousness, you might want to drain them. You will be thinner, no doubt, but you will miss the joy of putting a piece of bread into the oil and contentedly eating it.

YIELD: 6 SERVINGS

ENCHILADAS DE CANGREJO

Crab
Enchiladas

This was one of the dishes I learned when I was studying with Lillian Haines in California, trying to build an international repertoire of catering dishes. With some minor changes I have used it time and again.

According to Lillian, the recipe originated not in Mexico—but in U.S. regional rivalry. During a convention of U.S. mayors, an argument arose about who cooked crab better, people on the East or West Coast. As a result, crab-cooking contests were held on both coasts and the winners met for a final cook-off in San Francisco. The winning recipe was this one for crab enchiladas, developed by Ray Marshall of the Acapulco restaurant chain on the West Coast. It's a good example of the way the building blocks of Mexican cooking lend themselves to creative ideas in the *mestizo* climate of modern international cuisine. Dishes like this stimulated me in my own early experiments.

In this recipe, it is important to add the sauces and cheese to the enchiladas in layers. If you mix them all up together you will not experience the flavors as a sequence. Proportions as given are for a large party dish; the recipe can easily be halved, though you may need to increase the proportion of butter and sour cream slightly.

⅔ to ¾ cup (10 to 12 tablespoons) unsalted butter, or as needed
24 packaged corn tortillas
3 pounds lump crabmeat, picked over for cartilage
2 cups Crema Agria Preparada (see page 42)

2 cups Salsa de Tomatillo con Tortilla (see page 40)
2 pounds white cheddar or Monterey Jack cheese, shredded (about 8 cups)

Heat 3 tablespoons of the butter in a medium-size skillet over medium-high heat until hot and bubbling. Soften the tortillas by briefly heating them one at a time in the hot butter, cooking only until soft and removing at once. Stack the tortillas and set aside, covered, as they are done. Use more butter if necessary, about 1 tablespoon at a time.

In a large skillet, heat 5 to 6 tablespoons of the butter over medium-high heat until hot and bubbling and quickly cook the crabmeat, stirring, just until cooked through. (If more convenient, work in two batches.)

To assemble the enchiladas, take one softened tortilla at a time and spread thinly with the sour cream mixture. Cover with a thin layer of tomatillo sauce, then place about 2 tablespoons of crabmeat in the center. Sprinkle with shredded cheese and roll up into a fairly tight cylinder. As the enchiladas are filled and rolled, place them in an unbuttered 13 × 9-inch Pyrex baking dish.

Preheat the oven to 325°F.

When all the enchiladas have been rolled, spread the remaining tomatillo sauce evenly over them. Cover with the remaining sour cream and top with the remaining shredded cheese. Bake until the cheese is melted and the enchiladas are heated through, about 25 minutes. Serve immediately.

YIELD: 10 TO 12 SERVINGS

Variations:

Shrimp and scallops may be substituted for the crabmeat to make seafood enchiladas. Another change I often make—a big timesaver—is to convert the recipe into a layered casserole instead of filling and rolling the enchiladas. Place 8 of the softened tortillas on the bottom of the baking dish. Cover with a third of the sour cream sauce, a thin layer of tomatillo sauce, and half of the crabmeat. Sprinkle with a third of the shredded cheese. Repeat the sequence: 8 tortillas, half the remaining sour cream, a thin layer of tomatillo sauce, the remaining crabmeat, and half the remaining shredded cheese. Finish layering with the last 8 tortillas, the remaining tomatillo sauce, sour cream, and cheese. Bake as directed above.

TAMAL DE PESCADO

Fish in Corn
Husks

This belongs to one of the biggest surprises of my life—my invitation to prepare an outdoor luncheon for the international economic summit conference held in Williamsburg, Virginia, in 1983. That meal was very important to my career, not just because of the honor and the publicity, but because I felt that I had made a breakthrough in the kind of improvisation you only achieve with experience and knowledge.

The White House planners explained that the dish would have to be grilled on the spot. I needed to find a presentation that would suit the rest of my menu. I racked my brains with Harley Baldwin, the consultant and developer. (I had the honor of going last, after six other chefs and distinguished cooks who were to provide the previous days' meals.) Suddenly we turned to each other with the same inspiration: the ancient Mexican method of steaming inside corn husks. When done over coals, this results in a fish both perfectly moist and permeated with a delicate woodsy flavor— imparted by the charred husks, which do *not* impart a burnt taste.

These fish tamales are delicious plain. They can also be varied in any number of ways. At the summit conference we served red snapper fillets with a vivid cilantro sauce. You can substitute any firm-fleshed fish and any sauce that appeals to you. Salmon is good matched with *Salsa de Chipotle* (page 138), tilefish with the lime-cilantro sauce from *Pescado Estilo Playa* (page 135). What is important is that the fillets be of uniform size and not too much thicker at one end than the other, so that one *tamal* or end of a *tamal* does not cook faster than the rest.

½ cup olive oil
3 to 4 large garlic cloves, minced
   (about 2 tablespoons)
9 large corn husks (see page 7)
4 small fish fillets (about ¼
   pound each) from firm-fleshed
   fish such as red snapper, tile-

fish, or sea bass, skin removed
Salt and freshly ground white
   pepper to taste
1 cup Salsa de Cilantro (recipe
   follows)

In small bowl, combine the olive oil and garlic and let steep at least 4 hours or preferably overnight.

   Choose sound, unbroken corn husks. Cover with hot water and

let stand at least 1 hour (preferably 2), until pliable. Drain the corn husks and set one aside. Arrange the other 8 in pairs as follows: Line up 2 husks side by side, narrow ends next to each other. Partly overlap them so that the two form one big triangle. Check the fish fillets for any small bones, pulling them out with tweezers or your fingers. Place a fish fillet in the center of each triangle. Sprinkle with one fourth of the oil and garlic mixture. Season with salt and pepper.

Roll up the husks lengthwise to enclose the fish. Tear off 8 thin strips from the reserved corn husk and use as "string" to tie the tamales at both ends like party favors. The tamales can now be grilled immediately, or held refrigerated for up to 2 hours. To cook them, preheat a charcoal or gas grill. Place the tamales on the grilling rack and grill 3 to 5 minutes (depending on the intensity of the heat and the distance from the heat source). With two spatulas, carefully turn the tamales without squeezing them. Cook 2 to 4 minutes on the other side.

Place the tamales on serving plates. Remove the "strings" and open them. Serve at once with the sauce either spooned over the fish or on the side.

YIELD: 4 SERVINGS AS A FIRST COURSE. THE RECIPE CAN BE DOUBLED TO SERVE 4 AS A MAIN COURSE IF THE GRILLING RACK IS LARGE ENOUGH

SALSA DE CILANTRO

Cilantro Sauce

This is the sauce I served at Williamsburg with the fish tamales. I first tasted it with my mother at the restaurant Camino Real in Mexico City, where they made a very good version of a traditional seafood dish called *pescado al cilantro* (fish baked with cilantro sauce). My mother and I both have a passion for cilantro. While we were trying to duplicate the sauce, she developed this wonderful version.

Years later, while eating a totally unrelated squid dish at Elaine's in New York, I had a brainstorm that this sauce would be fabulous with fried squid. I tried it and it was. In fact, it was so good that it inspired me to try it with all kinds of fried seafood—shrimp, for example, or pieces of catfish dusted with cornmeal. The combination is always, in my opinion, great—though I should warn you that not everyone's taste for cilantro is as fanatic as my mother's and mine.

2 tablespoons butter
1 small onion, finely chopped (about ½ cup)
2 garlic cloves, minced
1 to 2 fresh jalapeño chiles (see page 225), or to taste, roasted (page 227), peeled, and finely chopped

1 medium-size ripe, red tomato, roasted (see page 14), peeled, seeded, and chopped
2 cups loosely packed fresh cilantro leaves (2 to 3 large bunches)
1 cup water or chicken stock
Salt to taste

Heat the butter in a medium-size saucepan over medium-high heat. When the foam subsides, add the onion and garlic and cook, stirring often, until the onion is translucent, 2 to 3 minutes. Add the chiles and tomato, reduce the heat to medium, and cook another 2 to 3 minutes, stirring occasionally, to concentrate the flavor.

While the mixture cooks, process the cilantro and water together in a blender or food processor until coarsely pureed, about 1 minute. Add the puree to the tomato-onion mixture. Season with salt and heat to just below the boiling point. Remove from the heat and serve at once. (The sauce can be held up to 2 to 3 hours at room temperature and rewarmed, but it turns an unappetizing khaki color.)

YIELD: ABOUT 2 CUPS

TAPADO TLAXCALA

Butterflied
Stuffed Beef
Fillet

Tapado literally means "covered," and it often refers to dishes smothered with a sauce. In the case of this dish, which was originally from the city of Tlaxcala near Mexico City, and which I first tasted at the restaurant El Paso del Norte in Ciudad Juárez, the sauce is covered by the meat. In Juárez they pounded the beef very thin before enclosing the filling.

The dish came to mind while I was coming up with ideas to meet the difficult circumstances—outdoor service, limited cooking facilities—of the Williamsburg economic summit meeting luncheon. However, I decided to dispense with pounding the meat in order to keep it more juicy and flavorful. My version made a big hit with the seven heads of state, who I think might have been oversupplied with seafood in the preceding days of meeting and eating. The dish later became a favorite at my restaurant.

6 filet mignons (9 to 10 ounces each)

4 fresh chiles, poblano or Anaheim (see pages 226 and 223), roasted or fried and peeled (page 227)

2 tablespoons lard (see page 19) or vegetable oil

1 medium-small onion, sliced into thin half-moons (about ¾ cup)

2 garlic cloves, minced

Salt and freshly ground black pepper to taste

10 ounces white cheddar cheese, shredded (about 2½ cups)

Vegetable oil for coating steaks

Have the butcher butterfly the steaks, or do it yourself by slicing horizontally almost completely through each steak as if slicing rolls for sandwiches.

Remove the seeds and veins from the chiles if desired, or leave them in for hotter flavor. Cut the chiles lengthwise into strips about ⅛ inch wide.

Heat the lard or oil in a medium-size skillet over medium-high heat until rippling. Add the onion and garlic and cook for 2 minutes, stirring occasionally. The onion should still be slightly crunchy. Add the chiles and cook another 2 minutes, stirring occasionally. Let cool.

To assemble, place the steaks on a counter and open each out flat. Season with salt and pepper. Place one sixth of the sautéed chile mixture on one butterflied half of each steak and cover with one sixth of the shredded cheese. Fold the other flap over to enclose the filling. If they look a little messy, secure with toothpicks. The steaks can be grilled at once, or held covered at room temperature 2 to 3 hours, or several hours longer in the refrigerator.

When ready to cook, preheat the charcoal grill or oven broiler. Lightly brush each steak on both sides with a little vegetable oil. Cook for approximately 4 minutes on each side for medium-rare steak, turning carefully with tongs. If a very rare steak is desired, cook only 3 minutes on each side, then open the *tapados* to expose

the filling (which still will not be cooked through) and finish cooking by placing the opened *tapados* under a preheated oven broiler just until the cheese is bubbling and the surface is cooked.
YIELD: 6 SERVINGS

LOMO DE PUERCO ADOBADO

Pork Loin with

Chile Sauce

The medical community of El Paso was my mainstay when I first started catering. It was a challenge to keep coming up with original ideas for menus, because they all were constantly going to each other's parties. You didn't want to repeat what everybody had just eaten six times. This recipe came to me from a beautiful American woman—I am terribly embarrassed to admit that I don't remember her name—married to a Mexican doctor. His mother had given her the recipe.

The large amount of Worcestershire sauce may seem surprising, but it is a flavor very much liked in Mexico.

¾ pound ancho chiles (see page 224)

1 small ripe, red tomato, peeled, seeded, and chopped (about ½ cup)

1 small onion, coarsely chopped (about ½ cup)

1½ cups Worcestershire sauce (one 10-ounce bottle plus ¼ cup)

1 cup red wine vinegar

¼ pound pitted dried prunes, halved

¼ pound jamón serrano (Spanish mountain ham) or prosciutto, cut into slivers

¼ pound Spanish chorizo or kielbasa, cut into slivers

¼ pound slab bacon, cut into slivers

1 boneless pork loin (about 3 pounds), rolled and tied for roasting

Salt and freshly ground black pepper to taste

¼ cup vegetable oil

Wash the chiles under cold water and remove the stems and seeds. Heat a heavy skillet or griddle over medium-high heat until a drop of water sizzles on contact. Toast the chiles on the griddle, a few at a time, just until the aroma is released, 30 to 60 seconds. Be careful not to burn them, or everything will taste bitter. As they are done, place them in a bowl. Cover the toasted chiles with boiling water and let soak until softened, about 10 minutes. Drain the chiles and discard the liquid.

Combine the chiles, tomato, onion, Worcestershire, and vinegar in a blender or food processor and process to a smooth puree. Set aside.

Preheat the oven to 325°F.

With a small, sharp knife, make incisions all over the roast and fill each with a piece of prune, ham, chorizo, or bacon, pushing them in well.

Season the roast with salt and pepper and brush with a little of the chile mixture. Heat the oil in a large, heavy sauté pan or skillet over high heat until rippling and quickly brown the pork on all sides. Transfer to a roasting pan and bake for 1 hour and 15 minutes, basting every 15 minutes with the chile mixture. An instant-reading thermometer inserted into the thickest part should register 160°F.

Remove the roast to a platter and pour off the excess fat from the roasting pan. Deglaze the pan drippings with a little hot water or chicken stock, stirring and scraping to get every bit. Add the remaining chile mixture and bring to a boil over medium-high heat. Serve at once, passing the chile sauce in a sauceboat.

YIELD: 6 TO 8 SERVINGS

FLAN—QUESO DE NÁPOLES

Naples "Cheese" Flan

My sister Marina contributed this version of a well-known dessert, like an intensely sweet crème caramel. It is an easy dish, popular in both Mexican homes and restaurants. I have no idea whether there is any real connection with Naples. Marina recommends cooking it in a pressure cooker (with enough water to come halfway up the sides of the mold) for 25 minutes, but I have never tried this since I'm scared to death of pressure cookers, much to my mother's chagrin.

1 can (14 ounces) condensed milk	4 large eggs
1 can (12 ounces) evaporated milk	1 teaspoon pure vanilla extract
	2 cups sugar

Place the condensed and evaporated milks, eggs, and vanilla extract in a blender and process until smooth.

Preheat the oven to 325° F. Have ready a 1-quart flan mold.

Heat the sugar in a heavy, medium-size saucepan over low heat, stirring, until it begins to melt, 8 to 10 minutes. Watching very carefully and continuing to stir, cook about another minute until golden brown but not dark. Carefully pour the hot caramelized sugar into the mold and tilt rapidly to coat the bottom and a little of the sides evenly before it cools and hardens.

Place the mold in a large pan and pour enough boiling water into the pan to reach 1 inch below the top of the mold. Bake for 1 hour and 15 minutes.

Remove the flan from the hot water bath. Let cool and refrigerate for at least 8 hours. To unmold, run a thin knife around the edges and invert onto a plate. Serve very cold.

YIELD: 6 SERVINGS

POSTRE DE MANGO

Mango Mousse

This is a basic dish with different variations—other popular versions are made with limes or lemons.

1 can (14 ounces) condensed milk	2 tablespoons fresh lime juice
1 can (32 ounces) mangos, drained, or 2 pounds fresh, ripe mangos, peeled, cored, and sliced	2 tablespoons dark rum, optional
	1 cup heavy cream, chilled

Place the condensed milk, mangos, lime juice, and rum in a blender or food processor and blend to a smooth puree.

Whip the cream until almost stiff and fold into the mango puree with a rubber spatula. Pour into individual dessert dishes or one large container. Chill for at least an hour before serving.

YIELD: 6 SERVINGS

What You Must Know to Understand Us:
Mexican Religion and Culture

RELIGION AND THE GIFT OF CORN

 How to explain that religion in Mexico has always meant corn and corn still means life? My mind reaches back to two scenes.

A few years ago, in a dusty, sun-baked region of the Mayan peninsula. . . .

Though it is nearly midday, there is almost total darkness in the hut. Outlined in its barely candelit shadows you can just make out the shapes of five hammocks, at different levels. But clearly visible on a large piece of cardboard on the floor lies a pregnant woman, in labor.

Two women attend her, one a midwife and the other Ruperta Loeza, the ninety-year-old healer who just this week cured my injured back with no medical aid but her two hands. Both are dressed in traditional Yucatecan style, in long, tuniclike garments, beautifully embroidered in brightly colored flowers at the neck, arms, and hem, with strips of cotton lace backing sewn under the embroidery. The darkness of the hut is a startling contrast to the brilliance of the cemetery—in the distance it seems for a moment to be a miniature golf course—that overlooks this small town. Within its walls is a vivid field of colors: pinks, yellows, greens, blues. It is filled with brightly painted tombstones in the shape of dollhouses but bigger, about five or six feet high, making a curiously urban skyline against a bright blue sky. Some are intricately decorated, most adorned with flowers. Just past it is a village of huts built on stilts, conical wooden frames thatched with palm fronds in symmetrical patterns. We are about an hour's journey from Mérida in northeastern Yucatán.

The midwife assisting, the woman gives birth, an easy delivery. A boy, apparently healthy and whole. They place him on his mother's stomach. Now Doña Ruperta hobbles over to the family altar, and as she turns her back to us I see the two long, thin gray braids falling to below her knees. The altar is covered with a starched embroidered white cloth. In the center is a wooden cross once painted bright pink but now faded, strips of dark wood showing through. A large rusted nail holds the cross together. On the altar votive candles light framed pictures of saints, a turquoise-blue wooden box, and a perfect ear of corn.

Doña Ruperta opens the box and takes out an obsidian knife about ten inches long. The candlelight reflects on the carved surface of the knife and on the dark, paperlike skin of her worn hands. She blesses herself and carries back the corn and the knife to the baby. The husk is still on the ear, but its kernels show through in perfect all-white rows.

The newborn boy lies nursing at the breast. The umbilical cord is not yet cut. Doña Ruperta places the cord on the ear of corn and cuts it with the obsidian knife, reciting prayers in the Mayan language. The blood drenches the corn. Doña Ruperta ties off the cord. She walks back to the altar and places the corn on a wooden tray painted black, with a painted red flower in the center. The blood mingles with the faded red of the flower.

Corn, the ancient gift of the gods, will sustain the child throughout his life. This ritual begins the lifelong relationship with the precious crop. The blood-soaked ear will be planted in a special plot called *la sangre del niño,* "the blood of the child." Its crop will feed the boy until he is old enough to grow his own.

Many years before, not fifty miles from the U.S. border. . . .
The valley where our ranch house is situated is surrounded by hills, steppingstones to the northern end of the Sierra Madre. My father built the simple wooden cross that stands on the nearest one. Before our time someone built three crosses of stone on the highest hill, but these are now in ruins. Only broken pieces re-

main. The stones lie where they've fallen over the years. At dusk, the stone ruins and the wooden cross are all silhouetted against the far horizon.

My parents explain to us that the cross protects the ranch from harm. Mother taught us to stop, bless ourselves, and say a prayer every time we ride our horses past the new cross or the ruins of the old ones. When we need rain she rounds up all available children to say a rosary kneeling before the wooden cross. On May 3, the Day of the Holy Cross, she goes with us to clean the cross and decorate it with a garland we have made of flowers—usually plastic flowers, since we don't have many fresh ones to choose from. When we have finished placing the flowers we pray in front of the cross. We return to the house for another ceremony: Mother or Socorro, the housekeeper, makes tamales and *atole,* a kind of sweetened gruel of prepared ground corn (*masa*). On that day, in every part of Mexico, people are honoring the cross in the same way, bringing garlands of flowers, decorating it with paper streamers, praying for what they are planting this spring, and offering or receiving *atole* and tamales.

Our modern, intellectual home was worlds away from the obsidian knife and the Mayan infant. But both these memories tell of something hard to explain to non-Mexicans—our matter-of-fact welcome to unseen powers that govern the cycles of life and food much as they did six hundred years ago. These forces may go by Christian or other labels. It doesn't really matter. Ours remains an agricultural religion. On May 3 my thoroughly up-to-date mother honored the central Christian symbol with our versions of *atole* and tamales, two corn dishes that might have been used as ceremonial offerings in the time of Moctezuma. And if you try to describe what is unique today about Mexican religion, you will find yourself coming back again and again to corn.

Though people in the United States boast of their corn, I find that ours has a more distinctive identity. In the United States "corn" usually makes people think of corn on the cob bred for sugar content and tenderness. To me this sweet corn often seems watery and insipid. The strains we use for corn on the cob are starchier, more like field corn. We harvest and eat it at a more mature stage. When you bite into an ear, it is substantial and chewy, with the true flavor of corn—richly satisfying and nourishing. If anything, it is more so when ground, dried, and made into a dough. This is the way maize tasted when the first European explorers began bringing it back under names like "Indian corn" or "Turkish wheat." When you eat Mexican corn, you know you are eating the staff of life.

What an amazing gift it is! It is beautiful and graceful, the tallest of the grain plants. The kernels come in natural shades from purest ivory to purple-black, red, or speckled. The Spaniards admiringly reported that there was no part of the maize plant that couldn't be used. (This is just as true today, In fact, modern industry has created whole new uses for every part of the plant, extracting fibers, pith, oils, sugars, and starches that can yield products from building materials and shoe polish to lubricants, dyes, detergents, medicines, and fuel-grade alcohols.) It did not seem strange to them that the native peoples held corn in such reverence as to consider it part of their identity. This attitude holds just as true today among the indigenous peoples in the villages.

A fascinating book titled *El Maíz,* based on a 1982 exhibit by the Museo Nacional de Culturas Populares, tersely sums up the case: *"Somos gente de maíz"* ("We are the people of corn"). Life in Mexico has always been ruled by the growing cycle of corn. It is the principal food of Mexican civilization as far back as anyone can determine. And it has always been a sacred mystery. Corn is the plant that gave life to the Mexican peoples. But even stranger, it was the peoples of the region who first gave life to corn. Without them it would never have existed.

The corn plant, *Zea mays,* is not found in the wild. Because the seeds are enclosed in the husk, they don't fall from the cob to germinate. In other words, the species as we know it cannot reproduce naturally. It has survived 5,000 years or more because it was propagated by man. Theories abound about how this happened. The most commonly accepted is that two or more wild grasses cross-pollinated, producing a new plant that primitive Mesoamerican peoples proceeded to sow by hand.

No wonder they thought it was a gift of the gods. It seemed to flourish everywhere under all conditions. Corn mutates rapidly, so it swiftly produced strains that people could depend on in the hottest or coldest parts of Mexico, on all types of soils, and with heavy or scarce rainfall. (Today this genetic flexibility makes corn a favorite target of plant geneticists breeding for different qualities like kernel size or starch or sugar content.) Because it could easily be grown in the same field as beans and cooked along with them, the Mesoamerican civilizations had what was probably the world's best supply of vegetable protein. Because they had learned to treat nearly all the corn they ate with alkali from ashes, limestone, or oyster shells, many of its nutrients were better assimilated, and the Aztecs and Mayas remained healthy on what the Spaniards thought was a very small amount of food. The alkalized corn was eaten whole as *pozole* (hominy) or ground to a paste that furnished porridge, beverages, sweets, the Mexican bread (tortillas), and the principal Mexican festive foods (tamales).

It is not farfetched to suggest that an important reason so many pagan religious practices survived the Conquest is that corn also triumphantly survived. The conquerors tried to stamp out the old religions. But when they had finished wrecking heathen images, ending human sacrifice, and eradicating the former priesthood, they found themselves explaining the new faith in the old vocabulary of traditions and beliefs. Of course, it helped that there were striking parallels between the existing religions and the beliefs of the missionaries. The Aztecs celebrated a form of communion, using amaranth-seed images sprinkled with sacrificial blood; several peoples observed some form of confession or penance. There were native Mexican traditions involving a divine mother and a miraculous conception. The inevitable result was a seamless syncretism, in which crops and especially corn continued to dominate most people's ideas of religion.

Every crop and vegetable, for the Indian peoples, was a gift of a specific god. So was everything about the growing season. A gift can be taken away, and man was impotent to prevent this except through keeping the givers happy and not leaving any of them out through ignorance or oversight. As they met other tribal religions the Aztecs adopted the foreigners' deities into their own pantheon—which, by the time the Spanish arrived, had become a large divine bureaucracy. The many pre-Columbian gods associated with rain, sun, fertility, and prospering crops were simply co-opted into the new order as saints. The supreme Christian God never seemed as real to the native peoples as the Virgin and especially the saints. The saints, to Mexicans, are ultimately individuals who can empower any worshipper able to establish good relations with them. They are human and comfortable. You can sing, dance, and celebrate with them. So the old holidays and sacred observances effortlessly became saints' days, according to where they happened to fall in the calendar.

For example, Tlaloc, the Aztec rain god, was conveniently merged with the cults of San Isidro Labrador and San Juan Bautista, whose feast days come at crucial times in the planting and growing seasons. The day of St. Isidore the Laborer, the patron saint of fields and harvest, is May 15, a time when everyone in my part of the North is getting ready for the new season and waiting for the all-important first rains. I remember visiting my godparents, Virginia and Bill Wallace, for this celebration at their magnificent hacienda of Corralitos and seeing the priest bless the planting implements and seeds that the field hands had brought to Mass. (In some towns it is also traditional to make mosaic images with the different seeds that will be used for planting.) Afterwards we made a joyful procession through the fields with a statue of San Isidro—taking him to see what he had to do—and a tractor decorated with flowers. The converted Mexicans also immediately associated St. John the Baptist with water for obvious reasons. By further coincidence, the rainy season is usually starting in many parts of the country just around St. John's Day, June 24. For Mexicans this is always a day to get into the water, preferably in a river or arroyo. We used to ride on horseback to a nearby dammed-up stream for a swim and a nice picnic under the *alamos* (elms).

The Aztecs believed that human affairs and the world itself would come to a ruinous end unless countermeasures were constantly taken—prayers, ritual observances, and many sacrifices. Today most Mexicans of the villages continue to believe that the success of the crops depends on the great powers being appeased. Everywhere they practice *costumbres*—literally "customs," a euphemism for pre-Christian rites.

At San Pedro de Ojitos I remember one of the ranch hands burying a chicken in the middle of the vegetable patch. I understood the reason years later when I read the chapter *"El Maíz Sagrado"* ("Sacred Corn") in *El Maíz*. Among other things it relates how the Mixtec Indians sprinkle cornfields at planting and harvest time with sugarcane juice and shed the blood of a freshly killed chicken or turkey onto the field. Or several animals may be sacrificed and buried at the four corners of a field. I highly recommend this account of the beliefs that the different peoples still practice with the sacred crop. A Nahua Indian explains how they set up a cross facing east in the cornfield when they go to plant, and how the adults never let the children help select and handle the kernels for planting, lest the new crop fail to develop fully.

Another section describes how the Tapehuas set up altars in their homes at planting time, with corn kernels and votive candles set before a saint's picture. At midnight on the day before planting, bread and coffee are placed on the altar next to the basket of kernels. The offering, the Tapehuas explain, is "to our god, to our life"—meaning corn. Harvest time is equally crucial. Some of the Yucatecan Mayas still appeal to the ancient weather gods, the Yuntzilob, to control the rain and winds. (The water table of the region is very low and rain is always a life-or-death chance, so crop rituals tend to be especially elaborate in Yucatán.) To thank the gods and ask their protection at the end of August when the crop is nearing maturity, many ritual offerings are presented in a ceremony called the *okatbatan.* A certain kind of corn gruel called *zaca* was the principal traditional offering. In the 1930s and 1940s the folklorist Frances Toor observed elaborate versions of the *okatbatan,* including thirteen gourds of *zaca* presented to the Yuntzilob and a larger bowl dedicated to Christ.

People in the villages take their obligations to the higher powers very seriously. But the powers above are not supposed to fall down on the job either. Cities, villages, even large ranches have their patron saint, who literally protects and nurtures the community. In times of drought, villagers may take the image from the church on a procession through the fields to show the saint the terrible state of affairs. This is repeated if rain is not forthcoming. There are accounts of villages taking the statue out to parch in the sun and suffer like everyone else when rain did not come in spite of prayers, or throwing it in the river to drown after too much rain. My grandfather, "Papá Lalito" Gabilondo, used to get disgusted with the patron saint of Santa Anita, his big ranch in Chihuahua and Sonora. When there had been no rain for a long time, he would march into the chapel and bawl her out: "Listen, you old lady, it's already the eighteenth of June and it hasn't rained! If it doesn't rain soon I'm going to take you out of your place of honor up there."

Even to intellectuals it does not seem incongruous to think that the gods (or God) and man are constantly involved in a mutual relationship. If man attends to the deities, they reciprocate. Prayer is as concrete as IOUs—hence the custom of *mandas,* vows to

perform some action if a favor is granted by a higher power (you do your part, I'll do mine). People have made *mandas* connected with good harvests for centuries, but they can take a more modern spin. I spent my student years in Jalisco, where people are devoted to La Virgen de Zapopan, a tiny image of the Virgin clad in splendid black and gold, housed in a lovely, very big church in a town bordering on Guadalajara. Ricardo, my boyfriend during my university years, was extremely religious and, I suspect, a poor student. He was always making deals with the Virgin, usually some variant on "If I pass this exam, I'll humble myself and walk to the altar on my knees." Unfortunately he always included me in his *mandas* and made me walk in on my knees down the long center aisle of the church in Zapopan. Remember, this was the first age of the miniskirt, and I would arrive with my knees torn and bleeding! He always did pass his exams.

On a more serious level, I remember my mother traveling to the shrine of St. Anne de Beaupré in Quebec when I was about sixteen, to fulfill a *manda* made eighteen years before when she lost her first child, my brother Antero.

Mandas are also involved in the fiestas that are probably the best-known symbol of Mexican religion and cultural life in this country. Virtually all fiestas are the observation of saints' days, some nationally important and some dedicated to a local heavenly patron. It is customary for prominent people in the community to promise to pay for the celebration. This is a great honor, a badge of status among fellow citizens, and a good practical move since the fiestas attract business. But all the money and work that the local *mayordomías* (civic associations) put into the fiestas still represent bargains with higher powers. When you help to bankroll a church holiday important to your community, you are building up a savings account of heavenly goodwill.

Fiesta has another aspect that may be hard to appreciate in non-Mexican societies. It is a kind of release from the forms and conventions so important in everyday Mexican life. Already the Spaniards noted that the Aztecs were a scrupulously polite and punctilious people, with elaborate standards of conduct. Not only did the correct observance of religious rituals assure them of the year's food supply, but behaving correctly in all situations was part of a godly person's general duties. Though the Spanish brutally imposed their own ways, they too honored traditions of courtly behavior. When the native peoples had been crushed and the present mingling of cultures had taken shape, one legacy was a society of polite self-disguise. Even everyday language in Mexico is filled with ceremonious formulas to cushion the impact of all dealings with others, from buying a newspaper to declining an invitation. People know how to act, they know what each situation calls for so that their true selves will remain somewhat hidden.

Escape from the rules and roles takes different forms. Our fondness for dirty language, even among very dignified people, is one such release. So is the Mexican tradition of private hospitality, welcoming family and friends into a circle where we feel understood, accepted, and free to enjoy ourselves. Fiesta, however, is different. It is an extravagant public release that is built into the Christian-pagan calendar and planned for by the whole community. Barriers go down and we express ourselves—in pageantry, dazzling costumes, reckless displays, drinking and eating, games of chance, and always the fireworks called *castillos,* revolving dizzily on high turrets.

No one knows how to celebrate better than Mexicans, who still are really pagan fatalists most of the time. Fatalism makes sense in a country still so close to the soil and the unpredictable elements. But that makes celebration all the more important. As Octavio Paz has written of Mexican fiestas, "Their frequency, their brilliance and excitement, the enthusiasm with which we take part, all suggest that without them we would explode."

St. Anthony's Feast and Candlemas Day—Oaxaca

Never having been to Oaxaca in winter, I walk into the market nor knowing quite what to expect. The usual women are not selling sautéed grasshoppers at the entrance. I do recognize the old woman sitting selling tamales wrapped in banana leaves just inside the entrance. She wears traditional Zapotec winter clothing, a hand-loomed woolen skirt held up by a brightly colored *fajo* (belt) and a tunic covered all over with red, green, and black geometric designs. She is warming herself over homemade charcoal smoldering in a brazier made out of a square tin shortening can.

A few steps farther to the right sits a young Zapotec woman whom I know. She makes and sells beautiful straw baskets in all shapes, with designs in purple and hot pink. Her children, except for the baby, are not with her this time. She tells me they are in school! She says that even a few years back this would have been out of the question for the kids of a market woman; they would have worked throughout their childhoods. While she is proud and happy about this new development, she is also concerned. Will there be jobs for them after they're educated? I reassure her, not revealing that I have mixed feelings about the end of old ways.

Now only the baby son sits with her on one corner of the *petate* (straw mat) where her baskets are artistically displayed. He wears tiny jeans and an undyed woolen tunic, an exact replica of what his father is probably wearing. I buy a heavy basket with a strong handle to carry the food I will buy in the market, and move on.

Without the intoxicating aroma of fresh melons and mangos, the fruit stands in the center aisle seem almost bare despite pyramids of oranges, limes, and grapefruits, along with apples, pears, and bananas, even some *tejocotes,* the small orange fruit used to make *calientitos,* the hot toddies served at the Christmas *posadas.*

Around the corner I'm greeted by my friend Doña Juana, the paper flower lady, surrounded by three rows of the Baby Jesus. The Christ Child comes in all sizes, from six inches to two feet, and is dressed in luxurious outfits, royal blue or turquoise velvet or satin overskirts, underskirts of cream or white lace or shiny taffeta, crowns of shiny paper or metal or garlands of small paper flowers. Hanging above where angels should be are bunches of miniature gold *huaraches* (sandals), tiny scepters, and cloth flowers marked "Made in China." Her daughters and daughter-in-law are all busy sewing little garments. Doña Juana is consulting with a young couple holding a small undressed statue that they have brought with them. She quotes a price of 50,000 pesos (about $20) to dress their Baby Jesus in one of the little velvet numbers.

This shocks me. So much money for poor peasants to dress a doll, sacred or not? And I protest as soon as the couple goes away. Doña Juana says the market would bear her price and if someone cannot afford to pay, they get—or try to get—a *madrina,* literally a godmother, to help pay the expenses for their Baby Jesus. It's important, it's worth it. The new purchase will travel with them to church in two weeks—I can go and see.

Doña Juana had become indispensable to me as a guide to the feasts of Oaxaca since I met her one late August and she suggested I go to church, any church, that afternoon—August 30, the feast day of St. Raymond. I don't remember anything special about this day from my childhood in the North. So I walk over to the large church next to the market and push open the creaking wooden door. The small altar in the vestibule is dedicated to Nuestra Señora del Sagrado Rosario, Our Lady of the Holy Rosary. She lies sleeping in a large glass case, the size of a small woman, clothed in lustrous white satin, in her hands a large gold filigree rosary. But she isn't the main business of the day. Something is happening on the other side of a wooden partition, where there seem to be cats meowing and other unidentifiable noises. I hurriedly bless myself and enter the main sanctuary. I think I must be seeing things.

Perhaps two hundred people are there, mostly children dressed in their Sunday best, and about two hundred animals. All the children are carrying their pets in their arms or leading them on leashes. There are dogs, cats, birds in cages, a small pig, and a baby lamb. They are decorated with ribbons and collars of the bright-colored Mexican tissue paper called *papel de China* ("China paper"). The animals and their masters sit politely through Mass until it is time for the benediction. Then they all proceed to the altar in surprisingly good order. The priest blesses the animals and urges them to guard the children and bring them joy. (In other parts of Mexico this celebration is held on January 17, the feast day of St. Anthony the Abbot, best known as the hermit who confronted wild beasts in the desert.)

On Doña Juana's advice I return to the church on February 2, Candlemas Day. It is filled to capacity and smells intensely of incense and candle wax. The aroma of wood smoke from hearths sticks to the clothes of everyone in the church. There are young and old couples, some wearing native dress of reds and shocking pinks, others in modern clothing and jewelry. The old ladies wrapped in heavy shawls in black and white patterns are widows—physically identical, each one indistinguishable from all the others except by the cut and quality of their clothing, precisely delineating each one's tribal identity and economic class. The men mostly wear work clothes—jeans and boots with handloomed woolen tunics, or white muslin pants and sandals showing the cracked skin of worn feet.

Many people are carrying figures of the Christ child dressed as royally as the one the young couple took away from Doña Juana's stand. Other people hold candles, many candles. All the men and some of the women carry baskets of various shapes and designs, some flat with a small trim, others deep and strong. All the baskets are decorated with tea towels, mostly embroidered and all freshly ironed. The contents are seeds—mixed together in one heap in some baskets, separated into different mounds in others. Some people have brought seeds of flowers and garden herbs, others vegetables, grain crops, and beans.

Candlemas celebrates the presentation of Christ at the temple by Joseph and Mary, as described in the Gospel of St. Luke. On that day the child was acclaimed by Simeon as God's true light. So this is the day when people bring candles to the church to be blessed. They will be kept at home on the family altar. Every time a special favor is needed from God you light one of the candles—Doña Juana has told me to bring plenty—and say a prayer. This special meaning of the day I remember from my childhood. But the elaborately dressed figures are new to me. Here each family keeps a figure of the Baby Jesus on the home altar. On Candlemas Day they reenact Joseph and Mary's visit to the temple by specially dressing their Christ child for the ceremonial presentation and bringing the little figure to be blessed.

The tradition of dressing religious images in special clothes is a powerful one in Mexico. The custom long vexed the Spanish religious authorities. In their climate of worship the image as it came from the sculptor or carver was supposed to be sufficient as a help to inward thoughts. But for the Indians this added external adornment was necessary to put concrete personal claims on the divine object.

The most important part of the ritual, for many of these families, is what is in the baskets. As each group in turn goes to the altar and kneels, the priest blesses the seeds, asking God that their crops be abundant. In many other Western countries people have forgotten that Candlemas was regarded for centuries as an augury of when spring would come—just like Groundhog Day, which continues an old tradition about badgers. So it is natural that in a country where February 2 is not far removed from the beginning of planting season in most regions, Candlemas is a day for trying to secure God's blessing of the crops. It is an example of how Mexicans still feel a living connection between the ecclesiastical calendar and the agricultural year that would have made perfect sense in medieval Europe or Moctezuma's empire.

AGUA FRESCA PARA LA CANDELARIA

Special Drink for Candlemas Day

This particular version is one that I learned in my Guadalajara student days. Related *aguas frescas* are served in many regions as part of the Candlemas celebration. Do not be dismayed at the strange-sounding combination of ingredients. It is something between a beverage and a soup or liquid salad—you drink the liquid and eat the other ingredients with a spoon. However, I must tell you that my children completely refuse to eat the fruits, nuts, and other ingredients—as far as they are concerned, these are foreign bodies floating around in an otherwise nice punch. I have to strain the *agua fresca* before they will drink it. You can do this too if you prefer; in that case, chop all the fruit and nuts very fine and steep them longer to extract more flavor.

1 cup sugar
2 quarts water
⅓ cup blanched almonds, coarsely chopped
½ cup dry-roasted unsalted peanuts
2 medium-size beets (about ¾ pound), cooked (see note below) and finely diced
¼ cup dark seedless raisins

8 ounces pitted dried prunes, coarsely chopped
1 small head iceberg lettuce, shredded
1 small jícama (see page 9—about ¾ pound), peeled and finely diced, or 2 green apples, peeled, cored, and diced

Stir the sugar into the water until completely dissolved. Add the remaining ingredients; place in a ceramic or glass container and refrigerate for at least 2 hours. Serve in pretty small bowls or cups.
YIELD: ABOUT 3 QUARTS WITH SOLID INGREDIENTS, 2 QUARTS STRAINED

NOTE: To cook beets, place them, in their skins with about 1 inch of tops, in boiling water to cover and cook until tender, about 45 minutes (cooking times can vary considerably, from 30 minutes to 1½ hours, so be sure to check on them occasionally). Once they cool a bit, peel them.

Los Días De Los Muertos

I think if I could choose one event to dramatize the spirit of Mexican religion, it would be the Day of the Dead, or actually Days—Los Días de los Muertos, November 1 and 2. To begin with, I assure you that this name does not sound in the least ghoulish or morbid to a Mexican. The Day of the Dead is perhaps our happiest, most life-affirming holiday. It is the celebration of memory, the time when we really feel we are speaking to and embracing those whom we have lost.

For me the Day of the Dead has been an important moment of the year since before I can remember. But even so, I don't think I took in the full dimension of meaning until I was a nineteen-year-old college student traveling—in an unchaperoned group of young people for the first time in my life!—to visit the ceremony on an island in Lake Pátzcuaro, in the state of Michoacán. It was a time in the late sixties when educated Mexicans from all over were suddenly "discovering" the richness of Mexican culture and descending in droves on previously untouched spots. So were many European tourists. So I have to say that the Day of the Dead celebration on the island of Janitzio, probably the most famous in all Mexico, already had a strong note of commercialism. But for me it was an astonishing and very moving pageant dedicated to the continuity of life.

We set out at dusk by motorboat, singing "María Isabel" to the strains of two guitars and one set of bongos and full of the famous local *pescado blanco* (white fish) caught in graceful "butterfly nets." The lake was soon a vast, chilly sea of darkness lit only by a few guide lanterns on canoes making the same journey. But even from far off we saw a yellow-white glow coming from the cemetery. We disembarked into a crowd of visitors and vendors that I couldn't match with anything in our sedate, private family celebration of the day. What a maelstrom! People were selling toys in the shape of laughing skulls; candies made like skeletons; chicle gums (cousins to our chewing gum) in all colors; black, yellow, or white candles; candleholders of shiny black pottery; *copal* (incense) burners. Streams of cheerful family parties pushed past us in the dark and confusion as if en route to a midnight picnic—which isn't too far off the mark.

Janitzio is a rocky island, and the hilly cemetery might have been hard to navigate had it not been so full of lights. It was a carnival lit by thousands of candles. Hundreds of brilliant orange-yellow shapes—high arches or crisscrossed squares—glowed in the darkness above every gravesite. They were *cempasúchil,* yellow marigold strung on ropes or strings, sometimes spelling out names. I had never seen or dreamed of such a fantasy of *cempa-súchil*. Huddled in shawls and *rebozos* against the chilly evening, the people settled down to sing and drink and chat on the ground by the graves, half-shadowed revelers watched from the darker shadows by crowds of German or Dutch tourists. They were Tarascan Indians, and for them the strings of flowers were arches framing a passage for the souls of their friends or relatives to return to their earthly resting place on a kind of social visit. This is the whole purpose of the celebration.

Yes, these people were having a nice reunion with their loved ones! They had brought food for the visit, including the favorite dishes of the deceased, and placed them—always in new pottery vessels bought for the occasion—before small altars erected at each grave with a picture of the loved one. They had also taken along any comforts the person might be missing in the next life, such as bottles of liquor and packs of cigarettes, toys and games, and new clothes. I was astonished at the practical range of *ofrendas* (offerings) laid on freshly ironed white embroidered tea towels. Of course we had always visited the family graves on the Day of the Dead, but our celebration had been limited to scrubbing the tombstones and decorating them with zinnias or other autumn flowers and sharing a silent moment of communion.

The full-blown Day of the Dead ceremony, which I was seeing that evening for the first time, is most common in Mexico among the Indian peoples and the more rural *mestizos*. Four hundred years ago it probably would not have seemed strange in most places. At that time many peoples in Mexico celebrated a festival in August and September to ask the intervention of departed ones in warding off early frost. The idea that individual personalities continue after death and can intercede for the living with the great powers fitted well enough with the Spanish Catholic faith to survive the Conquest without much change. The holiday conveniently migrated through the calendar to coincide with the Catholic feasts of All Saints and All Souls Day at the beginning of November. But only the date changed. Nothing disturbed the original basis of the celebration, the belief that dead souls spend a brief period each year on earth on a kind of holiday. It's an opportunity to catch up with those who are dear to you.

The Janitzio celebration begins after dark on November 1 and continues as a graveside vigil until dawn. In other villages there are usually two celebrations. November 1, All Saints, is when the souls of the children arrive home in the villages and are met by welcoming committees of the local mayor and dignitaries along with the town band. The procession leads the children through an arch of *cempasúchil* at the gate of the cemetery and helps them find their graves. Each grave is decorated with images or structures of *cempasúchil* and turned into party sites with candies, toys, new clothing, and white candles, always in new pottery candleholders. On the next day, All Souls, the souls of the adults are welcomed in the same way (except that the candles are black or yellow). Those without surviving relatives are not forgotten—their graves are decorated by townspeople. In some communities the altar with the *ofrendas* is set up at home instead of in the cemetery.

Beyond the favorite foods of the deceased, certain things are traditional for the Days of the Dead that date back to pre-Columbian times, including a sweet pumpkin dessert called *calabaza en tacha* and some forms of *tamal*. In Janitzio people had brought a special kind of *tamal* with duck filling, from the Lake Pátzcuaro wild ducks that are supposed to be harpooned (not shot) for this occasion. But the most famous specialty of the day throughout Mexico is of European origin. In one of those typical Indian-Spanish intermarriages that have shaped our culture, the native peoples came to celebrate the Days of the Dead with a rich, sweet yeast bread on the model of the altar breads that are special feast-day offerings everywhere in Europe from Spain to Sweden. The Mexican imagination put a new spin of fantasy on the idea by shaping the loaves into different images. The famous *pan de muerto* ("bread of death") comes in the shape of human figures, alligators, lizards, and other animals—but most often skulls and cross-bones or teardrops and crosses, gaily decorated with colored sugar crystals.

The following recipe is a typical modern version of the *pan de muerto*. Like the European altar breads, it was originally made with flour, yeast, eggs, sugar, and some aromatic flavoring like orange-blossom water. Today Mexican home bakers often enrich and sweeten the bread with condensed milk.

PAN DEL DÍA DE MUERTOS

Bread for the

Day of the

Dead

2 envelopes dry yeast
½ cup lukewarm water
3½ to 4 cups unbleached all-
purpose flour, or as needed
½ teaspoon salt
9 tablespoons (1 stick plus 1 tablespoon; 5 ounces) unsalted
butter, at room temperature
and cut into small pieces, plus
extra for greasing

3 large eggs (2 for the dough, 1
for glazing the loaves)
3 large egg yolks
½ of 1 can (14 ounces) condensed milk (about ⅞ cup)
1 tablespoon orange flower water (available in gourmet
stores and Italian and Middle
Eastern markets)
Sugar or colored sugar crystals
for sprinkling

In a small bowl, dissolve the yeast in the water and let sit in a warm place 5 minutes. Make a sponge by stirring in 4 to 5 tablespoons of the flour. Cover with a damp towel and let sit in a warm place until full of bubbles and about doubled in bulk, roughly 45 minutes.

Combine a scant 3½ cups flour with the salt in a large bowl or on a pastry board or clean counter. Cut or rub in the butter with a pastry blender or your fingers until the dough resembles the texture of coarse cornmeal.

Beat together 2 of the whole eggs and the 3 egg yolks. Have ready the condensed milk and orange flower water. Gradually add these ingredients to the dough, working them in with your fingertips. Add the yeast sponge and work it in, adding flour as necessary to make a soft but kneadable dough. Knead on a lightly floured work surface until smooth and silky, about 10 minutes. (Alternatively, use the dough hook of an electric mixer.) Lightly grease a large bowl with butter and place the dough in it, turning to coat both sides with butter. Let sit in a warm place, covered with a damp cloth or plastic wrap, until doubled in bulk, 1½ to 2 hours.

Punch the dough down. If not making decorated loaves, shape into 3 equal-sized round loaves. Or, to make 2 decorated loaves, proceed as follows: Cut off about one fourth of the dough and set aside. Divide the rest into 2 equal portions, shaping each into a ball. Place side by side on a greased and floured baking sheet, remembering that the loaves will expand in baking. With the remaining dough, shape skulls and crossbones: First divide the dough into 4 parts; roll 2 pieces between your palms into long, narrow strips for crossbones and cut each in half. Crisscross 2 strips over each loaf. Shape the remaining 2 pieces into 2 small balls for skulls. Lightly press them onto the loaves just above the crossbones (if you have difficulty getting them to stick, make gashes in the loaves with a small, sharp knife and press the balls into the gashes). Lightly cover with damp towels and let rise in a warm place until doubled in bulk, about 1 hour.

Meanwhile, preheat the oven to 375°F.

Beat the remaining egg and brush lightly over the loaves and decorations and bake 40 minutes. When done, the loaves will be golden brown and sound hollow when tapped. Sprinkle the loaves with sugar and return to the oven for about 1 minute to melt it.

YIELD: 3 PLAIN ROUND LOAVES (ABOUT 6 INCHES ACROSS) OR 2 DEC-ORATED LOAVES (ABOUT 7 INCHES ACROSS)

La Navidad

Once there was an elderly lady passing by a church in December just as a novice priest was setting out the *nacimiento,* the Nativity scene, in front. She walked up to him as he was placing the figures of a kneeling man and woman and asked who those were. The young priest explained about Joseph and Mary. Then she pointed to the manger and asked why that was there. When the priest told her, she went on to ask the meaning of the oxen, the angels and shepherds, the star, and the Three Wise Men. When every question was answered he had told her the whole Christmas story.

"How have you never heard this before?" asked the incredulous priest.

"Oh, I know it all," said the old lady. "But I love to hear it told because it is so beautiful."

That story was part of a sermon I heard preached on Christmas during my teens at the *misa de gallo,* "rooster's Mass," that is said at midnight. It shows the delight that Mexicans take in the whole Nativity season. Though most parts of Mexico do not celebrate Christmas Day itself exactly as people do in the United States, the entire time from mid-December through the first week in January is one of rejoicing.

The celebration of Christmas is supposed to begin December 16—but many people will have been celebrating since the first dawn of December 12, the feast of the Virgin of Guadalupe, when she is serenaded by assorted musicians and worshippers. Without her, Mexican Catholicism would not have its great symbol, the brown-skinned Virgin who appeared to a poor Indian in 1531 as if to tell the enslaved people that the Mother of God was one of them. By December 16 crèches have been set up in homes, and families and friends gather for the first *posada,* or "inn." Part of the group forms a candlelit procession bearing a litter of boughs with the figures of Mary and Joseph and the angel. They knock on the door of the house representing the inn, singing a *villancico* (a melody something like a plainsong chant) begging to be let in. From within the innkeeper answers with another *villancico* telling them to go away. They go from inn to inn until they find someone who finally admits them and they enter in triumph to kneel by the crèche. Then comes the part the children have all been waiting for. The singing becomes lively and tuneful and they all move to the piñata hanging from the ceiling of another room or in the courtyard.

Of course everyone knows what piñatas are, but it's almost as much fun to tell again as the Christmas story. They are the treasure-troves holding all good things for the *posadas* and also for birthday celebrations. They are made of clay jars covered with papier-mâché and a riot of colored decoration, made in shapes like "turkeys, horses, birds, monkeys—in fact, every beast, bird or fowl of the air that is known." So said the American visitor Fanny Chambers Gooch in 1887, but she never saw piñatas in the shape of cartoon characters and Muppets! On my twin sons' second birthday we got them piñatas made like Oscar the Grouch and Ernie, and both burst into tears when we reached the next fateful step. A guest is blindfolded, given a stick, spun around to disorient him, and given a shove toward (or away from) the piñata, which he is supposed to break. The others swing it out of reach until everyone has had enough fun and somebody is allowed to break the piñata. Out pours a rain of *colaciones*—sugar-coated coriander seeds in bright turquoise, pink, yellow, and white—and other candies.

The *posadas* are given every night until Christmas Eve. The crèches stay in place at least another two weeks (some people are as unwilling to put away the *nacimiento* as people in the United States are to take down the Christmas lights). Most of them are very elaborate, like an entire miniature village and stable. Families collect the figures over the years and lay them out lovingly.

Mexicans do not customarily give presents on Christmas Eve or Christmas Day, though my family always did. It is more strictly a religious observance, without the commercial overtones and carnival air present in this country. The *misa de gallo* is the most important Mass of the year. In Agua Prieta and Juárez they would bring entire mariachi bands to perform the Mass for mariachis and serenade the Baby Jesus with "Las Mañanitas," the Mexican birthday song. Christmas Day is usually spent visiting relatives and friends, especially the old ones. New Year's Eve always starts out with another late (or early) Mass to give thanks to God for another year of life.

The gift-giving day in Mexico is January 6, the celebration of the feast of the Three Kings. This is when families commemorate the gifts of gold, frankincense, and myrrh brought by the Magi to the Baby Jesus. Children write letters asking special requests of the Three Kings just as they do here to Santa Claus, and put their shoes outside the door to be filled with small presents. For this feast it is traditional to bake a yeast cake in the shape of a large ring (*rosca*) with a tiny clay figurine or a bean hidden inside. The one who gets the piece of the *rosca* with this symbol of the Magi's gifts must host the party for Candlemas Day on February 2, the day of the Presentation at the Temple (see page 201). Three Kings Day ends the Christmas season, and it is maybe a more beautiful sequence than the one here, where everything is an anticlimax after Christmas.

My personal memories of the Christmas season are probably different from those of southern Mexicans, for we had many Americanized customs in the North. The whole thing came back to me vividly a couple of years ago when the English-language Mexico City *News* printed an article on me and shortly afterward I received a letter from old family friends Lynch and Elizabeth Grattan, who used to spend part of the Christmas season with us at our ranch, San Pedro de Ojitos.

What happy times those were! Our preparations began months

before the holidays, when we started fattening a hog with all our food scraps, to be slaughtered a few days before Christmas and turned into all sorts of delicacies: chorizo, *chicharrones, carne adobada, revolcado* (braised pork in red chile sauce)—but mainly the traditional Christmas tamales.

Tía Elizabeth and Tío Lynch would arrive a few days before Christmas with their three sons, who were about our age. Mother would deck the halls with seasonal greenery and pretty decorations and lovingly set out our *nacimiento,* all except for the figure of the Child. We would help her make the same Christmas candies year after year: dates stuffed with a pecan half and rolled in sugar, prunes filled with fondant and topped with a pecan half, divinity with black walnuts gathered from our own trees, and fudge. Tía Elizabeth would arrive bringing her own sweets, and my grandmother's cook, Ramón, would send *bizcochos* (page 215), simple cookies rolled in cinnamon sugar. (There are many different shapes; Ramón used to form the *bizcochos* into miniature pretzels.) Fires were lit in all the fireplaces and we would drink hot buttered rum or *canela* (Ceylon cinnamon) tea.

The day after the Grattans arrived we would all turn out to cut the Christmas tree, children on horses and adults in a mule-drawn wagon. Father had previously combed the mountains for likely candidates and we would vote on our choice. We would sing American Christmas carols all the way and have a picnic in the cold. We also cut plenty of boughs to make wreaths and brought back a tree for each of the cowboys' families.

The Grattans would leave Christmas Eve to celebrate on their ranch about two hours' drive from San Pedro, and we would begin on our Christmas tamales from the year's chosen hog. The task and the tamales were shared with all the cowboys' families on the ranch. All the wives would come to our house on the morning of Christmas Eve and spend the day making the tamales with shredded pork and red chile sauce, laughing, singing, and chattering all the time. Late on Christmas Eve we would take presents to their houses—children's toys, flannel shirts, underwear, something pretty for the wives. Mother always made a shopping expedition to El Paso or Douglas, Arizona, for these gifts early in December. We loved to wrap them and take them over the icy field under the starlit winter night. They in turn would give us flaky cinnamon-covered *buñuelos* (fritters) and a cup of hot *atole* (a gruel of ground corn and Ceylon cinnamon).

Our Christmas Eve dinner was turkey. And throughout the land people eat turkey for this celebration, as they have for important feasts since Aztec times. After all, it was Mexico that gave turkey to the rest of the world! Late that evening our *nacimiento* would be completed when Mother placed the Baby Jesus in the cradle. We would sing carols accompanied by Father on the organ and Mother on piano—and usually sneak a look at our gifts because we couldn't wait until morning. I think we had the best of both worlds, the sacred holiday as it is observed in Mexico and the secular spirit of giving that makes Christmas such an exuberant time in this country.

TAMALES DE DULCE

Sweet Tamales

My mother often made us sweet tamales for special occasions, including Christmas. She would sometimes dye the *masa* pink and wrap the tamales like party favors, as is customary in many parts of Mexico. Mother used pink food coloring, though I have seen even pinker tamales in the state of Michoacán dyed with tiny wild fruits called *capulines*. If black walnuts or *piñones* (pine nuts) were in season, she would use them in place of the pecans.

20 to 25 large or 30 to 40 smaller
   dried corn husks (see page 7)
3 cups water
1 tablespoon plus 1 teaspoon
   aniseed
½ cup golden raisins
½ pound lard (1 cup plus 2 tablespoons; see page 19)
½ cup sugar, or to taste

1½ pounds masa (see page 49),
   fresh (ask for coarse-ground)
   or made from masa harina according to directions on page
   51
½ teaspoon salt
½ cup pecans, coarsely broken,
   optional

Place the corn husks in a large bowl and cover with boiling water. Let soak at least 1 hour. Bring the water and 1 tablespoon of the aniseed to a boil over high heat. Cook until reduced to 2 cups, about 15 minutes. Strain and use 1 cup of anise tea to soak the raisins until softened, about 15 minutes. Allow the remaining cup of tea to cool to room temperature. Reserve.

Beat the lard and sugar with an electric mixer at high speed until light and fluffy (or if beating by hand, follow the directions on page 51). Reduce the speed and add the *masa* a little at a time. When it is all added, beat for 3 minutes. Drain the raisins and add to the *masa*. (I like to reserve the drained liquid to use in steaming.) Beat for 1 minute. If the *masa* is stiff add ¼ to ½ cup of the reserved anise tea a little at a time while beating. Add the remaining aniseed and the salt and beat until light and fluffy. Fold in pecans.

Drain the corn husks. Put about 2 tablespoons filling in each husk, wrap, and steam the tamales as explained on pages 51–53. I like to make a little extra anise tea and add it to the water in the steamer, along with the raisin soaking liquid.

YIELD: ABOUT 20 LARGE OR 30 SMALLER TAMALES

PAVO BORRACHO

"Drunken Turkey"

My sister Aída is a wonderful cook with an assertive hand. She developed this recipe for one of our Christmas celebrations, and it is a new family favorite. It is actually oven-steamed rather than roasted, using the somewhat loosely named "roasting bags" (a type of plastic cooking bag available in most large supermarkets).

Be warned that it is delicious but does not look great. The cooking-bag method (decidedly untraditional) results in a very moist turkey with lots of natural gravy, but all this moisture may cause broken skin and exposed leg and wing bones. For the basting you will need a basting syringe with a thin metal injection nozzle.

If you find the amount of Grand Marnier in this recipe excessive, use the juice from 6 oranges and decrease the Grand Marnier to 1 cup.

1 turkey (12 pounds)
Salt and freshly ground black
  pepper
2 pounds mixed dried fruit
1 cup golden raisins
4 Granny Smith apples, cored,
  quartered, and cut into 1-inch
  wedges
Juice of 4 oranges

1 can (2.5 ounces) chiles
  chipotles en adobo (see page
  224)
3 cups dark tequila, preferably
  reposado (see page 117)
3 cups Grand Marnier
1 cup (2 sticks; ½ pound) un-
  salted butter

Preheat the oven to 325°F.

Rinse the turkey and pat dry inside and out. Salt and pepper the cavity and outside of the turkey. Set aside.

Combine the dried fruit, raisins, and apples in a medium-size bowl. Put the orange juice and chiles (with the sauce that clings to them) into a blender or food processor and process for 1 minute. Add 1 cup each of the tequila and Grand Marnier, then pour the mixture over the fruit and let rest 15 minutes. Drain the fruit, reserving the liquid. Cut half of the butter (1 stick) into ½-inch pieces and combine with the fruit.

Stuff the cavity of the turkey with most of the fruit. Place the turkey in the roasting bag, arrange the remaining fruit on top of the turkey and pour the reserved orange juice–liquor mix over it. Combine the remaining tequila and Grand Marnier. Have ready a basting syringe fitted with a metal injection nozzle and inject the mixture all over the turkey.

Melt the remaining butter (1 stick) and carefully pour over the turkey in the roasting bag. Seal the bag and cut a ¼-inch slit on the top to let the steam escape. Place in a roasting pan and roast for 2½ hours. Every 30 minutes open the bag (being careful to shield your face from steam) and inject more liquor, eventually using it up.

When ready to serve, slit open the bag, arrange the turkey on a platter, and scoop out the fruit stuffing. Place all the fruit in a serving bowl. Strain the juices that have accumulated in the bag, skim off any fat, and serve in a gravy boat.

YIELD: 8 TO 10 SERVINGS

BIZCOCHOS

Holiday
Cookies

As a child in the North I knew a crisper, less rich version of *bizcochos* (it's one of those not-very-definite words like "biscuits" in the British sense) served in my grandmother's household. This highly shortened version is probably familiar to more Mexicans.

This is one case where the United States "cinnamon" (actually cassia) will do. For once I prefer its sharpness. In Mexico and the American Southwest a whole array of decorative cutters is used for *bizcochos,* shaped like birds, flowers, and other fanciful images.

½ pound lard (1 cup plus 2 table-
    spoons; see page 19)
½ cup (generous) sugar
1 jumbo egg or 2 medium-size
Grated peel of 1 orange
3 to 3½ cups unbleached all-
    purpose flour

1½ teaspoons baking powder
¼ teaspoon salt
1 to 2 tablespoons fresh orange
    juice, optional
Cinnamon sugar made with 2
    tablespoons ground cinna-
    mon to each ½ cup sugar

Preheat the oven to 375°F. Have ready ungreased baking sheets.

In a large mixing bowl, cream the lard until light and fluffy, either by hand or with an electric mixer. Beat in the sugar a little at a time. Beat in the egg and grated orange peel.

Sift together 3 cups flour, the baking powder, and salt; add to the creamed lard mixture about 1 cup at a time, beating well after each addition. After 3 cups you should have a somewhat stiff but smooth, workable dough. Beat in up to another ½ cup flour if it seems too loose, or a little orange juice if it is too hard to mix. Refrigerate the dough until thoroughly chilled, 30 to 40 minutes.

You can shape the cookies either by rolling out the dough about ⅛ inch thick on a lightly floured surface with a lightly floured rolling pin and cutting with cookie cutters, or by placing the dough in a large pastry bag fitted with a no. 5 star tip and piping it onto the ungreased baking sheets. Space the cookies about an inch apart. Work in batches as necessary.

Bake until the edges are golden, 10 to 12 minutes. Transfer the cookies to racks. Roll in cinnamon sugar when cool enough to handle.

YIELD: ABOUT 3 DOZEN SMALL COOKIES (YIELD MAY VARY)

TAMALES CON CHILE COLORADO

Tamales with Red Chile

These festive red tamales are one of my earliest Christmas associations, and not mine alone. Right before Christmas last year, my friend Elisa's brother came into Zarela to see how I was going to celebrate the holidays. The first thing he asked was "Are you going to make tamales?" This was the kind he meant. To a northern Mexican it's the equivalent of "Have you bought your Christmas tree yet?"

Like most tamales, they are basically an assembly job. The different elements aren't difficult in themselves but add up to a long marathon if you don't have many willing hands to form a production line, as we did on the ranch. In fact, you can make any or all of the three major components (the red chile sauce, *tamal* dough, and cooked pork) the day before and just do the final assembly when you are ready. You will have the best flavor if you use some of the pork stock to moisten the *tamal* dough; if there is none on hand use *Caldo de Pollo* (see page 44).

2 cups Salsa de Chile Colorado (see page 31)
1 pound dried corn husks (see page 7)

1 recipe Basic Tamal Dough (see page 50)
3 cups shredded Carne de Puerco Cocida (see page 46) or other shredded cooked pork

Make the salsa and set aside to cool to room temperature.

Place the corn husks in a large, deep bowl, cover with boiling water, and let soak while you prepare the filling.

Prepare the *tamal* dough, preferably using pork stock to moisten it. When it is very light and fluffy, beat in ½ cup of the cooled salsa, mixing thoroughly to color the dough evenly.

In a mixing bowl, combine the shredded pork with the remaining red chile sauce.

Fill, fold, and steam the tamales as described on pages 51–53, using about ¼ cup of the red *masa* mixture for each husk and placing about 1 tablespoon of the shredded pork mixture in the center of the *masa*.

YIELD: ABOUT 45 TO 50 TAMALES

POLVORONES DE NUEZ

Walnut Cookies for Christmas

In Mexico these are wrapped in *papel de China,* the brightly colored tissue paper that we call "Chinese." I use salted butter because I think they need a little salt; add a pinch of salt if your butter is unsalted.

½ cup (1 stick; ¼ pound) salted butter or margarine
2 tablespoons confectioner's sugar, plus additional for dusting

½ teaspoon pure vanilla extract
1 cup sifted unbleached all-purpose flour
¾ cup very finely chopped (not ground) walnuts or pecans

Preheat the oven to 375°F.

Cream the butter until very light, either by hand or with an electric mixer. Add the 2 tablespoons sugar and vanilla and beat for 1 or 2 minutes more. Gradually beat in the flour; stir in the walnuts.

Shape the dough into 1-inch balls, using about 1 tablespoon of dough for each. You should have 24 cookies. Place them about an inch apart on an ungreased cookie sheet. Bake on the second highest shelf of the oven for 15 minutes, turning the cookie sheet once so that they will bake evenly. They should be only lightly colored.

Carefully transfer the cookies to a rack and let cool completely. Roll in sifted confectioner's sugar and wrap like party favors in colored tissue paper.

YIELD: 2 DOZEN COOKIES

CHILE

"Sin el chile los mexicanos no creen que están comiendo" ("Without chile, Mexicans don't believe they're eating"), observed Fray Bartolomé de las Casas in the sixteenth century, an eternal truth. Regardless of class, economic position, or anything else, all Mexicans eat chile at all times. It is culinary basic, junk food, medicine, drug, business, and recreation. If corn is the backbone of our cooking since prehistory, chile is its soul.

Do not try to tell me that the same is true of Hungary, North

Africa, or other places where they eat hot peppers. We are different because chile is the great gift of indigenous Latin American culture to the world that exterminated indigenous Latin American culture! It is a common denominator that defines what is Mexican.

No matter when, no matter who is at the meal, chile is always present on tables in Mexico. It is our standard stimulant and gets us going in the morning—maybe as *huevos rancheros* (eggs swimming in spicy chile sauce) or the pre-Columbian *chileatole* (a gruel made with corn *masa,* chile, and perhaps honey) that we still eat for breakfast. At night it is our standard mild sedative in the street snacks like *taquitos* or *tortas* (hot sandwiches with sauce) that are often the last meal of the day. Children (and adults) suck on candies with hot chile. It is indispensable for inducing pure enjoyment—or another kind of enjoyment that is a mixture of pleasure and pain! There has always been laughter at the sight of someone eating a really hot chile. The eaters turn red, they sweat profusely, they curse the little torpedo, *but* go on eating it.

Chile is history. It has outlasted religions and governments in Mexico. It is part of the landscape, literally: It grows wild in forest-sized ranges of bushes in some places. Botanically it is the fruit of *Capsicum annuum* and some other *Capsicum* species. It belongs to the holy trinity that has always been the basis of our diet: corn, beans, and chile. Without each other, none of the three would be what it is. Corn is an incomplete protein, beans are difficult to digest. Together they would be good basic sustenance, but hopelessly monotonous. Chile makes the gastric juices run for a dinner of beans and tortillas. It also provides the vitamins they lack, especially vitamins A and C. The combination of the three makes a nutritionally balanced meal. It's magic.

We have other kinds of chile magic, superstitions and beliefs that must go back to when the chile goddess was the sister of the rain god. When people make amulets of plants that are supposed to be good against spells and charms, chile is usually one of them. But sometimes it is feared, too. When I was pregnant, Kika, the housekeeper, was furiously certain that my baby was going to be born with *chilcual,* a rash supposedly caused by chile, because the only thing I wanted to eat was chile. (Funny—I couldn't stand the smell of chile roasting, but I craved the taste constantly.) There are a lot of beliefs about chile as the symbol of the male organ or some sort of sexual agent. In one central Mexican village about thirty years ago a researcher was told that a pregnant woman should never carry food seasoned with chile to her husband when he works in the special field for chile and tomato plants, or else she will be attacked by malicious spirits (*chaneques*) who will take away the food and fill her womb with water.

Chile is our medicine, too. It was earache remedy, cough medicine, antispetic, and toothpaste ingredient for the Aztecs. The Incas used it to increase the effect of coca by clearing the nasal passages of mucus. To wean children and young animals, chile was—still is—rubbed on the nipples. It is still supposed to protect against maladies caused by the evil eye and has always had a reputation for being an aphrodisiac. (I was encouraged to read of one 1938 study bearing this out—in male water fleas.) It is what makes people able to live and work in the hottest tropical regions of Mexico, because eating the hot chile makes you sweat enough to cool your skin.

Some Spaniards were interested enough in the ways of the Indians to report back on the plants and medicines of "New Spain" while the Spanish armies were busy destroying the ancient civilizations. Often botanists and doctors accompanied the explorers, searching for new herbs and remedies. Seeds, cuttings, and botanical descriptions went back and forth across the Atlantic during the first centuries of discovery—and among them was chile. The medical doctors did not know just what to make of its powers. The seventeenth-century physician Juan de Cárdenas tackled the mystery in *Problemas y Secretos Maravillosos de las Indias* (*Marvelous Mysteries and Secrets of the Indies*). Among other things, he pondered why chile seemed to have a laxative effect under certain conditions though it seemed not to be specifically a laxative, why it stimulated appetite, and why it appeared to afford much nourishment though it was really a spice rather than a food in its own right. As quoted in Janet Long-Solís's fascinating book *Capsicum y Cultura,* he came up with a theory that the spice helped "cook" and cleanse phlegmatic humors in the stomach. Fray José de Acosta took a more severe view in his *Historia Natural y Moral de las Indias* (*Natural and Moral History of the Indies*). In his opinion, chile was a good digestive taken in moderation, but could be dangerous because of its extreme "heat." He was referring not just to the burning sensation of chile *al entrar y al salir también* ("on going in and going out") but to the old physiological theory that all foods affect the human temperament according to their "hot" and "cold" properties. Chile, he warned, was very hazardous to the health of the young—especially their souls, because as a "hot" food it provokes lustful acts.

Would that he'd lived to see women carrying tiny spray cans of powerful chile extract—Mace—to fight off rapists! Modern science, by the way, bears out Acosta's praise of chile as a digestive aid. Two other medical properties also seem to stand out today: it is a good expectorant, helping to clear bronchial congestion, and eaten regularly it may help prevent the formation of blood clots. Meanwhile, it has acquired hundreds of industrial uses unknown to most consumers. It is a great source of coloring matters that meet USDA safety requirements—carotenoids, capsanthin, and a huge family of compounds called oleoresins that are composed of oil molecules joined to resins. Today oleoresins are used to color foods from gelatins to sausages to cornflakes. They add flavor to tobacco. Chile pigments—often the leftovers from canning pimientos—go into modern chicken feed; they help create the yellow color that consumers prefer in chicken skin and egg yolks. (Now I know why the cowboys on our ranch used to feed the chickens chile seeds and tops.) They also go into bird seed to help brighten the yellow in the feathers of canaries, parrots, and parakeets. And chile helps produce different tones of red in cosmetics.

But for me, the best part of the chile saga is the story of how it came out of Central and South America five hundred years ago and made itself at home on every continent. I am fascinated by the way ingredients and flavors move from one culture to another and are taken in and assimilated until people think they are indigenous. Chile is a fantastic example. It may be the most completely promiscuous vegetable there is.

Spain was the first channel. Everywhere the Spaniards went in the New World, they found people eating this strange spice. It was called *ají* in the Caribbean, *uchú* in Peru, and *chilli* in Mexico. Europeans took to the new seasoning right away, but not all imports were so popular. Potatoes and tomatoes were initially regarded by many as poisonous and/or aphrodisiac—in either case, not for polite consumption—and made their way into European cuisines in uneven fits and starts. But chile was an immediate hit.

The next line of distribution after Spain was the Turks. The Ottoman Empire, then at the height of its influence, ruled the principal Mediterranean trade routes. The Turks carried to different parts of Europe many goods that originated in both India and the Spanish Americas. So various American foods took on Turk-

ish associations in European languages: Maize was "Turkish corn," the bird we eat at Thanksgiving was "Turkey fowl," and Mexican chile made its European debut under the stage name of "Turkish pepper." It followed the Ottomans into present-day Bulgaria and somehow arrived in Hungary. This was "like the meeting of two people who seemed fated to fall in love," says George Lang in *The Cuisine of Hungary.* Today chile symbolizes Hungarian cuisine—except that they call it "paprika." (This goes back to *Piper,* the Latin name for the totally unrelated true peppercorns. The same confusion is found through every European language.) Apparently it spread like wildfire among humble people while the upper classes took a couple of centuries to get used to the idea. (I can't scientifically prove it, but I believe one reason chile is irresistibly popular among peasants and poor people all over the world is that it seems to give more dimension to food. A meager meal feels more satisfying with the addition of chile.) The Hungarians eventually learned to grow different sorts of chiles, from sweet to hot, string them on cords to make dried *ristras* in the Mexican way, and mill them into the fine powder used in all the classic Hungarian stews like *pörkölt, gulyás,* and *paprikás.* Escoffier put chile on the haute cuisine map in 1879 when he travelled to Szeged and unveiled his discoveries at Monte Carlo as *gulyás hongrois* and *poulet au paprika.* Today, according to Lang, "Paprika is to the Hungarian cuisine as wit is to its conversation." There is even a folklore figure called Jancsi Paprika, brash, clever, and as hot-headed as you'd expect seeing that he wears a big chile for a hat and a smaller one for a nose.

Meanwhile chile moved on, as both spice and sweet pepper. It spread around the Mediterranean until every land from Portugal and Algeria to Turkey and Albania reinvented the classic Aztec combination of peppers and tomatoes and considered it a triumph of local ingenuity. They all had some local spin to put on chile. In the south of France red chile became *rouille* (literally "rust"), the hot sauce served with fish soups. The Abruzzi region of Italy learned to steep tiny hot peppers called *diavolini* ("little devils") in olive oil. The beautiful red-orange garnish of Turkish dishes like Circassian chicken comes from paprika mixed with oil. Green peppers stuffed with rice and small hot peppers pickled in vinegar invaded what is now Yugoslavia.

Africa was a successful target. The Ottomans brought chile to present-day Morocco, Tunisia, and Algeria, where it was mingled with Old World spices to make the very hot sauce called *harissa* that accompanies couscous and other dishes. The Portuguese, who had the main trade routes around Africa and had broken the Turkish-Venetian monopoly on black pepper from India, were also busy colonizing Brazil. It happens that parts of Brazil, Africa, and India have very similar climates, and the Portuguese rapidly spread important plants such as maize, manioc, beans, and peanuts back and forth among the three locations. One of the major transplants was chile, especially an extremely hot species found in Brazil, *Capsicum chinense*. (Most Mexican chile is of the species *C. annuum,* which can vary from totally mild to blistering hot; some is the always hot *C. frutescens*.) New World chile turned the people into fire-eaters. From Nigeria to Uganda, Africans today season their food with such blazing hot peppers that foreign visitors may gasp in pain at one mouthful of a *mild* dish. In India, especially southern India, chile became one of the most important elements of the diet. The fiery vindaloo dishes are unthinkable without huge amounts of blowtorch-hot chile. The vindaloo seasonings are somewhat like the mixtures of spices called *berberé* in Ethiopia and used in all kinds of stews.

On it went, eastward from India with the Portuguese—and also westward across the Pacific with the Spanish who controlled the western routes. Even the Japanese, not known for hot food, learned to make a hot pepper marinade for fish from the missionary "barbarians." Other peoples frankly fell in love with it. Without chile Thailand would never have acquired its wonderful curry pastes or the hot sauces like *saus prik* and *nam prik*. Vietnamese food would not have its sweet-sour dipping sauces with their chile piquancy, and Indonesians would not eat the relishes called *sambal*. Can you imagine Sichuanese and Hunanese cuisine without chile? Inconceivable but true, until the Iberian powers brought chile to China in the sixteenth century. As for the Koreans, they are another people who hardly believe they're eating without chile. It appears as red pepper sauce served with almost everything, finely slivered fresh hot red or green peppers used as a garnish, and the ground red pepper that puts the fire in *kim chee* and other Korean pickled vegetables.

For all these world travels, no one has learned to grow so many varieties of chile pepper or to handle them in so many ways as the Mexicans. Other peoples have learned to cultivate kinds of peppers for this or that use, like the Italian frying peppers or the tiny hot ones grown in Japan, but I would still say that we wrote the book. Mexican chile is a whole spice cabinet in itself. I will not even try to list all of our varieties, but here is a short introduction to some important ones. Note that they can vary greatly in flavor and hotness! Chiles grown in the United States tend to have more water and less pungency than the same variety raised in Mexico. Even in Mexico, there are differences between growing regions, and names vary all over the place. For this reason shoppers can end up with very similar chiles sold under different names or something totally different under the same name.

Anaheim chile. A large, fleshy green chile developed in the United States, very close to varieties sold in southern Mexico as *chile chilaca* (see below) and in the north simply as *chile verde*. It is about 6 to 8 inches long and ranges from mild to very hot. Similar or identical varieties can be found as "California long green," "Texas long green," or "New Mexico" chiles. In the north of Mexico this general type is the favorite for stuffing. They are also sold dried under at least some of the same names (Anaheim, New Mexico; in Mexico the dried version is usually called *chile colorado*—see page 225). I sometimes call for a canned variety of this general type, which most often will be identified on the label as "long green chiles."

Banana peppers (also called "Hungarian wax peppers"). Long, bumpy-looking fresh chiles with pale yellow-green skin, developed in the United States from a Hungarian original. Fairly to very hot. Similar to the chiles known in Mexico as *chiles largos* ("long chiles"), especially used in Veracruz, where they often flavor fish soups or Veracruz-style red snapper.

Cayenne. General name for a group of small, very hot varieties mostly grown today in Africa, India, and Louisiana. In the United States it also refers to any dried ground red hot pepper, which means that you are making a leap in the dark any time you put something called "cayenne" into a Mexican recipe. The cayenne pepper sold in U.S. markets can be a mixture of different (and different flavored) chiles. The small fresh red or green hot peppers sold in Asian markets are often the cayenne type. See also *pure powdered red chile.*

Chile ahumado. General name for smoke-dried chiles. The best known is the chipotle. See also *chile pasilla* and *chile morita.*

Chile amarillo. A small yellow-red dried chile from Oaxaca, also called *chile chilcostle* or *chilcoztli.* It is used in *mole amarillo* and other Oaxacan dishes. Very hot.

Chile ancho. A large dried red chile with wrinkled skin, one of the most important in my cooking. The name means "broad chile." It is semihot and vaguely heart-shaped, dark red to reddish brown in color. When fresh the same variety is called *poblano* (see below). It is fairly interchangeable with another large dried variety, the *chile mulato.*

Chile árbol or de árbol. Little chiles about 1 inch long, skinny, pointed, and extremely hot. Eaten both dried and fresh, either green or red. Probably many of the chiles grown as cayenne chiles in different countries are close to this type. The Sichuanese cuisine of China uses dried chiles very similar to the árbol.

Chile cascabel. Round or oval dried red chiles about the size of a small walnut. The names means "jingle bells," from the rattling sound of the seeds in the pod. Fairly hot. Sometimes the name is applied to another pepper, a long thin dried chile that also has rattling seeds.

Chile chilaca. A long dark green semihot chile used like poblanos and Anaheims. When dried it is known as *pasilla,* though that name is also applied to other types (see below).

Chile chilhuacle. A dried chile from Oaxaca. In Nahuatl (the Aztec language) *chilhuacle* means "old chile." It is about the size of a small bell pepper and smooth-skinned when dried. The flavor is robust and very hot. A red variety, *chilhuacle rojo,* is used in Oaxacan *mole coloradito,* and the very dark-skinned *chilhuacle negro* is integral to the famous *mole negro.*

Chile chipotle. A variety of jalapeño that is dried in the smoke of a fragrant wood fire on bamboo screens. The smoky flavor is an indispensable, haunting note in many sauces. Do not substitute ordinary dried chiles for chipotles. Also widely sold in cans, in a thick, pungent, adobolike sauce. Chipotles are one of my favorite chiles.

Chile colorado. Any kind of chile that turns red when ripe, but the term is most often applied to the Anaheim type (see above).

Chile guajillo. Long thin dried chile, dark red to maroon. Semihot to hot.

Chile habanero. One of the hottest if not *the* hottest kind on record. Beware! It has a boxy shape that has been compared to a lantern or a child's top, and is orange to orange-red when ripe. It is originally from Brazil and is grown in different parts of Latin America, but in Mexico it is mostly used in Yucatán.

Chile jalapeño. A small fat chile, the best-known fresh hot variety in the United States. It is dark green (or bright red when ripe), smooth-skinned except sometimes for small rough striations, and about two inches long. Jalapeños can be quite hot, but the U.S. product is usually mild. Sometimes they seem a little tasteless, especially the ones from California. Many subvarieties of this important chile turn up in Mexico under different names like *chile gordo* or *chile jarocho.* It is available canned in several different forms, the most important being pickled (*en escabeche*). I recommend Mexican brands of pickled jalapeños when you can get them, because the U.S. versions are extremely vinegary, with an unpleasant aftertaste.

Chile manzano. A round chile, mostly used fresh after it turns reddish orange. It goes under many different names from its resemblance to the shape of an apple (*manzana*), pear, plum, etc. Used mostly in western and central Mexico. Very hot.

Chile mirasol. Applied to several kinds that grow with the fruit pointing upward instead of hanging down, hence the name "gaze-at-the-sun."

Chile morita. A version of small jalapeño that is sometimes smoke-dried. Can be extremely hot. The name means "blackberry," and they are dark blackish red.

Chile pasado. Literally, "sun-dried chile," from the dehydration process. Prepared from Anaheim or similar long semihot chiles. They resemble no other chile flavor because they are roasted and dried while still green.

Chile pasilla. Refers to several different dried chiles. In most places it is the dried semihot version of the *chile chilaca.* But in Oaxaca the *chile pasilla* is a small, very hot, smoke-dried chile of the jalapeño type, which lends its smoky flavor to vegetables pickled in vinegar and to different sauces such as *Salsa de Gusanitos* (page 249).

Chile piquín or pequín. Also called *chiltepín, chiltecpín, chilipiquín.* Tiny oval or round peppers eaten both fresh and dried throughout Mexico. In the North they grow wild, their seed spread by birds. They are stinging hot.

Chile poblano. Very important both fresh and, under the name *chile ancho,* dried. It is a large fruit, shorter and broader than Anaheim chiles and tapering sharply to a point. Poblanos can be a fairly mild chile, often used for stuffing and for *rajas* (cooked chile strips). They can be medium green or very dark, almost blackish. I find the small heart-shaped ones tend to be hotter than the larger poblanos.

Chile serrano. A small and sometimes very hot fresh red or green pepper, shaped like a little bullet.

Pure powdered red chile. This is just what it says: red chiles dried, roasted, and ground to a fine powder that looks like Hungarian paprika (though it does not have the same flavor). It is as mild or hot as the chiles that went into it. In shopping for it you will encounter a barrage of confusing names in stores. Do *not* accept chili powder (a mixture of different flavorings) or cayenne pepper. A reputable spice dealer or well-stocked gourmet shop will sell pure powdered red chile either under that name or as something like "ground hot red pepper." If the store has it in different grades of hotness, the one that is generally appropriate in my recipes is "hot" or (better) "medium-hot."

Yellow hots. Sold all over northern Mexico and the U.S. Southwest. Used only fresh, they are about the size of a thick jalapeño and are usually moderately rather than terribly hot. A pepper like this is sold in Mexico as *chile güerito* or *güero*.

Preparing Chiles for Cooking

Before cooking, chiles are often roasted on a griddle. This brings out a rich roasted flavor and makes the fresh chiles easier to peel. Usually the seeds and veins—the hottest parts of the chile—are removed at the same time, but not always. When handling any hot chile, be sure to wear rubber gloves. If your hands touch really hot chiles, wash them thoroughly before touching your face and *especially your eyes!* I pass on (though I have not tried) a suggestion from Jean Andrews, who says in her beautiful illustrated manual *Peppers: The Domesticated Capsicums* that she has taken the sting out of her hands by soaking them in a solution of household chlorine bleach.

I have a word of caution for anyone who is tempted to buy a huge quantity of dried red chiles in a Mexican or other market: They do not keep well, being extremely attractive to bugs and little visitors you probably don't want in your cupboard. It is better to buy in modest amounts and store them in carefully sealed bags.

To prepare fresh green chiles. Heat a griddle or cast-iron skillet over medium-high heat until a drop of water sizzles on contact. Working with a few chiles at a time so as not to crowd the pan, place them on the hot griddle and cook, turning occasionally with tongs, until they are blackened all over. (Chiles can also be held directly in a gas flame on a long-handled fork.) Place the hot chiles in a plastic or brown paper sack and let sit 2 to 5 minutes (no longer, or they get soggy). Remove them from the bag, peel by scraping off the blistered skin, and cut off the top with the seed core. Cut the chiles lengthwise into halves or thick strips (*rajas*) and scrape out the veins and any remaining seeds.

When chiles are left whole for stuffing, sometimes I fry them in hot oil, which leaves the texture crunchier. For this method, the chiles must be washed and thoroughly dried. Make a lengthwise slit in each chile to release steam while frying. Heat 1 inch of vegetable oil over high heat in a heavy medium-size skillet until very hot but not quite smoking. Add the chiles, one or two at a time. (Be careful—they will spatter violently!) Cook about 30 seconds on each side; they should be blistered and beige-colored. Remove from the pan as they are done and peel immediately under cold running water. Gently pull out the seeds through the slit, being careful not to tear the flesh.

To prepare dried red chiles. There are several methods. See the directions in individual recipes, but this is the general method for chiles that are to be pureed in sauces: Rinse under cold running water, shaking off excess water. Heat a griddle or cast-iron skillet over medium-high heat until a drop of water sizzles on contact. A few at a time, place the chiles on the griddle and roast 3 to 5 minutes, turning occasionally with tongs, just until the aroma is released. *Do not leave longer*—they will scorch and become miserably bitter! Large chiles like ancho chiles will usually be pliable after roasting and can be deseeded at once by cutting off the seed core at the top and scraping out the veins and any remaining seeds. Place the deseeded chiles in a large bowl and cover with boiling water. Let stand about 5 minutes; drain well. If the chiles are wrinkled and still brittle after roasting, place them in a bowl and cover with boiling water for 5 minutes before draining and seeding.

An alternative method is to pat the chiles dry after their initial rinsing and fry them in ½ to 1 inch of hot oil over high heat until fragrant and puffed up. Drain on absorbent paper, seed, and soak as described above.

With small chiles that are to be used whole, the rinsing and seeding is unnecessary. Or if chiles are not as *picante* as you would like, you may increase the hotness of the dish by leaving in the veins and seeds.

TAMALES

Al que ha nacido para tamal, del cielo le caen las hojas ("Leaves fall from heaven for the one born to be a *tamal*").

—Proverb quoted by Josefina Velázquez de León in *Mexican Cook Book Devoted to the American Home*

To "leaves" might be added "welcome" and "esteem," for tamales have been linked with celebrations and solemn offerings since Aztec times. A Mexican was traditionally—many still are—married, buried, christened, and fêted to the accompaniment of tamales. They were ritually offered at every sacred feast of the Aztec calendar, together with versions of the Aztec corn gruel, *atole.* Today Christmas, Easter, and saints' days are honored by those great Christian foods, tamales and *atole.* All these occasions are prefaced by *tamal*-making marathons for which every woman brings an ingredient—though only one person mixes the dough, because too many fingers in the pie are said to make it go sour.

Tortillas are the Mexican daily bread, a simple, quick-cooking food. The Spaniards had no trouble giving them a Spanish name ("little round cakes"). Tamales are a more complicated preparation and one the invaders found curious enough to keep the Náhuatl (Aztec) name *tamalli.*

What is a *tamal?* Well, just about anything that is cooked inside a leaf wrapping. Above all, it is a corn-husk packet enclosing a dollop of *masa* beaten until very light with lard, salt, and a little stock or water. This rich, delicate mixture may be used by itself, combined with other ingredients, or spread with a spicy meat, seafood, or vegetable filling. The husks are folded usually into a rectangle around the other ingredients and the tamales are steamed in or over a small amount of boiling water until the *masa* is light and succulent, not heavy and sticky. The steaming process keeps in and intensifies all the flavors of the food.

The Aztecs made tamales this way, minus the lard, packing the filled husks into narrow-necked clay pots to steam them. But they had dozens of variations that have survived and been added to over the centuries. Some are everyday fare sold at street stalls; some are rare and expensive, reserved for special occasions. The *masa* can be made from different kinds of corn—for the Day of the Dead there is one tradition of making the dough from blue corn. You can sweeten it with *piloncillo* (our flavorful brown sugar), spice it with chile, or leave it plain, with the basic lard flavor predominating. (One expression for a social gathering of all different types of people is *de chile, de dulce, y de manteca,* sort of like "vanilla, chocolate, and strawberry," only translating to "chile kind, sweet kind, lard kind.") You can make tamales from the *masa* mixture alone, with no meat or vegetable filling (*tamales blancos*). You can fold refried black or other beans into the *masa* for a simple, inexpensive, and popular version. You can eliminate the *masa* and use new corn kernels cut from the cob and ground (*tamales de elote*). You can vary the usual meats (pork, chicken, turkey, beef) with duck, iguana, iguana eggs, insects, rabbit, squirrel—but never *hacer de chivo los tamales* (make tamales from goat)! That's a popular expression for betrayal, especially going out on your mate.

You can leave out the *masa* altogether and simply fold the wrapping around a piece of meat or seafood. On the coasts, tiny fish are wrapped in corn husks, grilled, and eaten with a squirt of lime juice and a splash of a cold red chile sauce. Vegetables are cooked the same way. A takeoff on the idea appears in my *Tamal de Pescado* (page 183) and *Morralitos de Calabacitas* (page 311). Grilled tamales go back to an Aztec technique of cooking leaf-wrapped foods in hot embers. It has the flavor advantages of both roasting and streaming. Tamales are also pit-barbecued.

Everyone in the United States has seen some variation of the ordinary-sized (five or six inches long) rectangular husk-wrapped tamales, but that's just the beginning. There are tamales the size of a finger, and spit-roasted ones called *zacahuiles* that may be a yard long and enclose a whole haunch of pork or large pieces of turkey. There are ones in the shape of little round bundles gathered and tied at the top (*tamales de bola*). In Michoacán state there is a triangular version called *corundas* wrapped in corn leaves rather than husks. All sorts of leaves can be used for the wrapping, each imparting its own distinctive flavor to the food. A delicacy of Jalisco and other maguey-growing areas is meats in gathered bundles of *mixiote,* the parchmentlike outer covering of the maguey leaves, often baked in a barbecue pit. In Yucatán and other southern states tamales are usually flat packets wrapped in banana leaves, which release a delicate oil in steaming. For some versions the tamales are double-wrapped, with a layer of *hoja santa* (see page 8) inside the corn husks. In Baja California I've seen grape leaves used like the Middle Eastern *dolmades.* Then there is the option of no husk or leaf at all, for example, in the so-called *tamal de cazuela,* where the mixture is just baked in a casserole like a tamale pie. A similar dish is the *tamal Azteca* (definitely post-Conquest despite the name), made with alternating layers of sweet corn dough and *mole poblano,* baked in the oven. Commercial "Aztec pies" have alternating layers of either red or green tamales (cooked and removed from the husks), sautéed chicken, poblano strips, cream, and grated cheese.

Many or most *tamal* varieties are unknown outside their home region. Chiapas (sometimes known as "the *tamal* state") and Oaxaca are known for an incredible range of tamales, many of which I was lucky enough to sample. At Las Pichanchas restaurant in Tuxtla Gutiérrez I ate what I think is my favorite kind of all, made with goat cheese, a tomato-chile sauce, and a peppery-flavored herb called *chipilín* (*Crotalaria longirostrata*) that is unfortunately not available in the United States. It was also at Las Pichanchas that I tasted exotic tamales called *jacuanes* with a stuffing of refried black beans and dried shrimp (heads and all) in a green sauce, wrapped in *hoja santa* and then in corn husks. The sky is the limit in inventing different forms, and I hope you will be inspired to experiment after you have mastered some of my models—starting perhaps with my *Tamal de Pescado* (page 183), *Tamales Reales* (page 267), and *Cochinita Estilo Pibil* (page 280), and then trying the more elaborate *Tamales Miahuatecos* (page 253) and my grandmother's chicken tamales, *Tamales de mi Ana Linda* (page 99). Only be sure to be in a good mood and don't be mean to your kids! According to a superstition related by Teresa Castelló Yturbide, the tamales will get annoyed and stay uncooked if the cook is grumpy, or if a child is crying.

TAMALES CON ELOTE Y CHILE POBLANO

Tamales with
Corn and
Poblano
Chiles

I long for the flavor of *tamales de elote*, made with pureed fresh corn kernels. But our starchy, flavorful Mexican corn cannot be replaced with United States sweet corn, which creates a terribly insipid, watery effect. So I evolved something a little different using a regular *masa* mixture with fresh corn kernels and seasonings beaten in.

35 to 40 dried corn husks (see page 7)
2 tablespoons vegetable oil
1 medium-size onion, finely chopped (about 1 cup)
2 garlic cloves, minced
2 poblano chiles (see page 226), roasted (page 227), peeled, tops removed, seeded, and diced

2 cups fresh or drained canned corn kernels or 1 package (10 ounces) frozen
1½ tablespoons chopped fresh cilantro leaves
Salt to taste
½ recipe Basic Tamal Dough (see page 50)

Place the corn husks in a large bowl, cover with boiling water, and let soak while you prepare the filling.

Heat the oil in a large skillet over high heat until rippling. Add the onion and garlic and cook, stirring often, until golden, 2 to 3 minutes. Reduce the heat to medium; add the poblanos, stirring well to combine, and cook 2 minutes longer. Stir in the corn kernels and season with cilantro and cook until the moisture has evaporated, about another 3 minutes. Season with salt. Cool thoroughly.

Fold or beat the corn mixture into the prepared *tamal* dough, being sure it is evenly distributed. Fill, fold, and steam the tamales as described on pages 51–53, using about ¼ cup of the *masa*-corn mixture for each husk. Serve with a *picante* sauce such as *Pico de Gallo Norteño* (page 40) or *Salsa de Tomatillo con Chipotle* (page 301).

YIELD: 30 TO 35 TAMALES

ORIENTAL INFLUENCES

When the Spanish arrived in the Western Hemisphere, they believed they had landed in Asia, which was where they were headed by what they thought was a shortcut. From that time on, Asia has figured in the destiny of Mexico—and the food. We are a Pacific Rim nation, and not only our culture but our cuisine bears many traces of the fascinating movements from west to east as well as east to west that began with the Age of Discovery.

Once the conquest of America was firmly established, Pope Alexander VI divided the conquered lands and their routes to Europe between Spain and Portugal. The eastern route from Europe to Asia, around Africa and into the Indian Ocean, went to the Portuguese. The western route from Europe to Asia was Spain's. Eventually Spain ruled the Pacific from western South America to the Philippines, and shared the Far Eastern trade with Portugal. From the great Asian port of Manila, Oriental goods bound for Spain traveled to Mexico on the twice-yearly voyages of the powerful galleon called the *Nao de China.* This was how Mexico was introduced to silk, porcelains, and many spices.

The area most influenced by the Asian trade was Acapulco, the official western port city of Mexico. It was then considered a totally unlivable hellhole for most of the year. But when the *Nao* came in, a temporary population of merchants and carriers would appear in Acapulco to unload the cargo and prepare it for the overland journey to Mexico City and the eastern port, Veracruz. For several centuries the route between Mexico City and Acapulco was known as the "China Road."

The galleon was partly manned by sailors from China, the Philippines, and Southeast Asia. Over the years some put down roots in Mexico—mostly on the west coast, but Oriental influences can be traced elsewhere. The word "china" or "China" crops up in strange contexts. To this day Mexicans decorate their homes, churches, and public places for special celebrations with brightly colored tissue paper called *papel de China* ("China paper"), which is cut into intricate designs to form *papel picado,* "cut-up paper." Whether *papel de China* actually reached us from China or not, that is how we think of it. It is also curious that *china* (Chinese woman) came to mean a maidservant and that the national costume of Mexico, a long, full green-and-red skirt worn with an embroidered white blouse and a *rebozo,* bears the name of *china poblana* ("the maid from Puebla"). Various legends purport to trace the mystery back to the story of an Asian princess brought to Puebla as a servant. Other seldom recognized influences can be seen in the lacquerwork and glazed pottery that are thought of as typically "Mexican" but that actually incorporate styles and motifs derived from Oriental models during the golden age of the Asia-to-Mexico-to-Europe trade.

Just how much our food owes to Asia is a complex issue. The fact is that during the first centuries of European presence in the Americas hundreds of foods were brought to destinations halfway around the globe from their first homes in the Old or New World. Many or most were tropical plants. They were carried on Spanish, Portuguese, English, and Dutch ships by people who left no records of the strange plants they picked up. The voyagers also failed to note some of the dishes that they carried from one hemisphere to another. To trace these migrations would be the job of a scholar, but no scholar has really tried to research most of them. So I offer the following comments in the light of questions, not known facts.

Everywhere in Mexico rice is eaten as our "third bread" (along with the native corn tortillas and the European-introduced wheat breads). It is not the short-grain Valencia rice used in Spain for paellas but a long-grain variety more similar to some often used in China, and it is rinsed and washed as zealously in Mexican as in Chinese homes. It certainly looks as if rice arrived in our cuisine by the Pacific rather than the Atlantic route.

Then there is our fondness for strong, salty sauces used as condiments. U.S. visitors are often surprised to see us putting "un-Mexican" accents like soy or Worcestershire sauce into our cooking and think they must have come from later European immigrants. But it seems just as likely, or more so, that we were introduced to the original Asian ancestors of all such sauces directly from Asia or the Philippines some time during the more than two hundred years that the *Nao de China* traveled to our shores. The same can be said of fresh lime juice, which is almost a signature of Mexican cooking everywhere, from city street stalls to remote villages. It is not a particularly favorite ingredient in Spanish food—but it is just as common in Thai and other Southeast Asian cuisines. So is fresh coriander—cilantro—which is hardly used at all in Spain but figures prominently in Mexican—as well as Thai, Vietnamese, and Chinese—cooking. True, or Ceylon, cinnamon, originally one of the spices carried back to Europe from Southeast Asia, is so deeply rooted now in our cooking that the aroma almost conjures up a Mexican kitchen. It never came to pervade Spanish food in this way, but if you look at the spice mixtures of India and Thailand you will find cinnamon blending with a whole complex of seasonings much as it does in Mexican *moles* and some of the spice pastes.

Often the prevalence of an ingredient or cooking technique on the west coast of Mexico suggests that it came from the other side of the Pacific. Soy sauce is especially used in the state of Sinaloa. Fresh ginger occurs in the cooking of Chiapas. The most intriguing case of all is that of ceviche, raw fish or other seafood "cooked" by marinating it in fresh lime juice. This technique is known all over Southeast Asia, from Malaysia to the Philippines—and is also associated with the west coast of Latin America from Chile to

Mexico. It is not part of true Spanish cuisine, and despite the similarity of the name, it is not in the least like the Spanish *escabeche,* which involves already cooked fish placed in a vinegar marinade. In Mexico it is particularly associated with Acapulco and other western ports. I don't see how anyone can *not* conclude that our ceviche directly descends from the identical technique of the Orient.

CEVICHE DE CALLOS DE HACHA

Scallop

Ceviche

This version came originally from the port of Mazatlán, Sinaloa state.

1 pound sea scallops
7 large limes
1 large ripe, red tomato, peeled, seeded, and finely chopped
1 small onion, finely chopped (about ½ cup)

2 ripe avocados (preferably the black-skinned Hass variety), peeled, pitted, and finely diced
2 teaspoons dried Mexican oregano (see page 11)
Salt to taste

Squeeze the juice from 6 of the limes to make about 1 cup. Place the scallops in a nonreactive deep bowl (ceramic, glass, or stainless steel) and cover with the lime juice. Let marinate for 1 hour.

Drain the scallops and pat dry. In a large bowl, combine with the chopped tomato, onion, avocado, oregano, and the freshly squeezed juice of the remaining lime. Season with salt and serve.

YIELD: 4 SERVINGS AS AN APPETIZER

New Horizons: Regional Explorations

![decorative rule]

Until I moved for good to the United States, I would say that my knowledge of the regional Mexican cuisines was excellent in some regards and very spotty in others. I had lived for years in one of the important culinary capitals of the land; I had done some traveling after that; I had learned whatever I could from friends and relatives in many parts of Mexico. I knew what one can from books. But I had never set out on a systematic voyage or voyages of exploration to see the major provincial cooking styles at first hand.

It is strange that my success in this country is what enabled me to know more about my own, but that's how it happened. I had been working in New York only a short time when I decided that in order to keep developing as a cook I would have to start dedicating some time to research. My glimpses of the regional cuisines had made me aware of how much I didn't know—what other stimulating discoveries must be out there waiting for me? And so throughout the last seven-plus years I have visited many parts of Mexico, sometimes accompanied by my mother and reaping the benefit of her knowledge and insights, sometimes with other friends or on my own.

My first research trip was a marathon visit in the summer of 1985 that took me to seven states. It was a revelation. For me as a cook, it was like something you might read about in a nineteenth-century novel where the hero returns from the Grand Tour with every idea enlarged. Needless to say, no one can take in every dinner or every experience equally on such an ambitious journey. But I was absolutely charged with new ideas—new to me, anyhow. I could not wait to see how many things I had tasted could be re-created to my satisfaction at Café Marimba, with ingredients from New York markets or special chiles and herbs that I had packed up and carried with me as I traveled.

That was surely my most ambitious journey, but only the prelude to many visits in greater depth. I have said before that I feel privileged to understand and interpret Mexican food both as a Mexican and as a visitor. My travels have enriched this dual role, for I see what I encounter both as a part of my own heritage and as a process of culinary discovery. I have been exposed not only to ways of cooking but to ways of living far outside my own frame of reference.

I have listened to a popular poet improvise satirical verses in a Veracruz café and watched a midwife at work in a Yucatecan hut. I have swapped stories of local corn harvest traditions with sellers at market stalls in remote cities, watched church processions honoring events I had never paid attention to as a child, navigated slippery roads in the kind of terrain that shows you why Cortez, when asked by Charles V to describe the topography of Mexico, is supposed to have crumpled up a piece of paper in his fist. I have eaten, haunted markets, and asked questions from Mexico City to Tabasco to Tuxtla Gutiérrez. Every journey makes me insatiable for more. And even in New York I constantly explore distant parts of Mexico through the generosity of my dear Mexico City friend Pedro Luis de Aguinaga, who has shared books, sent me newspaper clippings, and told me stories from his own wide-ranging love and knowledge of Mexico.

Probably the two areas that have taught me the most in culinary terms are the southwestern and southeastern coastal states of Mexico. In the east, you sometimes feel as if Mayan cooking has held its identity intact since pre-Columbian times in the spice pastes and pit-barbecues of Yucatán. On the opposite side of Mexico, in Oaxaca and Chiapas, the two states I have returned to most often, other pre-Columbian remnants have joined forces with many later culinary elements—especially in the famous "seven *moles*" of Oaxaca and the innumerable varieties of tamales made throughout Chiapas. I would say that the present-day menu of Zarela is a combination of the food I grew up with in the North, the Guadalajara cooking I learned in my late teens, and the exciting influences of Yucatán, Chiapas, and, above all, Oaxaca and Veracruz. But I would also say that equally exciting discoveries lie ahead of me. Ten years ago I couldn't have imagined some of the directions my cuisine would have gone in. Now I think of myself as a prime example of learning-in-progress, and know that ten more years of travels and experiences will bring just as surprising kinds of enrichment.

The recipes that follow are a sampling of the regional dishes that I have loved most. I have not tried to cover all bases like a culinary Baedeker (something that has been done very well for Spanish-speakers in the volume *Gastronomía* of the *Atlas Cultural de México*). Nor have I filled in all the tourist attractions that you could find in any competent travel guide. What I would like to share with you from my travels is an album of impressions—glimpses that have touched me, telling details that capture the spirit of the places, moments where I have said to myself that before this I was not fully a Mexican.

OAXACA

When I think of the great Juárez Market of Oaxaca, I think of the delicious taste of crisp-fried *chapulines,* the red grasshoppers that are synonymous with high summer in that part of the world. I've been hooked since my first taste of them on a summer day about six years ago, which was also my first glimpse of the market.

It is July 16, the feast day of the Virgen del Carmen (Our Lady of Mount Carmel), just before the citywide festival called the Guelaguetza. I am staying with a friend at the Hotel Presidente, a great landmark that began as a sixteenth-century convent. In the nineteenth century it served as headquarters of Benito Juárez, a Zapotec Indian from Oaxaca who became Mexico's first Indian president. Later the place became a jail before being turned into an exquisite hotel. From the Presidente to the Juárez Market is a walk of five or six blocks through very clean cobbled streets filled with vendors—everywhere you look is another tray of wares. The streets are a shopper's paradise, but also a window on the fierce traditionalism of the Indians who live in and around this old southern city. Many tribes come to sell their goods, each clinging to its own language and tribal costumes. They also continue to cook their own foods. But Oaxaca is also home to a more assimilated population of *mestizos,* those of mixed Spanish and Indian blood.

We get no farther than around the corner from the hotel when we come upon a *mestizo* woman leaning against a wall. The little girl beside her stands up when she sees us coming and walks up to me smiling shyly, outstretched hands filled with handmade wooden combs, letter openers, bookmarks, and decorative little picks. The work is beautiful.

She gestures us over to her mother's stand. They are Hortensia Paz and her daughter Victoria, and Hortensia explains that her family has been doing this for generations. Her grandfather taught her father and aunts and uncles, they in turn taught their children, and now the younger generation is learning the trade. Most of them still whittle their lives away. As she talks, Hortensia is staining wide-toothed combs with a rag soaked in dye while Victoria sands away rough spots with a pumice stone.

A few steps away Margarita Ruíz, age thirteen, presides over an artistic arrangement of some pineapple-shaped fruit (but only the size of a walnut) heaped in pyramids on a wide, shallow hand-woven basket decorated with bunches of freshly cut alfalfa laid out in graceful arches. The fruit doesn't really look edible, and I ask if you can really eat it. She replies with a very dry yes. Thinking I'm about to make an exciting discovery, I ask, "And the alfalfa?" She disdainfully answers that only pigs eat it, it is only *para el lujo de la canasta*—to lend a more luxurious look to the basket. The fruit is *jiotilla,* she informs me, and is used in some Oaxacan versions of the *aguas frescas* (fresh fruit drinks) enjoyed throughout all the hot regions.

We make our way toward the market. But first we come to the Plaza Mayor, surrounded by government buildings. Today and every afternoon, it is a forest of vendors and offerings. I thread my way past Indians of many tribes in their different costumes, sellers with trays on their heads, civil servants taking an afternoon saunter, families on outings, students, tourists. The scope of different items for sale is overwhelming. So is the range within each category, whether it's toys or candies or corn. Dazed with the riot of colors and aromas, I partly stop comprehending what I'm seeing after I've noticed hot corn on the cob, small balloons like beach balls or huge ones like giant animated cartoon figures, colored *gelatinas* (jelled desserts) in jewellike tones, and some stuff for making bubbles.

I buy some of this last and start blowing bubbles. A young

family walks past and a little girl dressed in Sunday-best blue chiffon starts running after my bubbles, squealing with joy every time she catches one. I still have the photographs my friend Laurie took of her innocent and lovely pleasure.

Some of the crowd is here because today there is a concert. All over Mexico in every main plaza the government provides a free concert on Wednesdays and weekends. People from the surrounding villages come in, on foot or by bus, to enjoy the music. The band is playing on the second level of a kiosk accessible by an ornate, elaborate ironwork staircase. Here I get into a conversation with a young man of about thirty, dressed in white and wearing a Mixe Indian sarape. I have him figured as one who will be proud and suspicious of questions, the archetypal uncommunicative Indian of the villages. But Juan Luis Zamoras of Juquila Mixes surprises me by cooperatively opening up and talking about himself and his family. He tells me that he and his brother have come to enjoy the music with their young families. He translates my questions into the Mixe language and explains his relatives' answers in Spanish for me.

I ask him what he taught his little girl first, meaning which language. Juan Luis misunderstands my question. He answers, "I first taught my daughter to respect her elders and to say hello!"

The children, he tells me, still learn the history and legends of their people from the oldest person in a family, or sometimes the village elder. It is what has helped them survive as a people. Their food has also survived in nearly the same form for many centuries. In Juquila Mixes, as throughout this region, the villagers usually eat tamales, beans, chile, and *champurrado,* a gruel made with ground corn and cacao beans. These are the basic foods that their ancestors were eating when the Spanish set out to conquer Mexico. The tribes maintain an intense ethnic pride; the native foods of the Americas, and the still surviving pre-Columbian ways of cooking them, are a proud part of it. The attitude toward outsiders and other ways is not always warm in these isolated lands.

We resume our walk toward the market but are told that it is closed from three to five! We will not get a leisurely look at it until the next day. But meanwhile we decide to see the fair of the Virgen del Carmen. This is being held in the courtyard of the church of the Carmen Alto, with bands playing and people dancing and singing. Stalls selling drinks and food have been set up. We are taken with the delicious *quesadillas* at one place, but no one is willing to make one for us because we look foreign and the assumption is that we have come to observe them tourist fashion, like animals in a zoo. We have to get a local to intercede for us. The *quesadillas* are simple but good, made with epazote and the Oaxacan string cheese so curiously reminiscent of the kind made in Syria and Armenia. While we are eating, the cook's son, a boy of about eleven, comes back from some mission. We listen to their conversation and realize that he has been sent to look for work and is here to report success. "See, it was worth it!" his mother says encouragingly. Everyone is expected to do what they can for the family.

All this is only prelude to the adventure we have really come for: the *Mercado Juárez*, the main market of Oaxaca, set up with regular stalls selling anything from cradles to guitars. It justifies everything that has been said of it by visitors, D. H. Lawrence, for example, in *Mornings in Mexico.* You walk through the entrances set all about the four walls of the market and are propelled into a magical world of exotic sights and sensations—beginning with the shock of almost falling over a small woman selling something on the floor under your feet. What a burst of smells! At first it is all chaos, a feeling reinforced by the innumerable floor-level vendors in every aisle in among the stalls. I am bowled over not just by the diversity of wares but by the fact that I have never before seen most of the foods being offered all around the great square. I have no idea what they are.

My first encounter is with the women selling *tlayudas* or *clayudas,* large tortillas made with a special kind of very starchy yellow corn, on the floor near the entrance. The *tlayudas* are thick and chewy, with a rich, satisfying corn flavor, and served with various accompaniments. I taste them first with a simple spread called *asiento,* made from the layer that sinks to the bottom in rendering lard. People also eat *tlayudas* with the dried smoked *gusanos de maguey* (maguey worms) that are one of the true Oaxacan passions (you may have seen one in the bottom of a bottle of mezcal, the famous local maguey liquor). But maybe the best way turns out to be with the crunchy, freshly cooked insects that I find at the same spot. I have never tried anything of the kind.

The woman explains to me that these are *chapulines de milpa* ("grasshoppers of the cornfield"), harvested at daybreak with fine nets. First they are rinsed in very hot water to kill them, then picked over carefully. She cooks them by sautéing in hot lard and seasons them with garlic and powdered chile, finishing them with liberal amounts of fresh lime juice. Your first mouthful is a revelation—spicy and citrusy and deliciously crunchy all at once. There is nothing like them. No wonder Oaxacans are said to be about as devoted to fried *chapulines* as to soul and body!

It takes a while to see that the market is organized (if that's the word) into different areas selling various goods. There is a huge flower section. Just past it are the famous *nieves de Oaxaca* (ice creams in flavors like rose, avocado, and corn) and the fresh fruit drinks (*aguas frescas* and *preparados*). You pick your way through aisles of baskets, pottery, painted clay figurines, live birds, jewelry, musical instruments, leather and woodwork, cacao beans roasting on clay *comales* (griddles), sewing goods, piñatas, paper flowers, religious icons, herbs, remedies, maguey worms threaded on strings to be sold by the hundred. Among the riot of salesmanship in the aisles are Indian women selling brightly painted gourds of *pozol,* a slightly fermented beverage made with lime-treated dried corn, *panela* (Mexican brown sugar), and sometimes ground achiote. (Do not try this unless you subscribe to my mother's thinking that a little stomach trouble cleans your system and helps you lose weight!) Near the door and also at ankle level is another new experience, a blancmange-like dessert in layers of white and shocking pink. It turns out to be a kind of jelled pudding made by cooking corn many hours to extract the starch. When at last I reach the main produce stalls in the center of the market, I confront mountains of strange greens and other vegetables, fresh and dried red chiles unknown to me after a lifetime or eating chiles, palettes of *moles* and *recados,* the intoxicating smell of perfectly ripe mangos and bananas.

A separate building is taken up with restaurant stalls like mini-diners, interspersed with others selling fresh bread and produce like milk and eggs. Throughout my stay I have many an early morning cup of *champurrado* here with a freshly baked piece of sweet bread, starting my day with the city by watching everyone arrive and set up their wares. Our early evenings are spent in one of the many restaurants around the plaza where the play of life continues to unfold. There are fortune-tellers and strolling musicians, Indian families selling their weavings, and the roasted *camote* (sweet potato) cart that tells you it's almost time to turn in. One evening Laurie and I are approached at one of the restaurants by a couple of young men who take us to be American sightseers and offer their services as guide-gigolos. When I asked them where is their Mexican male pride, they explain that they are students with no jobs and this is how they manage to drink a few beers and sit in the marketplace cafés! Undoubtedly it's a good way for young guys to practice their English and get some meals out of squiring around lady tourists. (We decline their services.)

I come back again and again to the market but don't even begin to exhaust its riches. The stalls and cafés are my education in the distinctive flavors of Oaxaca. But I am frustrated in trying to understand what I am tasting until I find a mentor, Doña María Concepción Carballido de Portillo, who takes me through the market, explaining what the strange fruits and vegetables are and what ingredients are used to cook the dishes at the stalls. Then I begin to make sense of the experience.

I taste all sorts of chiles that are not grown in any other part of the country—the smoky dried *chile pasilla de Oaxaca,* the yellowish *chile amarillo* (also called *chilcostle*), and the large *chilhuacle rojo* and *chilhuacle negro.* Often the food is accented with the lemony-scented Oaxacan oregano. Some of the local dishes are as purely Indian in character as the food of the villages, others mingle native and Spanish elements. Many have a sweet-hot taste resulting from unusual combinations of fruits, nuts, and chiles. I seize the opportunity to learn what I can of *moles,* which are as much associated with Oaxaca as baked beans with Boston. In fact, the state is known as "the land of the seven *moles.*" Different people will argue about just what these are and other states can also claim some of the dishes as their own. But one listing that seems reasonable is *mole verde* (green, made with epazote, parsley, *hoja santa,* tomatillos, and green chiles), *mole amarillo* (yellow, made with amarillo chiles), *mole coloradito* (light red, made with both amarillo and ancho chiles), *mole colorado* (a deeper red), *chichilo* (involving several kinds of dried chiles and avocado leaves, with their wonderful anisey fragrance), *manchamanteles* (see page 95 for the recipe), and the richest and most elaborate of all, *mole negro* (see next page). I sample them all along with other beautiful dishes new to me, and ask Doña Concepción to teach me some of the Oaxacan specialties that, once tasted, I'm sure I can't live without.

I have been back to Oaxaca several times since and have pored over cookbooks as well to extend my knowledge. Probably no other cuisine has influenced my food as much—especially the multitude of sauces, which tempt me to privately christen the state "the land of the hundred sauces." But when I think of that teeming market and its wares, the first thing I taste is still the crisp succulence of *chapulines*.

MOLE ESTILO OAXACA

Oaxacan-Style Mole

What a sense of accomplishment I had when I first made the famous *mole negro oaxaqueño,* the state dish of Oaxaca! This adaptation (with ancho and guajillo chiles substituted for the characteristic *chilhuacle negro,* unavailable in this country) may not be the most difficult recipe in the entire book, but it's probably the most difficult-*looking.* Actually, if you have learned some of the basic techniques, you will see that the different stages of preparation here all make sense—especially the time-consuming process of grilling, browning, roasting, and toasting many sauce ingredients separately to intensify their flavors. Read the recipe carefully and have the different ingredients set aside in bowls after their preliminary handling so that all will be ready when you reach the stage of pureeing and combining them. You may think it couldn't possibly be worth the trouble when you look at the long list of ingredients and procedures, but I assure you that the end result is always rewarding.

The large amount of lard may not be to all preferences. I think it contributes a lot to the flavor, but if you wish you can use just barely enough to sauté the nuts and drain some of the fat from them before pureeing. Also, in the dish as I learned it, the seeds of the chiles are roasted on a griddle before several stages of soaking and rinsing. I don't recommend this for city dwellers because the fumes are so pungent that your entire apartment building will come down to complain! At least that's what happened to me.

FOR THE CHILES

8 ounces ancho chiles (see page 224), tops removed

8 ounces guajillo chiles (see page 225), tops removed

FOR THE SPICES

12 black peppercorns

6 cloves

1 piece (2 inches) true (Ceylon) cinnamon (see page 15), or 2 teaspoons ground U.S. "cinnamon"

2 tablespoons dried Mexican oregano (see page 11)

FOR THE NUTS

½ to 1 cup lard (see page 19) or vegetable oil

½ cup sesame seeds

½ cup dry-roasted unsalted peanuts

½ cup slivered blanched almonds

½ cup walnuts or pecans

FOR THE DRIED FRUIT

½ cup golden raisins

1 cup pitted dried prunes, sliced

1 cup pitted dried apricots, sliced

1 to 1½ cups dry sherry, heated

FOR THE PLANTAIN

1 large, very ripe plantain (see page 20), peeled and cut into ½-inch slices

2 tablespoons butter or lard

FOR THE VEGETABLES

½ head garlic (about 8 large cloves), unpeeled

1 large onion, unpeeled

1 pound firm ripe, red tomatoes (2 large or 3 to 4 medium-size)

¼ pound fresh tomatillos (see page 14)

FOR PUREEING

4 to 5 cups Caldo de Pollo (see page 44), or as needed

TO COMPLETE THE DISH

1 tablet (3 ounces) Mexican chocolate (see page 6), chopped

Rinse the chiles under cold running water, removing the seeds and veins. Heat a griddle or cast-iron skillet over high heat until a drop of water sizzles on contact. A few at a time, briefly toast the chiles on the griddle, turning once or twice, until their aroma is released, 1 to 2 minutes. Do not let them scorch or the dish will be ruined. As the chiles are done, place them in a large bowl or saucepan. Cover with boiling water and let soak until softened, no more than 10 minutes, while you prepare the spices. Drain and set aside. Rinse and dry the griddle, which you will need later.

Heat a small, heavy skillet over medium-low heat. Add the peppercorns and cloves; toast, shaking the pan and stirring constantly, until their aroma is released, about 1 minute. Set aside in a small bowl. Lightly toast the Ceylon cinnamon in the same pan for about 1 minute; add it to the pepper and cloves. (If using ground cinnamon, do not toast; just add to the other spices when you have finished toasting them.) Toast the oregano in the same pan until fragrant and add to the spices. Set aside while you prepare the nuts.

In a heavy, medium-size skillet, heat 2 to 4 tablespoons of the lard or oil over medium heat until rippling. Add the sesame seeds and cook, stirring, just until golden, 3 to 4 minutes; do not let them darken. Remove to a medium-size heatproof bowl. In the same pan, cook the peanuts in the same manner, stirring, until lightly browned, adding a little more lard. Add to the bowl with the sesame seeds. Cook the slivered almonds, then the pecans or walnuts, in the same way, using a little more lard each time and adding the toasted nuts to the sesame seeds and peanuts. Set aside.

Combine the raisins, prunes, and apricots in a bowl and pour the hot sherry over them. Set aside to soften.

Heat the butter or lard in a medium-size skillet over medium heat until hot and bubbling, then add the plantain slices and cook, stirring, until golden on both sides. Set aside.

Heat the griddle or cast-iron skillet over high heat until a drop of water sizzles on contact. Place the unpeeled garlic and onion on the griddle and roast, turning several times, until the onion is blackened on all sides and the garlic is dark brown and somewhat softened. Let cool slightly. Peel the onion and garlic; coarsely chop the flesh of the onion. Set aside. On the same griddle, roast the tomatoes, turning several times, until blackened on all sides. Place in a deep bowl to catch the juices. Let cool slightly and peel. Place the tomatillos in a small saucepan and cover with water. Bring to a boil over medium heat and cook, uncovered, until their color changes, about 5 minutes. Drain and set aside.

Now you are ready to puree the ingredients in sequence, working in batches according to the capacity of your blender and adding chicken stock as necessary to facilitate the blending.

Place as many of the drained chiles and toasted spices in the blender as it can comfortably accommodate, with about 1 cup of the chicken stock. Process until smoothly pureed, adding more stock if necessary. Repeat with the remaining chiles and spices.

With a wooden spoon or pusher, force the puree through a medium-mesh sieve into a bowl; discard whatever won't go through. Scrape the puree into a large, heavy saucepan or Dutch oven; rinse out the blender to wash away any hard or fibrous bits.

Puree the sesame seeds and nuts in several batches with just as much chicken stock as necessary to help free the blades. Add to the chile puree. Puree the dried fruit and sherry along with the sautéed plantain in the same manner, adding a little stock if necessary. Add to the saucepan with the chiles and nuts. Puree the onion, garlic, tomatoes, and tomatillos (they may not need added stock). Add to the other purees in the saucepan, along with the chocolate.

Bring the sauce to a boil over medium heat, stirring constantly. Reduce the heat to medium-low and simmer, uncovered, stirring often, for 30 minutes. Serve with chicken (either cooked separately or browned in a little hot lard and added to the sauce to finish braising) and sautéed sliced plantains. (The *mole* is also good with turkey.) Can be stored, tightly covered, in the refrigerator for 10 days or indefinitely in the freezer.

YIELD: ABOUT 3 QUARTS

MOLE AMARILLO

Oaxacan
Yellow *Mole*

This famous Oaxacan sauce (often called just *amarillo*) is one of my favorite tastes. Unfortunately, it is not easy to duplicate, and in this country I long ago worked out a liberal reinterpretation. The original recipe had lime juice and the fragrant herb called *hoja santa* (see page 8), which is very hard to find in the United States, although it can be ordered from Texas in some seasons. In the absence of *hoja santa,* I have done some rearranging, adding Ceylon cinnamon, cloves, and oregano (preferably the Oaxacan kind). The sauce is traditionally served with pork (sometimes beef), chayote, and green beans, but I prefer it with seafood or chicken. We have also cooked short ribs in it and they were delicious. I suggest beginning your acquaintance with *amarillo* by poaching shrimp and scallops in the sauce just until done (a few minutes). Another good introduction would be to brown chicken parts in a little vegetable oil and finish cooking them in the *amarillo* (20 to 25 minutes for a 3½-pound chicken). Another idea is to poach eggs just until set in the hot *amarillo*.

If you want to try to capture a little of the anisey flavor of the *hoja santa*, you can make an anise tea by boiling ½ teaspoon aniseed in 1 cup water until it is reduced to ½ cup; strain and add it to the onion-tomatillo mixture instead of the cinnamon, cloves, and oregano.

2 tablespoons lard (see page 19) or vegetable oil
2 garlic cloves, minced
1 medium-size onion, minced (about 1 cup)
1½ pounds fresh tomatillos (16 to 20 large tomatillos; see page 14), husks removed and cut in several pieces
3 large green tomatoes, sliced
1 piece (2 inches) true (Ceylon) cinnamon (see page 15) or 1 teaspoon ground U.S. "cinnamon"

2 teaspoons dried Oaxacan or Mexican oregano (see page 11)
5 cloves
10 black peppercorns
6 to 8 amarillo chiles (see page 224); if unavailable, substitute 3 to 4 dried guajillo chiles (page 225)
Salt to taste

Heat the lard or oil in a large, heavy skillet or saucepan over medium-high heat until very hot but not quite smoking. Add the garlic and onion and cook, stirring often, for 2 minutes. Add the tomatillos, green tomatoes, cinnamon, oregano, cloves, and peppercorns. Stir to combine; reduce the heat to low and simmer for 10 minutes. Let cool.

Rinse the chiles under cold running water; remove the tops and seeds. Place in a small bowl, cover with boiling water, and let soak 10 minutes. Drain.

Working in two to three batches as necessary, place the tomatillo mixture in a blender or food processor and process until partly pureed. Add the chiles, one at a time, and continue to blend, tasting after each addition, until it is as hot as you like it. Blend until smoothly pureed. Season with salt.

Can be stored, tightly covered, in the refrigerator for 1 to 2 days. Sauce will jell, but will regain the right consistency on reheating.

YIELD: ABOUT 3½ CUPS

SALSA DE BARBACOA CON CHILE COLORADO

Red Chile

Barbecue

Sauce

I developed this sauce based on a Oaxacan barbecue sauce. It is delicious with spareribs, short ribs, or on chicken. The original used the smoked Oaxacan pasilla chiles (hard to find in this country) and plain rather than sweet mustard. Dried (not canned) chipotles, if you can find them, have a similar smoked flavor.

½ pound dried chiles, either ancho, guajillo, New Mexico or dried (not canned) chipotle (see pages 223–225), tops removed and seeded

10 large garlic cloves, peeled

2 tablespoons red wine vinegar

2 teaspoons dried Mexican oregano (see page 11)

⅔ cup honey

½ cup sweet prepared mustard, or to taste

Salt and freshly ground black pepper to taste

Cover the chiles with boiling water and let soak until softened, about 10 minutes. Drain the chiles and discard all but ½ cup of the liquid. Place the chiles, reserved liquid, and garlic in a blender. Process for 1 minute and scrape down the sides with a rubber spatula. Add the vinegar and oregano and process again until smooth. With a wooden spoon or pusher, force the puree through a medium-mesh sieve into a bowl, discarding any solids. Whisk in the honey and mustard. Season with salt and pepper. Can be stored, tightly covered, in the refrigerator up to 2 weeks.

YIELD: ABOUT 1½ CUPS

SALSA DE GUSANITOS

Oaxacan

Maguey

Worm Sauce

Here is something you will be able to make only if you bring back the magic ingredient from Mexico (or get someone to send it to you). But it is so delicious that I include it anyhow. You may know of mezcal, the potent liquor made in Oaxaca from a kind of maguey or agave (a close cousin of the Jaliscan blue maguey that produces tequila). All over the city are *expendios de mezcal,* shops selling the fiery stuff along with accessories like colorfully painted gourds to serve as bottles (with ropes tied around for easy toting)

or painted ceramic shot glasses in unlikely shapes. (I have some in the shape of a woman's leg clad in a fishnet stocking that, in my house, have somehow turned into candle holders.)

People in Oaxaca are also crazy about the little worms that feed on the maguey plants. They are considered a delicacy and are very expensive. You can find them in stalls that sell herbs and remedies (they are commonly believed to be an aphrodisiac). They have a distinctive smell and a haunting, somewhat smoky flavor.

I brought some back with me to New York and saved them for a special occasion. When the day came, I invited friends over, cooked a suckling pig, and made this sauce as instructed by my Oaxacan teacher. As everyone walked through the buffet, I urged them to try the worm sauce. Everyone complied and pronounced the sauce delicious. As one of my guests was leaving, I asked him how he had liked the worms. He said, *"Worms?"*

"Yes, in the worm sauce," I told him.

"Worm sauce?" he said. "I thought you were saying *warm* sauce and couldn't pronounce it!"

1 pound fresh tomatillos (about 12 large tomatillos; see page 14), husks removed

2 dried chiles, either Oaxacan pasilla or dried (not canned) chipotle (see pages 226 and 224)

1 small onion, chopped (about ½ cup)

8 to 10 dried maguey worms (see page 10)

1 tablespoon dried Oaxacan or Mexican oregano (see page 11)

1 garlic clove, chopped

Salt to taste

Place the tomatillos and chiles in a small saucepan with water to cover. Bring to a boil and cook over medium-high heat until the tomatillos change color, about 5 minutes. Drain, reserving ½ cup of the cooking liquid.

Place the tomatillos, chiles, and reserved cooking liquid in a blender with the onion, maguey worms, oregano, and garlic. Process for 1 minute or until thoroughly pureed. Taste the sauce and add salt if desired. It will jell on chilling; serve at once or thoroughly reheat to reliquify.

Serve as the mood inspires—in Oaxaca it is usually a table sauce to accompany roast or other cooked meats, but it is also good as a sauce in which to serve lightly cooked scallops or shrimp or tiny new potatoes.

Can be stored, tightly covered, in the refrigerator for 2 to 3 days.
YIELD: ABOUT 3 CUPS

CHILES RELLENOS VEGETARIANOS

Vegetarian
Stuffed Chiles

This recipe is connected with memories of an idyll: my first visit to the sleepy fishing town of Puerto Escondido on the coast about two hundred miles southeast of Acapulco. That was in 1985. We reached it in an ancient DC-8 by way of an airport that then consisted of one palm-thatched structure and a dirt road and, because of the surrounding steep Oaxaca mountains, could not be flown into except in the evening or early morning. We prayed all the way—but once there had a glorious time.

We rented a bright pink and turquoise fishing boat and were taken out into the jade-colored ocean by a beautiful young Zapotec Indian who teaches in a Oaxacan mountain village during the school year and works in Puerto Escondido with his father, a fisherman, in summers. He told us a lovely Zapotec legend about the monarch butterflies that gather in Mexico every winter. The Zapotecs believe that all men killed in battle are turned into monarch butterflies and continue to visit their homeland once a year.

When we got out of the bay into deep water, the color of the sea turned a royal blue. We didn't resist. We jumped right in and watched dolphins and swordfish jumping in the distance, making graceful arcs against the bright sky and the deep blue of the sea. A large turtle swam by, and we levered it up onto the boat to marvel at it before letting it go back to its business. Our teacher-guide took us to a tiny beach, where we waded through the choppy waves and maneuvered our way barefoot over sharp cliffs to a palm-thatched restaurant where we had fried fish with corn tortillas, spicy chile sauce, and cold beer. This is the food typical of innumerable little beach-front eateries in Mexico, and it is one of the most satisfying meals there is.

There is not much to do in Puerto Escondido unless you are a surfer (it is considered one of the world-class surfing spots). We did nothing, to our heart's content. Our hotel, the Santa Fe—recommended by my late friend Albert Grossman, manager of the Rolling Stones, who first told me about Puerto Escondido—was ideal for this purpose. It has an open-air dining area facing the ocean. In this part of Mexico there usually are late-afternoon thunderstorms in summer, and we loved to have a late lunch there to the strains of a guitar and watch the lightning over the water in the distance.

The Sante Fe, owned by an American who happens to be a vegetarian, offers many meatless dishes on the menu. I brought back a souvenir in the form of this excellent vegetarian stuffed chile recipe.

Vegetable oil for frying
6 large poblano chiles (see page 226)
⅓ cup golden raisins
1 cup boiling water
¼ cup (½ stick) unsalted butter
2 large garlic cloves, minced (about 1 tablespoon)
1 small onion, finely chopped (about ½ cup)
1 cup converted rice

2½ cups water
⅓ cup slivered blanched almonds
¼ cup sliced pimiento-stuffed green olives
¼ cup chopped fresh Italian (flat-leaf) parsley
4 ounces white cheddar cheese, shredded (about 1 cup)
2 cups Caldillo de Tomate (see page 36)

Pour vegetable oil into a large, heavy skillet to a depth of about ½ inch and heat over high heat until very hot but not quite smoking. Make a small (1- to 1½-inch) lengthwise slit in each chile. Fry, 3 at a time, on both sides until beige-colored and puffed; remove as they are done and drain on paper towels. Peel the chiles and gently remove the seeds through the incision, being careful not to tear the flesh. Set aside.

Place the raisins in a small bowl and cover with the boiling water. Let stand until plumped, at least 20 minutes.

Heat 2 tablespoons of the butter in a medium-size saucepan over medium-high heat until fragrant and bubbling. Add the garlic and onion and cook, stirring, for 2 minutes. Add the rice and cook, stirring, for 2 more minutes. Add the water and bring to a boil. Reduce the heat to low, cover the pan tightly, and cook for 20 minutes. Let cool.

Preheat the oven to 325°F.

Heat the remaining butter in a small saucepan over medium-high heat until fragrant and bubbling. Add the almonds and cook, stirring, until golden, about 2 minutes. Drain on paper towels.

Combine the cooled rice mixture with the almonds, olives, parsley, shredded cheese, and drained raisins. Carefully stuff one sixth of the mixture (or as much as will fit comfortably) into the incision in each chile. Place the chiles (along with any leftover mixture) in an 8 × 8-inch Pyrex dish or shallow medium-size casserole, cover with the tomato sauce, and bake until the cheese is melted and bubbling, about 15 minutes.

YIELD: 6 SERVINGS

NOTE: For a nonvegetarian version, cook the rice in 2½ cups *Caldo de Pollo* (page 44).

TAMALES MIAHUATECOS

Oaxacan

Pumpkin

Tamales

These unusual tamales, made from a sweetened, pumpkin-flavored ground corn dough and filled with spicy bean puree, are from the Miahuatlán region in the state of Oaxaca. They have a rich, complex combination of flavors including smoked pasilla or chipotle chiles, Ceylon cinnamon, garlic, and the anise-flavored *hoja santa*. (This recipe substitutes an anise-based tea.) They make a wonderful accompaniment to roast pork or chicken.

In the original recipe the tamales are wrapped in corn husks. I like to use banana leaves, which add another level of fragrance and flavor.

Before beginning the recipe, have ready a steaming arrangement (see page 51).

1 pound banana leaves (available in Oriental and Latin American stores), thawed if frozen

FOR THE CORN DOUGH
2 heaping cups masa harina (see page 49)

2 to 2½ cups warm chicken stock or water

½ pound lard (1 cup plus 2 tablespoons; see page 19)

2 cups cooked or canned pureed pumpkin or winter squash (drain slightly if very watery)

1½ teaspoons ground true (Ceylon) cinnamon (see page 15), preferably freshly ground in a spice grinder, or ½ teaspoon ground U.S. "cinnamon"

3 ounces piloncillo (see page 20), grated or crushed, or ½ cup firmly packed dark brown sugar

1 teaspoon salt, or to taste

FOR THE BEAN FILLING
2 teaspoons aniseed

2 cups water

2 to 3 chiles, either dried Oaxacan pasilla or dried or canned chipotle (see pages 226 and 224)

2 to 2½ cups cooked (see page 43) or drained canned black beans

5 to 6 garlic cloves, peeled

2 tablespoons lard (see page 19) or vegetable oil

Salt to taste

Unfold the banana leaves, being careful not to split them unnecessarily. Wipe them with a clean damp cloth. With kitchen scissors, trim the leaves into 12 to 14 rectangles about 14 × 11 inches. Save some of the longer trimmings. Pat dry and set aside.

To make the corn mixture, mix the *masa harina* with enough warm stock to form a soft but not sticky dough. Beat the lard in a large bowl with an electric mixer on medium speed until very light and fluffy. Add the *masa harina* mixture and pumpkin puree a little at a time, beating on medium speed and stopping to scrape down the sides of the bowl as necessary. The mixture should be as light as buttercream. Beat in the cinnamon, *piloncillo* or brown sugar, and salt. (If beating by hand, see the directions on page 51.) Refrigerate while you make the bean filling.

Make an anise infusion by boiling the aniseed in the water until reduced by half. Strain and reserve. If using Oaxacan pasilla chiles or dried chipotles, cover with boiling water and let soak until softened, about 10 minutes; drain and remove the stems. Canned chipotle chiles can be used as they are. Working in batches if necessary, puree the beans in a blender or food processor fitted with the steel blade together with the chiles, garlic, and anise tea.

Heat the lard or oil in a heavy skillet or wide, shallow saucepan over high heat. When very hot, add the bean puree, watching out for splatters. Reduce the heat to medium and simmer, uncovered, stirring to prevent sticking, until most of the liquid is evaporated. Season with salt. Cool to room temperature.

To fill the tamales, place 1 or 2 banana-leaf rectangles at a time flat on the counter. Tear off some long, thin strips from the reserved banana-leaf trimmings to use as ties. Place a big handful (⅔ to 1 cup) of the *masa* mixture in the center of the leaf. With a spatula or your fingers, spread it out into an oval about 4 × 3 inches and about ½ inch thick. Place about 1 heaping tablespoon of the bean filling in the center of the oval.

Fold the right and left edges of the banana leaf toward the center to meet, overlapping a little to cover the filling, then fold the top and bottom edges toward the center to make a neat, flat package about 4 × 5 inches. Fasten by tying with a thin strip of banana leaf.

Place the tamales flat in the steamer, seam side up, arranging them in layers as necessary. Place some extra banana leaves on top to help absorb steam. Steam 1 hour over boiling water, replenishing with hot water as necessary.

YIELD: 12 TO 14 TAMALES

PASTEL SOLA DE VEGA

Oaxacan

Tamal

Casserole

This dish is served at weddings and other celebrations in the small town of Sola de Vega in Oaxaca. It is a great winter party dish and works particularly well for brunches. When I make this dish I simmer the pork and chicken together, proceeding as for *Caldo de Pollo* (page 44), and use some of the cooking broth to steep the saffron.

FOR THE FILLING

½ cup dry sherry, heated
½ cup golden raisins
Large pinch of saffron threads
¼ cup warm broth (see head-
note) or chicken stock
2 medium-large ripe, red tomatoes, roasted (see page 14)
and peeled
1 small onion, coarsely cut up
(about ½ cup)
2 garlic cloves, peeled
¼ cup vegetable oil
3 cups shredded cooked chicken
(meat from one 3½-pound
chicken)
1 pound cooked pork butt,
shredded
2 teaspoons ground true (Ceylon) cinnamon (see page 15),
preferably freshly ground in a
spice grinder, or ¾ teaspoon
ground U.S. "cinnamon"
Salt and freshly ground black
pepper to taste
1 cup toasted (see page 35) slivered blanched almonds

FOR THE MASA MIXTURE

¼ teaspoon saffron threads or to
taste
1½ cups warm broth or chicken
stock or as needed
1½ cups coarsely ground fresh
masa (see page 49), or 2 cups
masa harina reconstituted by
beating it with 2 to 2½ cups
warm water or chicken stock
(page 51)
1½ cups cooked (see page 43) or
drained canned chick peas,
skins removed
2 hard-boiled large egg yolks
2 teaspoons ground true (Ceylon) cinnamon, preferably
freshly ground in a spice
grinder, or ¾ teaspoon U.S.
"cinnamon"
½ cup lard (see page 19)
Salt and sugar to taste

TO COAT THE BAKING DISH

Butter
½ cup fine dry bread crumbs

For the filling, first pour the hot sherry over the raisins in a small bowl and let steep at least 15 minutes. Crumble the saffron into the warm broth or stock and let sit.

Puree the roasted tomatoes in a blender or food processor fitted with the steel blade, together with the onion and garlic. Heat the vegetable oil in a large skillet or sauté pan until very hot but not quite smoking. Add the tomato puree, reduce the heat to medium, and simmer, stirring occasionally, until slightly concentrated, about 5 minutes. Add the shredded chicken and pork, raisins and any remaining sherry, saffron and broth, and cinnamon. Season with salt and pepper. Cook over medium-high heat, stirring occasionally, until the liquid has evaporated and the flavors are well blended. Let cool to room temperature.

For the dough, crumble the saffron into the warm broth or stock and let steep a few minutes. Working in three batches, place the *masa,* chick peas, egg yolks, cinnamon, and saffron and broth in a blender or food processor fitted with the steel blade and blend with an on/off motion until smoothly pureed.

Beat the lard in a large bowl with an electric mixer on medium speed until very light and fluffy. Beat in the *masa*–chick pea mixture a little at a time, and continue beating until very well combined. Taste for seasoning; beat in a little salt and sugar.

To assemble, preheat the oven to 325°F. Butter a 13 × 9-inch Pyrex baking dish and sprinkle on all sides with a few tablespoons of the toasted bread crumbs; reserve the remainder.

Wet your hands in cold water and spread half the *masa* mixture across the bottom of the baking dish. Add the toasted almonds to the meat filling; pour the filling over the *masa* mixture and spread evenly.

Top with the remaining *masa* mixture; spread evenly and sprinkle with the remaining toasted breadcrumbs.

Bake until a knife inserted into the middle comes out clean, about 45 minutes. Serve with *Salsa Ranchera* (page 308) or *Caldillo de Tomate* (page 36).

YIELD: 8 SERVINGS

ALCAPARRADO DE POLLO

Chicken with
Caper Sauce

In this traditional Oaxacan sauce the capers have a surprisingly delicate effect in combination with the toasted pumpkin seeds, saffron, and aromatic seasonings. Ideally it would be made with Oaxacan oregano.

⅛ teaspoon saffron threads

1½ cups warm Caldo de Pollo
(see page 44)

5 to 6 tablespoons vegetable oil

3 ounces shelled raw pumpkin
seeds (about ¾ cup)

1½ tablespoons olive oil

1 small onion, coarsely chopped
(about ½ cup)

1 garlic clove, coarsely chopped

1 small crusty roll, cut into slices

4 black peppercorns

3 cloves

1 piece (1 inch) true (Ceylon) cinnamon (see page 15) or ¼
teaspoon ground U.S. "cinnamon"

½ teaspoon dried Mexican
oregano (see page 11)

6 ounces capers (2 small jars,
with brine)

Salt and freshly ground black
pepper to taste

1 chicken (3½ pounds), cut into
serving pieces

Crumble the saffron threads into the chicken stock and let steep a few minutes.

Heat 1 tablespoon of the vegetable oil in a medium-size skillet over medium-high heat until very hot but not quite smoking. Add the pumpkin seeds (carefully, since they tend to pop violently as they hit the hot oil). Cook, stirring constantly, until they are puffed and have a nutty fragrance, about 30 seconds. Do not let them burn or they will turn the whole dish bitter. Drain on paper towels.

In the same skillet, heat the olive oil over medium heat until very hot. Add the chopped onion and garlic and cook, stirring, 3 to 5 minutes. Add the sliced roll and cook, stirring, until golden brown on both sides. Add the peppercorns, cloves, cinnamon, and oregano and cook, stirring, until their aroma is released, about 2 minutes longer. Add the capers with their brine and stir well to combine. Simmer, uncovered, for 5 minutes on low heat; add the chicken stock with the saffron and simmer another 5 minutes.

Place the contents of the skillet in a blender and blend until well pureed, about 30 seconds. Add the pumpkin seeds and puree another 30 seconds.

Preheat the oven to 350°F.

Heat the remaining 3 to 4 tablespoons vegetable oil in a large, heavy skillet over medium heat until rippling. Salt and pepper the chicken pieces; brown well on both sides, a few at a time. Use a little more oil if necessary. Drain the chicken pieces on paper towels as they are browned.

Place the browned chicken pieces in a shallow baking dish. Pour

the sauce over the chicken, cover with aluminum foil, and bake until the chicken is tender, about 40 minutes.
YIELD: 4 SERVINGS

NOTE: This sauce is also delicious with grilled or broiled fish. Cook the fish separately and serve the sauce on the side.

CARNERO ENCHILADO

Lamb with Guajillo Chile Sauce

As I ate it in Oaxaca, this dish was blazing hot from the very strong guajillo chiles they have there. The guajillos we get in the North, and also the ones in the United States, are much milder, so you are not likely to set your hair on fire, though of course you could reduce the amount of chiles if you have qualms.

4 to 6 ounces dried chiles, either guajillo, ancho, or Anaheim (see pages 223–225)
4 garlic cloves, peeled
1 piece (2 inches) true (Ceylon) cinnamon (see page 15), or 1 teaspoon ground U.S. "cinnamon"
6 cloves
12 black peppercorns
1 cup water
2 tablespoons vegetable oil

2 pounds lean boneless lamb, cut into bite-sized cubes
1 medium-size onion, sliced (about 1 cup)
3 medium-large boiling potatoes (Red Bliss or other thin-skinned variety), about 1¼ pounds, peeled and cut into ½-inch slices
Salt and freshly ground black pepper to taste

Rinse the chiles thoroughly under cold running water, removing the seeds and veins. Heat a griddle or cast-iron skillet until a drop of water sizzles on contact. Place the chiles on the griddle and heat, turning once or twice, just until the aroma is released, 1 to 2 minutes. Be very careful not to burn them or the dish will be bitter. Place the chiles in a bowl or saucepan and cover with boiling water. Let soak until somewhat softened, about 10 minutes.

Drain, then place the chiles in a blender with 2 of the garlic cloves, the cinnamon, cloves, peppercorns, and water. Process until pureed, about 1 minute. With a wooden spoon or pusher, force the puree through a medium-mesh sieve, discarding the solids. Set aside.

In large, heavy saucepan or Dutch oven, heat the oil over medium-high heat until very hot but not quite smoking. Add the lamb cubes, onion, and remaining garlic and cook, stirring often, until the meat is browned on all sides, about 5 minutes. Drain off as much excess grease as possible. Pour in the chile mixture and add the potatoes. Season with salt and pepper. Simmer, covered, over low heat until the lamb is tender but not overcooked, about 25 minutes.

YIELD: 4 TO 6 SERVINGS

BUÑUELOS OAXAQUEÑOS

Oaxacan
Sweet Fritters

The Guelaguetza, also called Lunes del Cerro (Monday of the Hill), is held on the Cerro del Fortín in Oaxaca in July. In pre-Hispanic times it was one of the celebrations in which the Indian peoples honored the deity of corn, Centeotl, and prayed for good harvests. Like other pagan traditions, it survived by becoming mixed with Catholic practices. Even now members of the pre-Columbian civilizations would recognize parts of the celebration. During the festival the whole city parties, and magnificent cultural events are staged. Mixtec, Zapotec, Mazatec, Mixe Indians, and others converge on Oaxaca in native dress, bringing offerings of the foods they grow or products that they make. They dance the distinctive dances of each region, and then go to present the offerings to the local government officials. At the conclusion of the ceremonies they deliver the offerings to Centeotl—by throwing them at the stage!

A charming tradition is the stands set up around the cathedral where people go, mostly at night, to drink *atole,* the sweetened Mexican corn gruel, and eat the crispy pastries called *buñuelos*. The *buñuelos* are served in pottery bowls, either *roseados,* sprinkled with cane sugar syrup, or *ahogados,* "drowned" in the syrup. After finishing the *buñuelos,* you make a wish and throw the bowl against the cathedral wall. I think it works. My wish was partly granted.

Buñuelos are a traditional Christmas treat as well.

2 cups water

1 teaspoon aniseed

1 tablespoon sugar

Husks of 6 fresh tomatillos (if available)

2 pounds unbleached all-purpose flour (about 7½ cups)

1 teaspoon baking powder

½ teaspoon salt

4 large eggs

½ cup lard (see page 19) or vegetable shortening, at room temperature

Oil for deep-frying

Cinnamon sugar made with true (Ceylon) cinnamon (see page 15)

Bring the water to a boil in a small saucepan with the anise, sugar, and tomatillo husks. Reduce the heat to medium and simmer until reduced by half. Strain and let cool.

Sift the flour with the baking powder and salt into a large bowl. Make a well in the center and put in the eggs, anise tea, and lard. Work together with your hands until the mixture begins to form a dough. Knead the dough vigorously on a lightly floured surface, slapping it down on the work surface several times, until smooth and blistered. Let rest in a warm place, covered with a damp cloth, for 2 hours.

Lightly flour a rolling pin and work surface. Shape the dough into 20 balls. Keeping them covered with a damp cloth before and after working with them, roll out each into an 8- to 10-inch circle.

Choose a large, deep, heavy saucepan or deep-fryer; add oil to a depth of 3 inches, heat to 375°F, and deep-fry the *buñuelos* one at a time until golden, 1 to 2 minutes in all for each. Be careful not to let the temperature of the oil fluctuate while frying the *buñuelos*. Drain on paper towels; sprinkle while still hot with the cinnamon sugar.

YIELD: 20 FRITTERS

CHIAPAS

Chiapas is Mexico's southernmost state and its wildest, most remote region. The Spanish influence penetrated later there than most places. Looking at the fantastic geography of impassable mountains and canyons, you can see why. Even now Chiapas seems like a land of the Mayas, who ruled there for centuries. There are parts where hardly anyone speaks Spanish and you mainly hear the Mayan dialects, Tzotzil and Tzeltal. The sense of having traveled back in time strikes almost the instant you arrive.

My first glimpse of the state is the capital, Tuxtla Gutiérrez, a medium-sized city that strikes me as not old enough to be picturesque and not young enough to be modern. But how friendly everyone is! It is like a homely woman with a lovely smile. At once I sense something different and older-seeming about the vegetation here—not many trees, but the ones I see are strangely gnarled.

I am surrounded with hospitable and helpful people. A friend of my stepfather's eagerly introduces me to the many kinds of tamales in different leaf and husk wrappings for which Chiapas is renowned. Herb sellers in the market explain unfamiliar items. The owner of Las Pichanchas restaurant, which features specialties of Chiapas like game and the famous sausages, takes time to show me native fauna, from jaguars to crocodiles and quetzales (the iridescent-feathered birds worshipped by the pre-Columbian civilizations) at the Tuxtla Gutiérrez zoo. Experts at a big botanical research project tell me the correct scientific names of plants I ask about.

This will be my jumping-off point for a journey to the oldest city of Chiapas. This is San Cristóbal de las Casas, named for St. Christopher and for the Spanish bishop Bartolomé de las Casas, who registered a dramatic early protest against the slaughter and enslavement of the Indians. Nothing has prepared me either for San Cristóbal or for the route that takes me there. We come to the celebrated Cañon del Sumidero, where we are taken on a boat ride between majestic, towering walls of rock that rise almost beyond eyesight. I do not even think of being frightened; I am awestruck. We drive farther and farther into a terrain composed of mountains and rain forests, where switchbacks and dizzying ups and downs become even more treacherous every afternoon when it rains.

Our first intimation of the ancient culture we are entering comes as we start to notice scattered masses of impossibly vibrant color dotted throughout the landscape along the snaking road. We don't realize at first that the brilliant clusters are groups of people wearing their own everyday folk art, the famous woven cloth of the Chiapas highlands. The most striking notes are turquoise, lavender, and a kind of shocking pink, repeated everywhere in women's *huipiles* (a kind of overblouse) and men's fantastic vests and hatbands. No one can begin to describe the knowledge, skill, and passion that the women of these remote mountains pour into their weaving.

The Chiapanecans are considered among the greatest of Mexican weavers, if not *the* greatest. Years later I read a phrase that seemed to sum up their art: "The Tzotzil and Tzeltal women weavers produce clothes that cover their bodies but reveal their soul." No woman is considered marriageable until she has mastered every kind of garment. There is one local legend that the Virgin taught them to weave, but actually this craft reached great heights long before Christianity was introduced to Mexico, and the traditional patterns repeat motifs that are found in ancient Mayan art. The ritual aspect of weaving is still powerful; it is a vehicle of honor and celebration. I remember family friends from Chiapas telling us of a bishop of the diocese who was celebrating the silver anniversary of his ordination. The women of one village wove him an entire cape and soutane in their own patterns—every village has its own patterns that belong nowhere else. You feel as if the designs must be part of the gene pool.

We reach San Cristóbal by a dizzying descent into a high mountain valley. It is another time-travel experience, a small sixteenth-century city that is hard to relate to an old-new hybrid like Tuxtla. I have been lucky enough to secure lodging at the fascinating anthropological museum cum guest house, Na Bolom. A stay there is an education. Na Bolom is dedicated to the Indian peoples of Chiapas, and even the guest rooms have striking examples of the village weavings and artifacts. There is an important library used by visiting scholars from around the world, and a unique collection of religious art.

Of course I head as soon as possible for the market, my inevitable window on the soul of any Mexican city I visit. It is early morning when I set out from Na Bolom. It has rained during the light, and the cobblestones glimmer in the translucent mountain light. The air is crisp and cool. Everywhere I see women in the

ancestral pinks and lavenders sweeping sidewalks in front of their pink and turquoise-painted houses. The ritual of sweeping, by the way, is zealously carried out all over Mexico and is said to have been traced back to pre-Columbian ceremonies of temple sweeping. According to the scholar Jacques Soustelle, "in sweeping one opened the way for the gods." The sight of handmade twig brooms sweeping dampened dirt floors is one of my oldest memories from the ranch.

The market on first glance is small compared to the immense Mercado Juárez in Oaxaca, and far from picture-pretty. At first it is something of a disappointment—few colorful displays of toys and crafts, no every-day-a-holiday atmosphere. But then I start to see the rich offerings of local fruits and vegetables, and the little stands selling different foods. It is not easy to communicate with people since few of the vendors from the villages speak Spanish. I watch, full of questions but not able to put them to anyone.

Little girls in miniature replicas of their mothers' village costumes are there, selling wristbands of braided colored threads. A young man comes along in a vest of blinding pink and turquoise and a hat decorated with long ribbons of bright yellow, red, pink, and green. Anyone from the area would know at once that he has just come from the village of San Juan Chamula along with the merchandise he's pulling—four squealing piglets, all somehow tied up with one rope. It makes quite a picture. I catch sight of a woman in a shawl that seems related to the vest, repeating and somehow altering the same colors. As soon as I admire it she takes if off and I realize she is asking how much I would pay for it. But it is damp and chilly and I say I couldn't possibly deprive her of it.

I come to a pottery vendor who sells me a small mug, then to a woman selling chocolate and breads. She speaks Spanish, and I sit talking with her for a long time over a cup of chocolate and a piece of sweet bread. For some reason we get on the subject of corn-planting traditions, and discover that many of them are amazingly similar in her home state and mine.

She is a San Cristóbal *mestizo* woman, not one of the village Indians who travel miles to this market, and her little stand is typical of many here and around the country in its simplicity. It consists of a small table covered with oilcloth (red, with once-blue and yellow roses faded almost to a memory now) and an old Coca-Cola tray full of little pressed rounds of chocolate freshly ground with almonds and sugar. There is a glass display box full of sweet breads in a characteristic oval shape. That is the entire business. When I comment on the funny resemblance of the breads to the shape of a gigantic anchovy can, she tells me I'm not far wrong: The bread is made in sardine cans called *portolas*. Even in this stronghold of *indígenas* (native peoples), elements of different cultures mingle unexpectedly. The small altar at the back of the stand is another lesson in the same process: St. Anthony framed by vases of beautiful fresh flowers and a small votive candle—and just beneath the saint's picture a bright red good-luck charm with a scapulary and a lucky eye-shaped nut to ward off evil spirits. The best of Catholic and pagan, just in case.

I have come at the time of a major local festival, the feast of the city's patron, St. Christopher. The celebration begins a week before St. Christopher's day, July 25. Each of the seven major Indian villages of the region is in charge of conducting one procession at dawn to the church of San Cristóbal, to pay homage at the altar. The town band leads the way as the entourage carries the statue of the saint to the church, which is decorated for the day in the village colors. The last ten steps of the church are covered with fresh pine boughs, so that the purifying fragrance is released as you step on them.

St. Christopher's feast itself is one of the most beautiful fiestas I remember. We start out from Na Bolom at night, our way lighted by the *castillos* (revolving fireworks mounted on high towers) that punctuate every Mexican celebration like great pinwheels of fire.

It is a steep climb to the church, up hundreds of cobbled steps with (luckily) several landings where you can buy something to eat or drink. There are the inevitable and great roasted ears of corn with chile and lime juice. I stop to buy some *ponche*—not the innocent milkshakelike drink I grew to detest in Guadalajara, but a potent hot toddy made with pineapple, ginger, a cinnamon infusion, and a hefty dose of *aguardiente* (cane liquor) with *marque-*

sote, a type of pound cake, crumbled into it. We reach the top out of breath and flushed from the altitude, the exertion, and the liquor.

The church grounds are narrow and crowded, surrounded by a low wall to keep people from falling off the steep edge. Musicians are everywhere, playing different songs. People are dancing to the strains of a tropical band behind the church. Everybody is drinking too much, but nothing gets out of hand. We see many French and German tourists, few Americans. (Na Bolom's founders, Frans and Gertrude Blom, have created great interest in the Indian cultures of Chiapas among Europeans, but so far San Cristóbal has not attracted a great American throng.) I see games in progress, primitive games of chance like coin-tossing and a board game called *la lotería,* featuring cards divided into areas with pictured images like parrots, coins, soldiers. Each is called out as it is drawn and a bean is placed over that part of the card. Whoever fills his card up first wins.

I explore the beautifully arranged candy stands and their wares—*tejocotes en almíbar,* small syrup-drenched fruits that are said to be from a kind of hawthorn. They have little pulp and a large woody core that absorbs all the *aguardiente* syrup. *Cocadas,* blocks of snowy white coconut candy with shocking pink edges. *Jamoncillos* ("little hams"), pralinelike candies with a perfect pecan half in the center. I can't go away without trying the chicle gums displayed in tutti-frutti colors. Then there's the *churros* stand, where the woman is squeezing a batter through a pastry star-tube into hot oil and fishing out the crisp, ridged pastries to roll them in sugar—greasy and sweet and delicious. (Down in the plaza they sell a version of the same thing filled with chocolate.)

At last I go into the church and am overwhelmingly moved. It is lit with thousands of votive candles. Flowers are everywhere. At the foot of the altar an Indian family forms one of those incredible

blazes of color I will always associate with this part of Chiapas: They are holding bright red gladioli and wearing shocking pink shawls and vests. The man is on one knee, hat in hand, with the multicolored ribbons sweeping the floor. To one side of the altar four elderly men play religious songs on a worn harp, an out-of-tune violin, and two guitars. The melody pulls at my heart. Then I hear another note. It is a bird singing. Someone has left a cage with a *chonte,* a mockingbird, in front of the statue of the saint. I walk up and read the note fastened to the cage.

"Thank you for granting me special favors. I have nothing to give you but this song."

I kneel and bless myself and thank God for letting me be a part of it.

TAMALES REALES

"Royal"

Tamales

Why "royal?" Perhaps because they are elegant miniature tamales, on the expensive side because of the saffron. These fragrant morsels are a delicious hot party snack or hors d'oeuvre. I am a spendthrift with saffron and probably would use about 2 teaspoons.

Before beginning the preparation, see Tamales (pages 51–53) and decide on a steamer arrangement. This makes an army-sized amount; the recipe can easily be halved.

1 pound dried corn husks (see page 7)

1¼ cups golden raisins

1 scant cup dry sherry, heated

3 pounds fresh masa (see page 49) or an equivalent amount of reconstituted masa made by mixing 4½ cups masa harina with 4 to 5 cups warm Caldo de Pollo (page 44)

1 pound lard (see page 19)

1 teaspoon saffron threads, or to taste

1 cup lukewarm chicken stock, or as needed

2 teaspoons salt, or to taste

Place the corn husks in a large bowl or saucepan and cover with boiling water. Let soak for at least 1 hour.

In a small bowl, soak the raisins in the hot sherry until fully plumped, 20 to 30 minutes.

Prepare the *tamal* filling with the remaining ingredients, following directions for Basic Tamal Dough on page 50 but crumbling the saffron into 1 cup tepid chicken stock and letting it steep several minutes before beating it into the dough along with salt to taste. Add a little more stock if necessary. When the mixture is very light and silky, beat in the raisins with any remaining sherry.

Drain the corn husks. Discard the crinkled ones that are full of corn silk. Tear the husks lengthwise into pieces 2 to 2½ inches wide at the narrow end. (Pieces that are too narrow can be overlapped with each other). Form the tamales by putting about 1 tablespoon of the *masa*-raisin mixture on the lower (wider) half of each piece and rolling the husk up like a miniature cigar toward the narrow end to enclose the filling. Fold the *tamal* in the center to bring the two open ends of the cigar next to each other. If the edges are very uneven, trim them with scissors.

Arrange the tamales, open ends up, in a steamer basket or other steamer arrangement, leaning them against each other closely enough so that they will stay fairly upright. Steam, tightly covered, replenishing with boiling water if necessary, until the dough separates cleanly from the husk of a test *tamal,* 40 to 45 minutes.

YIELD: ABOUT 6 DOZEN TAMALES

BUTIFARRIA

Chiapas Sausage

The state of Chiapas is known for *embutidos,* sausages of all kinds. This is a classic example. It is traditionally served cold with a spicy sauce. Sometimes the sliced sausage is covered with mayonnaise and rolled in minced parsley. However, when we make it at the restaurant or for catered parties, we serve it hot with either the chipotle sauce from *Tortas Ahogadas* (see page 137) and grilled scallions or *Mole Estilo Oaxaca* (page 244). Usually I fill it into a long sausage casing to make one big ring and poach or braise it, but it is also good formed into patties and browned in lard or oil.

This is not a type of sausage that demands a high amount of fat. A mixture like ordinary ground pork from the market is fine.

I grind the bay leaf to a powder in a spice mill. If you don't have one, don't try doing it with a mortar and pestle; you will end up with sharp little pieces. It is better to make an infusion by boiling 1 cup of water and 5 to 6 bay leaves down to a few tablespoons and add the liquid to the mixture along with the brandy.

1 teaspoon aniseed
2 pounds ground pork, or a mixture of pork and beef
1 tablespoon freshly ground black pepper
2 large garlic cloves, minced
½ cup brandy
2 teaspoons salt, or to taste
½ teaspoon freshly grated nutmeg
1 sprig fresh thyme, leaves only, or ½ teaspoon dried

1 sprig fresh Mexican oregano, chopped (see page 11), or ½ teaspoon dried
2 bay leaves, ground to a fine powder in a spice grinder, any larger bits sifted out in a strainer and discarded
Juice of 1 lemon or lime
Sausage casings, optional

Toast the aniseed in a small, heavy skillet over medium heat, stirring constantly, just until the aroma is released, about 1 minute. Remove from the heat.

Place the ground meat in a large bowl. Add the toasted anise and all the remaining seasonings. Combine well with your hands. Let the mixture rest overnight in the refrigerator, tightly covered. The next day, fill into sausage casings (twist or tie at intervals with butcher's twine to make any desired size sausages, and tie securely at ends) or shape into patties the size of breakfast sausage cakes.

To cook sausages in casings, first prick in several places with a sharp knife, then either poach or braise. To poach, heat a large saucepan of water to boiling, add the sausages, and simmer, uncovered, over low heat for about 12 minutes. To braise, heat about 1 to 1½ cups water to a boil in a large heavy skillet over medium heat. Add the sausage and cook, covered, checking a few times, until the water is completely evaporated and the meat has partly rendered its fat. Continue to cook the sausage in its own fat, uncovered, turning once or twice, until well browned on both sides. Slice and serve hot with any preferred sauce or (as is done in Chiapas) let cool before slicing.

To cook patties, cook a few at a time in a little lard or vegetable oil (1 teaspoon for 4 patties) heated to rippling in a large or medium-size skillet over medium heat. Brown well on both sides, about 4 to 5 minutes per side. Be sure they are cooked through. Serve at once.

YIELD: 4 SERVINGS AS A FIRST COURSE, MORE AS AN APPETIZER

CHILES SERRANOS CURTIDOS

Pickled
Serrano Chiles

This recipe was given to me by the owner of a small taco stand in San Cristóbal de las Casas. It is very fiery—unusual in that it contains fresh ginger. Chiapas is one of the few states that use ginger. If serrano chiles are not available, substitute jalapeños.

2 pounds serrano chiles (see page 226)
5 tablespoons olive oil
5 garlic cloves, peeled
1 large onion, sliced into thin half-moons (about 2 cups)
10 cloves
1 stick (3 inches) true (Ceylon) cinnamon (see page 15), or 1 piece (1-inch) U.S. "cinnamon"

2 sprigs fresh thyme or 1 teaspoon dried
2 sprigs fresh Mexican oregano (see page 11) or 1 teaspoon dried
1 chunk fresh ginger (about 1 inch long), peeled and cut into slices
4 cups distilled white vinegar
1 tablespoon kosher salt

Rinse the chiles thoroughly under cold running water. Cut the tops off; prick the chiles in several places with a fork to help the flavors penetrate.

In a deep stainless-steel or enameled sauté pan or wide saucepan, heat the oil over high heat until rippling. Add the whole garlic cloves and cook, stirring, until golden, crushing lightly with the back of a wooden spoon. Add the onion, spices, herbs, and ginger and cook, stirring, until the onion is translucent but still slightly crunchy, about 2 minutes. Add the chiles and cook for 5 minutes, stirring often.

Meanwhile, heat the vinegar to a boil in a stainless-steel or enameled saucepan. Add to the chile-onion mixture, let boil, and stir in the salt. Pour into sterilized jars and seal according to manufacturer's directions. Or let cool and pour into ordinary refrigerator containers.

YIELD: ABOUT 4 PINTS

MOLE DE OLLA

Soup-Style

Mole

There was a small restaurant in San Cristóbal de las Casas called ¡Caldos! ¡Caldos! ¡Caldos! (Soups! Soups! Soups!) owned by a native of Mexico City, Jorge Ponce. All he served was two soups: a *puchero*—a delicious tripe stew similar to the *menudo* of the North—and this fabulous *mole de olla*. He graciously gave me his mother's recipe and I was thrilled to discover, when I finally made it, that it tasted exactly as I remembered.

In this case *mole* has a different meaning than the richly sauced dishes that usually go by that name. It is a hearty soup full of fresh vegetables, a perfect one-dish meal. The only drawback is that the vegetables must be separately cooked just until they are done.

In Mexico people often gild the lily by adding some *Arroz a la Mexicana* (see page 94) to the soup along with freshly made corn tortillas. A fresh salsa or two is great if you want to spice up the soup when it is served (try *Pico de Gallo Norteño,* page 40, or *Salsa Cruda de Tomatillo,* page 41). I consider the epazote integral to this dish—you can substitute fresh cilantro, but it will not be the same.

4 large ripe, red tomatoes, about 2 pounds

10 guajillo or dried red Anaheim chiles (see pages 225 and 223)

5 ancho chiles (see page 224)

1 medium-size onion (about 6 ounces), cut into 6 wedges

3 large garlic cloves

2 tablespoons lard (see page 19) or vegetable oil

3 pounds soup beef with bone in, either shin or short ribs

1 pound marrow bones (3 to 4 pieces)

4 quarts water

1 handful fresh epazote (see page 8) or ¼ cup dried

Salt and freshly ground black pepper to taste

1 pound new potatoes, scrubbed and cut in half

1 pound medium-size carrots, peeled and cut into thirds

4 medium-size turnips, peeled and quartered

1 pound fresh string beans, trimmed and strings removed if necessary

3 ears fresh or frozen corn, cut into thirds

1 pound zucchini, cut into 1½-inch slices

Heat a griddle or cast-iron skillet until a drop of water sizzles on contact. Roast the tomatoes until blackened on all sides. Place in a bowl to hold the juices; let cool, then peel. Set aside.

Rinse the chiles under cold running water, removing the seeds and veins. Heat a clean griddle or cast-iron skillet over high heat and place the chiles on the griddle a few at a time. Cook, turning once or twice, just until the aroma is released. Do not let them scorch! Remove as they are done. Place the toasted chiles in a bowl or saucepan and cover with boiling water. Let soak until softened, about 10 minutes. Drain well.

Working in batches if necessary, place the tomatoes, chiles, onion, and garlic in a blender or food processor fitted with the steel blade and process until pureed, adding water as needed. With a wooden spoon or pusher, force the puree through a medium-mesh sieve, discarding any solids.

Heat the lard or oil in a large Dutch oven or saucepan over medium-high heat until rippling. Add the chile puree and cook for 5 minutes, stirring occasionally. Add the meat, marrow bones, water, and epazote. Season with pepper and a little salt. Bring to a boil, reduce the heat to medium-low, and simmer, partly covered, until the meat is tender and broth is well-flavored, about 2 hours.

While the soup is cooking, cook each vegetable separately in a large saucepan of boiling water, cooking just until fork tender but still slightly crisp. As the vegetables are done, drain them at once, plunge into ice water to stop the cooking, and drain again. Set aside. The potatoes will take about 10 minutes to cook, the carrots and turnips 7 minutes, string beans 5 minutes, corn 3 minutes (add a minute or 2 if frozen), and zucchini 2 to 3 minutes.

Just before serving, add the vegetables to the soup and bring to a boil. Taste for seasoning and serve immediately.

YIELD: 8 TO 10 SERVINGS AS A MAIN COURSE

COCHITO CHIAPANECO

Chiapas-Style Roast Pork

This is one of my favorite pork dishes. It is sublime when made with suckling pig, because it has only a thin layer of meat that is quickly penetrated by the marinade. But a roasting cut of pork, such as Boston butt, is more practical for most people.

2½ pounds boneless pork butt
Vegetable oil or lard
1½ teaspoons salt, or to taste
1½ teaspoons freshly ground
    black pepper

FOR THE MARINADE
3 ancho chiles (see page 224),
    tops removed and seeded
5 garlic cloves, coarsely chopped
1 medium-size onion, coarsely
    chopped (about 1 cup)
1 chunk fresh ginger (about 1
    inch), peeled and coarsely
    chopped

¼ cup red wine vinegar or cider
    vinegar
½ cup dry sherry
1 small sprig fresh thyme or ¼
    teaspoon dried
1 large sprig fresh Mexican oreg-
    ano (see page 11) or ½ tea-
    spoon dried
1½ teaspoons ground allspice
1½ teaspoons sweet paprika
1½ teaspoons sugar
1 teaspoon salt, or to taste

Rub the meat all over with a few tablespoons of oil. Pierce at close intervals with the tip of a small, sharp knife. Rub thoroughly on all sides with the salt and pepper, rubbing them well into the incisions.

To prepare the marinade, place the ancho chiles in a bowl, cover with boiling water, and let soak until softened, about 10 minutes. Drain the chiles. Working in batches if necessary, puree the chiles, garlic, onion, and ginger in a blender with the vinegar, sherry, and all the seasonings. Rub the meat all over with the marinade, being sure that it penetrates into the incisions. Reserve any unused marinade. Let the meat marinate for 2 hours at room temperature or (preferably) overnight in the refrigerator.

Preheat the oven to 325°F.

Place the meat in a greased roasting pan and roast, basting with a little of the reserved marinade at 20-minute intervals, until a meat thermometer inserted into the roast registers a temperature of 160°F (pork is safe to eat at 140°F; most people prefer it at least 150°F), about 1 hour and 45 minutes.

YIELD: 4 TO 6 SERVINGS

YUCATÁN La Sobadora

I have learned much from the regional cuisine of Yucatán, a fantastic mixture of elements that still preserves both pre-Columbian cooking techniques of the Maya and a lot of influences that came with conquerors and traders from several parts of Europe. But I have to admit that my first-hand research trip was overshadowed by an entirely different experience. Every impression is filtered in my memory through a curtain of pain—real physical pain.

I am scarcely able to climb off the plane at Mérida airport. I can hardly walk as we emerge into the most paralyzing heat I can imagine. (It is early morning, but already the air hits your lungs like a blast furnace.) I am fresh from a disastrous, unplanned overnight stay at an airport in the state of Tabasco where, between lugging heavy purchases and sleeping on the airport floor, I somehow managed to wrench a muscle in my back. I am in agony, hardly able to take in the sight of the majestic *ciudad blanca* (white city) that is Mérida. My mother is with me, busily reminding me that she had warned me not to visit these parts in summer. Through my discomfort I half register the sunlit blaze of white buildings against a background of tropical vegetation, tall palm trees, and brilliant flowering plants.

I try to carry on in spite of the pain, but it's no good. Eventually I tell my mother that I think we need a *sobador,* a healer who cures pain by rubbing joints and muscles. I suppose the market is probably the best place to find one. So we make our way to the indescribable heat of the Mérida market. Everybody there is equipped with a real fan (I see pretty ones made out of paper flowers) or some kind of substitute like a palm leaf, a piece of newspaper, or a rag they twirl every once in a while. Even if fanning just moves the heat around, it's probably better than nothing. Despite my misery, I am amazed by the classic Maya faces on all sides—wide and flat, shining darkly like ebony, large-skulled. The Méridens are large, heavy, but not muscular, as if they sat a lot. This is understandable.

The market is not a beautiful wide square like others I've visited, but dusty and warrenlike. Many of the sellers are unceremoniously crowded into alleys and crooked passageways. Vendors seated on stools or on the ground are selling a kind of *tamal* unfamiliar to me, large (about six inches square) and soft, almost gooey inside. Hobbling through the labyrinth, I encounter people selling lizards, fabulous bright-colored birds, tropical fruits that look like hand grenades. There are medicine shows, but no *sobador*. We ask everywhere and receive a faintly suspicious response. No one is eager to share information with the strangers. Finally we obtain an address far away from the center of town in a new *colonia*. Our instructions are to go at dusk. We have no choice but to wait, pain or no pain.

The mission is a wild goose chase. We reach the area all right, a neighborhood of neat, well-kept houses in streets eerily empty at that hour, but cannot find the address. So we flag down a cab to get back to center city, and I ask the cab driver if he knows a *sobador*. Bingo! He knows old Ruperta Loeza, just the person, a *sobadora* in great demand who happens to live next to his parents. She is healer, midwife, wise woman. He undertakes to bring me to her the next morning at five, before the line forms at her place.

I sleep, after a fashion. We get up early and arrive at the *sobadora*'s as planned, but we are already too late. Even at this hour there are four other patients ahead of us, with no place to wait. But the cab driver's family welcomes us in for some coffee. None for me, though—they tell me to see the healer on an empty stomach. When my turn comes Ruperta's granddaughter comes next door to get me. She's no spring chicken herself, for Doña Ruperta is about ninety.

It is still dark. The Loeza house does not look ancient from outside, but its interior is primitive, with a dirt floor. People are still asleep in hammocks in the bedroom. The granddaughter ushers me behind a screen to undress and has me lie down on a much used piece of cardboard.

Ruperta comes in. I see a tiny woman, very thin and frail, in one of the long embroidered Yucatecan tunics. Thin gray hair, more than waist-length, haloes her flat, deeply lined Mayan face. Her skin is papery. Yet she is glowing. She tells me to lie down with my hands by my sides. Then her hands begin to move over my back, hands with the strength of a woman a third of her age. She manipulates different muscles in turn, firmly grasping folds of skin as her hands search for the right one. It is excruciating. Suddenly I feel a tremendous pull, and something releases deep inside my back like a rubber band, with a horrible *sprong*.

And that's all there is to it. I am still in pain, but something is obviously different. Doña Ruperta doesn't stand on ceremony—the next patient is waiting. She tells me to get up and get dressed, and when I ask about the fee, tells me to pay whatever I want.

I am not sure what's supposed to happen next, but Ruperta ushers me out with a succinct explanation: "You will feel pain for three days. Then you will be well."

She is as good as her word.

PAPADZULES

Tortillas in Pumpkin-Seed Sauce with Hard-Boiled Eggs

Every time I make this recipe I think of Craig Claiborne, because he loves this dish. It took me a while to try it because I am not a fancier of hard-boiled eggs, but in this case they are delicious. The pumpkin seeds and eggs have a lovely buttery effect together. The epazote is crucial, by the way—don't try to substitute anything else. This is a case of "Don't make the dish if you can't get the right ingredient."

In Yucatán the pumpkin-seed sauce is made in a different way; the sautéed ground seeds are soaked in water and squeezed between your hands in a lengthy process. Like the almonds in Arabic or medieval European cookery, pumpkin seeds contain a jelling agent that is brought out by grinding and soaking.

2 tablespoons lard (see page 19)
   or vegetable oil
1 cup shelled raw pumpkin seeds
2 cups Caldo de Pollo (page 44)
¼ cup chopped fresh epazote
   leaves (see page 8) or
   2 tablespoons dried
2 fresh chiles, either jalapeño or
   serrano (see pages 225 and
   226), or to taste

¼ cup vegetable oil
Salt to taste
8 thin commercial corn tortillas
3 large hard-boiled eggs, minced
Salsa de Tomate Asado (see
   page 316) or Salsa Ranchera
   (page 308)

Preheat the oven to 375°F.

Heat the lard or oil in a heavy, medium-size skillet until very hot but not quite smoking. Add the pumpkin seeds all at once and cook over high heat, stirring and shaking the pan constantly, until the seeds pop, about 3 minutes. Be careful—they tend to fly like unguided missiles! Do not let them burn, or the entire dish will be bitter; discard any that have gotten dark.

Place the fried pumpkin seeds, the chicken stock, epazote, and chiles in a blender and process until pureed. Pour the puree into a medium-size saucepan, season with salt, and bring to a boil. Reduce the heat to low and simmer for 5 minutes.

Heat the vegetable oil in a small saucepan over high heat until rippling. With tongs, dip the tortillas in the oil one at a time to soften them. Do not let them brown; lift out onto paper towels as they are done. Dip each tortilla in the pumpkin-seed sauce. Place a little of the minced hard-boiled eggs in the center of each and roll the tortillas around the egg. Place in an 8 × 8-inch baking dish, cover with the remaining sauce, and bake until heated through, about 12 minutes. Serve with a dab of the *salsa de tomate* or *salsa ranchera*.

YIELD: 4 SERVINGS

ADOBO PIBIL

Pibil-Style Achiote Marinade

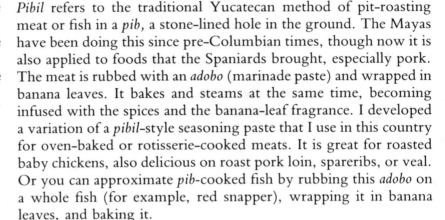

Pibil refers to the traditional Yucatecan method of pit-roasting meat or fish in a *pib,* a stone-lined hole in the ground. The Mayas have been doing this since pre-Columbian times, though now it is also applied to foods that the Spaniards brought, especially pork. The meat is rubbed with an *adobo* (marinade paste) and wrapped in banana leaves. It bakes and steams at the same time, becoming infused with the spices and the banana-leaf fragrance. I developed a variation of a *pibil*-style seasoning paste that I use in this country for oven-baked or rotisserie-cooked meats. It is great for roasted baby chickens, also delicious on roast pork loin, spareribs, or veal. Or you can approximate *pib*-cooked fish by rubbing this *adobo* on a whole fish (for example, red snapper), wrapping it in banana leaves, and baking it.

½ cup **Pasta de Achiote (see page 26)**
½ cup **fresh orange juice**
2 tablespoons **orange liqueur**
2 tablespoons **fresh lime juice**
2 large **garlic cloves, minced (about 1 tablespoon)**

¼ cup **honey**
2 tablespoons **cumin seed, briefly toasted in a skillet over medium heat and ground**
2 teaspoons **dried Mexican oregano (see page 11)**

Combine all the ingredients and mix thoroughly. Rub on meat, poultry, or fish and let sit overnight (or at least 2 to 3 hours) before cooking.

Can be stored, tightly covered, in refrigerator up to 10 days.
YIELD: ABOUT 2½ CUPS

ADOBO YUCATECO

Yucatecan Barbecue

I ate this with delicious pork chops at a hotel in Mérida. I often substitute country-style ribs here. The *adobo* can also be used to coat a pork loin roast (baste frequently with pan juices). I have used it with great results on baked chicken wings.

If you have no ancho chiles, substitute any dried chile except *chile árbol* or chipotle. For a hotter flavor, leave in the seeds and veins.

3 ancho chiles (see page 224), tops removed	**1 teaspoon dried Mexican oregano (see page 11)**
½ cup Pasta de Achiote (see page 26)	**¼ cup red wine vinegar**
½ cup fresh orange juice	**½ teaspoon sugar, optional**
2 garlic cloves, peeled	**1 teaspoon salt, or to taste**
	2 pounds country-style pork ribs or thick pork chops

Rinse the chiles under cold running water, removing the seeds and veins. Heat a griddle or cast-iron skillet over high heat until a drop of water sizzles on contact. Place the chiles on the griddle and heat until their aroma is released, 1 to 2 minutes on each side. Do not let them burn or they will make the dish horribly bitter. Place the toasted chiles in a small bowl or saucepan, cover with boiling water, and let soak until somewhat softened, about 10 minutes.

Place the softened chiles, achiote paste, orange juice, garlic, and oregano in a blender or food processor fitted with the steel blade and process for 1 minute. Scrape down the sides with a rubber spatula, add the vinegar, and process again until smooth. Taste for seasoning; add a little sugar, if desired, and the salt.

Rub the ribs or pork chops with the marinade and let rest in the refrigerator, covered, overnight (or for at least 4 hours).

Preheat the oven to 350°F. Choose a roasting pan large enough to allow a little space between the pieces and bake the ribs or chops until no pink shows in the center, 20 to 30 minutes.

YIELD: 4 SERVINGS

Variation:

Use 2½ to 3 pounds of chicken wings instead of pork ribs. Coat well with the marinade, let rest overnight or for at least 4 hours, and bake for about 45 minutes.

COCHINITA ESTILO PIBIL

Pibil-Style Pork

It may be a bit impractical for most people in this country to dig pits and roast whole suckling pigs or large cuts of pork as is done for the real *cochinita pibil* in Yucatán. But a good dish can be made with another approach: individual-sized portions wrapped in banana leaves with the appropriate seasonings and baked until tender. One thing that will definitely be different is the citrus flavor. The fruit that would be used in Yucatán is not like an orange, a lemon, or a lime, though it is called *lima*. It is sweeter than U.S. lemons and limes, so I substitute orange slices.

FOR EACH SERVING	Salt
1 large piece of banana leaf (see page 15)	2 to 3 tablespoons Pasta de Achiote (see page 26)
1 pork chop (about 6 ounces)	4 orange slices

Preheat the oven to 325°F.

Trim the banana leaf into a neat rectangle about 13 × 8 inches. From the trimmings, tear off a few strips to use as "string."

Rub the pork chop well with salt, then rub it generously on all sides with the achiote paste. Place 2 of the orange slices close to one end of the banana leaf; place the pork chop over them and the remaining orange slices on top. Fold the leaf up over the pork chop and around. Tuck in the ends neatly. (If it rips, fold another piece of banana leaf around it.) Tie securely with strips of leaf. Place on a baking sheet and bake for 35 to 40 minutes. Serve with *Escabeche de Cebolla* (page 282).

YIELD: 1 SERVING

PESCADO CON ESCABECHE

Fish with Escabeche

When I first discovered the *recados* of Yucatán, I tried different ways of using them with fish and came up with the following simple idea—red snapper or other fillets rubbed with *recado*, lightly grilled, and served topped with a vegetable *escabeche* that adds a wonderful dash of acidity. We serve it often as a special.

Salt
4 red snapper or swordfish fillets
   or boneless skate wings (6
   ounces each)
⅓ cup (approximately) Recado
   de Adobo Blanco (see page
   27) or Recado de Adobo Colorado (page 28)

Escabeche de Verduras or Escabeche de Cebolla (recipes
follow)

Lightly salt the fish fillets. Rub them all over with the *recado* and let rest in the refrigerator at least 1 hour, preferably 2.

Meanwhile, prepare the grill or preheat the broiler.

Grill or broil the fish for 2 to 3 minutes on each side, depending on the thickness. The fish should still be somewhat firm to the touch, not overcooked. Arrange on a serving plate and place the *escabeche* on top. Serve immediately.

YIELD: 4 SERVINGS

ESCABECHE DE VERDURAS

Pickled
Vegetables

I prefer to julienne the vegetables, but if time is short you can dice them instead. At Zarela we use this as a garnish on or an accompaniment to fish.

2 teaspoons aniseed
⅓ cup extra virgin olive oil
8 garlic cloves, peeled
1 large sprig fresh rosemary
   or ½ teaspoon dried
1 large sprig fresh thyme or
   ½ teaspoon dried
4 bay leaves
1 tablespoon black peppercorns
4 small carrots, peeled and finely
   julienned or diced

1 large red onion, cut into thin
   slivers (about 2 cups)
2 medium-size zucchini, finely
   julienned or diced
2 poblano chiles (see page 226),
   roasted (page 227), peeled,
   seeded, and julienned
Salt to taste
¾ cup red or white wine vinegar

Heat the aniseed in a small, heavy skillet over high heat, shaking the pan often, until toasted and fragrant, 3 to 5 minutes. Remove from the heat and set aside.

Heat the oil in a large skillet or sauté pan over high heat until very hot but not quite smoking. Add the garlic, fresh rosemary, fresh thyme, bay leaves, peppercorns, and carrots. Reduce the heat to medium-high and cook, stirring often, for 2 minutes. Add the onion, zucchini, and chiles and cook, stirring, for 2 minutes more. (If using dried rosemary and thyme, add along with the onion.) Season with salt. Add the vinegar and bring to a rapid boil. Remove at once from the heat. The vegetables should be somewhat crunchy. Stir in toasted aniseed and let cool.

Pour the *escabeche* into a nonreactive container (glass, stainless steel, glazed pottery) and let sit at room temperature, loosely covered, at least 2 to 3 hours before serving to meld the flavors. Serve at room temperature.

Can be stored, tightly covered, in the refrigerator for up to 1 week.

YIELD: ABOUT 4 CUPS; 4 TO 6 SERVINGS AS A SIDE DISH

ESCABECHE DE CEBOLLA

Pickled Red

Onion Garnish

¼ cup olive oil
8 garlic cloves, peeled
1 large sprig fresh rosemary or
 ½ teaspoon dried
1 large sprig fresh thyme or
 ½ teaspoon dried

2 bay leaves
1 tablespoon black peppercorns
2 medium-size red onions, thinly
 sliced (about 2 cups)
Salt to taste
½ cup red wine vinegar

Heat the oil in a medium-size skillet or sauté pan over medium-high heat until very hot but not quite smoking. Add the garlic, fresh rosemary, fresh thyme, bay leaves, and peppercorns. Stir to combine and cook, stirring, for 1 minute. Add the onions and cook, stirring, for 2 minutes. (If using dried rosemary and thyme, add along with the onions.) Season with salt and stir in the vinegar. Bring to a rapid boil and remove from the heat at once. The onions should still be slightly crunchy. You can serve it at once, but I would more often serve it at room temperature after giving the flavors a few hours to meld.

Can be stored, tightly covered, in the refrigerator for up to 1 week.

YIELD: ABOUT 2 CUPS

VERACRUZ

It is before nine in the morning when I stumble through the boarding procedure in Mérida, Yucatán, on my way to Veracruz. It is extremely hot, I am still taking it very easy on my back despite Doña Ruperta's amazing cure, and I am seldom at my best at such an hour anyway. I take my seat without paying much attention to my fellow passengers. When the stewardesses come by with beer, I take one, hoping the flight won't be too bad.

The next thing I know, a man stands up and shouts, *"¡Bomba!"* We are 30,000 feet over the Gulf of Mexico

While my brain is taking in this threat, the man recites a four-line stanza full of double entendres and fun. Everyone laughs and applauds. Someone else stands up and extemporaneously responds with another stanza ending with the first verse's first line. Three more stand up in turn and invent verses, each ending with a successive line of the first one. They complete a round and I feel much better.

I have loved some cities immediately, like Oaxaca, and found that others grow on me. Veracruz is the first one I loved before I set foot in it, just from the folks on the plane—who turn out to be a goodwill delegation from Veracruz to Havana, now on their way back home and whiling away the flight with one of the famous pastimes of the city. But I don't learn the mystery of the *bomba* until I've been there a bit.

The people of Veracruz, *jarochos* as they are popularly called, have the reputation of being the friendliest in all of Mexico. As we arrive I see that the city is not particularly beautiful. But it is still a busy, exciting port—the oldest in Mexico. It was here that Cortez landed from Cuba in 1519, and the city was Mexico's gateway to Europe for centuries. Today there are few foreign tourists but lots of Mexicans. Overwhelmed with the street bustle, I am astonished to see groups of smartly uniformed cadets everywhere I look—not ordinarily the first thing you notice in most Mexican cities, but Veracruz is a great naval base and home to a large naval academy.

The food of Veracruz is probably the most Spanish-influenced in Mexico, with much use of olive oil as well as olives and capers. Some dishes make you think of the Moorish and Persian elements in Spanish cooking, for example the mixture of flavors in the baked rice dish called *Budín de Arroz* (see page 293). The seafood of Veracruz is excellent, and the *Salsa Veracruzana* served with red snapper and other fish (see page 37) has become celebrated all over Mexico. (The city is also the home of a thriving seafood packing and canning industry.) I head for the famous Restaurant Pardiños, whose spinoff restaurant in Mexico City I already know. There and in other spots I have a wonderful time dining on shrimp served in coconut halves, tender baby octopus, and stuffed squid.

But meals are not the main memory I take away with me from Veracruz. The real adventure begins when I wander into the Zócalo and sit down in what turns out to be the best place in the city to take in the action.

What a scene! Musical duels between marimba bands. An old drunk dancing, unable to resist the beat, while people clap and urge him on. Waiters carrying well-worn pots in each hand—one full of steaming milk, the other of instant-energy coffee—to tables of old men exchanging stories and gossip in one well-populated corner of the Zócalo filled with the noise of spoons clicking against thick cups and calls for refills. This is La Parroquia, Veracruz's oldest café. They mostly sell sweet bread, flan, and their rightfully famous coffee. It is a Veracruz institution, practically a way of life. People come in at the same hour every day—for years, decades, most of a lifetime. They wouldn't dream of not showing up at the regular time, to sit for hours at the same table chewing the fat with the same crew of friends. There must be many like the incredibly aged Don Manuelito, who performs the same dignified shuffle to and from La Parroquia every day at the same time for an hour-and-a-half stint, led by his granddaughter and dressed in a white suit that stands out like a flag among the *guayaberas*—tropical shirts—favored by most people. ("Do you always dress all in white, Don Manuelito?" I inquired after we'd been introduced. "No," he replied, "in December and January I dress all in gray.") And it's

not just the old guard, either. Young men have their tables at La Parroquia as well.

Here is where I know I will learn something of the people of Veracruz. I ask an old man to tell me stories. Surprised, he asks, "What kind?" I tell him I want to hear whatever stories he has to tell. He points me to a table where an even older gent is holding court. "Go talk to him." Thus begin three enchanting days in the company of Paco Píldora, a political satirist, poet, and the most popular man in Veracruz. I hold the memory of these few days close to my heart.

Francisco Rivera, "Paco Píldora" to his readers, is a charming, learned man of nearly eighty who has been writing a column in verse for the newspaper in Veracruz since before I was born. I pump him for information about everything—politics, history, and the *bomba* of the plane. He replies with story after story of this city for which he serves as unofficial muse.

The delegation coming back from Cuba, Paco tells me, was nothing unusual. Havana and Veracruz are sister cities. There have been close ties since colonial times, when many Spaniards who had settled in Cuba moved on to Mexico. Veracruz music has the Cuban beat, and the subjects of the popular songs are the same in Havana and Veracruz.

The *bomba* was nothing out of the way, either. Paco explains that it is a word game played in many of the port cities. It belongs to the Mexican tradition of poetry extemporized on the spot. This is something that died out of most European cultures centuries ago. But in parts of Mexico, especially the ports and more international cities, there remains a very strong tradition of true popular poetry recited in cafés or written for the newspapers on all kinds of topical subjects. I learn that Paco has written an entire history of Veracruz state, *Veracruz en la Historia y la Cumbancha* (*Veracruz in History and Celebration*), in rhyme. Veracruz natives like to contend that their state history is *the* post-Conquest history of Mexico—and with reason, since it was here that it all began. The *jarochos* half-accuse themselves of having let the invaders in.

With joy, I seek out the book in the tiny newspaper stand next to La Parroquia. (When I travel I always go to bookstores and buy cookbooks, histories, guides, any sort of local literature. Most places have countless volumes on local customs, celebrations, and legends—but all I find in Veracruz is ten copies of Paco's book at the ridiculously low price of 300 pesos, not even a dollar. I buy them all.) It is written in a version of *décimas,* the ten-line stanzas used for much popular narrative poetry in Mexico. The *bomba* game I heard was in *cuartetas,* quatrains.

At our table in La Parroquia, Paco illustrates the a-b-b-a *cuarteta* scheme with the following story, which regrettably loses some of its double meanings in translation. It seems there was a young lady called Lupe la Pela-Huevos (Lupe the Egg-Sheller, supposedly so called because she shelled the hard-boiled eggs for field hands to take to lunch—but *huevos* is also slang for testicles, which gives you some idea), who attracted the amorous attention of the town leper, a courtly soul despite his affliction. He went around barefoot because his toes were falling off, and Lupe thought she was cleverly getting rid of his unwanted attention by telling him that she certainly couldn't go out with someone who didn't wear shoes. He removed his toes with an ax, put on brand-new shoes, and pressed his suit. Lupe had run out of excuses and had to give herself to him. But at the great moment he was devastated to discover that he was not her first. So he composed the following verse:

Cuando me diste entrada	When you let me enter
en el jardín de tu amor	In the garden of your love
me ofriste una flor	You offered me a flower
que ya estaba deshojada.	That had been deflowered before.

In this way he poured out his love and wounded pride, but still remained a gentleman!

In "polite conversation" and much of the popular written poetry the ten-line *décima* is used. *Décima* is also sometimes used to "reply" to *cuarteta* in the game of *bomba.* Four *cuartetas* or *décimas,* each answering one line of the original *cuarteta,* complete a round. Paco's column is often composed in *décimas*—for example, the thank-you he published some years back when he was recovering from a heart attack and literally the whole city rallied round. Incentives to keep living showered down on him. That he should live for many more years, the city of Veracruz gave him a house. A shoemaker undertook to send him new shoes every month that he stayed alive. His local baker sent him bread every day. To help him get out and about, a taxi driver took him every day at no charge to La Parroquia or anywhere else he wanted to go. The luxury hotel gave him a suite. And someone wrote him a song. In return Paco wrote:

Tengo una casa que es mía
Me la dio el Ayuntamiento.
Beto Torres, muy contento,
me dio una zapatería.
Coyo me pasea de día,
Hualco me manda panes.
Chino tiene en sus planes
brindarme una habitación.
Y ya tengo hasta un danzón
que me hizo Kiko Centanes.

I have a house that's my own,
City Hall gave it to me.
Beto Torres happily
Gave me a whole shoestore.
Every day Coyo gives me a lift,
Hualco sends me bread.
Chino has in mind
To offer me quarters.
And I even have a song now
That Kiko Centanes made for me.

Paco's recovery from his heart attack was long and difficult. He got around in a wheelchair for quite a long time but eventually got up on a walker. From there he graduated to crutches and, finally, to a cane, which he still uses today. On one of his first excursions with his cane, a young girl tripped and bumped into him, and yelled at him as if it was his fault. He responded in a quiet voice, but in case she didn't hear him he wrote in his next column:

Por culpa de un tropezón
vino a dar una chamaca,
con todo y su chiche flaca,
muy cerca de mi mentón.
Esto causó confusión
a la inquieta chamaquita
y, demonstrando su qüita,
"Cojo"★, me gritó enojada.
Y le dije en voz pausada
"¿Cuánto cobras, mamacita?"

Thanks to an unfortunate stumble,
There I had a young lass,
Flat little tits and all,
Right up against my forehead.
This caused great confusion
To the agitated little miss,
And venting her spleen,
She shouted, "Fuck!" in a rage.
And I quietly responded,
"Little momma, what's your fee?"

★ *Cojo* means "gimp," but also recalls the slang verb *cojer*, "fuck."

I am sorry to say that Paco's columns of the last forty years have not been preserved and he hasn't ever been translated.

I spend every moment I can in Veracruz listening to Paco and his cronies talk of local trivia and Mexican history and major political issues. On the last two, the dominant note is fatalism, disenchantment. I get the sense that since the Spaniards invaded Veracruz to conquer "New Spain" and decimate the Aztec empire, life has moved on—not forward, just on. I try to point out what I think is a more positive look toward the future, but it's the *jarocho* poet who caps the argument as we speak of local economic discontent, the chances of Cuban-style revolution, and the dangers of a one-product economy after the Gulf of Mexico oil runs out. I have a lot of practical suggestions for revitalizing things: encourage tourism, train service personnel, develop products to attract new foreign customers to the region.

Paco Píldora looks at me and quietly puts things in proper perspective. "What," he asks, "is so wrong with a city where you can dance, drink coffee, recite poetry and song?"

ALMEJAS A LA MEXICANA

Clams
Mexicana

2 pounds fresh clams in shell (I use cherrystones)
1 cup dry white wine
1 cup water
2 tablespoons olive oil
2 garlic cloves, finely minced
1 small onion, finely chopped (about ½ cup)
2 large ripe, red tomatoes, peeled, seeded, and chopped
4 sprigs fresh cilantro, leaves only, finely chopped

2 sprigs fresh Italian (flat-leaf) parsley, leaves only, finely chopped
½ teaspoon dried marjoram
½ teaspoon ground coriander
1 to 2 fresh jalapeño chiles (see page 225), tops removed, seeded, and chopped (for extra hotness, leave the seeds in, or use more chiles or substitute serranos—page 226)
Salt and freshly ground white pepper to taste

Before cooking the clams, let them sit at least 2 hours in a large pot or bucket of very cold salted water. Scrub them thoroughly under cold running water, discarding any that are open. Place in a large, deep saucepan or Dutch oven with a tight-fitting lid. Add the wine and water, cover tightly, and bring to a boil. Reduce the heat to medium and cook, shaking the pot occasionally, just until the shells open, 5 to 8 minutes. Remove the clams from their shells and set aside. Discard any clams that do not open. Rinse the shells and reserve the best-looking half-shells.

Heat the oil in a medium-size saucepan over high heat until very hot but not quite smoking. Add the garlic and onion and cook 2 minutes, stirring often. Add the chopped tomatoes, cilantro, parsley, marjoram, coriander, and chiles. Season with salt and white pepper. Reduce the heat slightly and cook another 5 minutes, stirring occasionally. Add the clams and cook just until heated through, another 2 to 3 minutes. Serve on the reserved half-shells.

YIELD: 4 SERVINGS AS AN APPETIZER

ESCABECHE DE MEJILLONES

Mussels in

Escabeche

This is a versatile basic recipe that works well with any seafood. Cooked fish and shellfish in this type of vinegar marinade are a favorite preparation in Veracruz. In the North, my grandmother used to make something very similar with mountain oysters, and they were delicious. In Mexico it is usual to serve this sort of appetizer with saltines.

2½ pounds mussels in shell
1 teaspoon cumin seed
1 teaspoon dried Mexican oregano (see page 11)
¼ cup extra virgin olive oil
12 garlic cloves, peeled
10 bay leaves
1 teaspoon black peppercorns

¼ cup dry white wine
1 medium-size or 2 small carrots, peeled and diced
1 medium-size red onion, diced (about ¾ cup)
1 medium-size zucchini, diced
Salt to taste
¼ cup red wine vinegar

Before beginning to cook, let the mussels sit at least 2 hours in a large pot or bucket of very cold salted water, then scrub them well and debeard them under cold running water, discarding any that are open.

Heat the cumin and oregano in a small, heavy skillet over high heat, tossing frequently, just until they begin to smoke. Remove at once from the heat and reserve.

Heat the olive oil in a medium-size skillet over medium-high heat until very hot but not quite smoking. Add the garlic, bay leaves, and peppercorns and cook, stirring frequently, until the garlic is golden brown and the oil is infused with the flavors, about 5 minutes. Remove from the heat and strain. Reserve the infused oil.

In a large Dutch oven or deep saucepan with a tight-fitting lid, bring the wine to a simmer over high heat. Add the mussels and cover tightly. Steam the mussels just until the shells open, about 5 minutes. When they are cool enough to handle, remove the meat from the shells and reserve. Discard any that do not open. Strain the cooking liquid through cheesecloth and reserve separately.

Heat the strained oil in a large sauté pan over medium-high heat until rippling. Add the carrots and cook, stirring, for 3 minutes. Add the onion, stirring to combine, and cook, stirring, for 2 minutes. Add the zucchini, stirring to combine, and cook, stirring, for 1 more minute. The vegetables should be barely cooked, still crisp. Add the mussels and cook, stirring, 1 minute. Add the toasted cumin and oregano and season with salt. Stir in the vinegar and reserved cooking liquid, bring to a boil, and remove at once from the heat.

Let the *escabeche* cool. Place in a glass or stainless-steel container and refrigerate, tightly covered, overnight or for at least 2 hours before serving. Serve with tortilla chips or (more authentically) saltines.

YIELD: 4 SERVINGS AS AN APPETIZER

CALAMARES RELLENOS

Stuffed Squid

1 pound fresh squid with ink sacs (about 8 medium-size squid) or 8 pre-cleaned medium-size squid

¼ cup olive oil

¼ pound jamón serrano (Spanish mountain ham) or prosciutto, finely chopped

1 medium-size onion, finely chopped (about 1 cup)

2 garlic cloves, finely chopped

1½ teaspoons flour

1 large ripe, red tomato, roasted (see page 14), peeled, seeded, and finely chopped (about 1 cup)

1 sprig fresh parsley, leaves only, finely chopped

1 teaspoon dried Mexican oregano (see page 11)

1 canned chile chipotle en adobo (see page 224), finely chopped

2 tablespoons plain bread crumbs

Freshly ground black pepper to taste

Salt, optional

½ cup water

Clean the squid, removing the intestines, transparent quill, and thin outer skin but being careful to leave the bodies intact. Carefully cut out the ink sacs; squeeze out the ink into a small bowl and reserve. Cut off the tentacles and chop them fine. Reserve the squid bodies.

Heat 2 tablespoons of the olive oil in a medium-size skillet or sauté pan over high heat until very hot but not quite smoking. Add the chopped tentacles, ham, onion, and garlic and cook 3 minutes, stirring often. Add the flour and cook, stirring, another 2 minutes. Add the tomato, parsley, oregano, and chipotle chile. Simmer over medium heat 5 minutes, until most of the liquid has evaporated. Add the bread crumbs and stir well to combine. Season with pepper. The ham is very salty, so the mixture will probably need no salt.

Fill the squid bodies with the mixture and secure them with toothpicks. Heat the remaining oil in a medium-size skillet over high heat until rippling, then carefully brown the squid on all sides until golden, about 5 minutes. Add the reserved ink to the pan along with the ½ cup water and any leftover stuffing mixture. Reduce the heat to medium-high and simmer about 3 minutes more. Do not cook any longer or the squid will toughen.

NOTE: If the squid do not have much ink or you are using them pre-cleaned, use a little fish stock (¼ to ½ cup) to simmer them in. A good variation is to add a smoked Oaxacan or canned chipotle chile to the cooking liquid.

YIELD: 8 SERVINGS AS AN APPETIZER

ENSALADA DE PULPO

Octopus
Salad

Most Mexican recipes for octopus require cooking times of about an hour. But the baby octopus can be cooked very quickly—3 to 5 minutes—with good results. My friend Giorgio Petracco showed me the trick of putting a cork in the cooking liquid to tenderize the octopus—a technique I'd heard of for tough cuts of meat but had never tried on seafood.

The baby octopus, not much bigger than a walnut, are often available in Chinese fish markets. If you have to clean them yourself, cut around the central sac with a small, sharp knife, turn them inside out, and carefully pull and cut out the hard "beak" and viscera. Rinse thoroughly.

1 quart water
1 lemon, thinly sliced
2 bay leaves
1 teaspoons salt, or to taste
1 medium-size carrot, scrubbed
    but unpeeled and quartered
2 celery stalks with leafy tops
1 small onion, unpeeled
2 garlic cloves, unpeeled
1 pound whole baby octopus
    (weight after cleaning)

FOR THE DRESSING
1 medium-size onion, minced
    (about 1 cup)
2 garlic cloves, minced
2 teaspoons finely chopped fresh
    cilantro leaves
2 fresh chiles, either jalapeño or
    serrano (see pages 225 and
    226), tops removed, seeded,
    and finely chopped
¼ cup extra virgin olive oil
Juice of 2 limes
Salt to taste

In a medium-size saucepan, bring the water to a boil over high heat with the lemon, bay leaves, salt, carrot, celery, onion, garlic, and the cork from a wine bottle. Reduce the heat to medium-low and simmer, partly covered, 10 minutes. Add the whole baby octopus and cook until tender, about 3 minutes. Remove the octopus from the stock and allow to cool. Cut the tentacles and heads into convenient-sized serving pieces and place in a salad bowl or a platter.

Meanwhile, have all dressing ingredients ready, combined in a small bowl. Toss the octopus with the dressing and serve at room temperature.

YIELD: 4 SERVINGS AS AN APPETIZER, 2 TO 3 AS A MAIN-DISH SALAD

BUDÍN DE ARROZ

Rice Casserole

Try to find the true Ceylon cinnamon for this dish. The cinnamon and sugar should completely cover the casserole, so the wrong flavor of the cassia usually sold as cinnamon in this country would really stand out.

2 tablespoons butter
1 small onion, finely chopped (about ½ cup)
2 garlic cloves, minced
1 cup converted rice
2 cups Caldo de Pollo (see page 44) or water
1 cup milk

6 large eggs, separated
½ recipe Picadillo Dulce (see page 47)
1 tablespoon ground true (Ceylon) cinnamon (see page 15), preferably freshly ground in a spice grinder
1 tablespoon sugar

Melt the butter in a heavy 2-quart Dutch oven or saucepan over medium heat. When fragrant and bubbling, add the onion and garlic and cook 3 minutes, stirring often. Add the rice and cook, stirring often, until the rice is golden, about 3 more minutes. Add the chicken stock and bring to a boil. Reduce the heat to low and simmer, partly covered, 10 minutes. Stir in the milk, cover tightly, and cook about 15 minutes longer. Let cool.

Preheat the oven to 325°F. Beat the egg whites until stiff but not dry. Add the egg yolks one at a time, beating well after each addition. Fold the beaten eggs into the cooled rice mixture.

Butter a 1½-quart Pyrex baking dish and spread half the rice mixture over the bottom. Top with the *picadillo* and then with the remaining rice. Sprinkle the top with the combined cinnamon and sugar. Bake until the top is golden, about 25 minutes.

YIELD: 4–6 SERVINGS

MARISCOS CON AGUA DE COCO

Seafood with Coconut Water

The model for this dish was a spectacular presentation called *coco relleno* (stuffed coconut), with the seafood piled into two coconut halves. You scoop out a little of the coconut meat with each bite, and it is a wonderful complement to the flavor of the salmon and shellfish. Unfortunately, it is difficult to whack a coconut into two neat halves without much practice, so this version uses only the liquid drained from the coconut; reserve the meat for some other purpose such as *Camarones con Coco* (page 323). You can substitute ¼ cup canned unsweetened coconut milk for the coconut water, but the flavor will not be as delicate. Be sure to buy a coconut that sounds as if it has a lot of liquid sloshing around inside, not a dried-out one.

1 coconut
2 to 3 tablespoons unsalted butter (or a mixture of butter and vegetable oil)
1 cup Salsa Verde de Tampico (see page 324)
1 cup loosely packed fresh mint leaves stripped from stems (1 large bunch), finely chopped after measuring

½ pound sea scallops
¼ pound medium-size shrimp, peeled and deveined
1 salmon fillet (about 6 ounces), skinned and cut into 1-inch cubes
½ cup good fish stock
Salt to taste

With an ice pick or corkscrew, pierce two of the "eyes" in the coconut. Drain the coconut water into a small bowl, strain, and reserve. (You want at least 1 cup of liquid; if it is much less add enough cold water to make 1 cup.)

Heat the butter in a large skillet over medium-high heat until fragrant and bubbling. Add the salsa and chopped mint and cook for 2 minutes, stirring often. Add the scallops, shrimp, and cubed salmon and cook, stirring constantly, 2 to 3 minutes. Add the coconut water and fish stock and season with salt. Simmer, uncovered, just until the fish is cooked through and opaque, another 2 to 3 minutes.

YIELD: 4 SERVINGS

Zarela

S ome important wishes of my life have come true as if the gods had pulled strings to have me in just the right place at the right time, request in hand. My first restaurant, Café Marimba, was an example. Of course it wasn't really "my" restaurant, but it gave me the thrill of creation on a new level, at an exciting time for the whole restaurant business in New York. I was lucky to come there at the right moment—and lucky to have several years of practical restaurant experience under my belt just when another once-in-a-lifetime opportunity came along.

It was 1987, and I was saying to myself that I was ready for another big leap. "Consultant" and later "executive chef" was my title. If you are familiar with the structure of big, ambitious city restaurants under investment partnerships, you will guess that I was only one cog in a complicated, politics-ridden scene. After a time I knew that I was frustrated. I had so much to say now in my cooking, and I needed to say it on my own terms. What would I not give to start a restaurant of my own from scratch, with the unique spirit of Mexican hospitality!

This is a subject I have hardly touched on. When people in this country talk about warmth and hospitality, often I have felt the words are empty. But in Mexico when we invite guests into our homes there is nothing, truly nothing, that we would not do for their well-being. We are not figuratively but literally at their service. If they do not like a dish, you go and rustle up something else for them. It is a privilege to cook for guests. Isn't this one of the most important things anyone can do for another? Can there be anything more pleasant than the *sobremesa,* the time spent simply savoring each other's company? But often in New York I would feel that this was the last thing people thought of—business considerations and the right contacts were the real reason for having someone to dinner. And then I would visit Mexico on one of my research trips and be reminded again that hospitality itself, at least as much as cooking, is one of the highest treasures of civilization.

Once again the gods were with me. While I was hatching the idea of a place that would present Mexican food in the welcoming, unstinting Mexican spirit, I learned of a prime East Side restaurant spot being vacated by the previous business, a wine bar called Tastings. I pounced! And miraculously everything materialized at the very moment I needed it: a loan from my aunt and uncle, Tía Panchita and Tío Ernesto Ellis, and supplies advanced on credit by purveyors we had used at Marimba who somehow believed my assurances that I could repay them in a month or two.

I knew just what I wanted the new place to be: a personal statement. The timid young woman who told Paul Prudhomme she couldn't even chop an onion the right way was long gone. Now I had a profound belief in myself and what I had to contribute. I was more excited about Mexican food and culture than I ever had been, more eager to sweep aside the clichés and fashion a menu based on my own family's table and my own voyages of exploration.

The décor would have to be whatever I could come up with on a shoestring. A little at a time, we acquired a half-funky, half-rustic, wholly delightful collection of the Mexican crafts that are one of my great passions, from *papel picado* (colored tissue paper cut-outs) to surrealistic figurines in all mediums. (It has now been described as being like the inside of a piñata.) But at first we just festooned a lot of colored ribbons over the previous English-pub furnishings, and my artist friend Mary Jo Schwalbach-Gitler made me the surreal, figureheadlike multimedia assemblage that greets you by the bar (quickly christened Juana the Tortilla Lady). My main attention went to the food.

By now I had arrived at a cuisine representing, I felt, not just the *mestizo* character of Mexican food generally but my own personal process of *mestizaje,* synthesis. I was making dishes true to their origins—whether simple, hearty ranch food, tropically flavored *recados,* or lavish *moles*—but I was also experimenting by juxtaposing different elements. I might, for example, take a thick blue corn tortilla from the state of Mexico, top it with a version of braised pork I'd known all my life from Sonora, and serve it with a Oaxacan sauce and Yucatecan *escabeche de cebolla*. In this way the layers of flavors that diners encountered in one of my meals reflected the depth of possibilities in Mexican cooking. I was convinced that the best way to make people experience the complex orchestration of flavors in my cooking was the simple, unpretentious family-style service that you see in a Chinese restaurant: the dishes placed in the middle of the table, with people helping themselves to a little of several things.

The name I chose? Zarela. I knew right away that it would have to stand or fall by the sum of myself I had put into it.

Actually, opening my own restaurant felt like walking off a precipice. But my instinct had told me truly. Don't ask me how I knew, but I walked into this tremendous gamble knowing absolutely, from the first minute, that it would work. What I was trying to say in Zarela struck an immediate chord with a large public. From the moment we opened we were not just a success but a kind of New York fixture—despite a complete lack of advance fanfare, in no time at all people were talking as if we had always belonged there.

Zarela has been the sum and substance of all my life's experiences and training, from my childhood on the ranch to the present. In a way, it's an outgrowth of my college education in modern communications. It gives me the small businessperson's satisfaction of providing value and marshaling every resource to best advantage. I am conscious of putting to best use everything Eddie Schoenfeld taught me about day-to-day operation and making a restaurant concept work. I love the challenge of motivating a staff, encouraging people to do their best. I love being my own public-relations woman. I love surrounding the scene with Mexican objects I think funny or rare and beautiful. But the best part is the people.

Now I must confide that all my life I have thought I would like nothing better than to have a sort of old-fashioned salon where my friends felt free to drop by on a regular basis for nourishment, nurturing, and civilized talk. My parents' home was like this in many ways—and in a sense my restaurant is a testimony to their upbringing. Even beyond the praise of satisfied customers, I am rewarded by the atmosphere of friendship and celebration that is maybe an even bigger attraction than the food at Zarela.

My parents taught me to enjoy people and help them enjoy themselves. I don't know whether the customers or I am having a better time—and that's the essence of what I wanted to convey about Mexican hospitality. Many times people walk in and look around and ask, "Is this a private party?" Perhaps it is—*my* private party. "Is it always so much fun here?" someone once asked me. I told him it depended on my mood. He said he thought in that case maybe he better call ahead next time to check the current mood. "No," I said, "my mood can change in a minute." Where else could I dance and sing (as I often do) or be serious, as the fancy strikes, in my own surrogate-salon? Where else could I have the pleasure of continuity, of seeing people who had their first dates at Café Marimba now bringing their children to Zarela?

I have been lucky to work with many talented and loyal people like Jackie Brassil who walked those first tentative steps with me, and our chefs, Gary Jacobson and Ed Bonuso. I am lucky in having with me a precious part of my earlier life—my stepdaughter, Marissa Sánchez, my right hand. But what makes me feel the luckiest is that through food I have been able to communicate with so many people, if I may pun as my father might have, on a visceral level. My own memories and discoveries are the foundation of the menu at Zarela, and with every meal we serve I hope that they will now become someone else's memories and discoveries.

VAMPIRO

For long years sangrita, usually a combination of tomato, lime, and orange juice and red powdered chile with a few seasonings, was the most popular accompaniment to tequila—drunk as a chaser, a shotglass of each. Then someone had the happy idea of combining the liquor and the sangrita. The result is Vampiro, which is very popular in Acapulco and starting to be a favorite with U.S. restaurant-goers. It promises to become the Mexican Bloody Mary—and I would be delighted, because the sangrita flavors are too good to be only served as a chaser.

FOR EACH SERVING

¼ cup (2 ounces) white tequila, preferably Sauza or Herradura

¼ cup tomato juice

2 tablespoons fresh orange juice

1 tablespoon fresh lime juice

½ to 1 teaspoon powdered red chile (see page 226) or cayenne pepper

Dash of kosher salt

Freshly ground black pepper to taste

1 cup crushed ice

2 lime wedges

Combine all the ingredients, except the lime wedges, in a shaker or blender and mix thoroughly. Squeeze the wedges into a tall glass and fill with the tequila mixture.

YIELD: 1 SERVING

GUACAMOLE

Everyone has their own guacamole recipe and this is mine. It is crucial that the ingredients be as fresh as possible and at their peak of ripeness. I prefer the dark, rough-skinned Hass variety of avocado. Fuerte avocados are also good. The large green, smooth-skinned Florida avocados do not work as well. They are watery and fibrous, not buttery.

4 very ripe medium-size avocados, peeled and seeded

1 firm medium-size ripe, red tomato, peeled, seeded, and chopped

¼ cup finely minced onion

¼ cup finely minced fresh cilantro leaves

1 teaspoon dried Mexican oregano (see page 11), crumbled

2 fresh jalapeño chiles (see page 225), tops removed, seeded, and finely chopped

2 tablespoons fresh lime juice

Salt to taste

In a large bowl, mash the avocados with a fork. They should still be chunky. Stir in the remaining ingredients until well blended. Serve at once, if possible.

Can be held, tightly covered and refrigerated, up to 30 minutes, but in that case do not add the salt until ready to serve.

YIELD: 6 TO 8 SERVINGS

SALSA DE TOMATILLO CON CHIPOTLE

Tomatillo Sauce with Chipotle Chiles

This is an excellent dipping sauce for crudités or tortilla chips. The chipotle adds a smoky, intriguing note. You can use more chiles for a spicier sauce.

½ pound fresh tomatillos (see page 14), husks removed (about 6 large tomatillos)

1 to 2 canned chiles chipotles en adobo (see page 224)

½ small onion, finely chopped

½ teaspoon dried Mexican oregano (see page 11)

½ teaspoon salt, or to taste

Pinch of sugar, or to taste

Place the tomatillos in a small saucepan, cover with water, and bring to a boil. Simmer, uncovered, until they change color, about 5 minutes. Drain, reserving ½ cup of the liquid.

Place the chipotle chiles (with the sauce that clings to them) in a blender or food processor fitted with the steel blade with the tomatillos, reserved ½ cup liquid, onion, and oregano. Process until smoothly pureed, about 1 minute. Taste the sauce; season with salt and a pinch or two of sugar.

Can be stored, tightly covered, in the refrigerator for 2 to 3 days.

YIELD: ABOUT 1½ CUPS

ENSALADA DE BERENJENA

Eggplant Salad

This is one of my New York improvisations that started when Tony Calicchio, a very young chef who was working for me at Café Marimba, brought in an eggplant salad his mother—a fabulous cook—had made. We made sandwiches out of it with fresh mozzarella and all fell in love with it. It inspired me to try a version with Mexican seasonings, which we introduced at Zarela and which is one of our most popular dishes.

3 medium-small eggplants (total 1½ to 2 pounds), peeled, and cut into ½-inch dice

1 tablespoon plus 1 teaspoon salt, or to taste

1 teaspoon coriander seed

1 cup water

1 cup distilled white vinegar

2 poblano chiles (see page 226) (for hotter flavor use 2 fresh jalapeño or serrano chiles, see pages 225 and 226), roasted (page 227), peeled, seeded, and finely chopped

1 medium-size onion, sliced into thin half-moons (about 1 cup)

1 garlic clove, minced

½ cup extra virgin olive oil, or to taste

1 teaspoon dried Mexican oregano (see page 11), crumbled

Toss the diced eggplant in a bowl with the 1 tablespoon salt. Let rest 45 minutes to an hour. Meanwhile, toast the coriander seed over high heat in a small, heavy skillet, shaking the pan frequently, until fragrant and slightly brown, 3 to 5 minutes. Set aside.

Drain off the salty liquid from the eggplant. In a large saucepan, heat the water and vinegar to a rolling boil over high heat. Working in two or three batches, add the eggplant and cook 2 minutes, until barely cooked but still firm. Remove each batch quickly and drain in a colander, pressing with the back of a spoon to squeeze out as much liquid as possible.

Combine the chiles, onion, garlic, olive oil, oregano, and toasted coriander seeds in a large bowl. Add the eggplant and remaining salt and toss to combine. Let rest at room temperature at least 1 hour before serving to meld flavors.

YIELD: 4 TO 6 SERVINGS

ENSALADA DE CORPUS CHRISTI

Corpus Christi Salad

The feast of Corpus Christi falls on a Thursday between May 20th and June 20th. In the city of Puebla I encountered a beautiful, unusual salad served during the fiesta with an assortment of fruits and vegetables that are then at their peak. Vendors were selling it in the streets, in little paper cones. Everything ripens at a different time here, but you may be able to come close to the original in late summer. For this salad I would avoid extra virgin olive oil, which drowns out the fruit flavors.

1 cup fresh corn kernels
1 medium-small zucchini, finely diced
1 small cucumber, finely diced
1 pear (preferably Comice), peeled and finely diced
1 firm, sweet peach, peeled and finely diced
1 cup fresh blueberries

Seeds of 1 pomegranate
2 small, ripe avocados (preferably the black-skinned Hass variety), peeled and finely diced
¼ cup olive oil
Juice of 3 limes
1 teaspoon salt, or to taste

Combine all the diced vegetables and fruits in a large salad bowl. In a small bowl, whisk together the olive oil and lime juice and season with salt. Pour the dressing over the salad ingredients and toss thoroughly. Serve at once.

YIELD: 6 TO 8 SERVINGS

ENSALADA GIRASOL

Sunflower Salad

The idea for this dish came to me when I took Aarón and Rodrigo, my twin sons, to eat at a Caribbean restaurant in the East Village called Sugar Reef. We ordered a side dish of mango, onion, lime juice, and chile, and it suddenly brought back to me the wonderful mangos that they sell both ripe and green all over Mexico—cut in decorative patterns, sprinkled with lime juice, salt, and powdered red chile. It occurred to me then to try combining them with grilled chicken and smoky chipotle chiles, and thus was born one of the most popular dishes at Zarela.

At the restaurant we partly grill the chicken over charcoal (about 5 minutes on each side) and finish it in a preheated 400°F oven (another 15 to 20 minutes). Since many people will find this cumbersome and chicken breasts are hard to keep from drying out if cooked only on the grill, I have substituted an all–oven method.

½ cup Pasta de Chipotle (see page 35), or to taste

2 large whole boneless chicken breasts with skin

2 to 4 tablespoons vegetable oil, or as needed

1 large ripe mango (about 1 pound), peeled, seeded, and thinly sliced

2 cups Vinagreta de Chipotle (recipe follows)

Preheat the broiler to 500°F.

Brush the chipotle paste over both sides of the chicken breasts. Brush a little oil over the chipotle paste. Place on a broiler pan and broil, skin side up, 4 minutes. Turn and broil another 4 minutes. Turn off the broiler, reduce the heat to 400°F, and bake the chicken in the oven 10 minutes longer or until cooked through. Slice on the bias (remove the skin first if desired).

Toss the sliced mango in the chipotle vinaigrette; lift out, letting the dressing drain back into the bowl. Arrange the mango slices around 4 serving plates, sunflower-fashion. Toss the sliced chicken breasts in the remaining vinaigrette and pile in the center of the serving plates.

YIELD: 4 SERVINGS

Variation:

Peel a large jícama (see page 9) and cut into fine julienne or dice. After slicing the chicken, toss the jícama in the vinaigrette and lift out with a slotted spoon, letting the dressing drain back into the bowl. Arrange the jícama in the center of the serving plates. Continue with the recipe, arranging the sliced chicken on top of the jícama.

VINAGRETA DE CHIPOTLE

Chipotle Vinaigrette

This is a good dressing to experiment with. It would be great with a grilled duck salad or any green salad.

½ cup red wine vinegar
1 garlic clove, minced
1 teaspoon dried Mexican oreg-
    ano (see page 11)
3 canned chiles chipotles en
    adobo (see page 224), minced
    (or use fewer for milder
    flavor)

Salt and freshly ground black
    pepper to taste
1½ cups olive oil

In a medium-size bowl, whisk together the vinegar, garlic, oregano, chiles, salt, and pepper. Add the olive oil a little at a time, whisking well after each addition.

Can be stored, tightly covered, in the refrigerator, 2 to 3 days.
YIELD: ABOUT 2 CUPS

CALDO DE HUITLACOCHE

Huitlacoche Soup

I must have encountered something like this in Mexico City in my early recipe-gathering days, but the present variation is one I came up with a few years ago and have become very fond of. Served in demitasse cups, it makes a great appetizer on cold winter nights.

3 tablespoons lard (see page 19) or vegetable oil

1 medium-size onion, sliced in thin half-moons (about 1 cup)

2 cloves garlic, minced

3 fresh chiles, either poblano or Anaheim (see pages 226 and 223), roasted (page 227), peeled, seeded, and diced

1 can (8 ounces) huitlacoche (see page 9)

2 tablespoons dried epazote (see page 8) or minced fresh cilantro leaves

8 cups Caldo de Pollo (see page 44), or as needed

1 cup heavy or light cream

Salt and freshly ground black pepper to taste

Heat the lard or oil in a large skillet over medium-high heat until very hot but not quite smoking. Add the onion and garlic and cook, stirring occasionally, until the onion is golden and translucent, about 5 minutes. Add the diced chiles and cook for another 3 minutes, stirring occasionally. Add the *huitlacoche* and epazote, reduce the heat to medium, and simmer, uncovered, stirring occasionally, for about 5 minutes.

Let cool slightly. In two or more batches, process the mixture to a smooth puree in a blender or food processor fitted with the steel blade, adding enough chicken stock to facilitate blending. Pour the puree into a large, heavy saucepan and bring to a boil, stirring. Add the remaining chicken stock a cup or two at a time until the mixture is the consistency of a thin cream soup. Stir in the cream, bring to a boil, reduce the heat to medium, and simmer another 5 minutes. Season with salt and pepper and serve hot.

YIELD: ABOUT 10 CUPS (6 TO 8 REGULAR OR 10 TO 12 DEMITASSE SERVINGS)

MOUSSE DE HUITLACOCHE

Huitlacoche

Mousse

I developed this dish—a very rich and sumptuous use of the exquisite *huitlacoche*—for a reception given by the noted Mexican photographer Eugenia Rendón de Olazábal at the International Center for Photography in New York City. The occasion was the publication of her book *Espinas,* a volume of striking black-and-white photographs of cactus.

At the party we used the mixture as a filling for tiny puff pastry shell—*volovanes*, as they are called in Mexico. As you might guess, *volovanes* are the Mexican version of vol-au-vents, one of many French specialties introduced in the nineteenth century and considered particularly elegant. We garnished the little pastries with a few grains of salmon roe. For a simpler presentation, serve the mousse as a spread with tortilla chips or as a rich first course chilled in tiny ramekins.

1 envelope (1 tablespoon) plain gelatin

¼ cup cold water

1 cup heavy cream

2 tablespoons corn oil

2 garlic cloves, minced

1 small onion, finely chopped (about ½ cup)

2 poblano chiles (see page 226), roasted (page 227), peeled, seeded, and diced

1 fresh chile, either jalapeño or serrano (see pages 225 and 226), roasted (page 227), peeled, seeded, and diced

2 cans (8 ounces each) huitlacoche (see page 9)

2 tablespoons dried epazote (see page 8) or minced fresh cilantro leaves

Salt to taste

Stir the gelatin into the cold water and let soften at least 5 minutes. In a small saucepan, heat the cream over medium heat until hot but not boiling. Add the gelatin and stir to dissolve completely. Let cool while you prepare the remaining ingredients.

Heat the oil in a medium-size skillet over high heat until very hot but not quite smoking. Add the garlic and onion and cook, stirring often, for 2 minutes. Add the diced chiles and cook for 3 minutes, stirring often. Add the *huitlacoche* and epazote; reduce the heat to medium and cook another 10 minutes, stirring often. Let cool slightly.

Transfer the *huitlacoche* mixture to a blender or food processor. Add the gelatin-cream mixture and process until smooth, about 1 minute. Pour into a glass serving container or 8 small individual ramekins. Let cool completely and refrigerate, covered, until set (2 to 3 hours).

YIELD: 8 SERVINGS

COLIFLOR EN SALSA RANCHERA

Cauliflower

with

Ranch-Style

Sauce

2½ teaspoons salt, or to taste
1 small cauliflower (about 1¾
    pounds), cut into large florets
½ cup flour
Freshly ground black pepper to
    taste

3 large eggs, separated
Vegetable oil for deep frying
3 to 4 cups Salsa Ranchera
    (recipe follows)

Bring a large saucepan of water (at least 2 quarts) to a boil; add 2 teaspoons of the salt. Add the cauliflower and cook at a rolling boil about 3 minutes. Drain and plunge into ice water to stop the cooking at once. Drain again and dry on paper towels.

Combine the flour with the remaining salt and a generous grinding of pepper in a shallow tray or deep-rimmed plate. Choose a large, heavy saucepan or deep-fryer; add oil to a depth of 3 inches and heat to 375°F. While it is heating, beat the egg whites in a large bowl until stiff but not dry. Add the yolks, one at a time, beating well after each addition. Have the salsa ready, heated just to a simmer.

Roll the florets in the seasoned flour. When the oil is heated, shake off any excess flour, dip the florets in the egg mixture, and fry in batches until golden. Do not crowd the pan; watch the temperature to be sure it stays close to 375°F. Remove each batch as it is done and drain on paper towels. Pour the salsa over the hot cauliflower and serve at once.

YIELD: 4 TO 6 SERVINGS

SALSA RANCHERA

Ranch-Style

Sauce

This is wonderful with the fried cauliflower in the preceding recipe, but I use it in many other ways. It is a great accompaniment to corn fritters or any grilled fish. I use it to make a "red" version of *Chilaquiles* (see page 312) with a light tomato sauce instead of a creamy tomatillo sauce. It is delicious on pasta as well.

3 tablespoons lard (see page 19) or vegetable oil

2 garlic cloves, coarsely chopped

1 medium-size onion, sliced (about 1 cup)

1 can (28 ounces) whole tomatoes (choose a brand without added puree; do not drain)

3 fresh chiles, either jalapeño or serrano (see pages 225 and 226), or to taste, tops removed and coarsely chopped

5 sprigs fresh cilantro

Salt and freshly ground black pepper to taste

Heat the lard or oil in a medium-size saucepan over medium-high heat until rippling. Add the garlic and onion and cook 3 minutes, stirring often. Crush the tomatoes with your hand and add to the garlic and onion. Add the chiles and cilantro; stir well to combine. Reduce the heat to low and simmer, stirring often, another 10 minutes. Let cool about 10 minutes.

Working in batches if necessary, puree the mixture in a blender or food processor fitted with the steel blade. Season to taste with salt and pepper. Return the sauce just to the boiling point when ready to use, stirring often to keep it from sticking.

Can be stored, tightly covered, in the refrigerator 2 to 3 days.

YIELD: ABOUT 4 CUPS

ELOTES ASADOS CON MANTEQUILLA ENCHILADA

Grilled Corn
on the Cob
with Chile
Butter

This is the taste of Mexico, vivid and true. It is our two great gifts to world kitchens, corn and chile, in combination with two of our more beloved Old World imports, butter and fresh limes. Lime is so Mexican it's hard to believe it didn't originate here. It seems as if lime juice and Mexican chile must always have been waiting for each other.

These roasted corn ears appear around six in the evening on streets in practically every town in Mexico, sold by vendors pushing carts with a little hibachi-type grill or an oil can cut out to make a grill. Our corn is starchier than the U.S. sweet corn, and it grills better, though it takes longer to cook. The idea is always the same: grill or roast the corn over charcoal, rub it with butter, roll it in powdered chile (sometimes also spreading it with mayonnaise), and finally, always, sprinkle it with lime juice. A marriage made in heaven! My mouth is watering.

In the version of *elotes asados* that we serve at Zarela, the butter and powdered chile are combined. The mixture isn't just good on corn, either. It's great on freshly grilled fish and other grilled or steamed vegetables. You can use it to (gently) sauté seafood or vegetables. We like to combine it with minced garlic, but feel free to add other herbs or spices as the spirit moves.

4 large, fresh white ears of corn in husks
Mantequilla Enchilada (recipe follows)

Lime wedges
Salt, optional

Remove the tough outer husks of the corn, leaving the two inner layers intact. Carefully remove the corn silk.

Grill the corn over very hot charcoal or mesquite, turning several times, a total of 6 to 10 minutes for average-sized ears. (The timing may vary even more depending on the freshness of the corn and the starch content of the variety.) Serve with the chile butter, lime wedges, and a sprinkling of salt, if desired.

YIELD: 4 SERVINGS

NOTE: Mother taught me a trick to remove the corn silk. Have a bowl of water next to you. Wet your hand and run it over the ear of corn and the silk will stick to your fingers. Dip your hand in the water and the silk will rinse off.

MANTEQUILLA ENCHILADA

Chile Butter

Be sure not to use chili powder (a Tex-Mex blend of spices) instead of pure powdered chile, or your corn will faintly resemble a chili cook-off! If powdered red chile is not available, use a small amount of good-quality cayenne pepper or red pepper flakes (start with 1 teaspoon and add more to taste). If using a food processor, be sure butter is well chilled and don't overprocess, or it will become greasy.

½ cup (1 stick; ¼ pound) butter

2 garlic cloves, finely minced

1 tablespoon pure powdered red chile (see page 226), or to taste

Salt to taste (if unsalted butter is used)

Cream the butter with the minced garlic in a food processor fitted with the steel blade (or by hand in a small bowl) until light and fluffy. Add the powdered chile to taste. Season with salt if desired. Let the mixture sit at least 1 hour, refrigerated, to blend the flavors. Can be stored, tightly covered, in the refrigerator for up to 1 week.

YIELD: ABOUT ½ CUP

MORRALITOS DE CALABACITAS

Zucchini Bundles

Morralitos are literally little bundled-up packages like a hobo's pack. You will recognize this as another takeoff on the endless possibilities of the grilled *tamal*, like *Tamal de Pescado* (page 183). I developed the recipe some years ago for an article Barbara Costikyan was writing on summer entertaining for *New York* magazine.

8 large unbroken dried corn husks (see page 7), plus 1 medium-size husk

1 to 2 tablespoons butter or vegetable oil

1 small onion, finely chopped (about ½ cup)

2 small garlic cloves, minced

2 fresh chiles, poblano or Anaheim (see pages 226 and 223), roasted (page 227), peeled, seeded, and finely diced

¾ cup fresh, frozen, or drained canned corn kernels

1 tablespoon dried epazote (see page 8) or minced fresh cilantro leaves

Salt and freshly ground black pepper to taste

3 medium-size zucchini (about 1 to 1¼ pounds total), cut into ¼-inch dice

4 ounces white cheddar cheese, shredded (about 1 cup)

About 1 hour before beginning to cook, place the corn husks in a large bowl or kettle and cover with hot water. Let soak until softened. Remove any loose corn silk. Drain and pat dry.

Heat the butter or oil in a medium-size skillet or sauté pan over medium-high heat until very hot but not quite scorching. Add the onion and garlic, and cook, stirring, until the onion is translucent, about 2 minutes. Add the chiles, corn, and epazote or cilantro and cook, stirring often to combine, for 5 minutes. Season with salt and pepper and let cool. Stir in the diced zucchini and shredded cheese.

To assemble the *morralitos,* place 2 large corn husks end to end so that the wide ends are lined up against each other (barely overlapping) and the narrow ends face away from each other. Place one quarter of the filling in the center. Carefully roll up lengthwise like a fat cigar. Tear two thin strips from the medium-size husk and tie the two ends like a party favor. Repeat with the remaining large husks and filling.

Grill over charcoal about 3 minutes on each side. Be very careful in turning them, so that the juice does not drip out. Alternatively, broil under a preheated broiler about 6 inches from the heat source, allowing 3 minutes per side.

YIELD: 4 SERVINGS

CHILAQUILES

Tortilla Casserole

In Mexico, *chilaquiles* are eaten for breakfast. I used to make them as a brunch dish at home. But at Zarela, they have become our most popular luncheon and dinner appetizer, which I suppose says something about different breakfast preferences. The dish is a simple one, traditionally made by cooking tortilla strips in a simmering sauce that is enriched with grated cheese, cream, and an optional cooked meat (often chicken) and baked until heated through. My version is quite rich, though it could be lightened some by using the regular version of *Salsa de Tomatillo* (page 38). I also prefer to fry the tortillas before adding them to the mixture, so that they will remain somewhat crisp and crunchy. Omit this step, if desired, but the tortillas will be soggier.

12 commercial corn tortillas

2 cups vegetable oil

1 pound white cheddar cheese, shredded (about 4 cups)

3 cups Pollo Guisado (see page 45)

2 cups Crema Agria Preparada (see page 42)

1½ cups Salsa de Tomatillo con Crema (recipe follows)

Preheat the oven to 325°F.

Cut the tortillas in half; stacking them a few at a time, cut them into ¼-inch strips at right angles to the first cut. In a large, heavy saucepan or deep-fryer, heat the oil to 350°F. (A tortilla strip dropped into the oil should sizzle at once.) Fry the tortilla strips in batches, a large handful at a time (do not try to do more or the oil temperature will drop). With a skimmer, remove each batch immediately as soon as it stops sizzling; tortilla pieces will scorch if left in longer. Drain on paper towels and let cool completely.

Combine the tortilla strips, shredded cheese, and chicken in a large bowl; toss to distribute the ingredients evenly. Place the mixture in a 13 × 9-inch Pyrex baking dish or other wide, shallow ovenproof container. Spread the sour cream over the top and bake until heated through, about 25 minutes.

In a small saucepan, heat the tomatillo sauce just to a simmer, stirring often to keep it from scorching. Pour the sauce over the casserole and serve immediately.

YIELD: 6 TO 8 SERVINGS

SALSA DE TOMATILLO CON CREMA

Tomatillo Sauce with Cream

Canned tomatillos are really a last resort here. They taste nothing like the real thing.

Chilaquiles are only the beginning of what you can do with this sauce. It is wonderful with grilled or poached fish, especially salmon, or pan-fried chicken cutlets.

1 pound fresh tomatillos (see
page 14; about 12 large tomatillos), husks removed, or 1
can (15 ounces) tomatillos,
drained
¼ cup vegetable oil
1 commercial corn tortilla
1 small onion, chopped (about
½ cup)
2 garlic cloves, chopped

2 fresh chiles, either jalapeño or
serrano (see pages 225 and
226), or to taste, tops removed
1 cup loosely packed fresh
cilantro leaves (1 large bunch
cilantro, leaves stripped)
1 teaspoon sugar
2 tablespoons unsalted butter
1 cup heavy cream
Salt to taste

Place the fresh tomatillos in a medium-size saucepan and add water to cover (about 3 cups). Bring to a boil over high heat and
cook, uncovered, until the tomatillos have changed color, about 5
minutes. Drain, reserving ½ cup of the cooking liquid. If using
canned tomatillos, omit this step.

Heat the oil in a small, heavy skillet over high heat until almost
smoking and fry the tortilla until crisp and golden. Drain it on
paper towels, and when cool enough to handle, break into pieces.

Place the cooked tomatillos with the reserved liquid in a blender.
(If using canned tomatillos, no extra liquid is necessary.) Add the
chopped onion, garlic, chiles, cilantro, broken tortilla pieces, and
sugar. Process for about 1 minute, or until smoothly pureed.

Heat the butter in a medium-size saucepan over high heat until
hot and bubbling. Add the tomatillo mixture and heavy cream and
season with salt. Bring to a boil, then reduce the heat to low and
simmer until somewhat thickened, about 5 minutes. Can be kept,
tightly covered, in the refrigerator up to a week. It may jell and
look curdled but will smooth out when reheated.

YIELD: 3 TO 3½ CUPS

POBLANOS RELLENOS

Stuffed
Poblano
Chiles

One of the crowning glories of Mexican cuisine is *chiles en nogada,*
which hail from the state of Puebla. To make this famous dish,
poblano chiles are stuffed with a mixture of braised meat (usually
pork) and assorted dried and fresh fruits, then usually dipped in
beaten egg and deep-fried. The chiles are then covered with a

sauce made with a type of cream cheese and ground unripe pecans or walnuts and garnished with pomegranate seeds. The dish has the most patriotic associations because the red, white, and green of the pomegranate seeds, sauce, and poblanos are also the colors of the Mexican flag. People always serve *chiles en nogada* on the national holidays of September 15 and 16, as well as St. August-ine's Day (August 28).

Patriotic or not, I do not try to serve the real *chiles en nogada* at the restaurant because you cannot get all the crucial ingredients here at the same time—pomegranates are not ripe at the time when young walnuts are on the tree, even supposing you could buy the walnuts here at the right stage. It was partly to compensate for the absence of this dish that I developed another version of stuffed poblanos, baked instead of batter-fried, that is filled with a mix-ture of cooked chicken and dried fruits and is one of our most beloved dishes at Zarela. The sauce is a cream-enriched variation on the basic combination of roasted tomato, onion, and garlic that underlies so many Mexican sauces.

6 large poblano chiles (see page 226)

Vegetable oil for frying

½ cup (1 stick; ¼ pound) un-salted butter

1 medium-size onion, chopped (about 1 cup)

2 garlic cloves, minced

½ cup pimiento-stuffed green olives, sliced

½ cup pitted prunes, coarsely diced

½ cup dried apricots, coarsely diced

½ cup dried peaches, coarsely diced

1½ teaspoons ground cumin

1½ teaspoons ground true (Cey-lon) cinnamon (see page 15), preferably freshly ground in a spice grinder, or ½ teaspoon U.S. "cinnamon"

¼ teaspoon ground cloves

2 cups shredded cooked chicken (see page 45)

Salt to taste

Salsa de Tomate Asado (recipe follows)

Preheat the oven to 500°F.

Make a small (1 to 1½ inches long) lengthwise slit in each chile. Pour the oil into a large, heavy skillet to a depth of about ½ inch and heat over high heat until very hot but not quite smoking. Fry the chiles, two at a time, turning once or twice, until they puff up and take on an olive-beige color. Remove from the pan as they are done. Carefully peel the chiles under cold running water. Very gently pull out the seeds through the slit in each chile, being sure not to tear the flesh. Set aside.

Melt the butter in a large skillet over medium heat until very hot and fragrant. Add the onion and garlic and cook, stirring, for 3 minutes. Add the olives and dried fruit and cook, stirring, another 3 minutes. Add the spices and chicken and cook, stirring to combine, for 2 minutes more. Season with salt.

Carefully fill the chiles with the mixture through the slit in each. Bake on a greased baking sheet or shallow pan for 7 minutes.

Spoon the tomato sauce onto individual plates or a large serving platter and arrange the chiles on top.

YIELD: 6 SERVINGS

SALSA DE TOMATE ASADO

Roasted

Tomato Sauce

I love the combination of smoothness (from the cream) and intensity (from the preliminary roasting of the vegetables). It's a versatile sauce, which I serve also with *Papadzules* (page 276), pasta, crêpes, and roast or grilled pork.

1½ cups heavy cream
8 large garlic cloves, unpeeled
1 medium-size onion, unpeeled, halved crosswise

3 to 4 large ripe, red tomatoes (about 2¾ pounds total)
Salt

Cook down the cream in a small, heavy saucepan over medium heat until reduced by about a third. Set aside.

Heat a heavy cast-iron griddle or skillet over high heat until a drop of water sizzles on contact. Roast the unpeeled garlic cloves and onion, turning several times, until the garlic is dark on all sides and somewhat softened and the onion is partly blackened and fragrant. Set aside. Roast the tomatoes in the same way, turning several times, until blistered on all sides. Let cool until just cool enough to handle. Peel the garlic cloves and place in a blender. Peel the onion, rubbing away any charred bits, and add to the garlic. Peel the tomatoes directly over the blender so as not to lose any juice and add to the garlic and onion. Puree on medium speed until smooth. Add the cream and process until blended. Season with salt. Place the sauce in a heavy, medium-size saucepan and bring to a boil over medium heat. Reduce the heat to low and simmer the sauce for 10 minutes, stirring often.

Can be stored, tightly covered, in the refrigerator for 2 to 3 days. I don't recommend freezing.

YIELD: ABOUT 4 CUPS

CHULETAS DE POLLO

Chicken
Cutlets

This is a simple, quick low-cholesterol dish that I developed for *"La Familia de Hoy"* ("Today's Family"), a series of brief Spanish-language spots on Univision, the Hispanic cable television company.

4 small boneless chicken breast
   halves, skin removed
1 large garlic clove, minced
1 teaspoon dried Mexican oregano (see page 11)
Salt to taste

1 medium-size onion, sliced in
   thin half-moons (about 1 cup)
2 tablespoons distilled white
   vinegar
¼ cup olive oil

With a wooden mallet or veal pounder, pound the chicken breasts as thin as you can get them without tearing the meat. Rub them with the garlic, oregano, and a little salt. Combine the onion, vinegar, and 2 tablespoons of the oil in a shallow dish or plate. Turn the chicken breasts in the mixture and let rest for 30 minutes. Lift the chicken and onion from marinade, letting drain briefly.

Heat the remaining oil in a large skillet over high heat until rippling. Add the chicken and cook for 2 minutes on each side. Remove the chicken to a heated serving platter and quickly stir-fry the onion over high heat for 3 to 4 minutes. (It will still be a little crunchy.) Scatter the onion over the chicken. Serve immediately, plain or with a table sauce like *Pico de Gallo Norteño* (page 40).

YIELD: 4 SERVINGS

POLLO CON CHILE ANCHO

Braised Chicken with Ancho Chiles

This recipe was created by my dear friend Xavier Esqueda, a great raconteur and a great cook who also happens to be one of Mexico's distinguished artists.

4 ancho chiles (see page 224), tops removed and seeded
½ cup vegetable oil
1 tablespoon dark Oriental sesame oil
1 chicken (3½ pounds), cut into serving pieces
Salt and freshly ground black pepper to taste

1 large onion, sliced (2 cups)
2 garlic cloves, chopped
3 bay leaves
10 allspice berries
1½ cups Caldo de Pollo (see page 44) or water
1 tablespoon sugar
1 cup red wine vinegar, or to taste

Rinse the chiles under cold water. Heat a griddle or cast-iron skillet over high heat until a drop of water sizzles on contact. Add the chiles and cook, turning once or twice, just until they are turning slightly red and beginning to release their fragrance. Do not burn or they will become bitter. Remove, dice, and set aside.

In a large Dutch oven, combine the oils and heat over medium-high heat. Salt and pepper the chicken and brown very thoroughly on all sides. Remove to a platter.

Pour off all but 2 tablespoons of fat from the pan. Add the onion and garlic and cook, stirring, over medium heat until the onion is translucent, about 5 minutes. Add the chiles, bay leaves, allspice, chicken stock, and sugar. Add the vinegar a little at a time, tasting until you like the balance of sweet and sour. Bring to a simmer. Return the chicken to the pan, cover, and simmer over low heat until the chicken is tender, 20 to 25 minutes.

YIELD: 4 SERVINGS

LOMO DE PUERCO RELLENO DE FRUTAS

Rolled Loin of
Pork Stuffed
with Fruit

1 boneless loin of pork (about 3 pounds)
Salt and freshly ground black pepper to taste
¼ to ⅓ cup **Pasta de Chipotle** (see page 35)
Fruit Stuffing (recipe follows)
2 tablespoons vegetable oil
2 medium-size carrots, cut into 1-inch pieces

2 celery stalks, cut into 1-inch pieces
1 medium-size onion, coarsely chopped (about 1 cup)
4 garlic cloves, chopped
2 bay leaves
1½ cups **Caldo de Pollo Casero** (see page 45)
1½ cups heavy cream
¾ cup dry sherry

Have the pork loin trimmed and butterflied so it can be opened out flat to roll around the stuffing. Salt and pepper it lightly on both sides. Rub the chipotle paste over both sides. Spread the stuffing over the inside. Roll it up like a jelly roll and tie securely with butcher's twine.

Preheat the oven to 325°F.

In a heavy skillet large enough to hold the meat and vegetables with plenty of room to spare, heat the oil over high heat until rippling and brown the roast on all sides for 5 to 7 minutes, adjusting the heat as necessary. When almost brown, push the roast to one side, add the carrots, celery, onion, garlic, and bay leaves and cook, stirring, over high heat until well colored, another 3 to 5 minutes. Transfer the roast and vegetables to a roasting pan and set aside. Pour the chicken stock into the skillet and scrape with a wooden spoon to deglaze the pan drippings. Add the cream and sherry; bring to a boil over medium-high heat. Cook until sauce is slightly thickened, about 5 minutes. Season with pepper and salt (remember that salt will concentrate in cooking). Pour the sauce into the roasting pan and bake the pork for 50 minutes to an hour (an instant-reading thermometer inserted into the thickest part should read 160°F).

Transfer the pork to a serving platter and let rest for 20 minutes. To finish the sauce, puree the contents of the roasting pan by pushing the sauce and vegetables through a sieve or food mill. Pour into a medium-size saucepan and bring just to a simmer. Cook over very low heat or a Flame-Tamer for 5 minutes. (The sauce will break down if cooked over high heat.)

To serve, cut the roast into 1-inch-thick slices and pass the sauce on the side.

YIELD: 8 SERVINGS

Fruit Stuffing

Another mixture of many uses, a wonderful stuffing for all sorts of roast poultry. I also like to turn it into a filling for tamales to accompany roasts. If you cook the fruit down to a slightly softer consistency, it also makes a good compote.

½ cup golden raisins
1 cup dry sherry, heated
¼ cup (½ stick) unsalted butter or corn oil
1 medium-large onion, finely chopped (about 1½ cups)
4 to 5 garlic cloves, minced (about 2 tablespoons)

1 cup dried apricots, sliced
1 cup pitted prunes, sliced
1 cup pimiento-stuffed green olives, sliced
½ cup toasted (see page 35) slivered blanched almonds

In a small bowl, combine the raisins and sherry and let soak at least 20 minutes to plump the raisins.

In a large skillet, heat the butter or oil over medium-high heat until very hot but not quite scorching. Cook the onion and garlic, stirring often, until the onion is translucent, about 3 minutes. Add the raisins with any remaining sherry, the apricots, prunes, and olives. Cook, stirring occasionally, about 5 minutes, or until the fruit is slightly soft. Add the almonds and cook 1 minute longer. Let cool for about 15 minutes before using.

YIELD: ABOUT 5 CUPS

TINGA DE PUERCO

Shredded Pork

This is a great way to use not only leftover roast pork but also beef or chicken. If you have no suitable leftovers, it is worth roasting or braising a piece of meat just for this purpose. I love to make *tinga* with leftover *Cochito Chiapaneco* (page 273) and often make the recipe from scratch just to have the meat for the *tinga*. The meat from *Carne de Puerco Cocida* (page 46) is also excellent. Any sort of *tinga* can be used to make tacos or burritos. If you do not have any canned chipotles, use any other chile you have—fresh poblanos, jalapeños, or Anaheims—to season the dish to your taste.

2 large ripe, red tomatoes
3 canned chiles chipotles en
    adobo (see page 224)
¼ cup water or chicken stock
⅓ cup vegetable oil
4 large garlic cloves, finely
    chopped
1 large or 2 medium-size onions,
    thinly sliced in half-moons
    (about 2 cups)

2 teaspoons ground cumin
1 teaspoon freshly grated
    nutmeg
2 pounds shredded leftover
    roasted pork butt or any other
    cooked meat
Salt and freshly ground black
    pepper to taste

Heat a griddle or cast-iron skillet over high heat until a drop of water sizzles on contact. Roast the tomatoes, turning several times, until blackened on all sides. Let sit until cool enough to touch; working over a bowl to catch any juices, peel off the black skin. Seed the tomatoes, chop the flesh roughly, and set aside.

In a blender or food processor fitted with the steel blade, puree the chipotle chiles and the sauce that clings to them with the water or stock. Set aside.

In a large skillet, heat the oil over high heat until very hot but not quite smoking. Add the garlic and onion and cook, stirring, 2 to 3 minutes. Add the tomatoes, cumin, nutmeg, and pureed chipotles and cook, stirring, another 3 minutes. Reduce the heat to medium, add the shredded meat, and simmer, uncovered, until most of the liquid has evaporated, about 10 minutes. Season with salt and pepper and serve at once.

YIELD: 4 SERVINGS AS A MAIN DISH; MORE AS A FILLING FOR TACOS, GORDITAS, OR BURRITOS

CAMARONES AL CHIPOTLE

Prawns with

Chipotle

This recipe was developed by Gary Jacobson, chef at Zarela. Gary grew up in the Boston area and is a master seafood cook. He has taught me much about the ways of the sea and its creatures, and our menu is the richer for it. The Worcestershire sauce, by the way, is not an inauthentic "Americanization." It is a ubiquitous seasoning in Mexico.

At the restaurant we make these with freshwater prawns, which I really prefer in this case. Substitute shrimp if necessary. The dish as served at Zarela is extremely spicy, though you can lower the amount of chiles for a milder version or cut back some on the rosemary. It's definitely finger food—picking up the prawns and sucking out the last bit of sauce is half the fun, but finger bowls are essential! I like to serve this with plain rice or *Arroz con Crema y Poblanos* (page 172).

¼ cup (½ stick) unsalted butter
8 medium-size garlic cloves, peeled
5 bay leaves
10 black peppercorns
1 tablespoon dried rosemary, or to taste
4 canned chiles chipotles en adobo (see page 224), finely chopped (for milder sauce, use 2 to 3 chipotles)
½ cup chicken stock

½ cup Worcestershire sauce
1½ pounds medium-size fresh-water prawns or shrimp in shell, bought with heads on if possible (about 32 if bought with heads on; more if bought headless), rinsed and drained
2 scallions, green part only, finely chopped
Salt and freshly ground black pepper to taste

Heat the butter in a large, wide skillet or sauté pan over high heat until fragrant and bubbling. Add the garlic, bay leaves, pepper-corns, and rosemary, and cook, stirring often, until the butter is well infused with their flavor, about 3 minutes. Add the chipotles and cook another 3 minutes, stirring; adjust the heat as necessary to prevent scorching. Add the chicken stock and Worcestershire sauce; bring to a boil and reduce until slightly thickened. Add the prawns and cook for 2 minutes on each side. Sprinkle with the scallions and season with salt and pepper.

YIELD: 4 SERVINGS

CAMARONES CON COCO

Coconut

Shrimp

This is a takeoff on something that I first encountered at Restaurante Diligencias in Tampico. I fell in love with their spicy version of a *salsa verde,* served on the side with fried shrimp or baked fillet of fish. You will see the family resemblance of this sauce to others like *Pico de Gallo Norteño* and *Salsa Cruda de Tomatillo* (pages 40 and 41)—fresh uncooked sauces with a jolt of chile, meant to be used as table sauces from which diners help themselves according to their tolerance for chiles.

I became crazy about the sauce, which I adapted in a cooked version. I enriched the flavor by my favorite re-sautéing technique and used the sauce to poach or sauté seafood, making it an integral part of the dish instead of a condiment. But the spiciness of the sauce limited the number of ways I could use it, until I found that garnishing the dish with grated coconut and fresh lime did wonders in mellowing the strong *picante* flavor.

This version, with the shrimp, is also a perfect party dish—easy to prepare ahead and quickly cook at the last moment.

3 tablespoons butter or olive oil	1 pound shrimp, peeled and
1 cup (approximately) Salsa	deveined
Verde de Tampico (recipe fol-	½ cup freshly grated coconut
lows)	Lime wedges

Heat the butter in a heavy skillet or sauté pan over high heat until the foam subsides and the butter is almost ready to brown. (If using olive oil, heat until very hot but not quite smoking.) Quickly add the salsa and cook, stirring, until heated through, about 2 minutes. Reduce the heat to medium-high. Add the shrimp and stir well to combine. Reduce the heat a little more and simmer until the shrimp are opaque and cooked through, about 3 minutes longer. Do not overcook. Arrange the shrimp and sauce on a serving platter, sprinkle with the grated coconut, and garnish with lime wedges.

YIELD: 4 SERVINGS

SALSA VERDE DE TAMPICO

Tampico Green Sauce

I serve this versatile sauce with everything from grilled fish to fried crab nuggets and even eggs, either scrambled or poached, on mornings when only a strong dose of chile can get me going. As with *Camarones al Ajillo* (page 179), a little commercial soup base makes a big effect here. The powdered stock bases are much used in Mexican homes and restaurants.

If this amount of chile makes you gulp, use only 2 to 4 for a less explosive sauce. Deseeding them will further temper the heat. In *Camarones con Coco* (preceding recipe) I re-sauté the sauce, but it is also excellent served fresh.

8 fresh chiles, either jalapeño or serrano (see pages 225 and 226), or to taste, tops removed, halved crosswise
1 medium-size onion, quartered
5 garlic cloves
¼ cup vegetable or olive oil

½ cup loosely packed fresh cilantro leaves
1 teaspoon dried Mexican oregano (see page 11), crumbled
1 teaspoon powdered chicken base

Place all the ingredients in a blender or food processor fitted with the steel blade and pulse until coarsely chopped, then process to desired consistency. (It is nicest when slightly coarse.) Can be stored, tightly covered, in the refrigerator for up to 2 weeks, though it will discolor.

YIELD: ABOUT 1½ CUPS

PEZ ESPADA CON SALSA DE CHILE POBLANO

Swordfish with Poblano Sauce

Though any fish will work with this recipe, I suggest swordfish because its flavor goes well with the poblano sauce. It is very important that the fish not overcook. The poblano sauce is also a natural for pasta.

4 swordfish steaks (about 7 ounces each)
Salt and freshly ground white pepper to taste
2 tablespoons olive oil

2 tablespoons unsalted butter
3 garlic cloves, peeled and crushed
Salsa de Chile Poblano (recipe follows)

Season the swordfish steaks with salt and pepper and set aside.

Heat half of the oil and butter in a large skillet or sauté pan over high heat until hot and sizzling. Add half the garlic and cook, stirring constantly, until it softens, 1 to 2 minutes. Add two of the swordfish steaks and cook for 2 minutes on each side. Remove from the pan. Repeat with the remaining ingredients.

Serve immediately with the poblano sauce.

YIELD: 4 SERVINGS

SALSA DE CHILE POBLANO

Poblano Chile Sauce

Poblano chiles can vary a lot in hotness. If you prefer a milder sauce, replace part or all of the poblanos with California long green or Anaheim chiles. If you want it hotter, add one or two jalapeños.

2 tablespoons lard (see page 19), butter, or vegetable oil
1 medium-size onion, chopped (about 1 cup)
2 garlic cloves, minced
8 poblano chiles (about 1 pound; see page 226), roasted (page 227), peeled, seeded, and coarsely chopped

1 tablespoon dried epazote (see page 8) or 3 sprigs fresh cilantro
1 cup chicken stock
½ cup heavy cream
Salt to taste

Heat the fat in a medium-size saucepan over high heat until very hot but not quite smoking. Add the onion and garlic and cook, stirring occasionally, for 2 minutes. Reduce the heat to medium and cook, stirring, another 3 minutes, or until the onion starts to color. Add the poblanos and epazote or cilantro and stir to combine. Cook, stirring occasionally, for another 5 minutes.

Place the mixture in a blender or food processor fitted with the steel blade, add the chicken stock, and process until smooth, about 1 minute. Return the mixture to the saucepan and bring to a simmer over low heat. Add the cream. Taste for seasoning, add salt if desired, and simmer for 3 minutes.

Can be stored, tightly covered, in the refrigerator 2 to 3 days.
YIELD: ABOUT 3 CUPS

SALMÓN AHUMADO AL CHIPOTLE

Grill-Smoked
Salmon with
Chipotle
Mayonnaise

Of course, salmon is not a Mexican fish, but living in New York I have learned to treasure it. This is just one example of how I use simple canned chipotle puree as a seasoning paste to coat grilled foods—try it on any grilled or broiled fish and experiment with other meats.

For this dish, choose a grill with a high rack and have the wood or charcoal very hot. I like a mesquite fire, started an hour before the salmon is to be cooked. The heat should just be starting to diminish.

2 sides of a 6- to 9-pound salmon, skin on
4 to 5 large garlic cloves, minced (about 2 tablespoons)
2 to 3 canned chiles chipotles en adobo (see page 224)
3 tablespoons dried Mexican oregano (see page 11)

Salt to taste
2 to 4 tablespoons olive oil, or as needed
1 cup Mayonesa de Chipotle (recipe follows)
Jícama Escabechada (see page 163)

Run your fingers over the salmon to find any pin bones and pull them out with tweezers.

In a food processor fitted with the steel blade or blender, puree the garlic and chipotles (with the sauce that clings to them) with 1 tablespoon of the oregano. If too thick to blend, add 1 to 2 tablespoons of water. Brush the paste over the salmon on both sides. Use the full amount for the spiciest effect, less for a milder flavor. Sprinkle the remaining oregano over the salmon on both sides. Season with salt. Brush with olive oil and let rest at room temperature at least 15 minutes before grilling.

Add some mesquite chips or a small piece of wood to the coals; when it starts smoking, place the salmon on the grill, skin side down. If your grill does not have a cover, cover with a baking tray or disposable roasting pan to trap the smoke. Cook for approximately 6 to 7 minutes on each side. The outside should be nice and brown, the center just barely cooked (very slightly translucent).

Serve at room temperature with the mayonnaise and the *jícama escabechada* on the side.

YIELD: 8 TO 10 SERVINGS

MAYONESA DE CHIPOTLE

Chipotle
Mayonnaise

1 cup prepared mayonnaise   **Salt to taste**
3 tablespoons Pasta de Chipotle
(see page 35), or to taste

Combine the mayonnaise and chipotle paste. Taste for seasoning and add salt if desired. Refrigerate unless using at once.

Can be stored, tightly covered, in the refrigerator up to 1 week.

YIELD: ABOUT 1 CUP

PERAS CON CHIPOTLE

Chipotle Pears

I developed this recipe one lazy afternoon when I had a surplus of pears. It is a variant on a side dish that my cousin Hector makes with cling peaches. I have since tried the formula with apples and quinces with equally good results. Tightly covered, they keep for weeks in the refrigerator and make a nice addition to a holiday buffet as a side dish with pork, turkey, or brisket.

¼ cup water	2 canned chiles chipotles en
¼ cup distilled white vinegar	adobo (see page 224)
2 tablespoons fresh lime juice	4 medium-size pears (about 1½
¼ cup sugar	pounds), peeled, quartered,
½ teaspoon salt, or to taste	and cored

Combine the water, vinegar, lime juice, and sugar in a small saucepan. Bring to a boil over medium heat, stirring to dissolve the sugar. Add the chiles, whole if you want to remove them later, or chopped if you want to leave them in for a more intense flavor. Season with salt.

Add the pears to the boiling marinade. Remove from the heat and let cool to room temperature. If not using at once, pour into a lidded storage container or jar and store in the refrigerator. Serve chilled.

YIELD: ABOUT 1 PINT

PEPIÁN VERDE DE TAMPICO

Tampico Pumpkin-Seed Green Sauce

I first ate and loved this sauce at the Restaurante Diligencia in Tampico, Tamaulipas. They serve it with pan-fried fish fillets and fried fish roe, accompanied by steaming hot tortillas. I have found it marvelous with grilled fish, chicken and duck breasts, fried shrimp, and roast lamb. It is great in the fillings for *Sopes* (see page 124). The sauce should be very buttery and make your mouth tingle!

6 tablespoons (¾ stick) unsalted butter
2 cups shelled raw pumpkin seeds
1½ cups Caldo de Pollo (see page 44), or as needed
1 cup heavy cream
½ cup loosely packed fresh cilantro leaves
2 fresh chiles, either jalapeño or serrano (see pages 225 and 226), roasted (page 227), tops removed, and peeled, or use 2 canned jalapeños
Salt to taste

Heat 4 tablespoons (½ stick) of the butter in a large, heavy skillet over medium-high heat until hot and bubbling. Add the pumpkin seeds, which should fit in one layer (fry in two batches if necessary). Cook over medium-low heat, shaking the pan and stirring constantly for about 3 minutes, until the seeds start to pop. (Watch out—they can really fly!) Do not let them darken or the whole sauce will be bitter; remove any that have browned. Let cool slightly.

Place the seeds in a blender along with the butter in which they were cooked. Add 1 cup of the chicken stock, the cream, cilantro, and chiles. Blend for 1 minute; scrape down the sides with a rubber spatula, adding more chicken stock and blending a little longer if necessary. The consistency should be creamy. Season with salt.

In a medium-size saucepan, heat the remaining butter over high heat until the foam subsides. Add the sauce, give it a good stir, and bring the mixture to a boil, stirring. Immediately reduce the heat to low and simmer for 3 minutes, stirring often.

Can be stored, tightly covered, in the refrigerator up to 1 week.
YIELD: ABOUT 3 CUPS

MAYONESA DE JALAPEÑO

Jalapeño
Mayonnaise

A useful accompaniment where you would use tartar sauce (with fried oysters or fish) or with Mexican-style sandwiches (*tortas*).

1 cup mayonnaise
4 pickled jalapeño chiles (see page 225), seeded and finely chopped

1 garlic clove, minced

Combine all the ingredients in a small bowl and let rest 30 minutes before using. Can be stored, tightly covered, in the refrigerator up to 1 week.

YIELD: ABOUT 1 CUP

Menus

MAKE-YOUR-OWN-TACO-PARTY

One of my favorite ways to entertain is to have a make-your-own-taco party. My guests love to stuff the assorted fillings into freshly made corn or flour tortillas and top them with hot salsa, shredded lettuce, and grated cheese.

Carne con Chile Colorado (page 105), *Picadillo de Pollo* (page 48), and *Ropa Vieja* (page 175) are other good choices.

SALPICÓN DE HUACHINANGO

(Red Snapper Hash)

PICADILLO DULCE

("Sweet" Spiced Ground Meat)

PAPAS CON CHILE VERDE

(Potatoes with Green Chile)

POLLO GUISADO

(Poached and Sautéed Chicken)

FRIJOLES REFRITOS

(Refried Black Beans)

PICO DE GALLO NORTEÑO

(Uncooked Tomato Salsa)

SALSA DE TOMATILLO CON CHIPOTLE

(Tomatillo Sauce with Chipotle Chiles)

TORTILLAS DE HARINA

(Flour Tortillas)

TORTILLAS DE MAÍZ

(Corn Tortillas)

BACKYARD SUMMER BUFFET

CALDO FRÍO DE AGUACATE MARGARITA

(Margarita Jameson's Cold Avocado Soup)

SALMÓN AL CHIPOTLE

(Grill-smoked Salmon with Chipotle Mayonnaise)

JÍCAMA ESCABECHADA

(Jícama Relish)

PASTEL RÁPIDO

(Quick Butter Cake)

RANCH BREAKFAST OR BRUNCH

CHILAQUILES

(Tortilla Casserole)

HUEVOS A LA MEXICANA

(Scrambled Eggs with Salsa)

PAPAS CON CHORIZO

(Potatoes with Homemade Sausage)

SEMITAS

(Little Biscuits)

VAMPIRO

(Mexican Bloody Mary)

BUFFET DINNER

This is one of my most successful menus both for entertaining at home and for catering. The dishes represent a wide range of flavors and textures. Only the shrimp have to be done at the last minute. Everything else can be assembled and reheated just before serving.

CHILES ANCHOS NANA LUZ RELLENOS DE PICADILLO DULCE

(Marinated Ancho Chiles Stuffed with "Sweet" Spiced Ground Beef)

ENSALADA GIRASOL

(Sunflower Salad)

CAMARONES CON COCO

(Coconut Shrimp)

SOPA DE CREPAS

(Layered Crêpe Dish)

ARROZ CON CREMA Y POBLANOS

(Creamy Rice Casserole with Poblano Chiles)

ENSALADA DE JÍCAMA Y BERROS

(Jícama-Watercress Salad)

BOLITAS DE CHOCOLATE

(Chocolate Balls)

APPETIZER PARTY

ALITAS DE POLLO EN SALSA DE CHIPOTLE

(Chicken Wings with Chipotle Sauce)

FLAUTAS

(Rolled Chicken Tacos)

GUACAMOLE

BUTIFARRIA

(Chiapas Sausage)

SOPES CON SALSA DE TOMATILLO Y QUESO FRESCO

(Masa Tartlets with Tomatillo Sauce and Fresh Cheese)

PICO DE GALLO NORTEÑO

(Uncooked Tomato Salsa)

TORTILLA CHIPS

FESTIVE SEATED DINNER

CALDO TLALPEÑO

(Soup from Tlalpan)

ENCHILADAS DE CANGREJO

(Crab Enchiladas)

LOMO DE PUERCO RELLENO DE FRUTAS

(Rolled Loin of Pork Stuffed with Fruit)

ENSALADA DE BERENJENA

(Eggplant Salad)

TORTA DE ELOTE

(Savory Corn Bread)

PASTEL DE NUEZ

(Pecan Cake)

CASUAL RANCH DINNER

ALBÓNDIGAS DE MI MAMÁ

(Meatballs like Mama Makes)

ARROZ A LA MEXICANA

(Rice Mexican-Style)

CALABACITAS CON QUESO

(Zucchini with Cheese)

FRIJOLES DE LA OLLA

(Pot-cooked Beans)

TORTILLAS DE HARINA

(Flour Tortillas)

Mail-Order Sources

Unless otherwise indicated, most of the companies listed will give ordering information by mail or telephone. A word of advice: with the rapid expansion of Mexican immigration into many regions of the United States, you may be surprised to find that retail sources for Mexican ingredients are fairly close at hand. Look through local telephone books and do some inquiring.

El Aficionado, Ltd.
2365 N. Quincy St.
Arlington, VA 22207
800-622-4317

Supplies fresh *huitlacoche* in season.

Dean & DeLuca
560 Broadway
New York, NY 10012
212-431-1691

Frieda's by Mail
P.O. Box 58488
Los Angeles, CA 90058
800-241-1771

Mail-order branch of Frieda's Inc., a major distributor of specialty ingredients to supermarkets nationwide. Several dried chile varieties and packaged corn husks for tamales.

Great Southwest Cuisine Catalogue
206 Frontage Rd.
Rio Rancho, NM 87124
800-869-9218

Old Southwest Trading Co.
P.O. Box 7545
Albuquerque, NM 87194
505-836-0168

Carries "true" or "Ceylon" cinnamon (ask for "soft-stick" cinnamon).

Pendery's
304 E. Belknap St.
Fort Worth, TX 76102
817-332-9896

Another source for "true," "Ceylon," or "soft-stick" cinnamon.

Penzey's Spice House, Ltd.
P.O. Box 1633
Milwaukee, WI 53201
414-768-8799

Knowledgeable source of information on spices; carries "true" or "Ceylon" cinnamon. Interesting catalogue.

Quaker Oats Co.
Consumer Response
P.O. Box 049001
Chicago, IL 60604-9001
312-222-7111

Information on local distributors for *masa harina*.

Santa Cruz Chili and Spice Co.
P.O. Box 177
Tumacacori, AZ 85640
602-398-2591

Very good quality pure powdered red chile.

Santa Fe Chili Co.
218 Old Santa Fe Trail
Santa Fe, NM 87501
505-988-1289

Stop One Supermarket
210 W. 94th St.
New York, NY 10025
212-864-9456

One of the largest New York City area sources for hard-to-find ingredients (no mail order).

Tianguis Supermarkets
3610 North Peck Rd.
El Monte, CA 91731
818-459-4716

Central address for information on the large Tianguis chain of stores in the Los Angeles area.

Selected Bibliography and Suggested Reading

Andrews, Jean. *Peppers: The Domesticated Capsicums*. Austin, TX: University of Texas Press, 1990.

Ávila Hernández, Dolores, *et al. Atlas Cultural de México: Gastronomía*. Mexico City: Secretaría de Educación Pública/Instituto Nacional de Antropología e Historia, 1988.

Bayless, Rick, with Deann Groen Bayless. *Authentic Mexican: Regional Cooking from the Heart of Mexico*. New York: William Morrow and Company, Inc., 1987.

Bedford, Sybille. *The Sudden View: A Mexican Journey*. New York: Harper & Brothers, 1953.

Benítez, Ana M. *Pre-Hispanic Cooking/Cocina Prehispánica* [bilingual edition with English translation by Mary Williams Varela]. Mexico City: Ediciones Euroamericanas Klaus Thiele, 1974.

Blom, Gertrude. *Gertrude Blom/Bearing Witness,* edited by Alex Harris and Margaret Sartor. Chapel Hill, NC, and London: University of North Carolina Press (for Center for Documentary Photography, Duke University), 1984.

Caballero Hernández, María del Socorro. *Costumbres del Estado de México*. Mexico City: Secretaría de Educación Pública, 1986.

Carbia, María A. de. *México en la cocina de Marichu*. Mexico City: Editorial Epoca, 1969.

Castelló Yturbide, Teresa. *Presencia de la Comida Prehispánica*. Mexico City: Fomento Cultural Banamex, 1986.

Coe, Sophie. "Aztec Cuisine." *Petits Propos Culinaires,* number 19 (March 1985): 11–22.

———. "Aztec Cuisine, Part II." *Petits Propos Culinaires,* number 20 (July 1985): 44–59.

———. "Aztec Cuisine, Part III." *Petits Propos Culinaires,* number 21 (November 1985): 45–56.

Dewitt, Dave, and Nancy Gerlach. *The Whole Chile Pepper Book*. Boston: Little, Brown and Company, 1990.

Díaz del Castillo, Bernal. *The Conquest of New Spain,* translated and edited by J. M. Cohen. Baltimore: Penguin Books, 1963.

Directorio Nacional Gastronómico. Mexico City: Secretaría de Turismo, n.d.

Fiestas in Mexico: A Complete Guide to Celebrations. First English edition. Mexico City: Ediciones Lara, 1978.

Flores Estrada, Francisco. *Cocina Exótica de Chiapas*. San Cristóbal de las Casas: Editorial La Noticia, 1986.

Gabilondo, Aída. *Mexican Family Cooking*. New York: Fawcett Columbine, 1986.

Gooch, Fanny Chambers. *Face to Face with the Mexicans*. Carbondale, IL: Southern Illinois University Press, 1966.

Guerrero Guerrero, Raúl. *Toneucayotl: El Pan Nuestro de Cada Día*. Mexico City: Colección Divulgación/Instituto Nacional de Antropología e Historia, 1987.

Iglasias y Cabrera, Sonia. *El Pan Popular*. Mexico City: Fondo Nacional para el Fomento de las Artesanias, 1982.

Iturriaga de la Fuente, José N. *De Tacos, Tamales y Tortas*. Mexico City: Editorial Diana, 1987.

Kennedy, Diana. *The Cuisines of Mexico*. New York: Harper & Row, 1972.

———. *Recipes from the Regional Cooks of Mexico*. New York: Harper & Row, 1978.

Long-Solís, Janet. *Capsicum y Cultura, La Historia del Chilli.* Mexico City: Fondo de Cultural Económica, 1986.

El Maguey, Árbol de las Maravillas. Mexico City: Museo Nacional de Culturas Populares, 1988.

El Maíz, Fundamento de la Cultura Popular Mexicana. 3rd edition. Mexico City: Museo de Culturas Populares, 1987.

Minutiae Mexicana: Tequila, Mezcal y Pulque. Mexico City: Minutiae Mexicana, 1971.

Paz, Octavio. *The Labyrinth of Solitude* and other works, translated by Lysander Kemp and others. New York: Grove Press, 1985.

Piñeda, Dolores Sánchez de. *Comida Tradicional de San Cristóbal de las Casas.* Mexico City: Luz Olivia Piñeda Sánchez, 1988.

Porter, Eugene O. *Lord Beresford and Lady Flo.* El Paso, TX: University of Texas Press, 1970.

Recetario Mexicano del Maíz. Mexico City: Museo de Culturas Populares, 1983.

Riding, Alan. *Distant Neighbors.* New York: Vintage Books, 1985.

Rivera, Francisco ("Paco Píldora"). *Veracruz en la Historia y la Cumbancha.* Mexico City: Viñetas de Alberto Beltrán, 1976.

Soustelle, Jacques. *Daily Life of the Aztecs on the Eve of the Spanish Conquest,* translated by Patrick O'Brian. Stanford, CA: Stanford University Press, 1970.

Taibo, Paco Ignacio. *Breviario del Mole Poblano.* Mexico City: Editorial Terra Nova, 1981.

Toor, Frances. *A Treasury of Mexican Folkways.* New York: Bonanza Books, 1947.

Las Tradiciones de Días de Muertos en México. Mexico City: Secretaría de Educación Pública/Dirección General de Culturas Populares, 1987.

Velázquez de León, Josefina. *Mexican Cook Book Devoted to the American Homes* [bilingual edition with English translation by Concepción Silva Garcia]. Mexico City: Ediciones Velázquez de León, 1947.

Index

Corn (cont.)
crêpes, 86
religion and, 191–99
tamales with poblano chiles and,
231–32
tortillas, 54–55
tomatillo sauce with, 40
Corn husks
about, 7–8
tamales in, 51–53
Corn smut. *See huitlacoche*
Corpus Christi salad, 303
Courtship and marriage, 118–23
Crab enchiladas, 181–83
Crema
salsa de tomatillo con, 313–14
Rajas con, 178–79
Crema agria preparada, 42
Crema fresca, 21
Crepas
de chicharrón, 158
de huitlacoche, 173–74
de maíz, 86
sopa de, 84–85
Crêpe(s)
corn, 86
dish, layered, 84–85
filled pork cracklings, 158
with *huitlacoche,* layered, 173–74
Crescents, jam-filled, 123–24
Cucumber, jícama, and fruit salad,
128–29
Cuernitos de mermelada, 123–24
Cuitlacoche. See huitlacoche
Cumin, about, 19
Cuquita, Doña, 134

Date-nut roll, 147
Dátil, rollo de nuez y, 147
Desprecio (horse), 73–75
Desserts. *See* Cakes; Sweets
Días de los Muertos (Days of the
Dead), 204–8
Díaz, Porfirio, 62, 69
Díaz del Castillo, Bernal, 1–2
Díaz de León, Joel, 151

Egg(s)
hard-boiled, in pumpkin-seed
sauce, 276–77
scrambled, with salsa, 110
string beans with, 91
Eggnog, Mexican, 141

Eggplant salad, 301–2
Ejidos, 87
Ejotes con huevo, 91
Ellis, Ernesto, 149, 159, 297
Ellis, Panchita, 149, 159, 297
El Maíz, 194, 196
Elote(s)
asados con mantequilla enchilada,
309–10
tamales con chile poblano y, 231–32
torta de, 139–40
El Paso (TX), 150–52, 154, 156
El Paso del Norte (Ciudad Juárez), 185
Enchiladas, crab, 181–83
Enchiladas de Cangrejo, 181–83
Ensalada
de berenjena, 301–2
de chicharrón, 164
de Corpus Christi, 303
girasol, 303–4
de jícama y berros, 165
pico de gallo, 128–29
de piña y chile morrón, 166–67
de pulpo, 292–93
Epazote, about, 8
Caldo de huitlacoche, 305–6
Crepas de huitlacoche, 173–74
frijoles de la olla, 43–44
Huitlacoche mousse, 306–7
Mole de olla, 271–73
Escabeche
de cebolla, 282–83
fish with, 280–81
de mejillones, 289–90
pescado con, 280–81
de verduras, 281–82
Espinacas, 92
Esqueda, Xavier, 128–29, 318

Fajitas, 177–78
Fideos, sopa caldosa de, 83–84
Fiestas, 198–217. *See also specific
fiestas*
Fish. *See also specific fish*
with *escabeche,* 280–81
in sauce Jalisco-style, 135–36
tamales, 183–84
Flan, Naples "cheese," 188–89
Flan (Queso de Nápoles), 188–89
Flautas, 174–75
Florida ("Lady Flora"), 59–60
Flour tortillas, 56–58
Fresa, preparado de, 142–43